Cheeky Angel ™

Vol. 7
Story and Art by
Hiroyuki Nishimori

Cheeky Angel
Vol. 7
Action Edition
Story and Art by
HIROYUKI NISHIMORI

Translation/Joe Yamazaki
English Adaptation/Gary Leach
Touch-Up Art & Lettering/Gabe Crate
Cover and Interior Design/Izumi Evers
Editor/Michelle Pangilinan

Managing Editor/Annette Roman
Director of Production/Noboru Watanabe
VP of Publishing/Alvin Lu
Sr. Director of Acquisitions/Rika Inouye
VP of Sales & Marketing/Liza Coppola
Publisher/Hyoe Narita

Printed in the U.S.A.

Published by VIZ, LLC
P.O. Box 77010
San Francisco, CA 94107

Action Edition
10 9 8 7 6 5 4 3 2 1
First printing, June 2005

store.viz.com

RATED T+ FOR OLDER TEENS

PARENTAL ADVISORY
CHEEKY ANGEL is rated T+ for Older Teen. Contains strong language, violence and sexual themes. Recommended for older teens (16 and up).

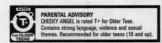

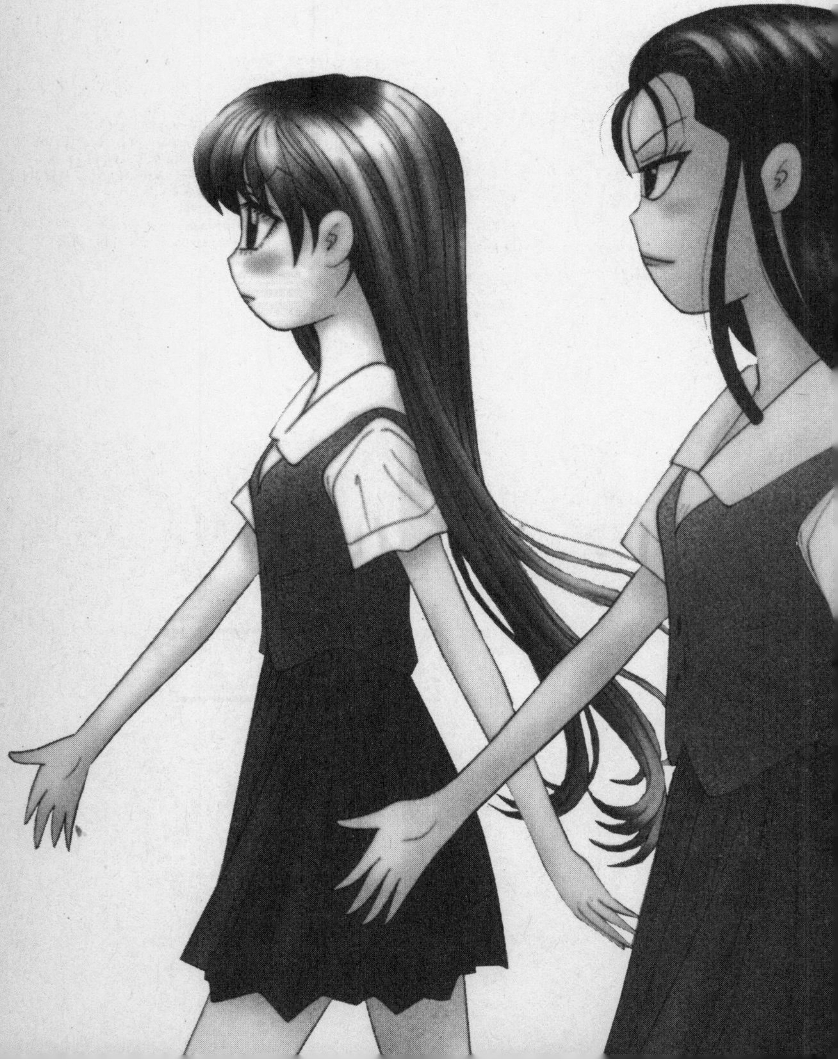

STORY THUS FAR

When she was younger, beautiful Megumi Amatsuka was turned into a girl by a genie from a magic book.

Megumi yearns to be a boy again, yet continues to draw attention from other boys who have formed "Meg's Musketeers."

To add salt to injury, Megumi's main rival from her junior high days transfers to her high school. This rival, Keiko, exploits her femininity to the fullest, and Megumi decides to compete in the same way. The result is an unexpected come-from-behind victory!

But there is little time to celebrate—she now has to deal with the heightened interest of Genzo, a hulking thug who finds her irresistible. Worse, she must deal with the shock of feeling reassured by his presence during a very tense and awkward situation...

Contents

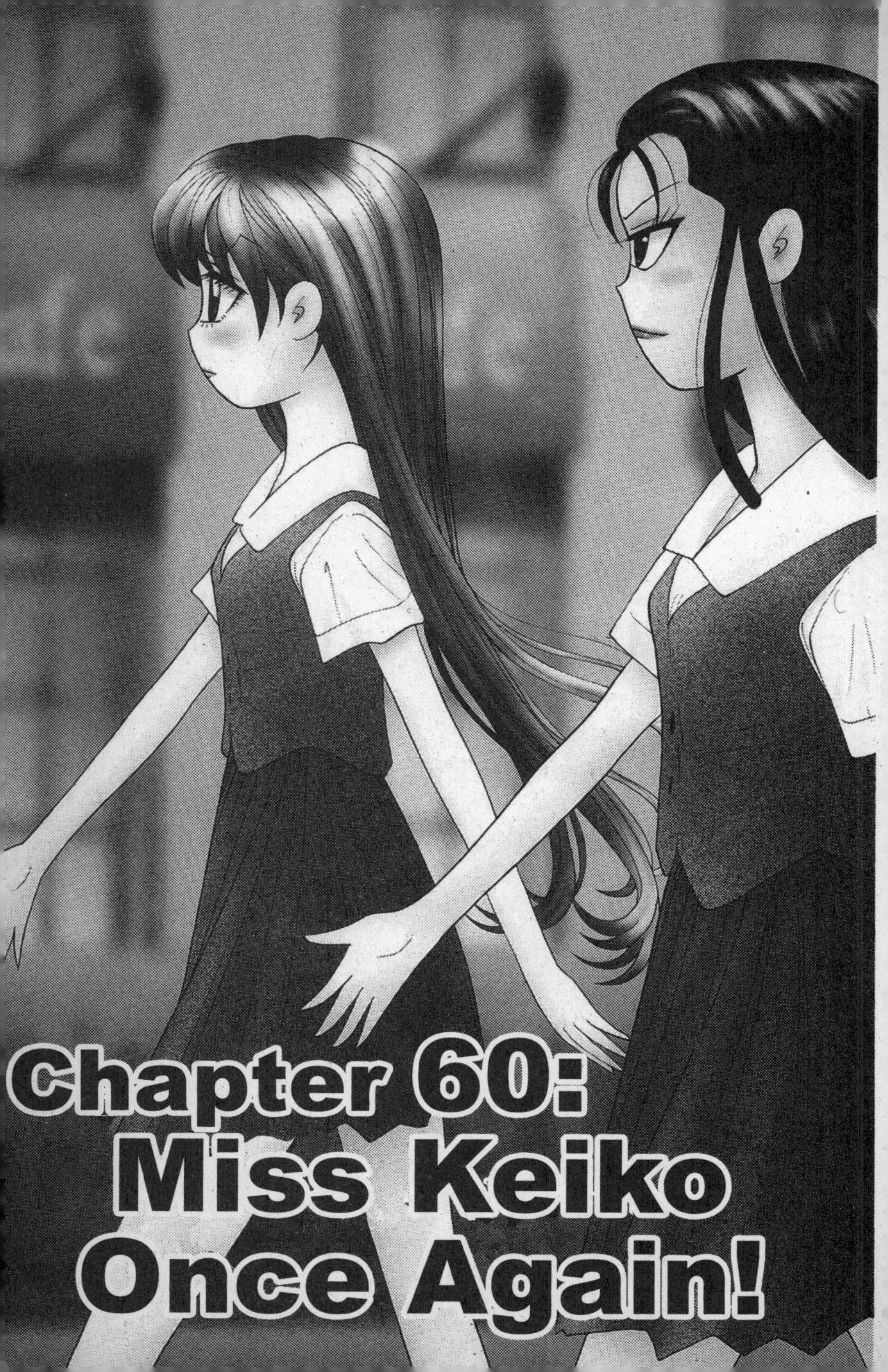
Chapter 60:
Miss Keiko
Once Again!

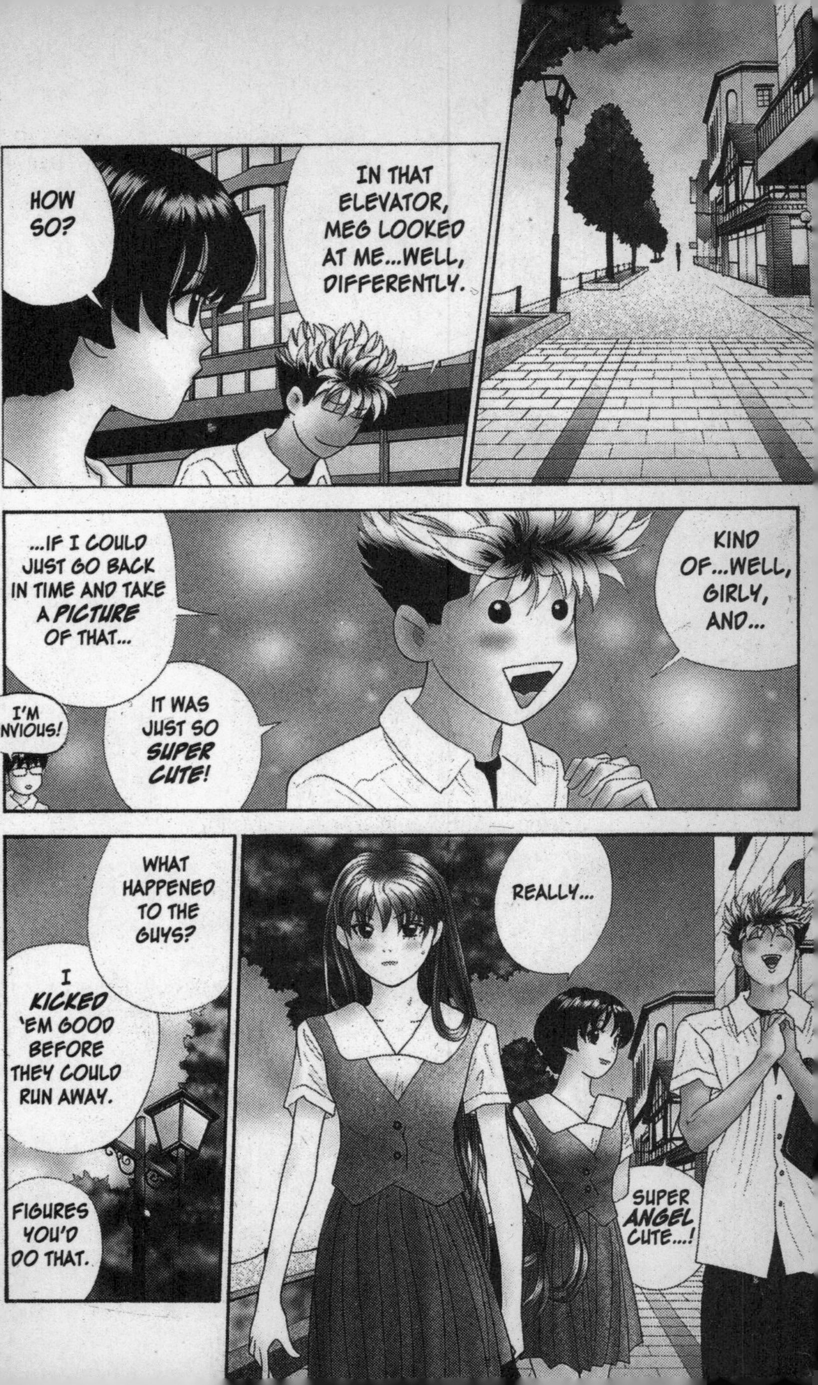
IN THAT ELEVATOR, MEG LOOKED AT ME...WELL, DIFFERENTLY.
HOW SO?
KIND OF...WELL, GIRLY, AND...
...IF I COULD JUST GO BACK IN TIME AND TAKE A *PICTURE* OF THAT...
IT WAS JUST SO ***SUPER CUTE!***
I'M ENVIOUS!
REALLY...
SUPER ***ANGEL*** CUTE...!
WHAT HAPPENED TO THE GUYS?
I ***KICKED*** 'EM GOOD BEFORE THEY COULD RUN AWAY.
FIGURES YOU'D DO THAT.

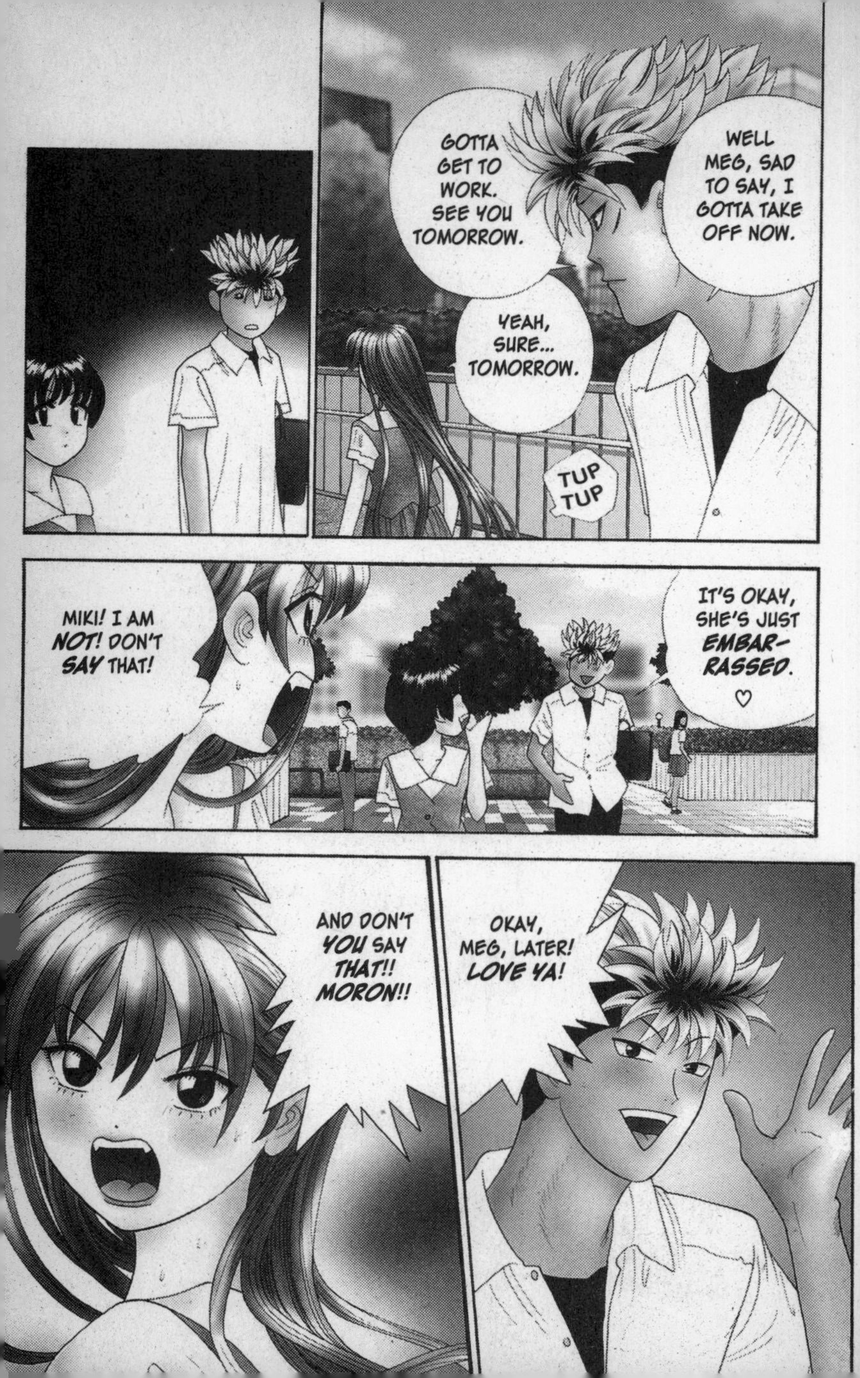
WELL MEG, SAD TO SAY, I GOTTA TAKE OFF NOW.
GOTTA GET TO WORK. SEE YOU TOMORROW.
YEAH, SURE... TOMORROW.
TUP TUP
IT'S OKAY, SHE'S JUST *EMBARRASSED.* ♡
MIKI! I AM *NOT!* DON'T *SAY* THAT!
OKAY, MEG, LATER! *LOVE YA!*
AND DON'T *YOU* SAY THAT!! *MORON!!*

天使な小生意気
A Cheeky Angel

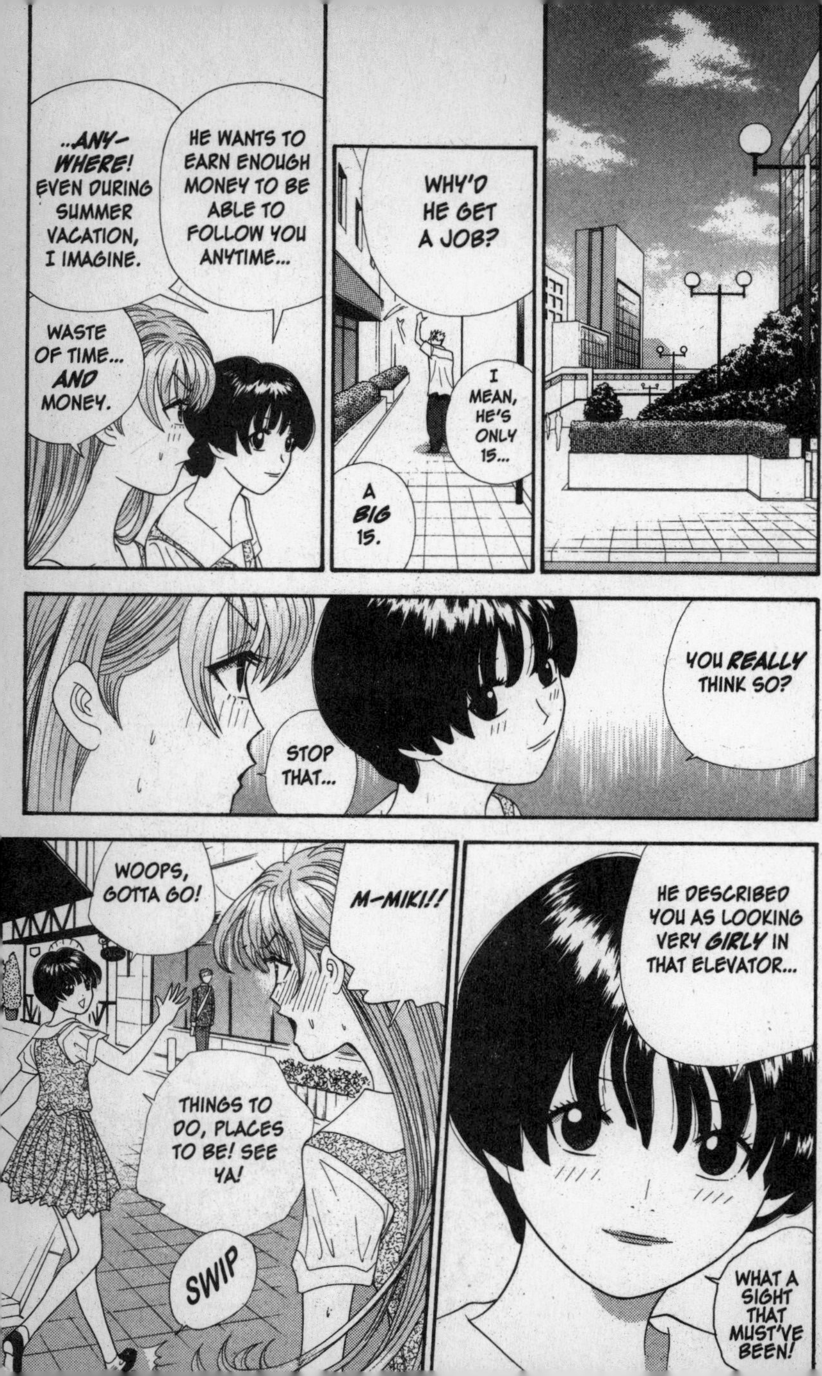
WHY'D HE GET A JOB?
I MEAN, HE'S ONLY 15...
A BIG 15.
HE WANTS TO EARN ENOUGH MONEY TO BE ABLE TO FOLLOW YOU ANYTIME...
...ANY-WHERE! EVEN DURING SUMMER VACATION, I IMAGINE.
WASTE OF TIME... AND MONEY.
YOU REALLY THINK SO?
STOP THAT...
HE DESCRIBED YOU AS LOOKING VERY GIRLY IN THAT ELEVATOR...
WHAT A SIGHT THAT MUST'VE BEEN!
M-MIKI!!
WOOPS, GOTTA GO!
THINGS TO DO, PLACES TO BE! SEE YA!
SWIP

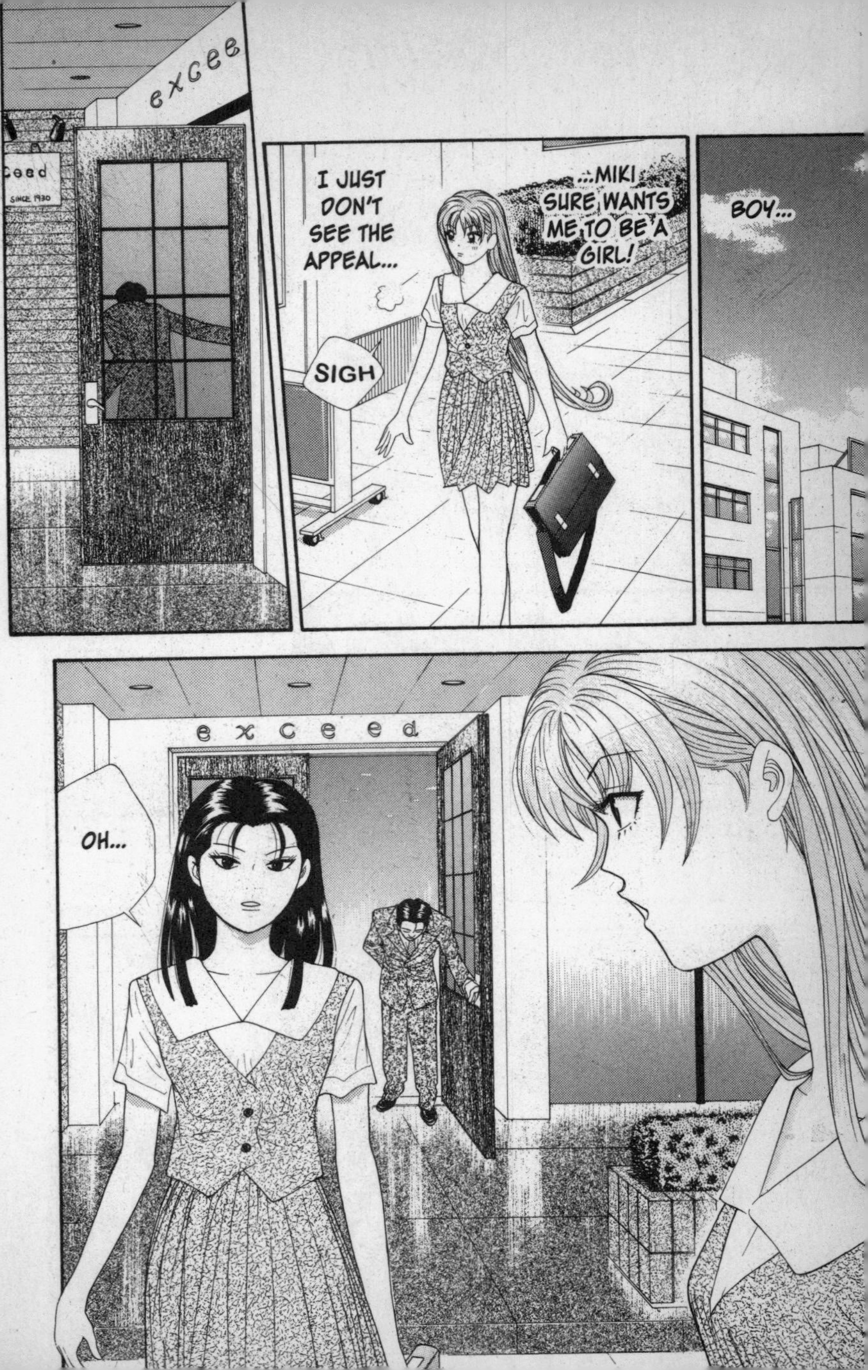
BOY...
...MIKI SURE WANTS ME TO BE A GIRL!
I JUST DON'T SEE THE APPEAL...
SIGH
excee
ceed
SINCE 1930
exceed
OH...

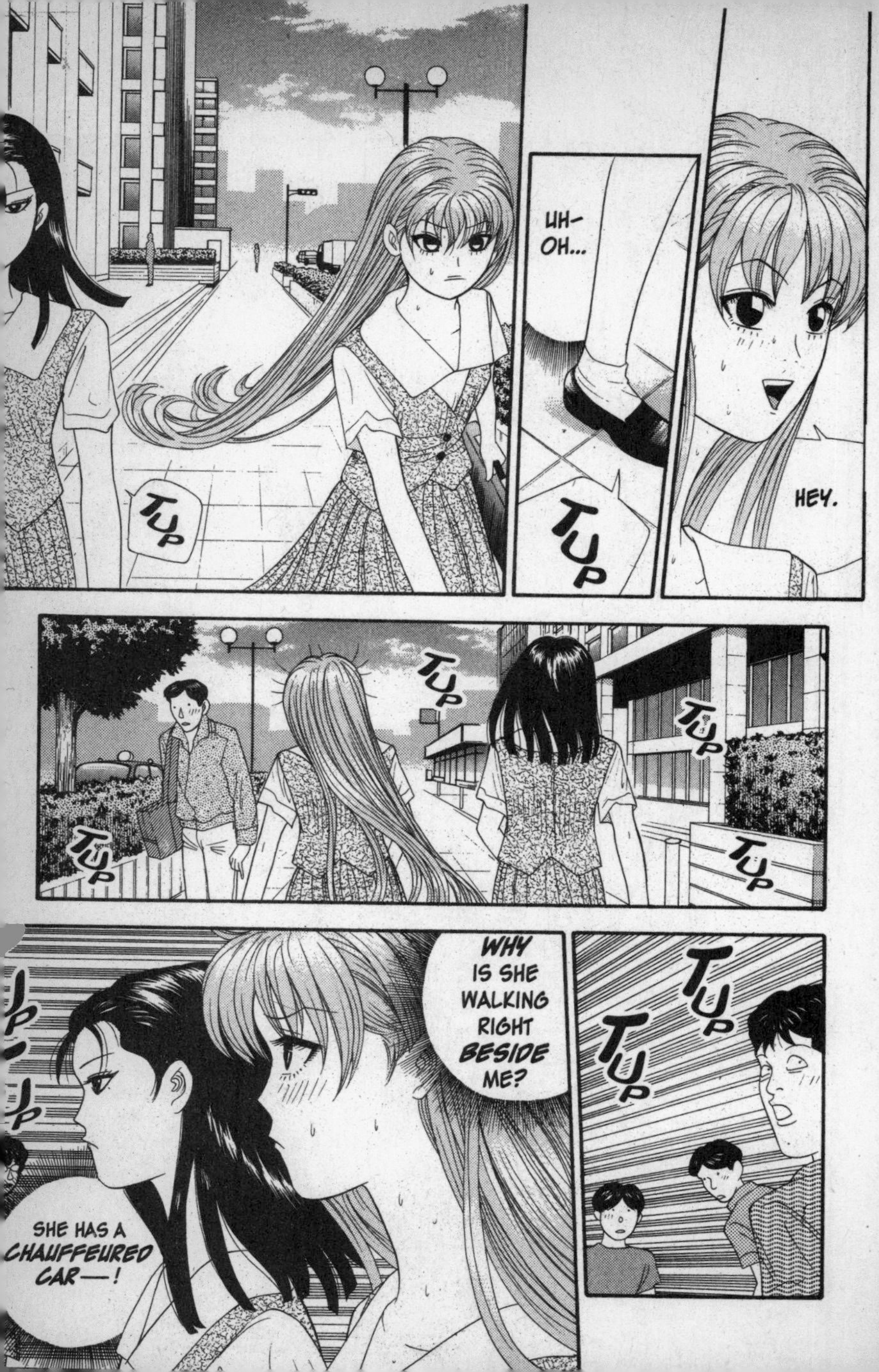
HEY.
UH-OH...
TUP
TUP
TUP
TUP
TUP
TUP
TUP
TUP
WHY IS SHE WALKING RIGHT BESIDE ME?
SHE HAS A CHAUFFEURED CAR—!

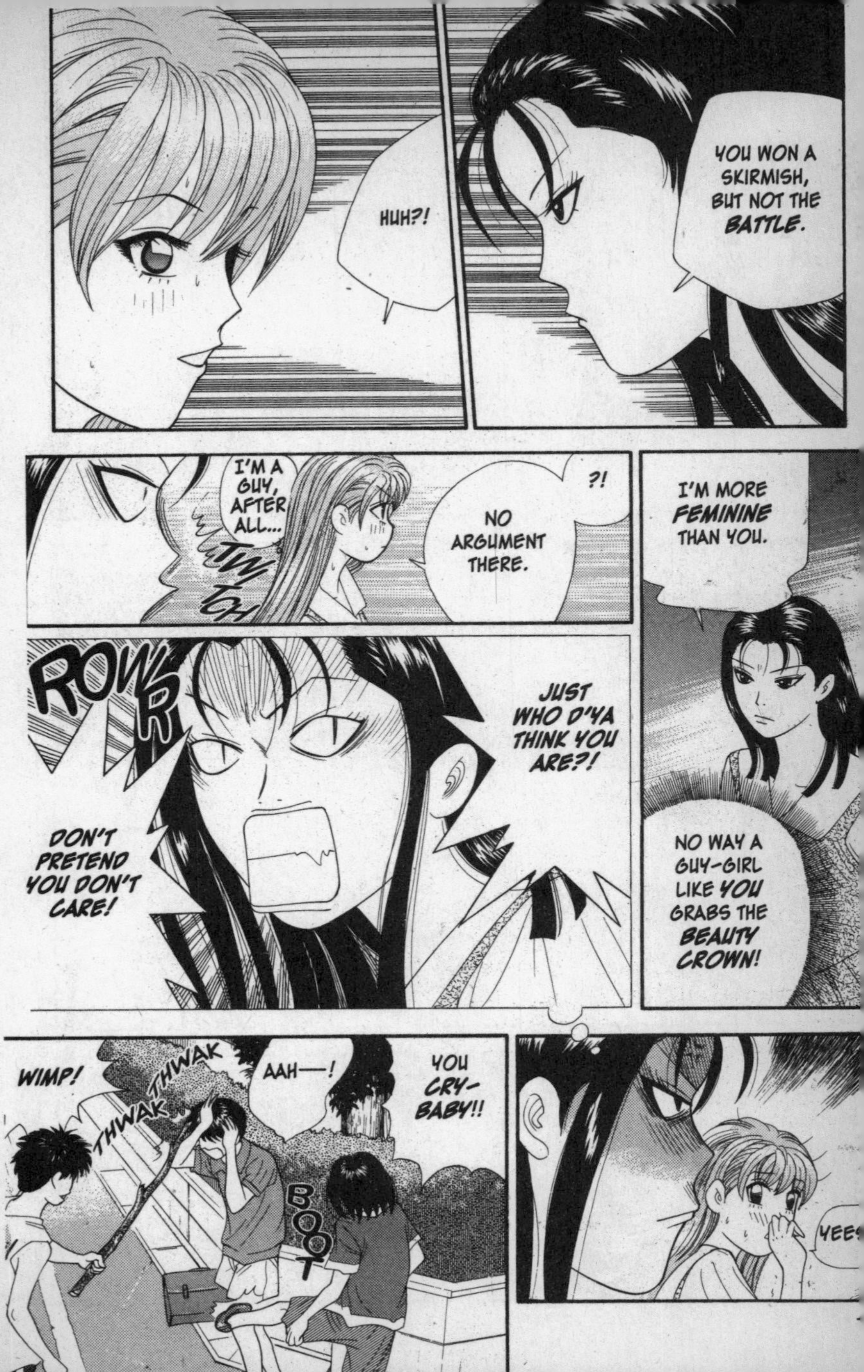
YOU WON A SKIRMISH, BUT NOT THE BATTLE.
HUH?!
I'M MORE FEMININE THAN YOU.
NO WAY A GUY-GIRL LIKE YOU GRABS THE BEAUTY CROWN!
?!
NO ARGUMENT THERE.
I'M A GUY, AFTER ALL...
TWITCH
JUST WHO D'YA THINK YOU ARE?!
ROWR
DON'T PRETEND YOU DON'T CARE!
YEES
YOU CRY-BABY!!
AAH—!
THWAK THWAK
WIMP!
BOOT

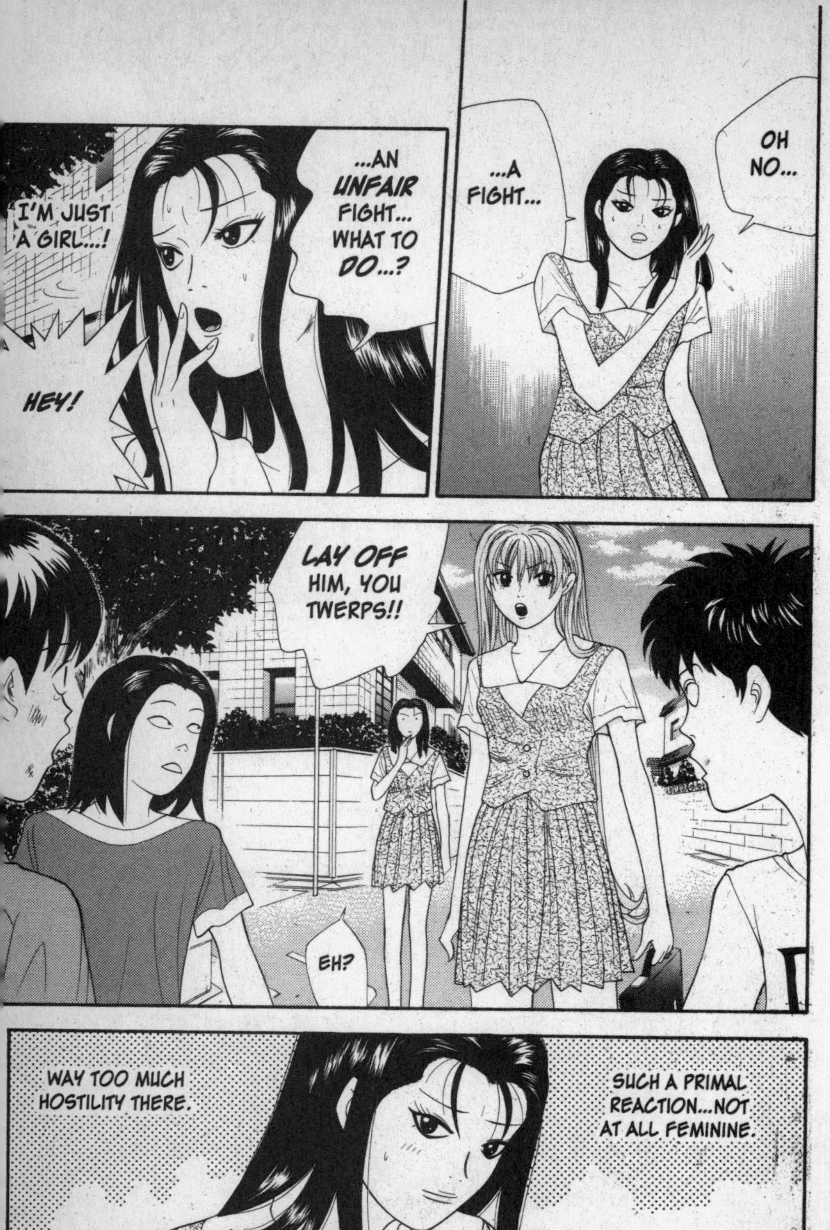
OH NO...
...A FIGHT...
...AN UNFAIR FIGHT... WHAT TO DO...?
I'M JUST A GIRL...!
HEY!
LAY OFF HIM, YOU TWERPS!!
EH?
SUCH A PRIMAL REACTION...NOT AT ALL FEMININE.
WAY TOO MUCH HOSTILITY THERE.

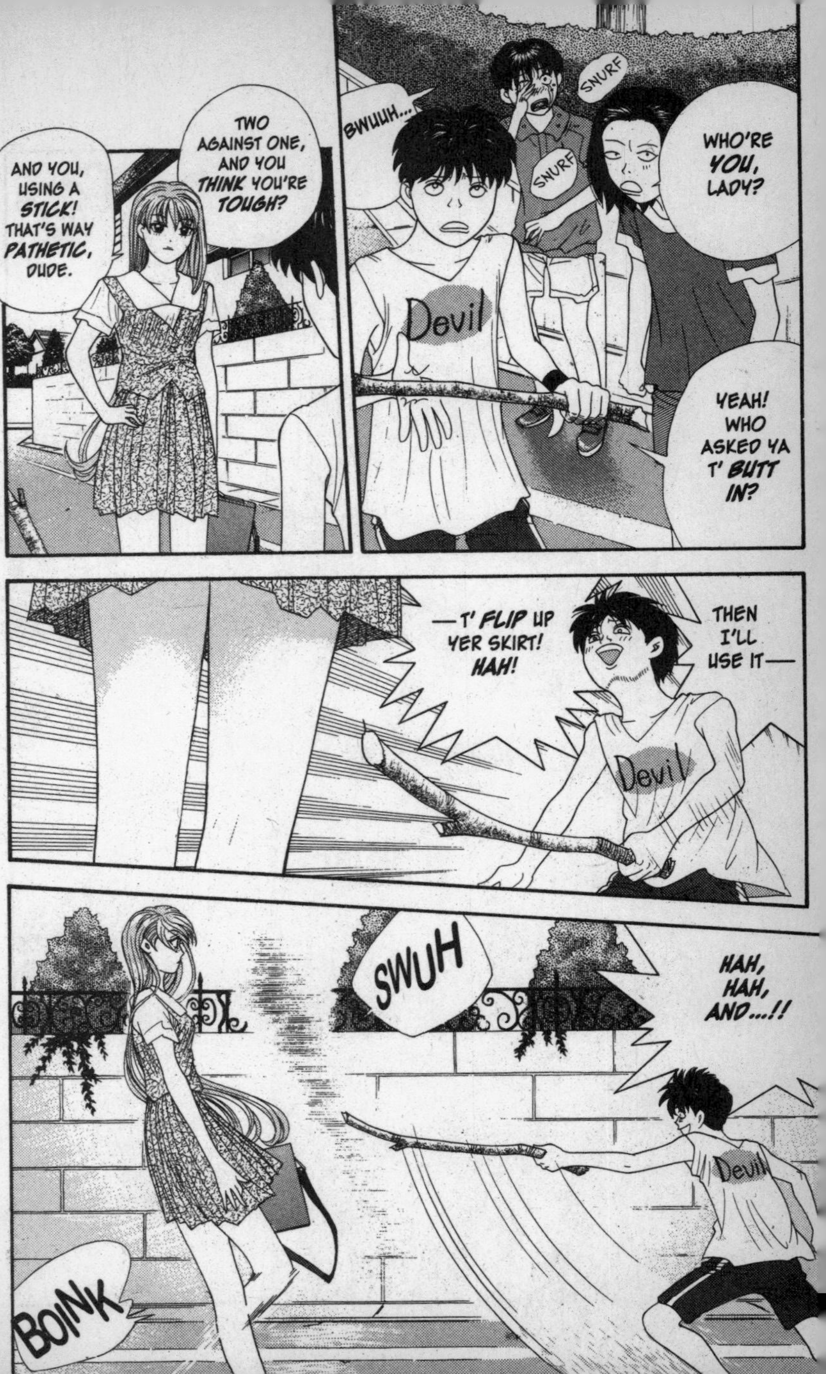
SNURF
WHO'RE YOU, LADY?
BWUUH...
SNURF
YEAH! WHO ASKED YA T' BUTT IN?
TWO AGAINST ONE, AND YOU THINK YOU'RE TOUGH?
AND YOU, USING A STICK! THAT'S WAY PATHETIC, DUDE.
THEN I'LL USE IT—
—T' FLIP UP YER SKIRT! HAH!
HAH, HAH, AND...!!
SWUH
BOINK

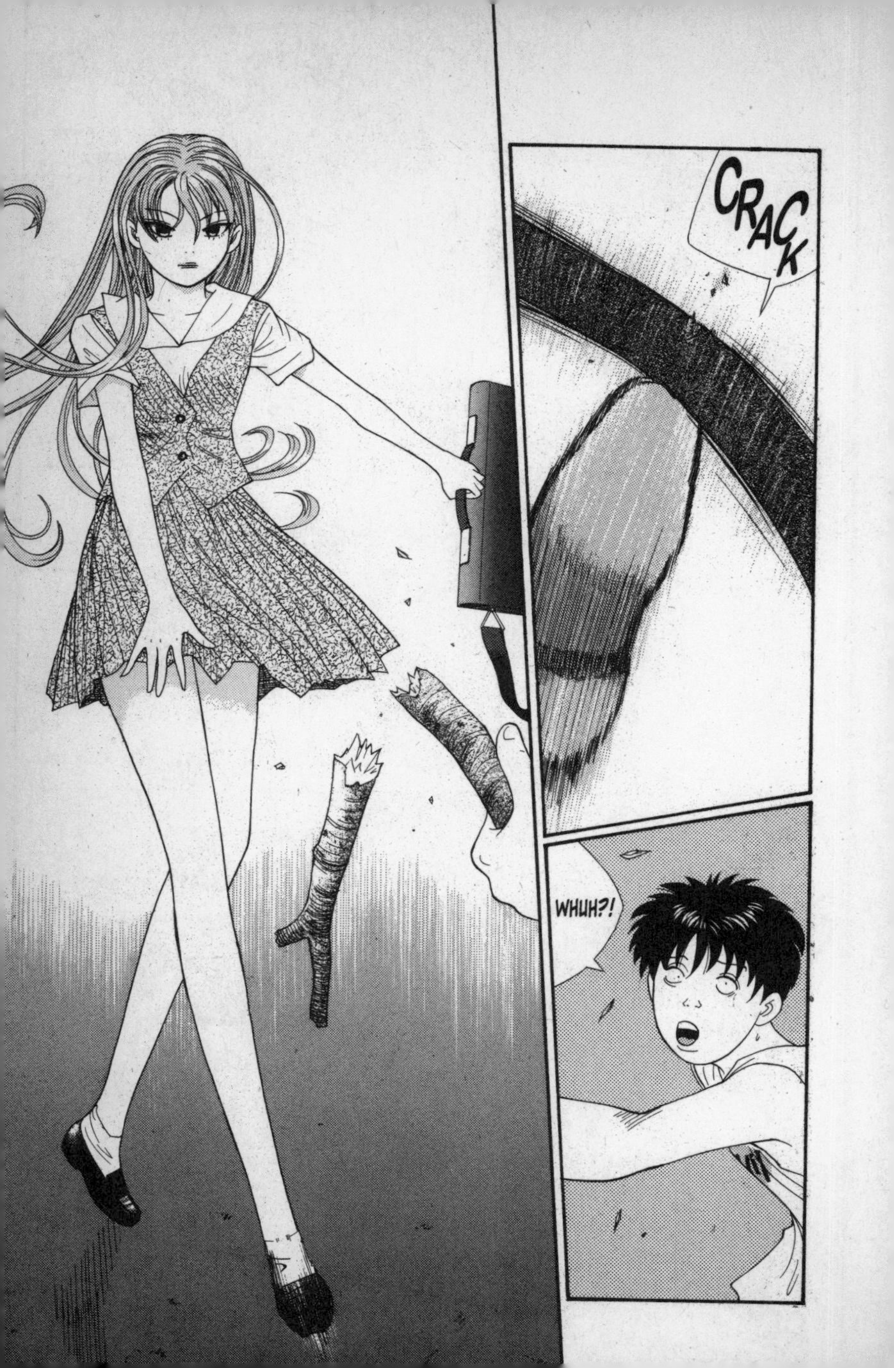
CRACK
WHUH?!

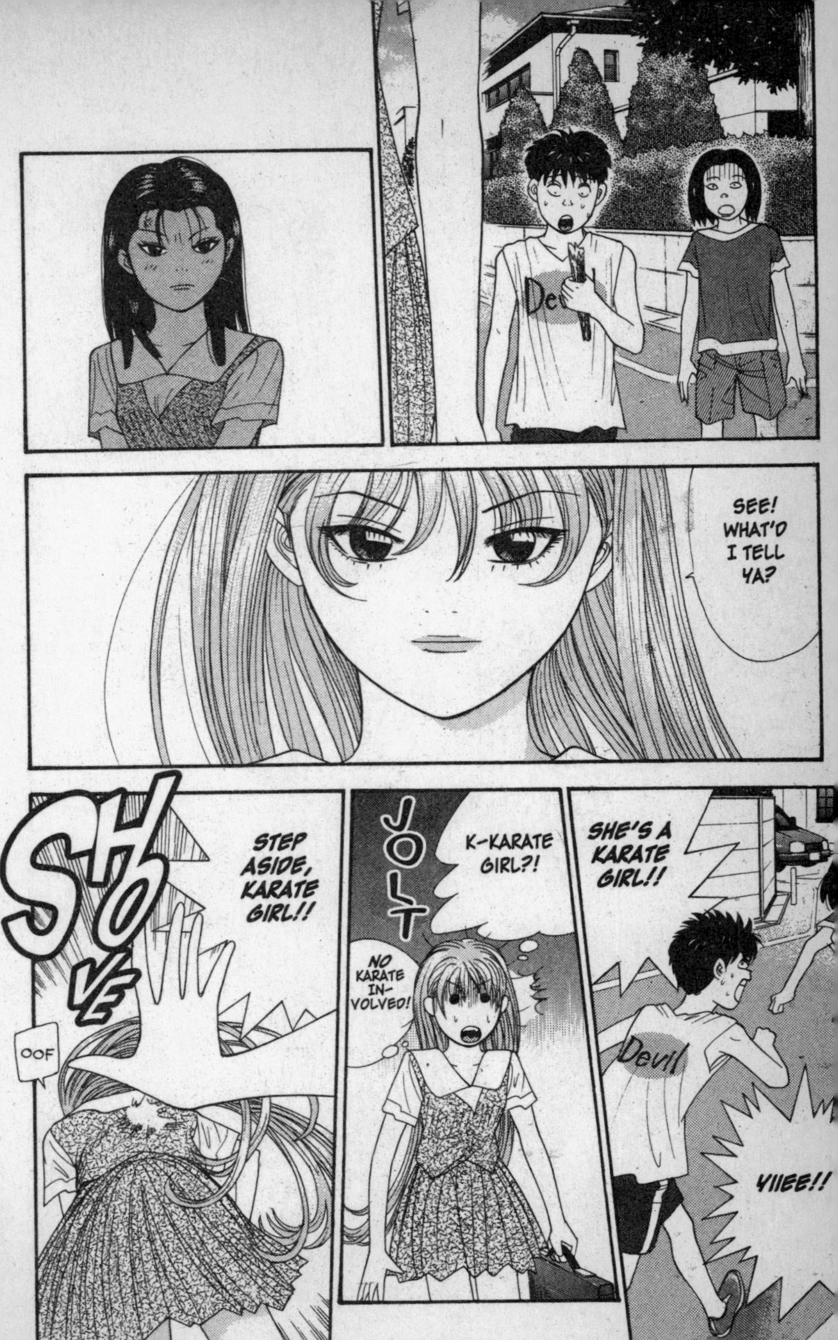
Devil
SEE! WHAT'D I TELL YA?
SHE'S A KARATE GIRL!!
Devil
YIIEE!!
JOLT
K-KARATE GIRL?!
NO KARATE INVOLVED!
SHOVE
STEP ASIDE, KARATE GIRL!!
OOF

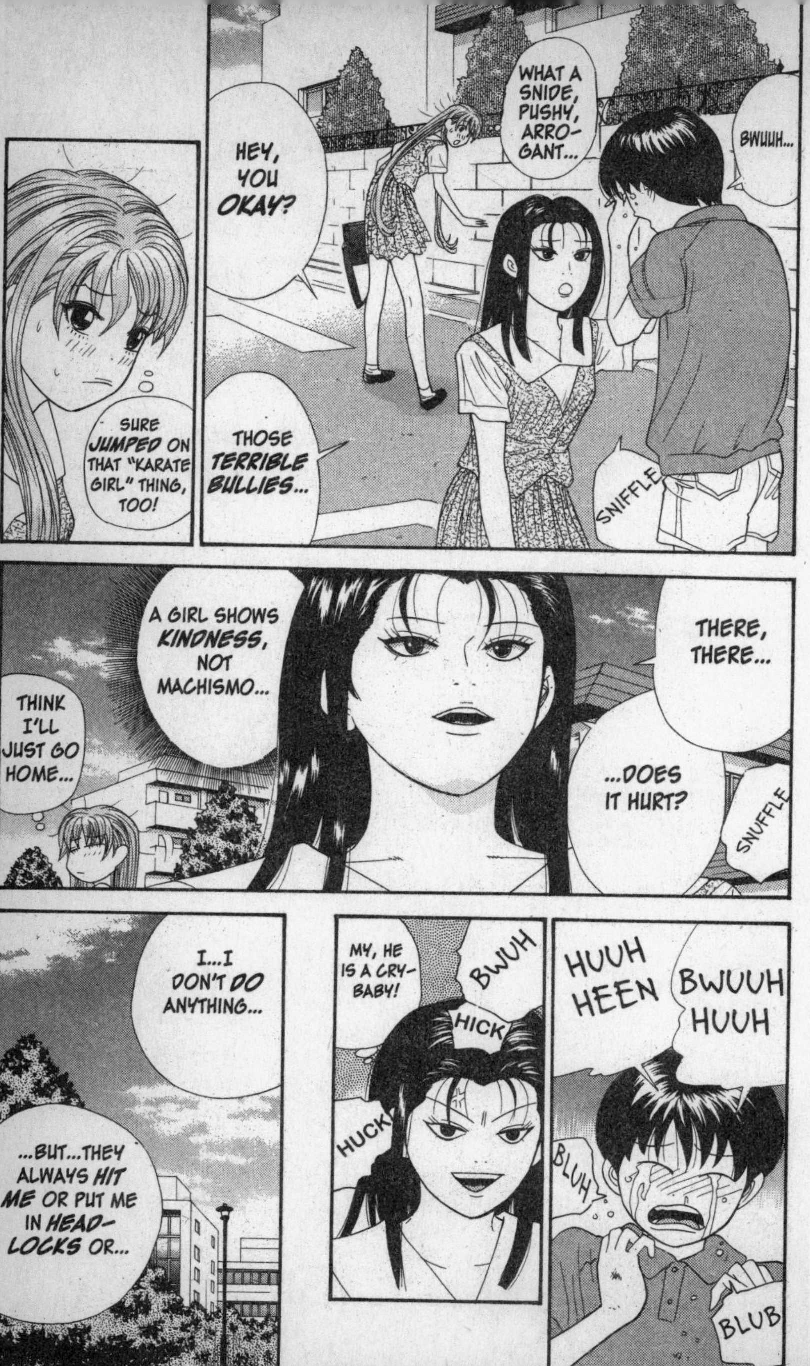
BWUUH...
WHAT A SNIDE, PUSHY, ARRO-GANT...
HEY, YOU OKAY?
SNIFFLE
THOSE TERRIBLE BULLIES...
SURE JUMPED ON THAT "KARATE GIRL" THING, TOO!
THERE, THERE...
SNUFFLE
...DOES IT HURT?
A GIRL SHOWS KINDNESS, NOT MACHISMO...
THINK I'LL JUST GO HOME...
BWUUH HUUH
HUUH HEEN
BLUH
BLUB
BWUH
MY, HE IS A CRY-BABY!
HICK
HUCK
I...I DON'T DO ANYTHING...
...BUT...THEY ALWAYS HIT ME OR PUT ME IN HEAD-LOCKS OR...

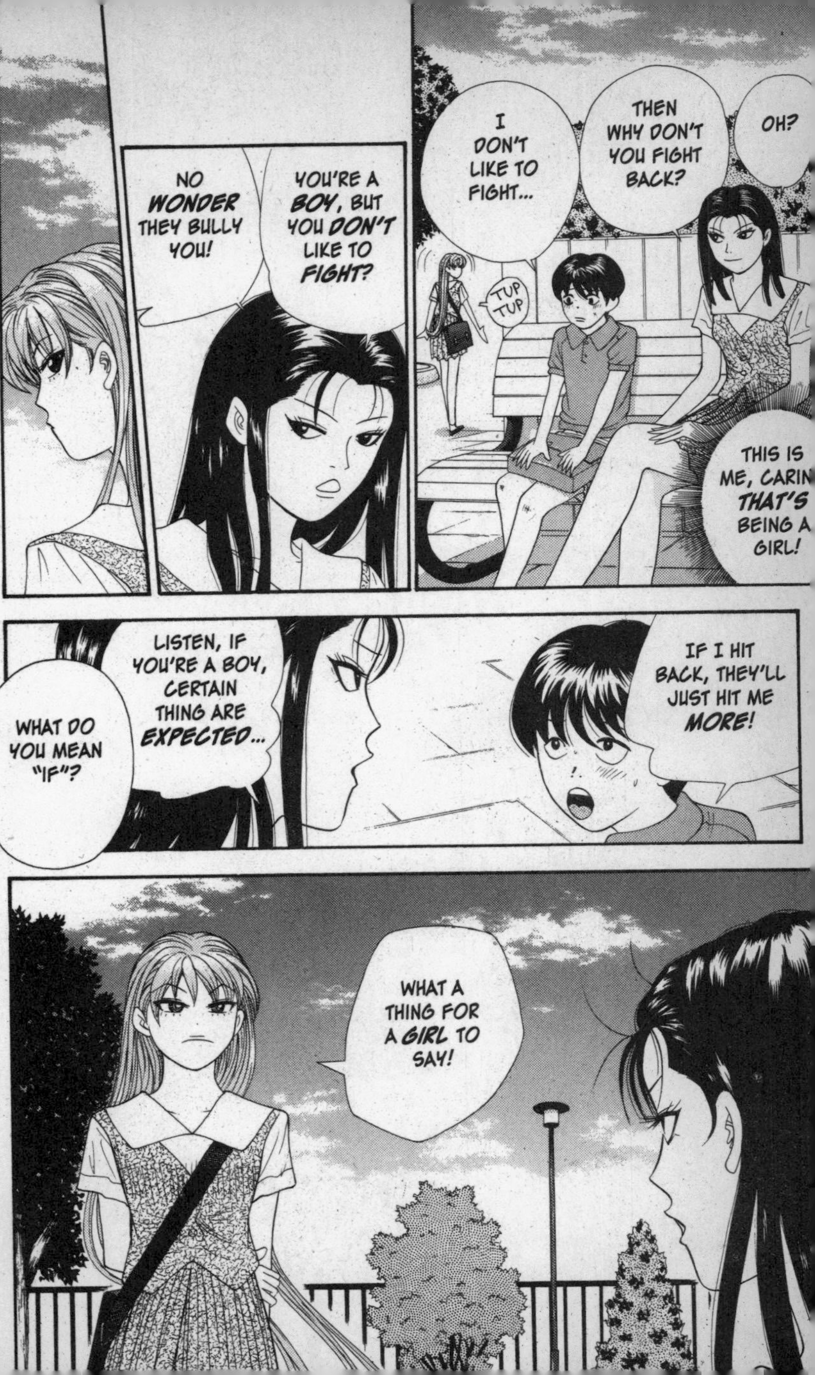
OH?
THEN WHY DON'T YOU FIGHT BACK?
I DON'T LIKE TO FIGHT...
TUP TUP
THIS IS ME, CARIN THAT'S BEING A GIRL!
YOU'RE A BOY, BUT YOU DON'T LIKE TO FIGHT?
NO WONDER THEY BULLY YOU!
IF I HIT BACK, THEY'LL JUST HIT ME MORE!
LISTEN, IF YOU'RE A BOY, CERTAIN THING ARE EXPECTED...
WHAT DO YOU MEAN "IF"?
WHAT A THING FOR A GIRL TO SAY!

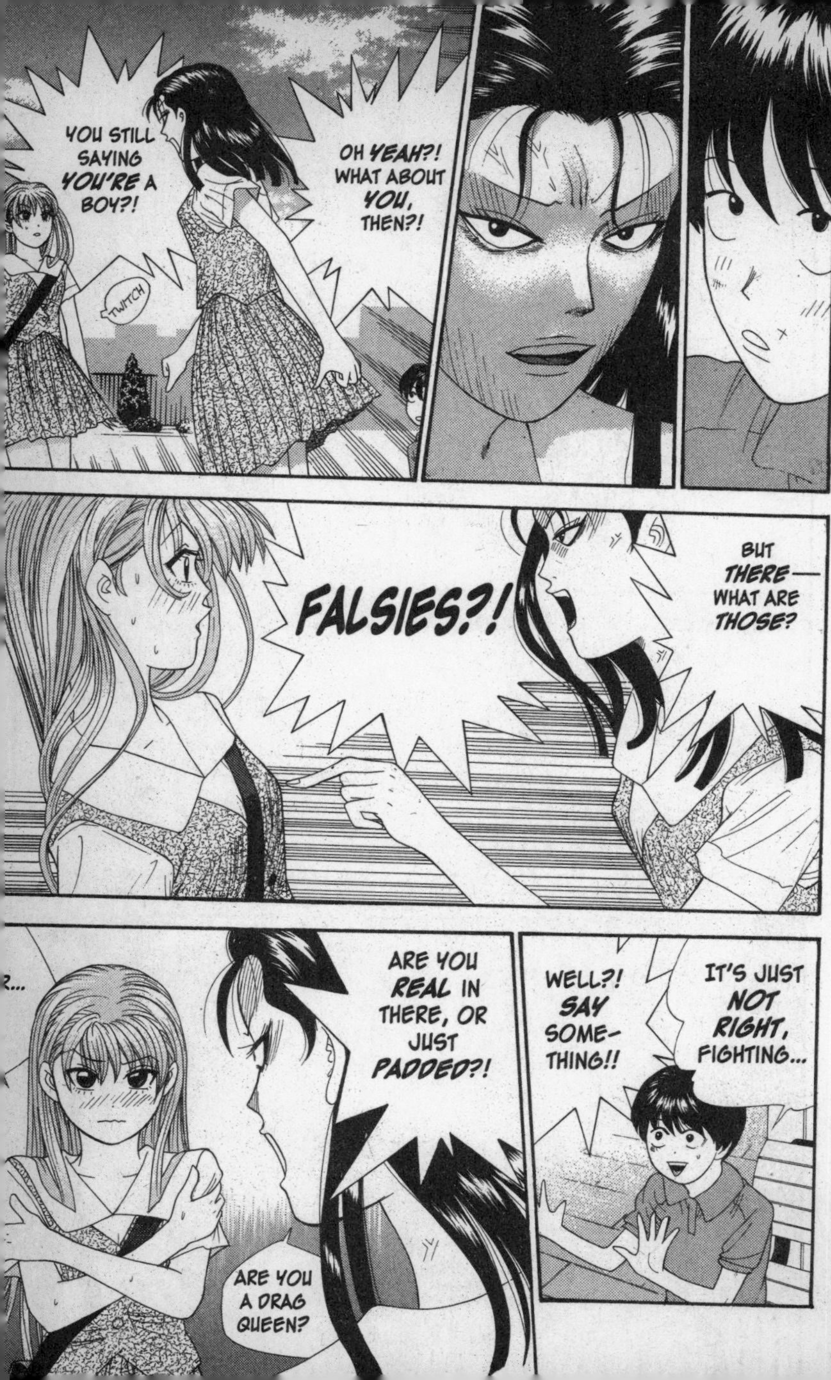
OH YEAH?! WHAT ABOUT YOU, THEN?!
YOU STILL SAYING YOU'RE A BOY?!
TWITCH
BUT THERE— WHAT ARE THOSE?
FALSIES?!
IT'S JUST NOT RIGHT, FIGHTING...
WELL?! SAY SOME-THING!!
ARE YOU REAL IN THERE, OR JUST PADDED?!
ARE YOU A DRAG QUEEN?

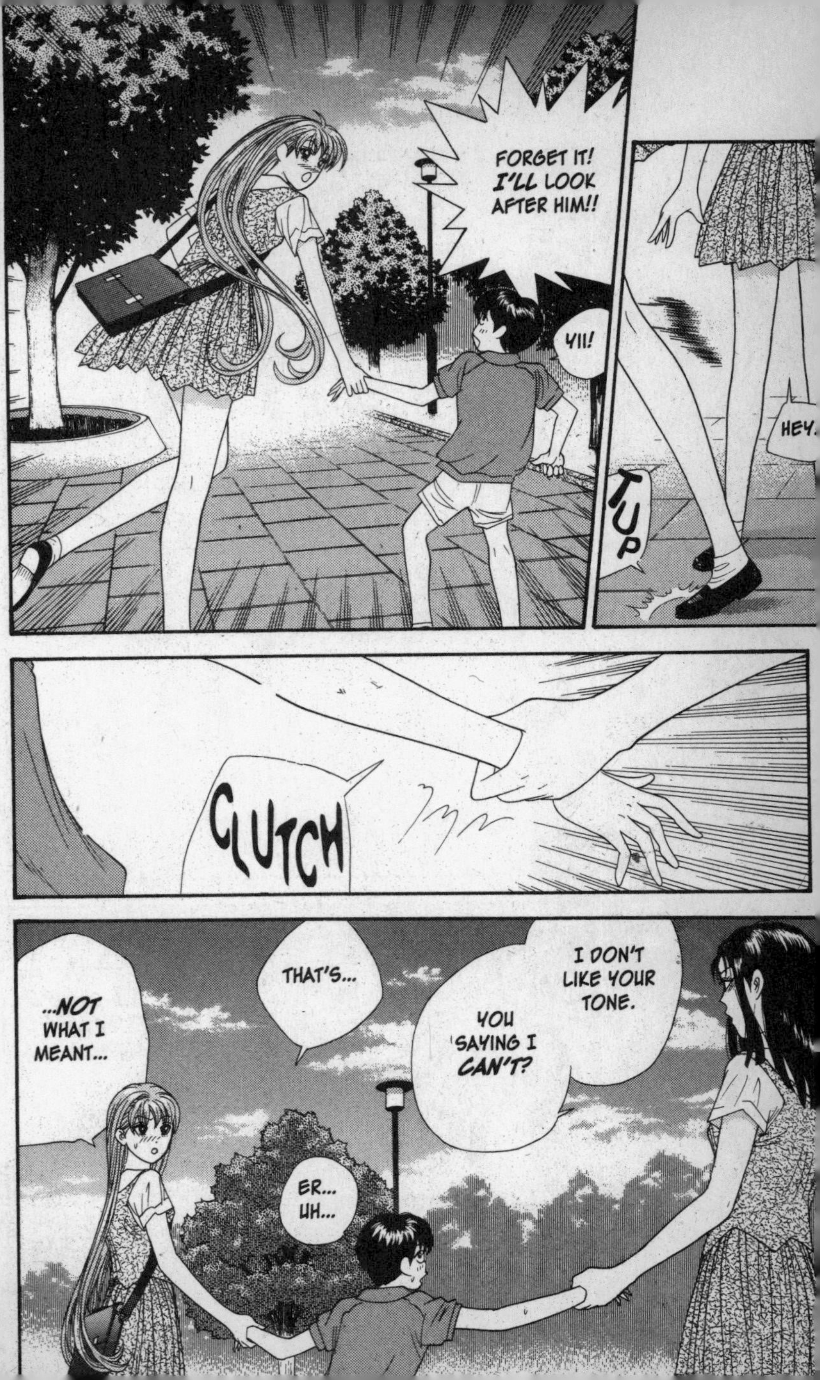
HEY.
TUP
FORGET IT! I'LL LOOK AFTER HIM!!
YII!
CLUTCH
I DON'T LIKE YOUR TONE.
YOU SAYING I CAN'T?
THAT'S...
...NOT WHAT I MEANT...
ER... UH...

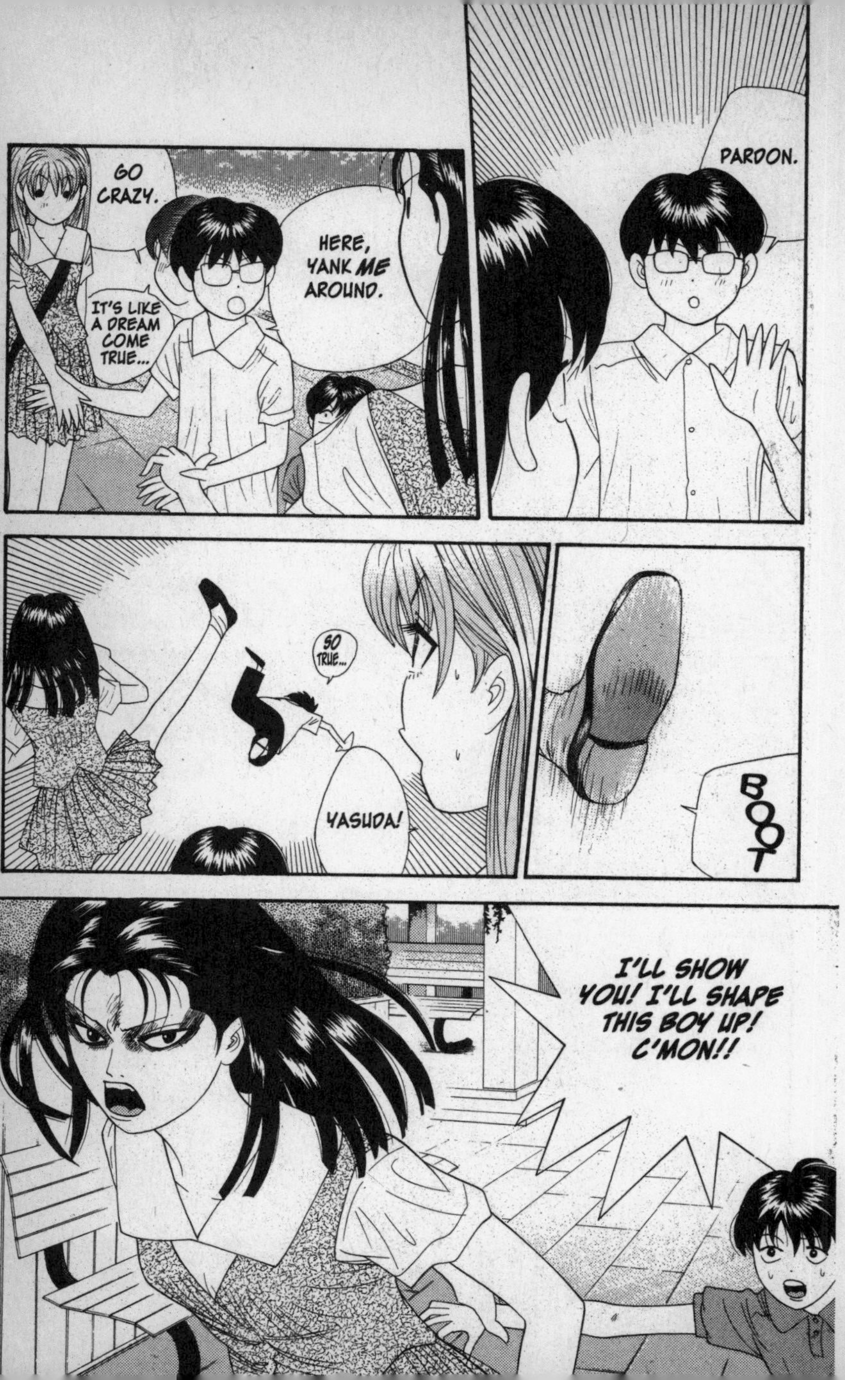
PARDON.
HERE, YANK ME AROUND.
GO CRAZY.
IT'S LIKE A DREAM COME TRUE...
BOOT
SO TRUE...
YASUDA!
I'LL SHOW YOU! I'LL SHAPE THIS BOY UP! C'MON!!

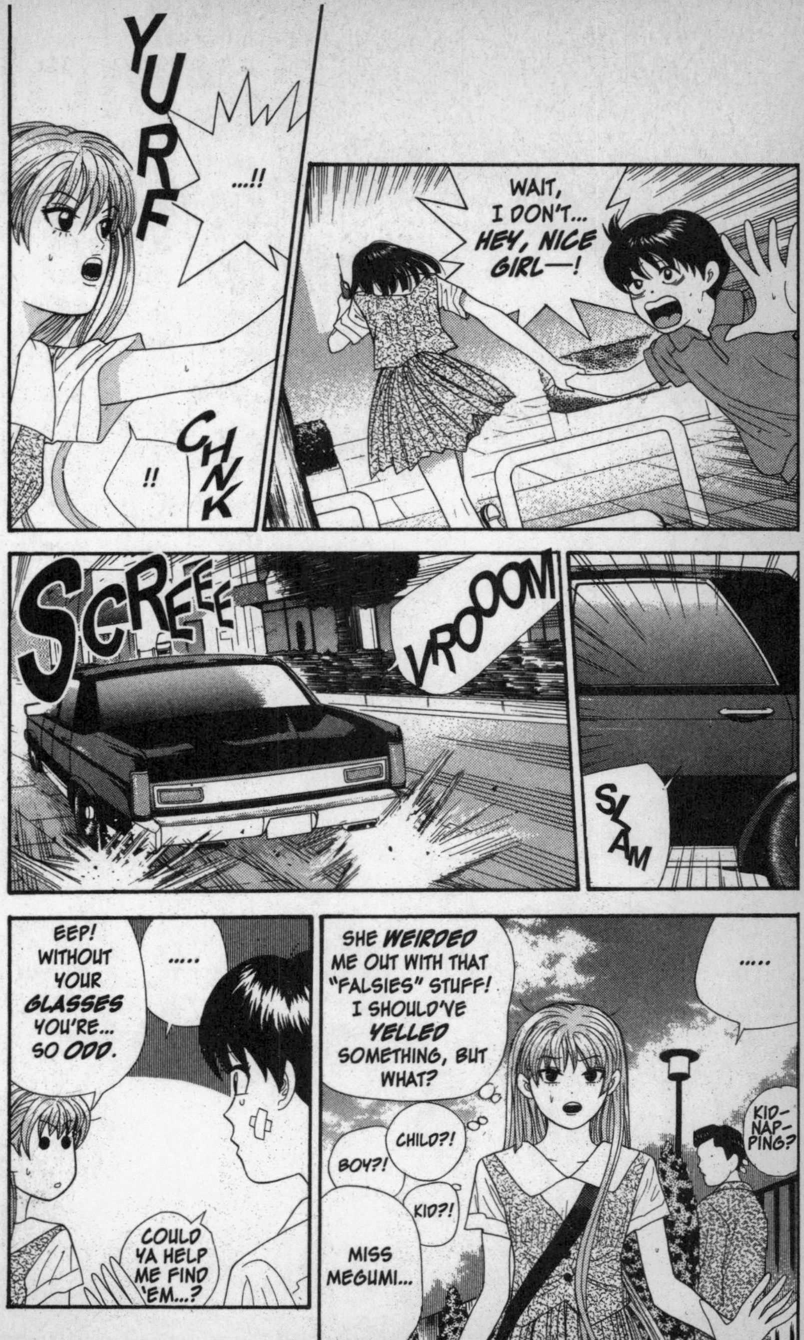
WAIT, I DON'T... HEY, NICE GIRL—!
YURF
...!!
CHNK
!!
SLAM
VROOOM
SCREEE
.....
SHE WEIRDED ME OUT WITH THAT "FALSIES" STUFF! I SHOULD'VE YELLED SOMETHING, BUT WHAT?
KID-NAPPING?
CHILD?!
BOY?!
KID?!
MISS MEGUMI...
.....
EEP! WITHOUT YOUR GLASSES YOU'RE... SO ODD.
COULD YA HELP ME FIND 'EM...?

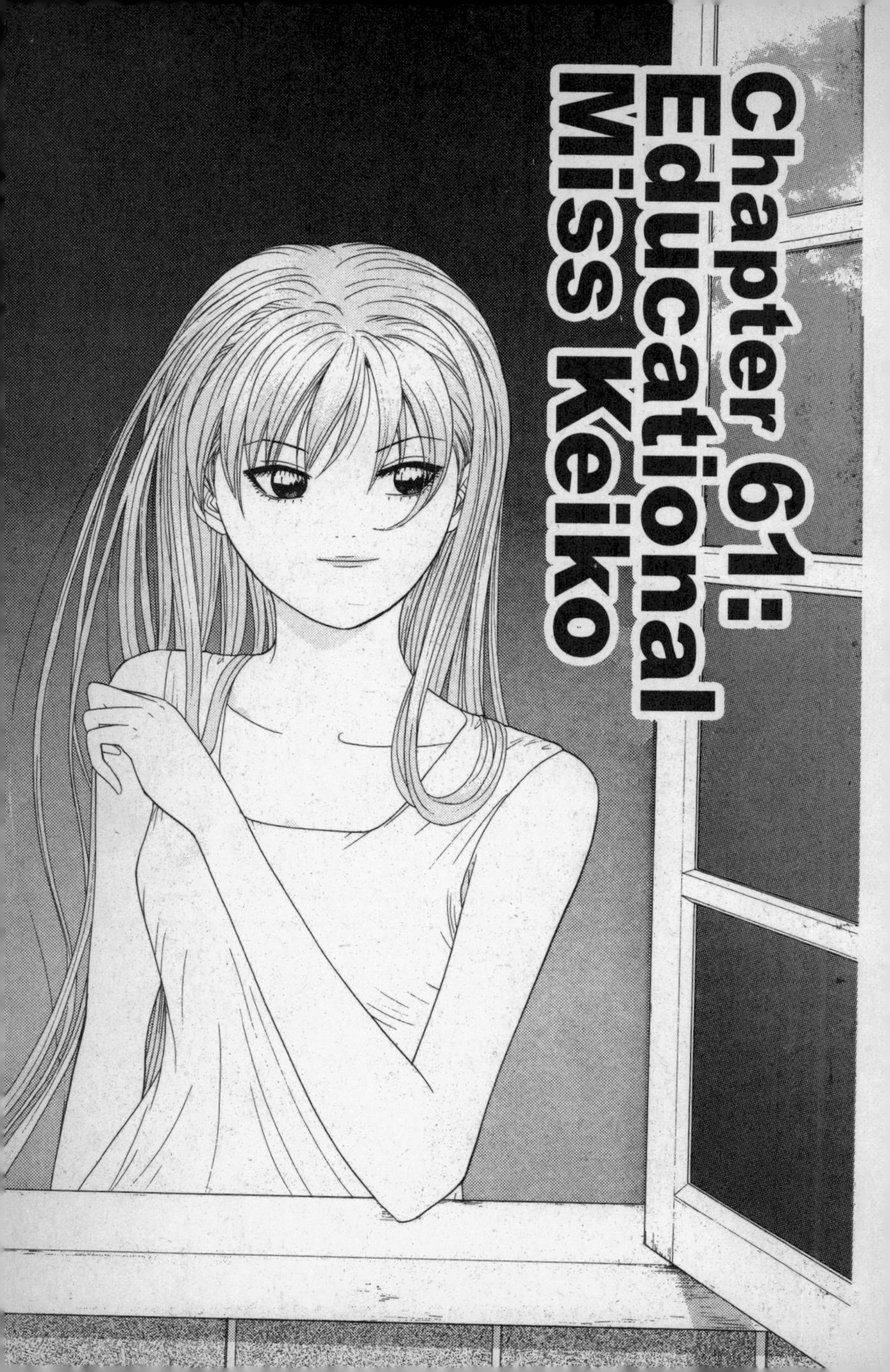
Chapter 61:
Educational
Miss Keiko

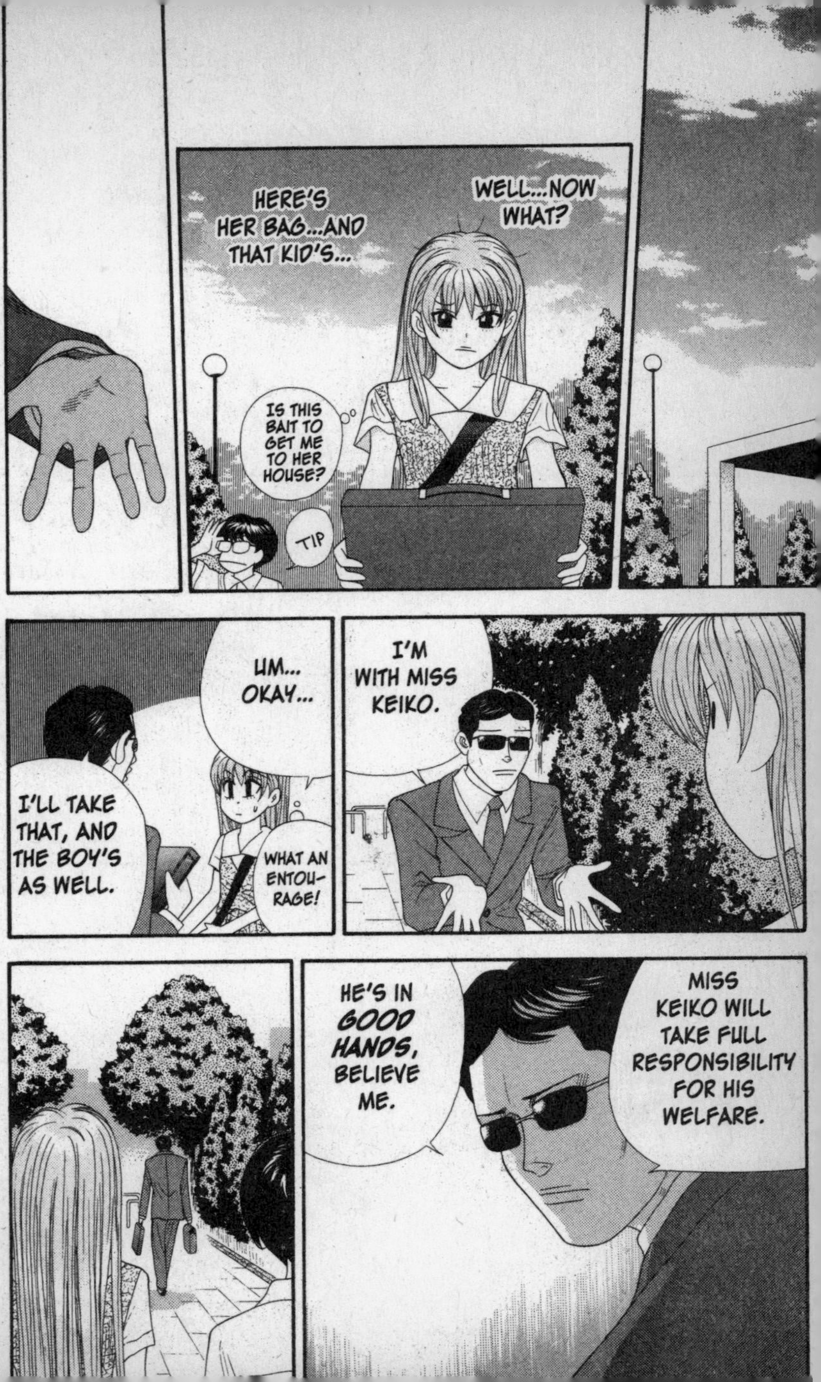
WELL...NOW WHAT?
HERE'S HER BAG...AND THAT KID'S...
IS THIS BAIT TO GET ME TO HER HOUSE?
TIP
I'M WITH MISS KEIKO.
UM... OKAY...
WHAT AN ENTOU-RAGE!
I'LL TAKE THAT, AND THE BOY'S AS WELL.
MISS KEIKO WILL TAKE FULL RESPONSIBILITY FOR HIS WELFARE.
HE'S IN *GOOD HANDS*, BELIEVE ME.

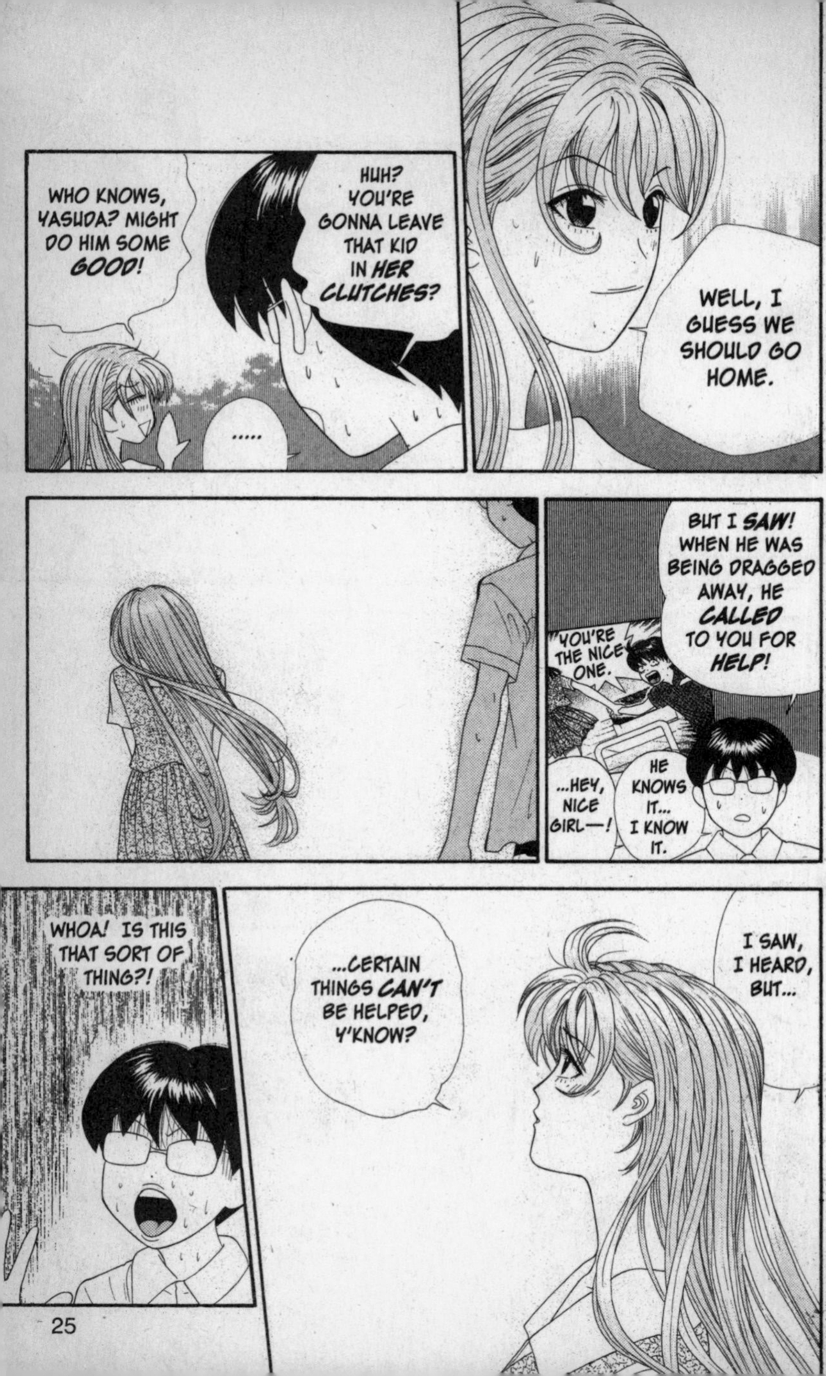

WELL, I GUESS WE SHOULD GO HOME.
HUH? YOU'RE GONNA LEAVE THAT KID IN *HER* CLUTCHES?
WHO KNOWS, YASUDA? MIGHT DO HIM SOME *GOOD*!
.....
BUT I *SAW*! WHEN HE WAS BEING DRAGGED AWAY, HE *CALLED* TO YOU FOR *HELP*!
YOU'RE THE NICE ONE.
HE KNOWS IT... I KNOW IT.
...HEY, NICE GIRL—!
I SAW, I HEARD, BUT...
...CERTAIN THINGS *CAN'T* BE HELPED, Y'KNOW?
WHOA! IS THIS THAT SORT OF THING?!

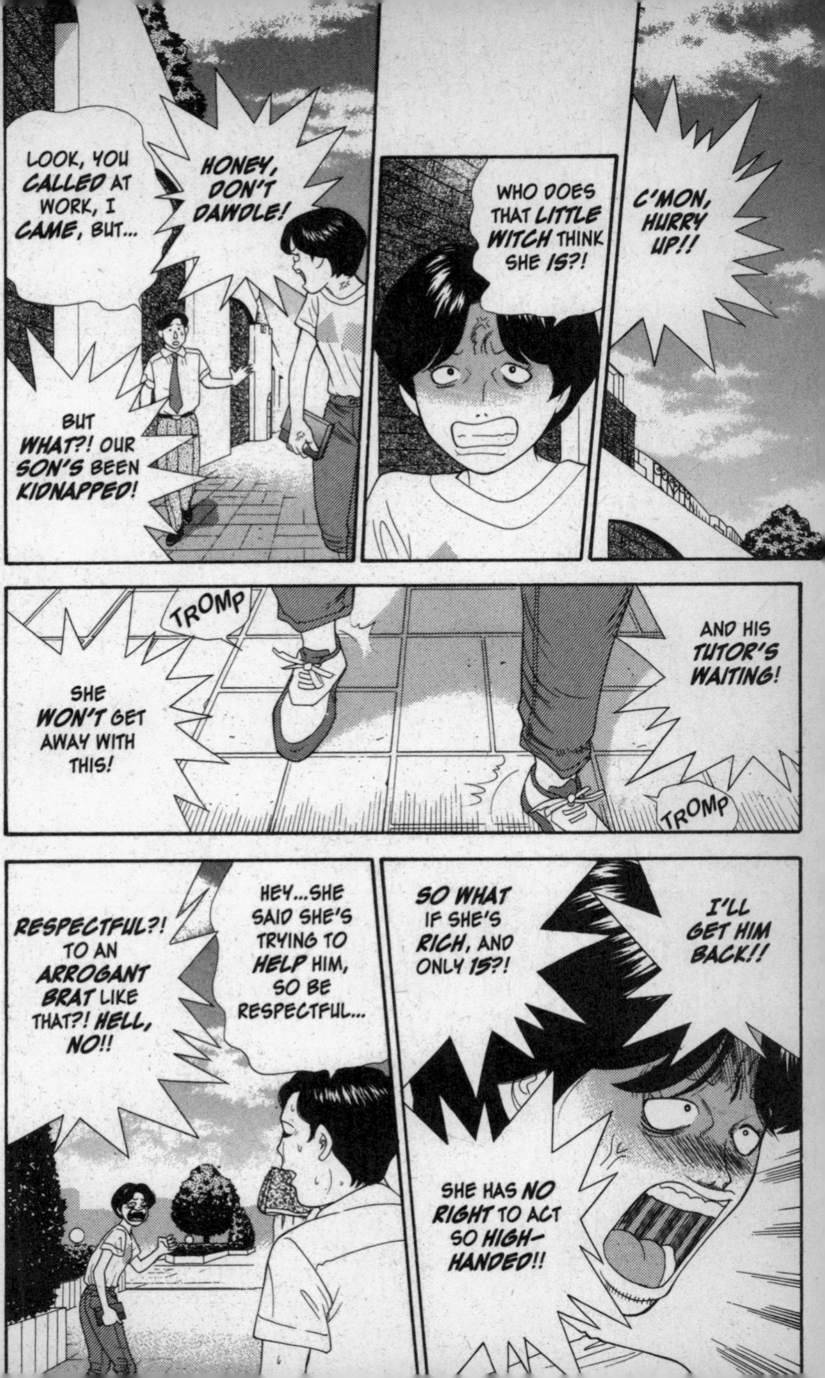
C'MON, HURRY UP!!
WHO DOES THAT LITTLE WITCH THINK SHE IS?!
HONEY, DON'T DAWDLE!
LOOK, YOU CALLED AT WORK, I CAME, BUT...
BUT WHAT?! OUR SON'S BEEN KIDNAPPED!
AND HIS TUTOR'S WAITING!
TROMP
TROMP
SHE WON'T GET AWAY WITH THIS!
I'LL GET HIM BACK!!
SO WHAT IF SHE'S RICH, AND ONLY 15?!
SHE HAS NO RIGHT TO ACT SO HIGH-HANDED!!
HEY...SHE SAID SHE'S TRYING TO HELP HIM, SO BE RESPECTFUL...
RESPECTFUL?! TO AN ARROGANT BRAT LIKE THAT?! HELL, NO!!

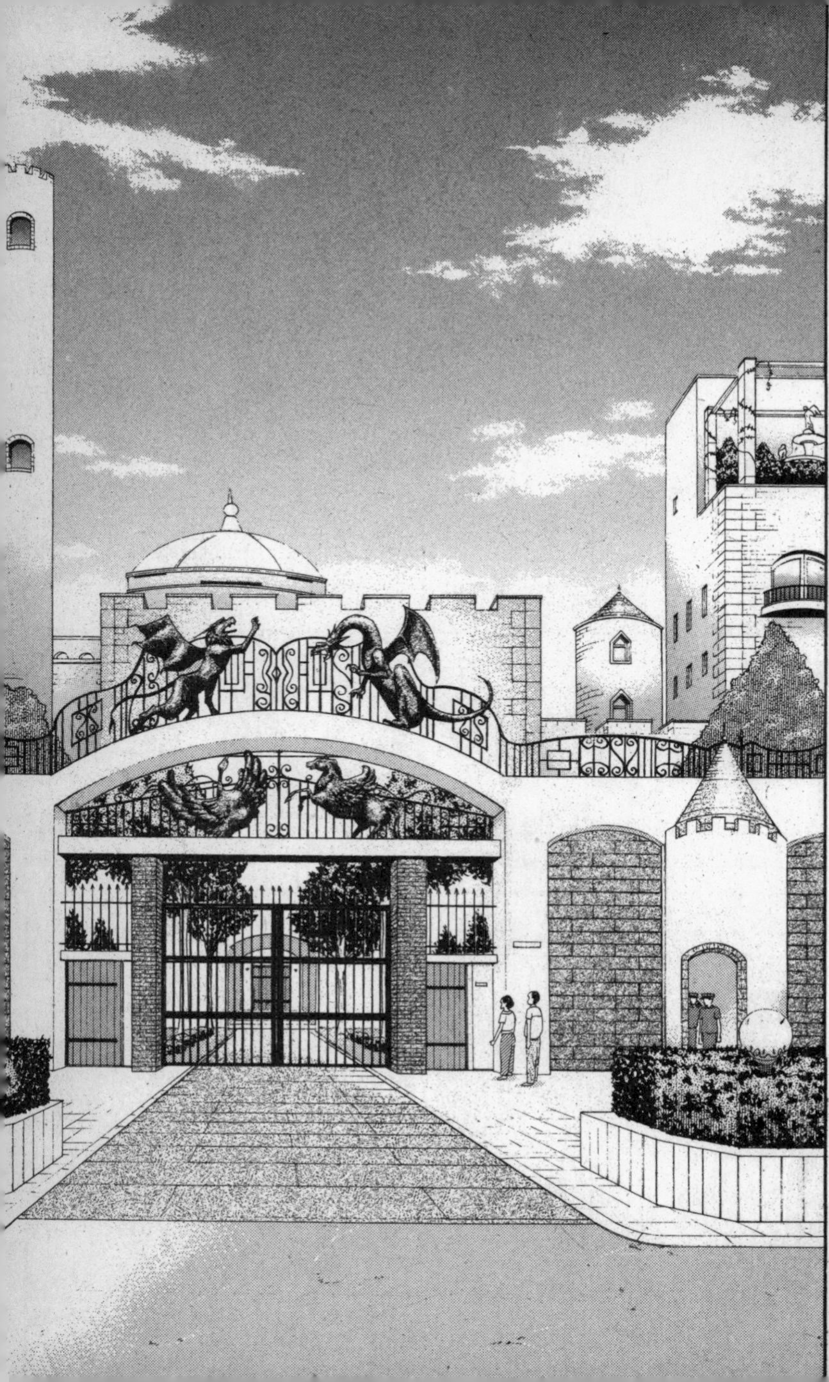

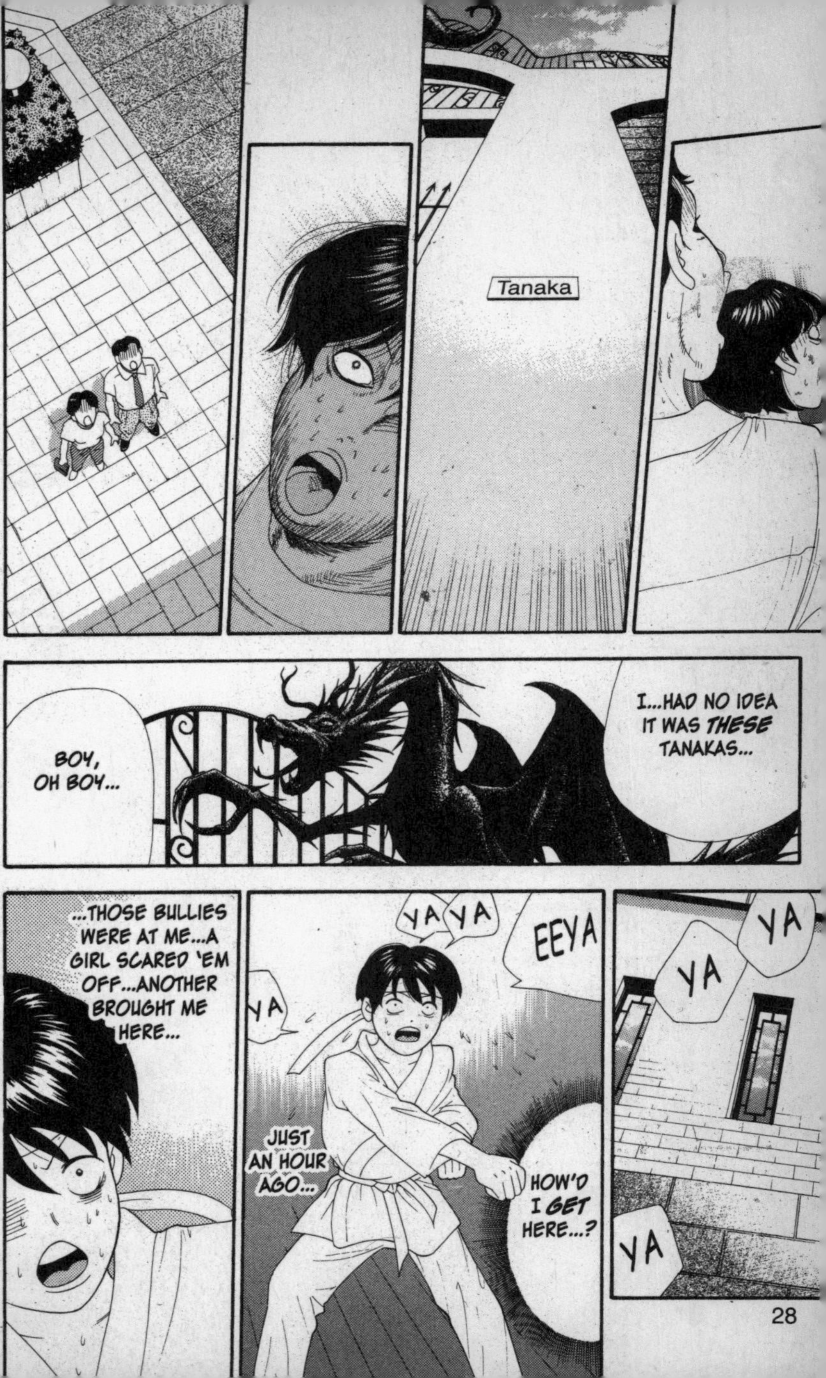
Tanaka
I...HAD NO IDEA IT WAS *THESE* TANAKAS...
BOY, OH BOY...
YA
YA
YA
EEYA
YA YA
YA
HOW'D I *GET* HERE...?
JUST AN HOUR AGO...
...THOSE BULLIES WERE AT ME...A GIRL SCARED 'EM OFF...ANOTHER BROUGHT ME HERE...

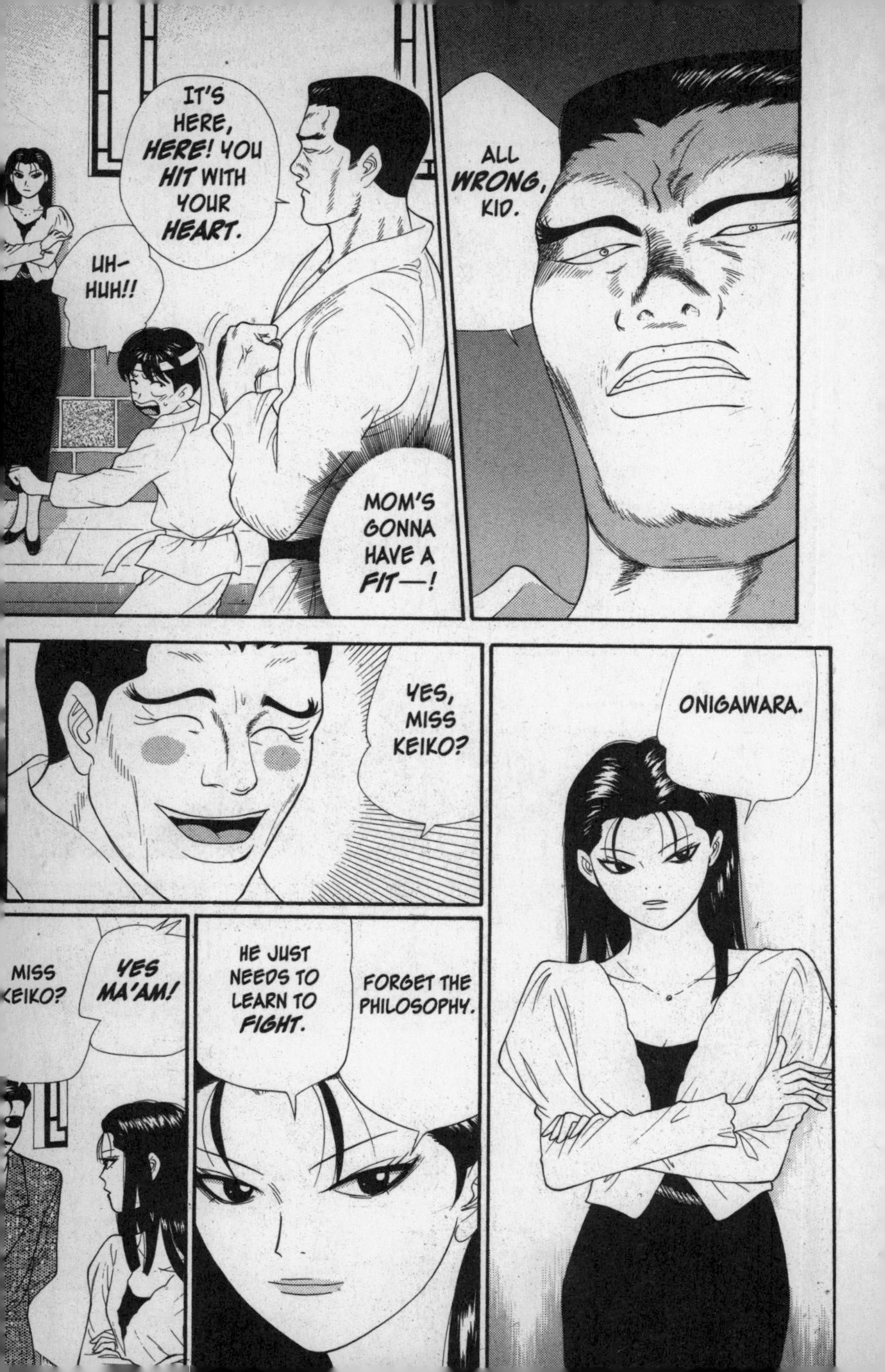
ALL WRONG, KID.
IT'S HERE, HERE! YOU HIT WITH YOUR HEART.
UH-HUH!!
MOM'S GONNA HAVE A FIT—!
ONIGAWARA.
YES, MISS KEIKO?
FORGET THE PHILOSOPHY.
HE JUST NEEDS TO LEARN TO FIGHT.
YES MA'AM!
MISS KEIKO?

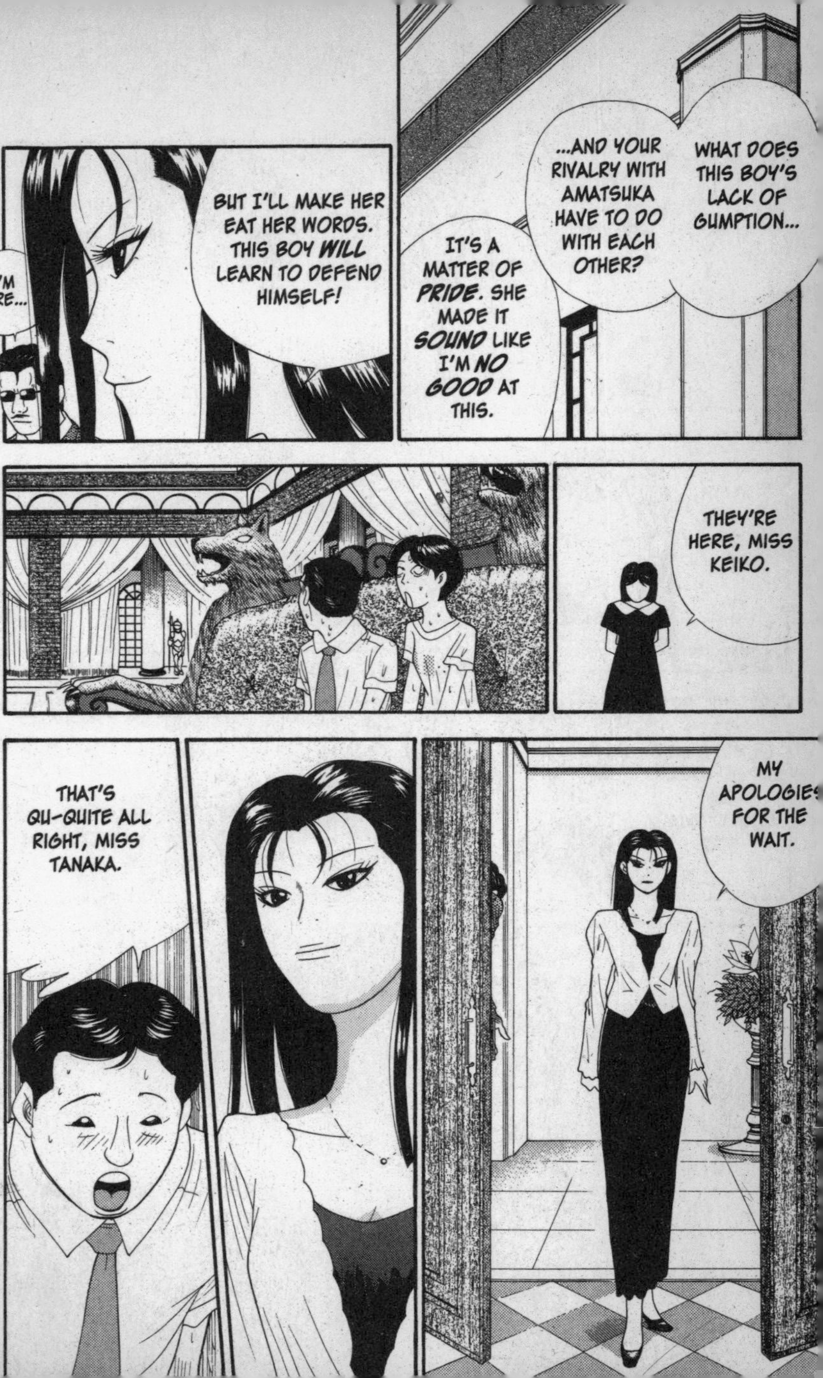
WHAT DOES THIS BOY'S LACK OF GUMPTION...
...AND YOUR RIVALRY WITH AMATSUKA HAVE TO DO WITH EACH OTHER?
IT'S A MATTER OF PRIDE. SHE MADE IT SOUND LIKE I'M NO GOOD AT THIS.
BUT I'LL MAKE HER EAT HER WORDS. THIS BOY WILL LEARN TO DEFEND HIMSELF!
I'M SURE...
THEY'RE HERE, MISS KEIKO.
MY APOLOGIES FOR THE WAIT.
THAT'S QU-QUITE ALL RIGHT, MISS TANAKA.

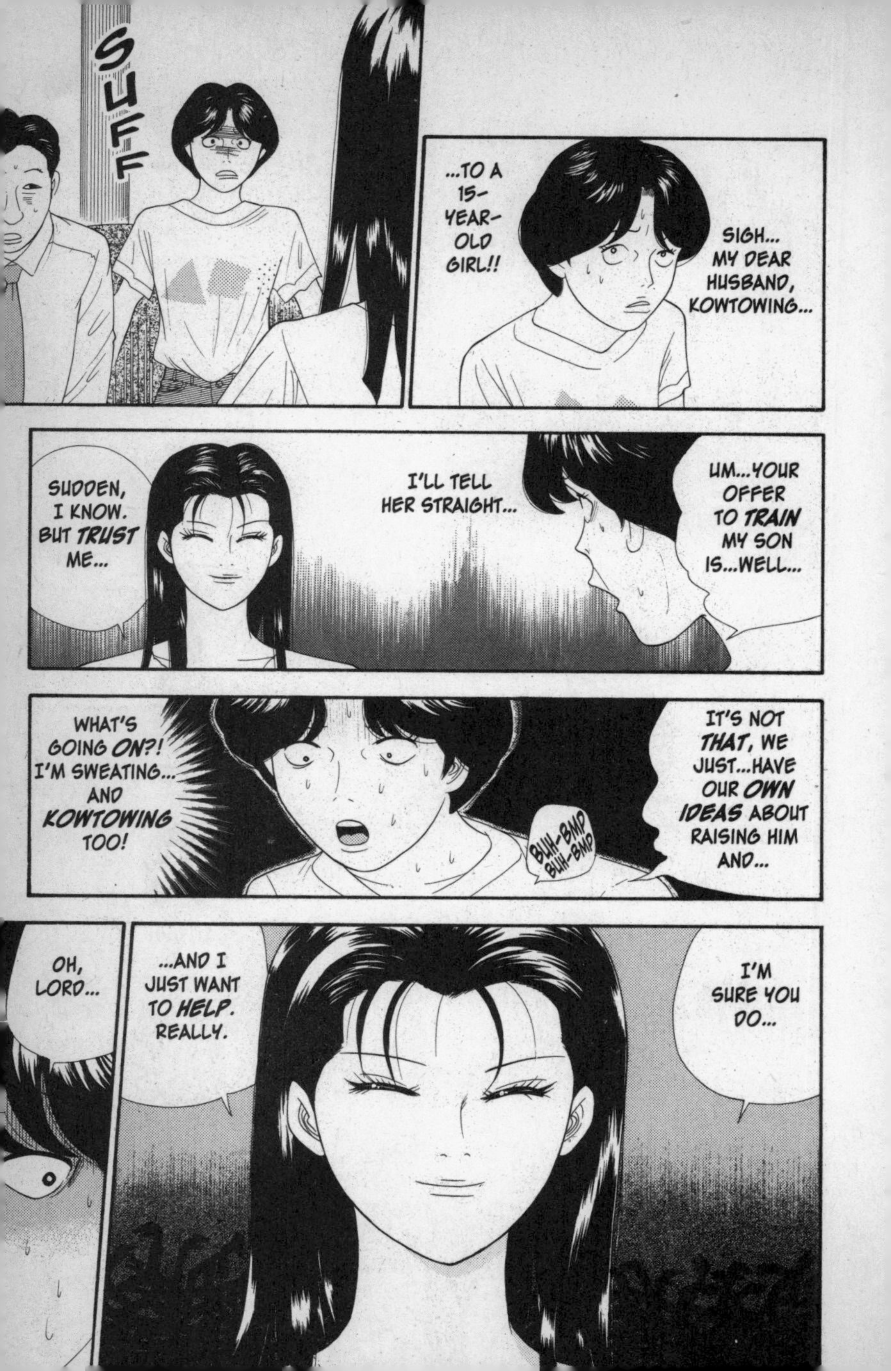
SIGH... MY DEAR HUSBAND, KOWTOWING...
...TO A 15-YEAR-OLD GIRL!!
SUFF
UM...YOUR OFFER TO TRAIN MY SON IS...WELL...
I'LL TELL HER STRAIGHT...
SUDDEN, I KNOW. BUT TRUST ME...
IT'S NOT THAT, WE JUST...HAVE OUR OWN IDEAS ABOUT RAISING HIM AND...
BUH-BMP BUH-BMP
WHAT'S GOING ON?! I'M SWEATING... AND KOWTOWING TOO!
I'M SURE YOU DO...
...AND I JUST WANT TO HELP. REALLY.
OH, LORD...

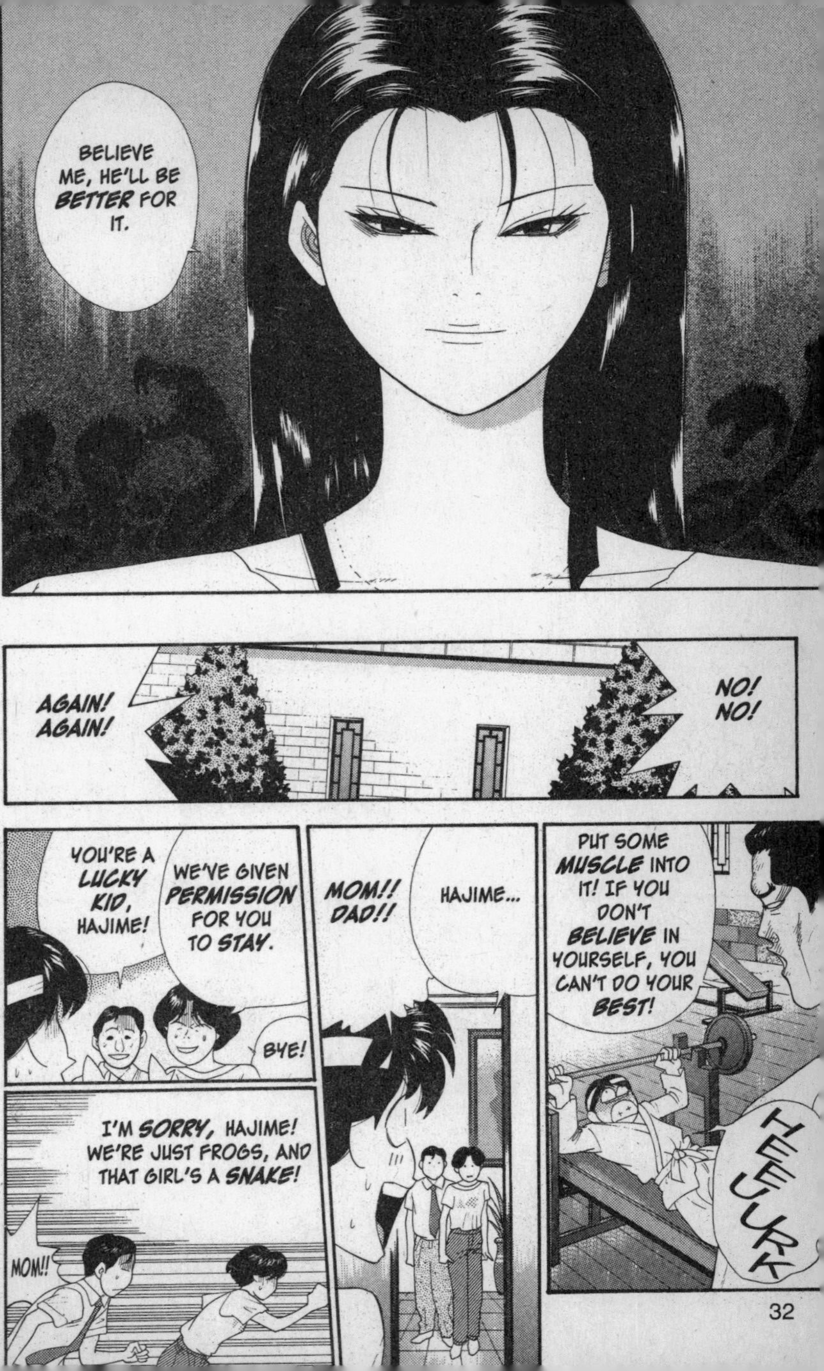
BELIEVE ME, HE'LL BE BETTER FOR IT.
NO! NO!
AGAIN! AGAIN!
PUT SOME MUSCLE INTO IT! IF YOU DON'T BELIEVE IN YOURSELF, YOU CAN'T DO YOUR BEST!
HEEURK
HAJIME...
MOM!! DAD!!
WE'VE GIVEN PERMISSION FOR YOU TO STAY.
YOU'RE A LUCKY KID, HAJIME!
BYE!
I'M SORRY, HAJIME! WE'RE JUST FROGS, AND THAT GIRL'S A SNAKE!
MOM!!

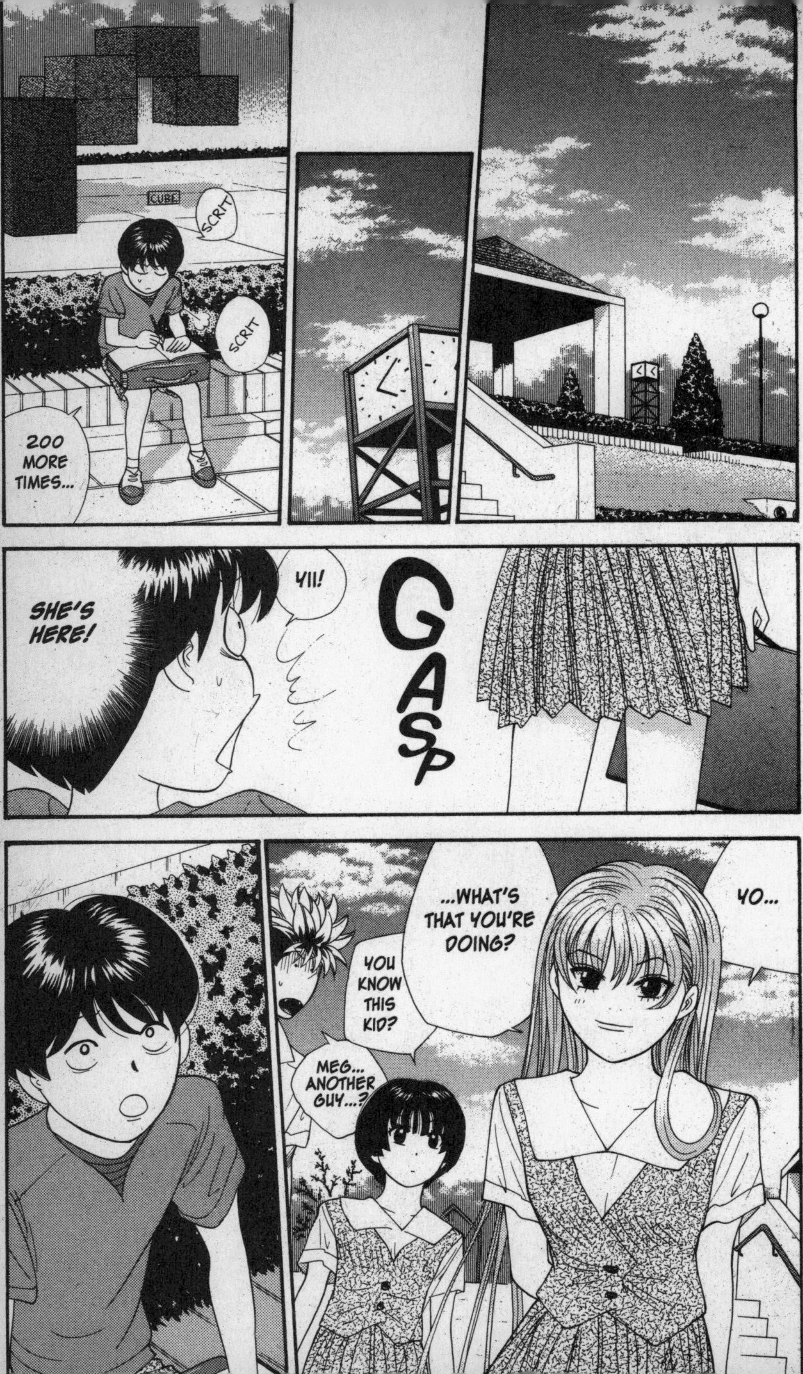
CUBE
SCRIT
SCRIT
200 MORE TIMES...
GASP
YII!
SHE'S HERE!
YO...
...WHAT'S THAT YOU'RE DOING?
YOU KNOW THIS KID?
MEG... ANOTHER GUY...?

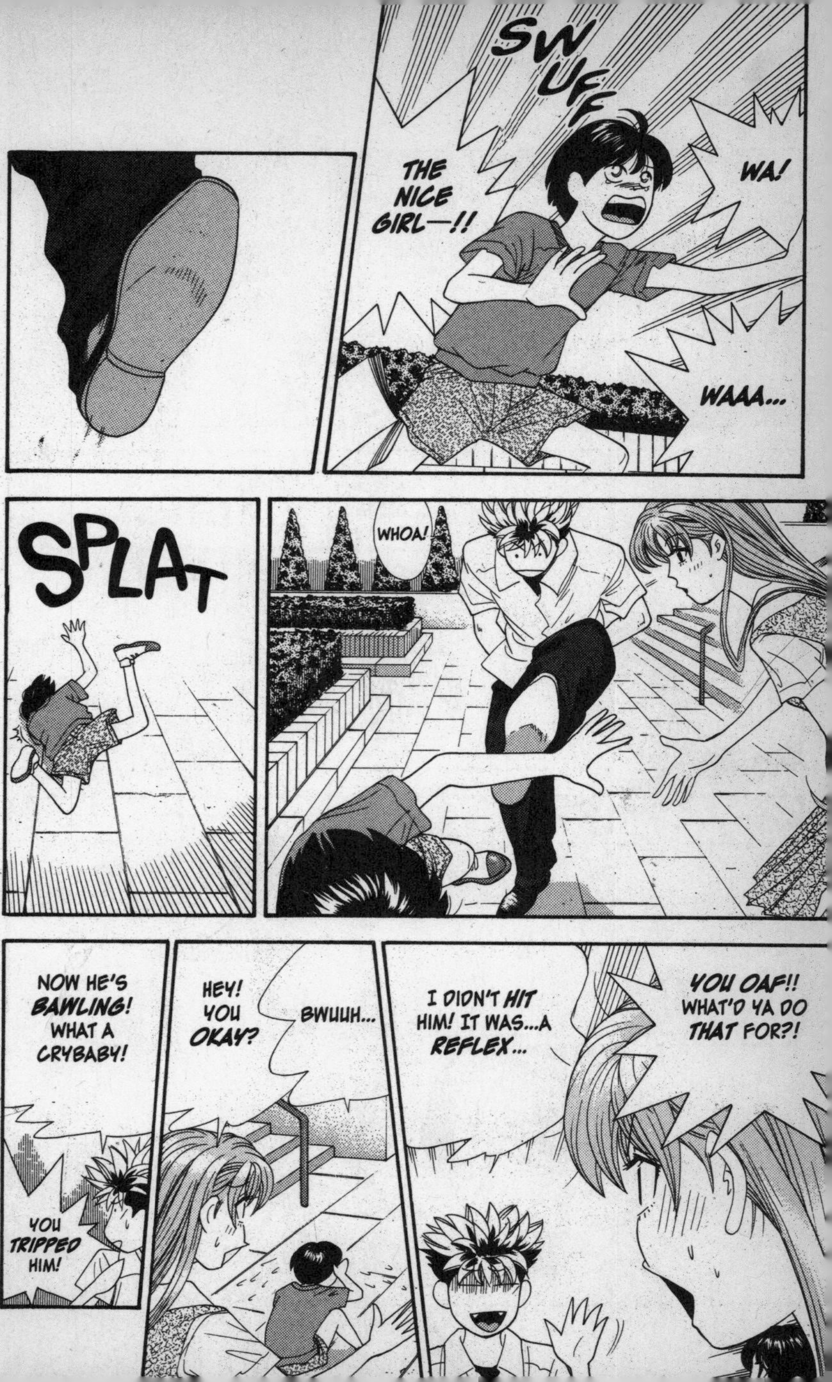
SWUFF
WA!
THE NICE GIRL—!!
WAAA...
WHOA!
SPLAT
YOU OAF!! WHAT'D YA DO THAT FOR?!
I DIDN'T HIT HIM! IT WAS...A REFLEX...
BWUUH...
HEY! YOU OKAY?
NOW HE'S BAWLING! WHAT A CRYBABY!
YOU TRIPPED HIM!

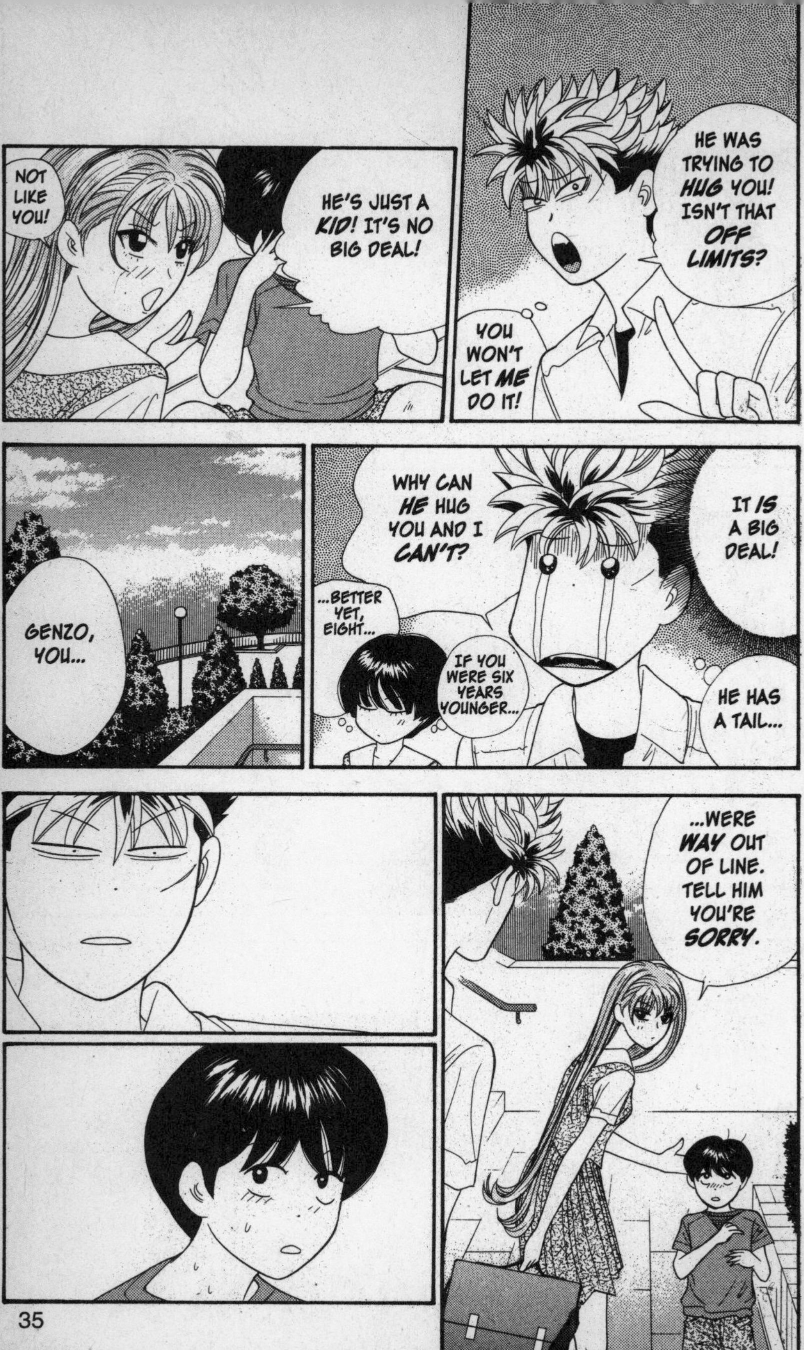
HE WAS TRYING TO HUG YOU! ISN'T THAT OFF LIMITS?
YOU WON'T LET ME DO IT!
HE'S JUST A KID! IT'S NO BIG DEAL!
NOT LIKE YOU!
IT IS A BIG DEAL!
WHY CAN HE HUG YOU AND I CAN'T?
HE HAS A TAIL...
IF YOU WERE SIX YEARS YOUNGER...
...BETTER YET, EIGHT...
GENZO, YOU...
...WERE WAY OUT OF LINE. TELL HIM YOU'RE SORRY.

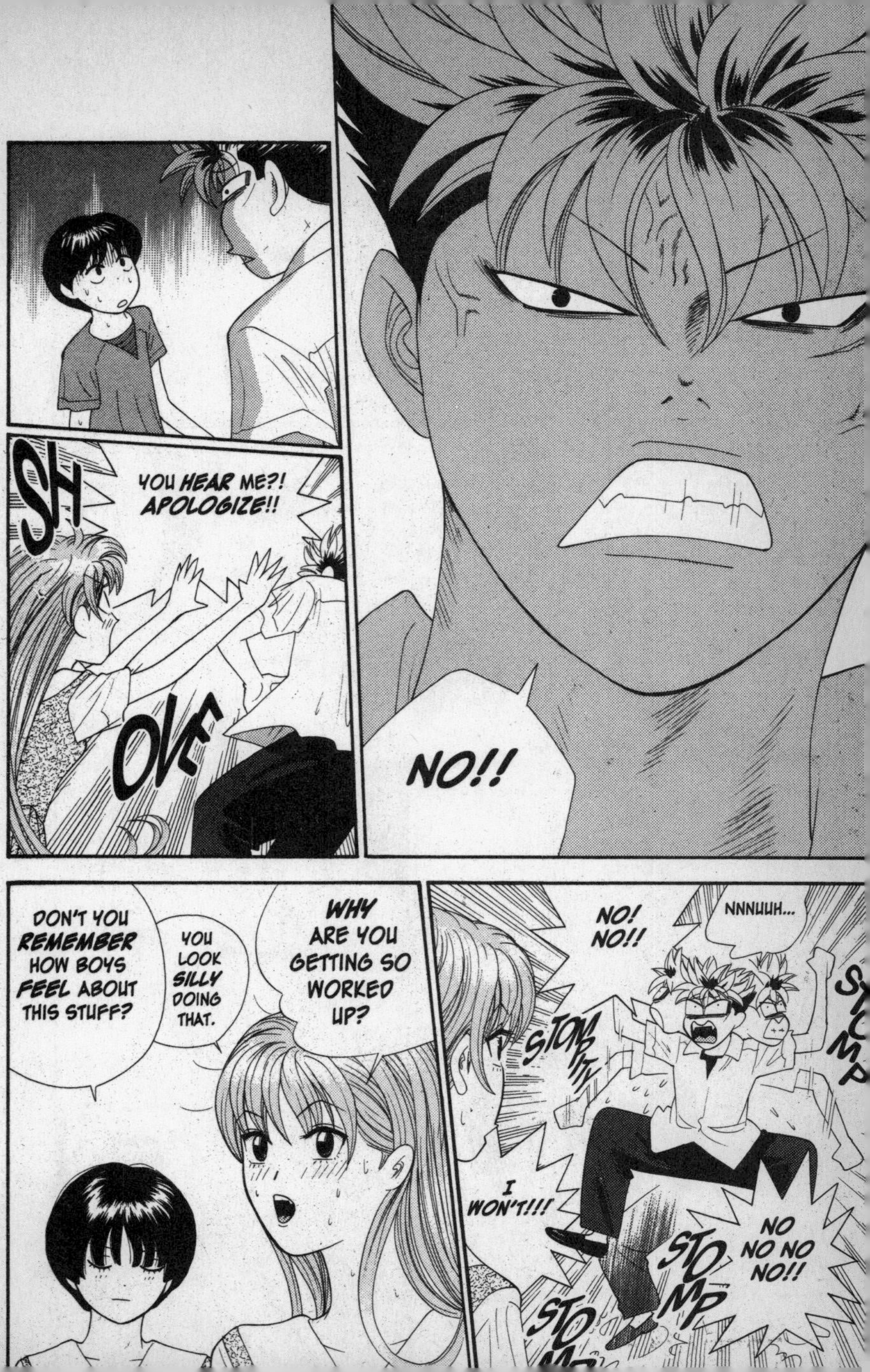
NO!!
SHOVE
YOU HEAR ME?! APOLOGIZE!!
NNNUUH...
NO! NO!!
STOMP
STOMP
I WON'T!!!
NO NO NO NO!!
STOMP
STOMP
WHY ARE YOU GETTING SO WORKED UP?
YOU LOOK SILLY DOING THAT.
DON'T YOU REMEMBER HOW BOYS FEEL ABOUT THIS STUFF?

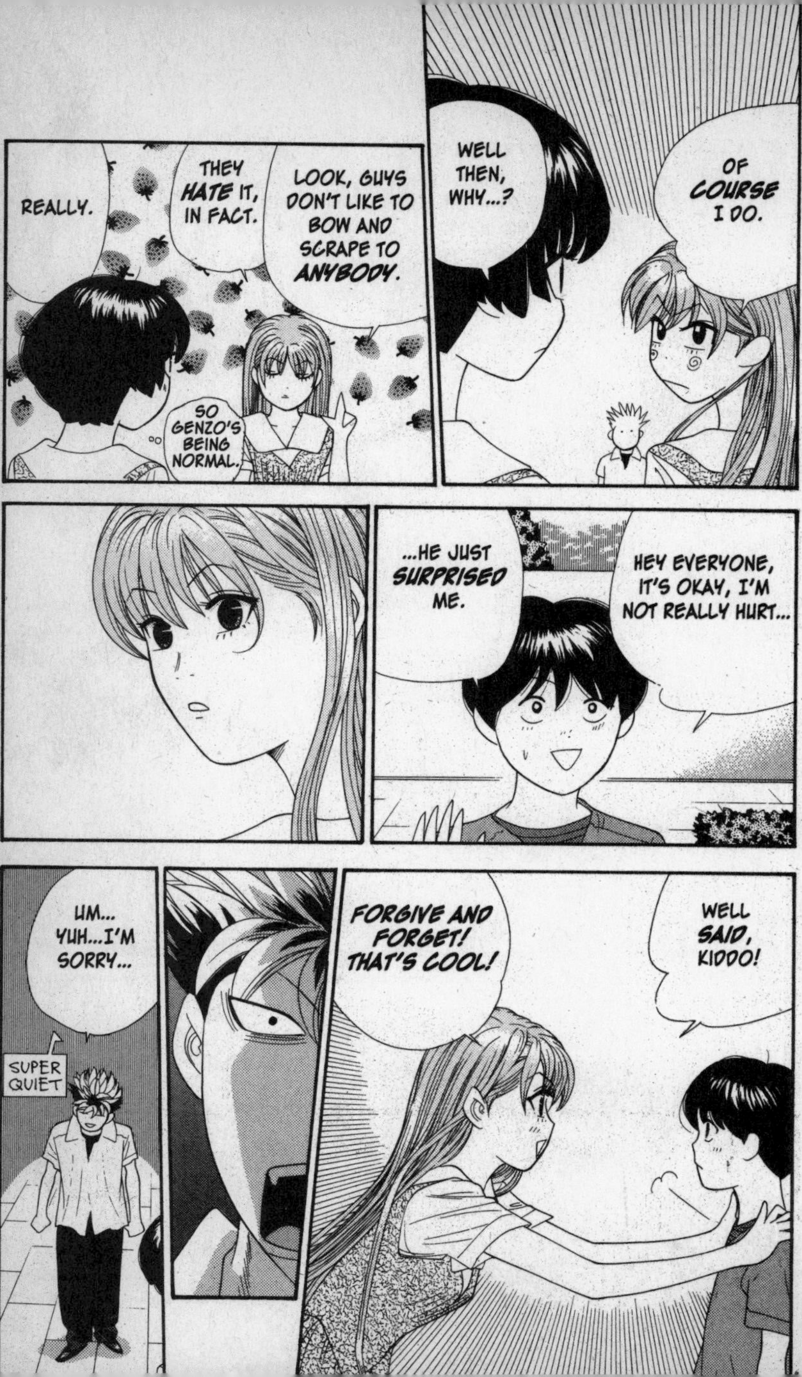
OF COURSE I DO.
WELL THEN, WHY...?
LOOK, GUYS DON'T LIKE TO BOW AND SCRAPE TO ANYBODY.
THEY HATE IT, IN FACT.
REALLY.
SO GENZO'S BEING NORMAL.
HEY EVERYONE, IT'S OKAY, I'M NOT REALLY HURT...
...HE JUST SURPRISED ME.
WELL SAID, KIDDO!
FORGIVE AND FORGET! THAT'S COOL!
UM... YUH...I'M SORRY...
SUPER QUIET

BUT *THEY* SAID I SHOULDN'T CRY...

HUH? *WHO* SAID?

.....

HOW'S THAT GOING?

OH, THAT'S RIGHT, *KEIKO'S* TRAINING YOU.

WOW...

I am strong I am strong I am strong I am strong I am strong I am strong I am strong I am strong I am strong I am strong I am strong I am strong I am strong I am strong I am strong I am strong I am strong I am strong I am strong I am strong

WHAT'S THIS?

.....

...YEAH, BUT I'M *NOT* STRONG.

WELL...

IS *THIS* PART OF YOUR TRAINING?

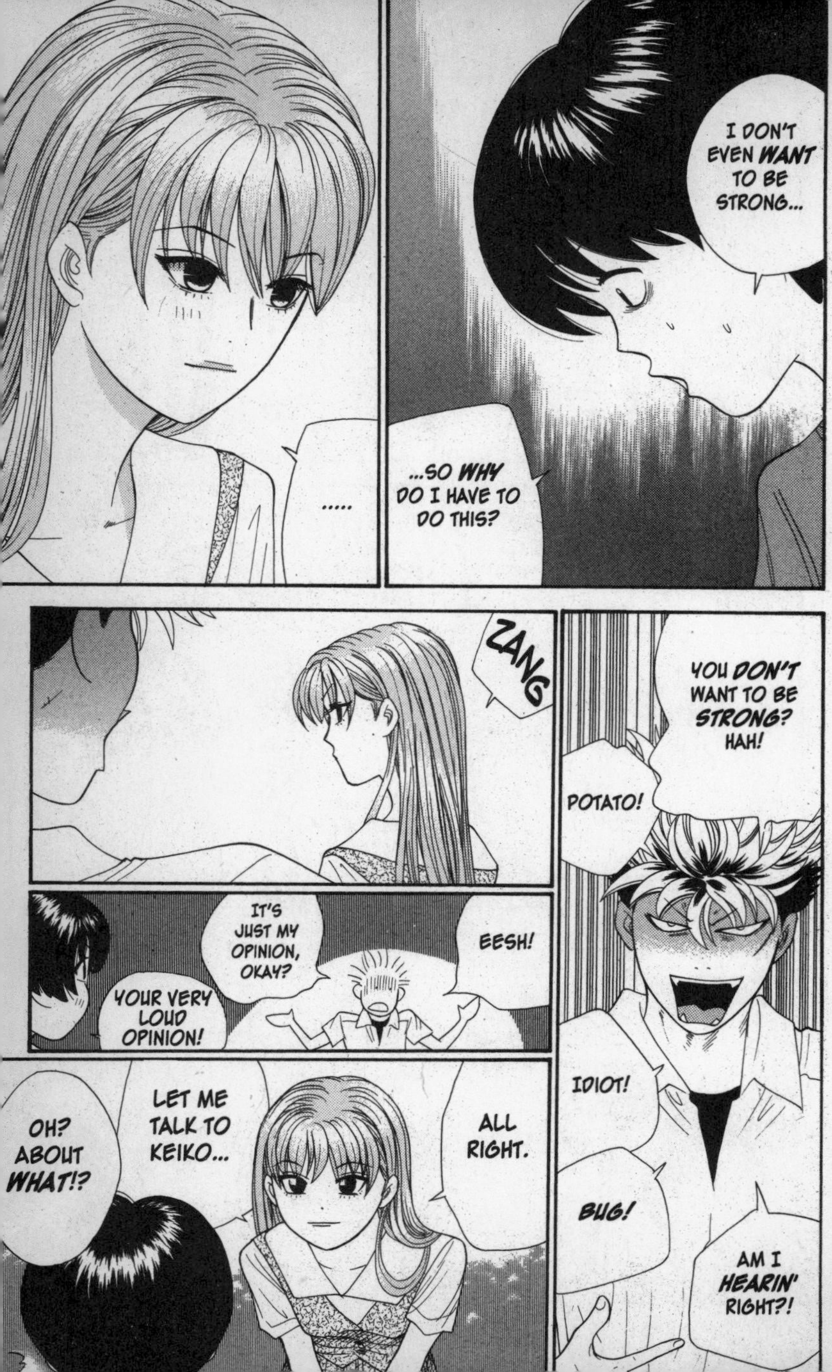
I DON'T EVEN WANT TO BE STRONG...
...SO WHY DO I HAVE TO DO THIS?
.....
YOU DON'T WANT TO BE STRONG? HAH!
POTATO!
IDIOT!
BUG!
AM I HEARIN' RIGHT?!
ZANG
EESH!
IT'S JUST MY OPINION, OKAY?
YOUR VERY LOUD OPINION!
ALL RIGHT.
LET ME TALK TO KEIKO...
OH? ABOUT WHAT!?

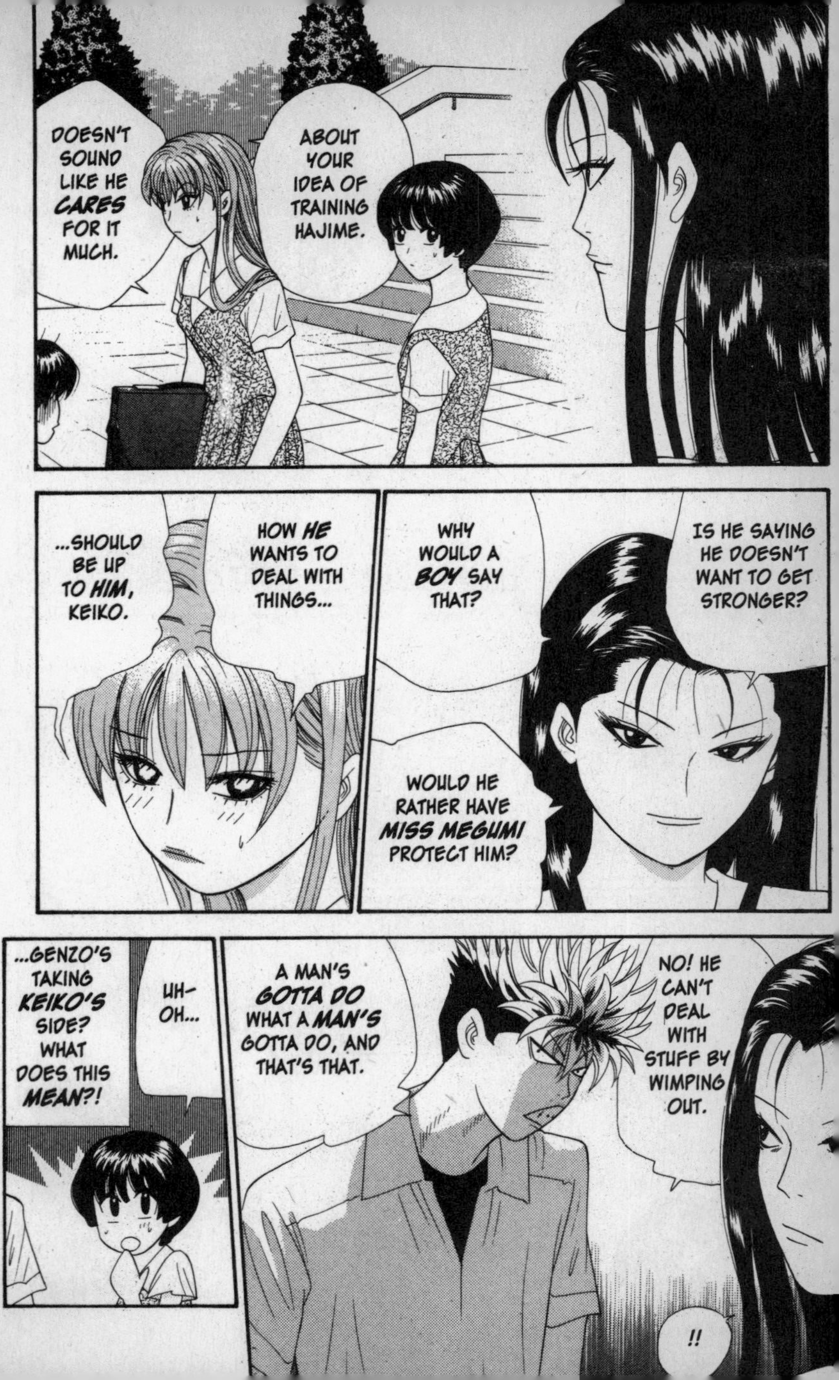
ABOUT YOUR IDEA OF TRAINING HAJIME.
DOESN'T SOUND LIKE HE CARES FOR IT MUCH.
IS HE SAYING HE DOESN'T WANT TO GET STRONGER?
WHY WOULD A BOY SAY THAT?
WOULD HE RATHER HAVE MISS MEGUMI PROTECT HIM?
HOW HE WANTS TO DEAL WITH THINGS...
...SHOULD BE UP TO HIM, KEIKO.
NO! HE CAN'T DEAL WITH STUFF BY WIMPING OUT.
A MAN'S GOTTA DO WHAT A MAN'S GOTTA DO, AND THAT'S THAT.
!!
UH-OH...
...GENZO'S TAKING KEIKO'S SIDE? WHAT DOES THIS MEAN?!

Chapter 62: Disappointed

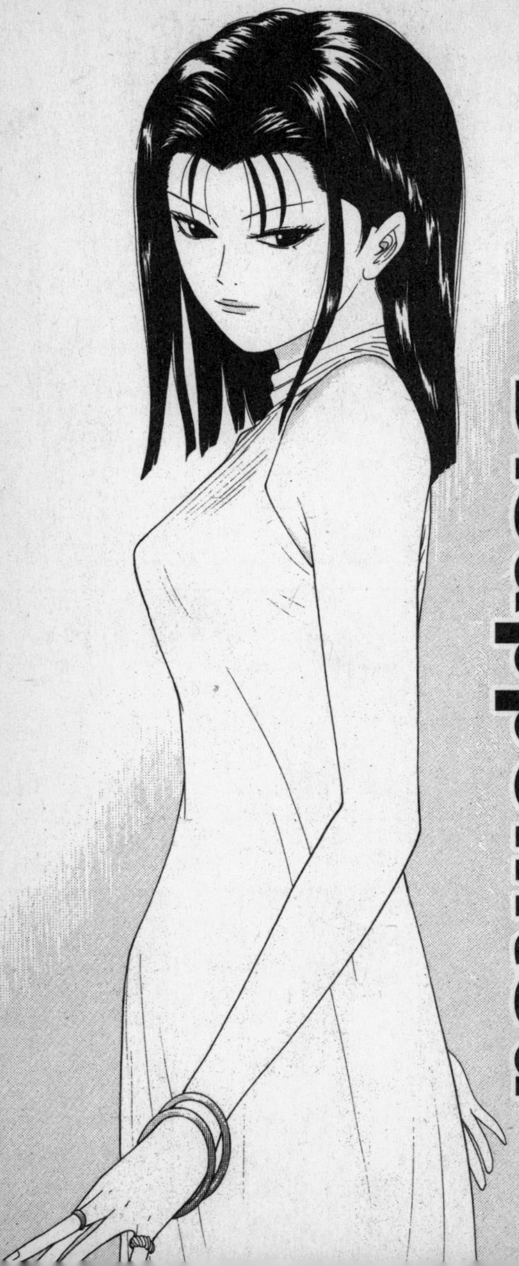

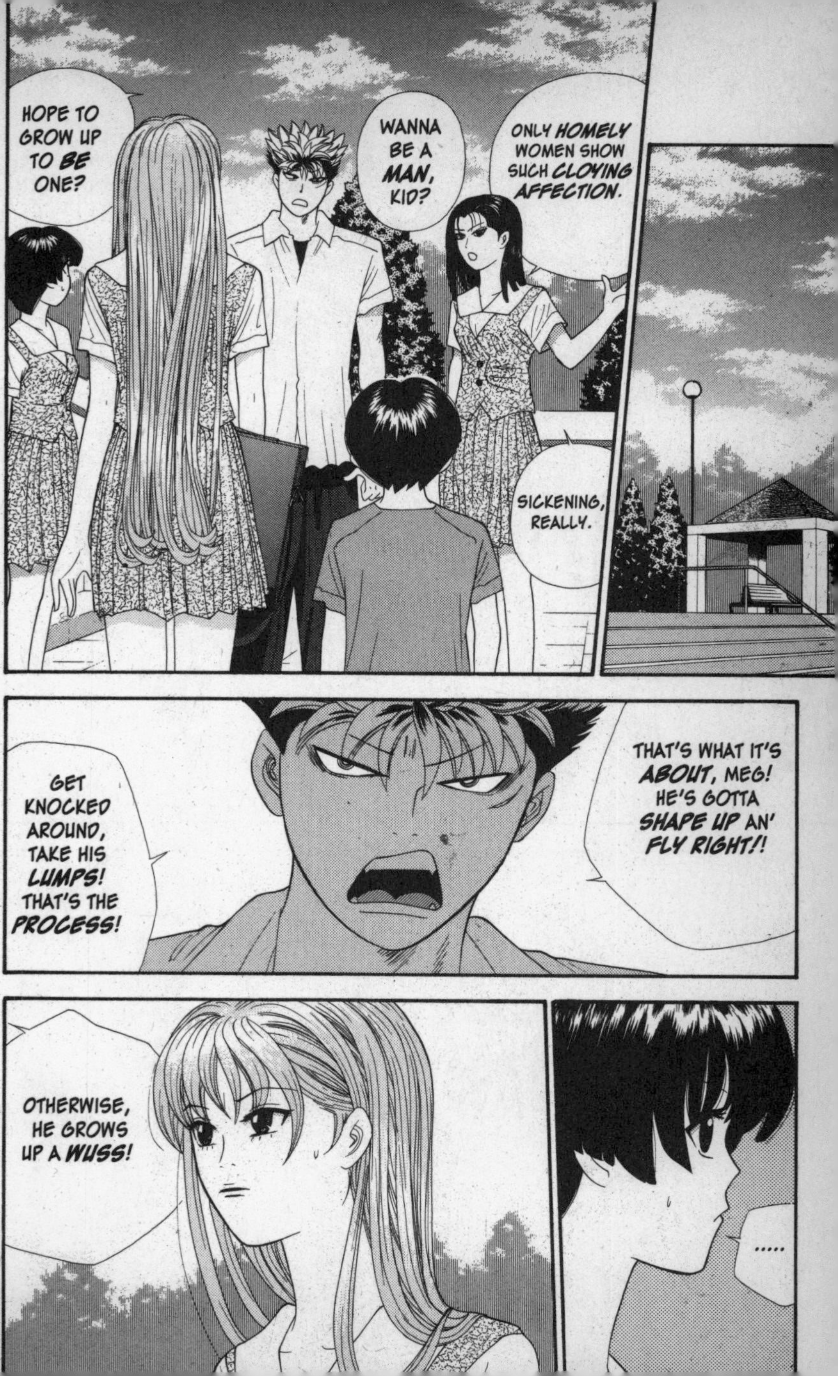
ONLY HOMELY WOMEN SHOW SUCH CLOYING AFFECTION.
WANNA BE A MAN, KID?
HOPE TO GROW UP TO BE ONE?
SICKENING, REALLY.
THAT'S WHAT IT'S ABOUT, MEG! HE'S GOTTA SHAPE UP AN' FLY RIGHT!!
GET KNOCKED AROUND, TAKE HIS LUMPS! THAT'S THE PROCESS!
.....
OTHERWISE, HE GROWS UP A WUSS!

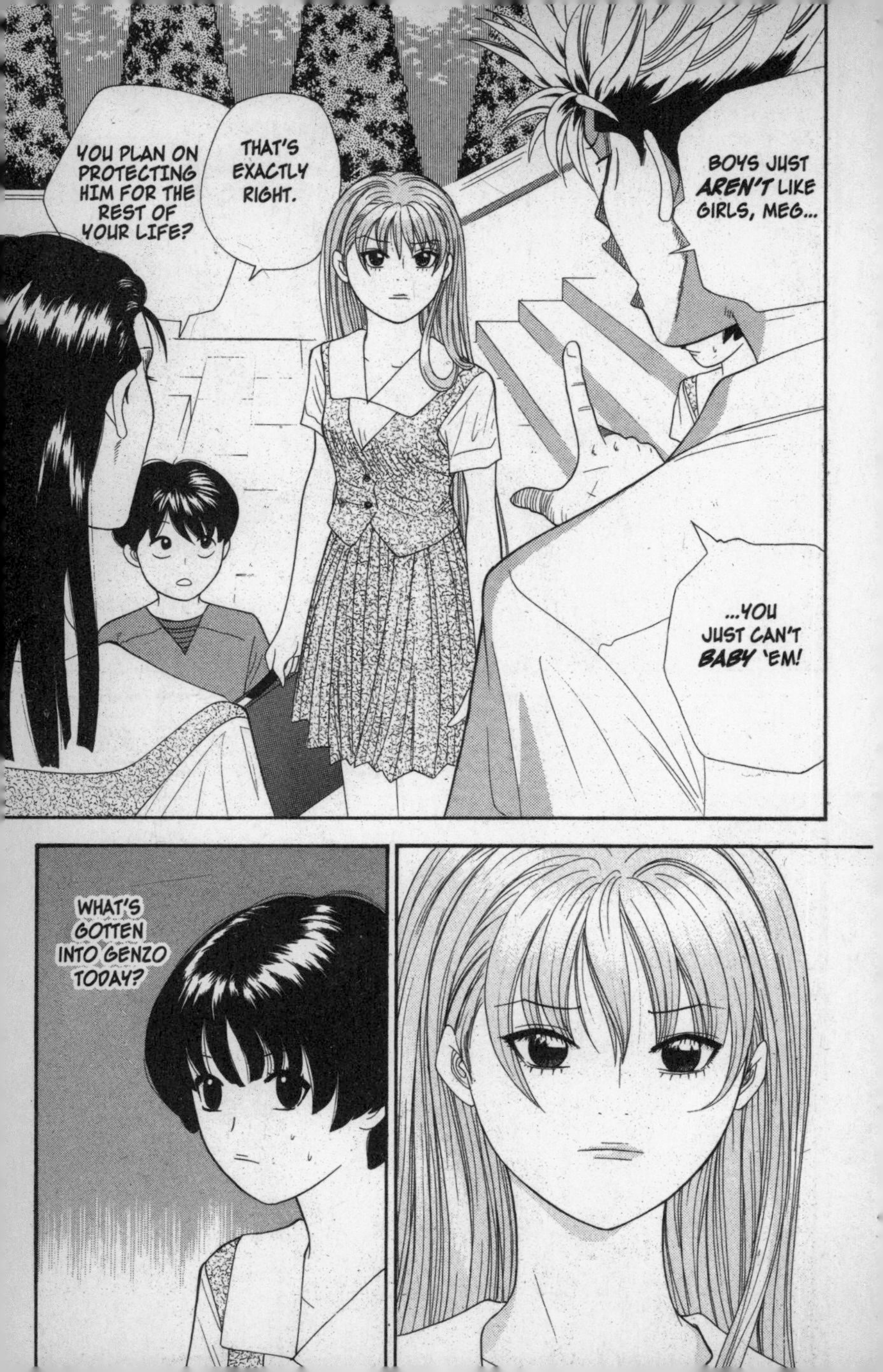
BOYS JUST AREN'T LIKE GIRLS, MEG...
...YOU JUST CAN'T BABY 'EM!
THAT'S EXACTLY RIGHT.
YOU PLAN ON PROTECTING HIM FOR THE REST OF YOUR LIFE?
WHAT'S GOTTEN INTO GENZO TODAY?

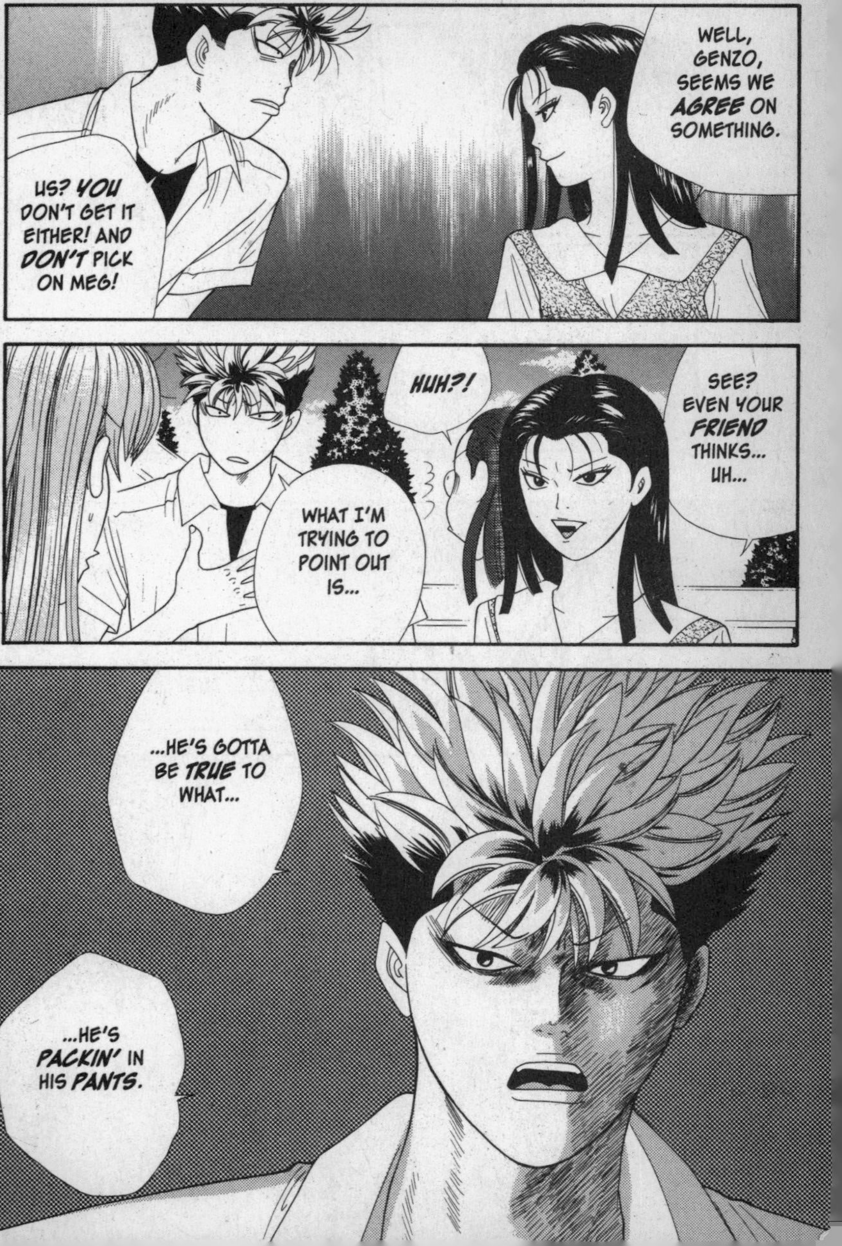
WELL, GENZO, SEEMS WE AGREE ON SOMETHING.
US? YOU DON'T GET IT EITHER! AND DON'T PICK ON MEG!
SEE? EVEN YOUR FRIEND THINKS... UH...
HUH?!
WHAT I'M TRYING TO POINT OUT IS...
...HE'S GOTTA BE TRUE TO WHAT...
...HE'S PACKIN' IN HIS PANTS.

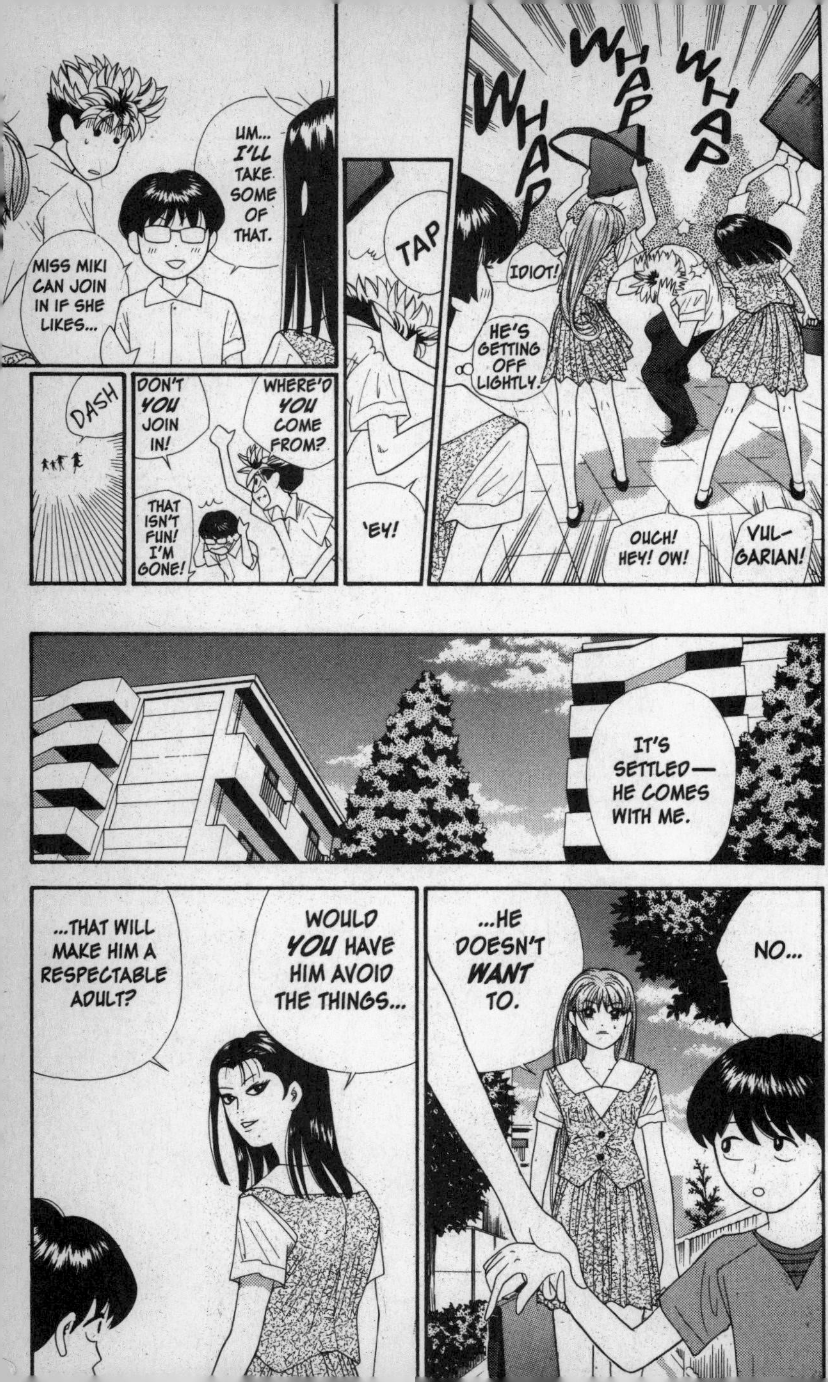
WHAP
WHAP
WHAP
IDIOT!
HE'S GETTING OFF LIGHTLY.
VUL-GARIAN!
OUCH! HEY! OW!
TAP
'EY!
UM... *I'LL* TAKE SOME OF THAT.
MISS MIKI CAN JOIN IN IF SHE LIKES...
WHERE'D *YOU* COME FROM?
DON'T *YOU* JOIN IN!
THAT ISN'T FUN! I'M GONE!
DASH
IT'S SETTLED— HE COMES WITH ME.
NO...
...HE DOESN'T *WANT* TO.
WOULD *YOU* HAVE HIM AVOID THE THINGS...
...THAT WILL MAKE HIM A RESPECTABLE ADULT?

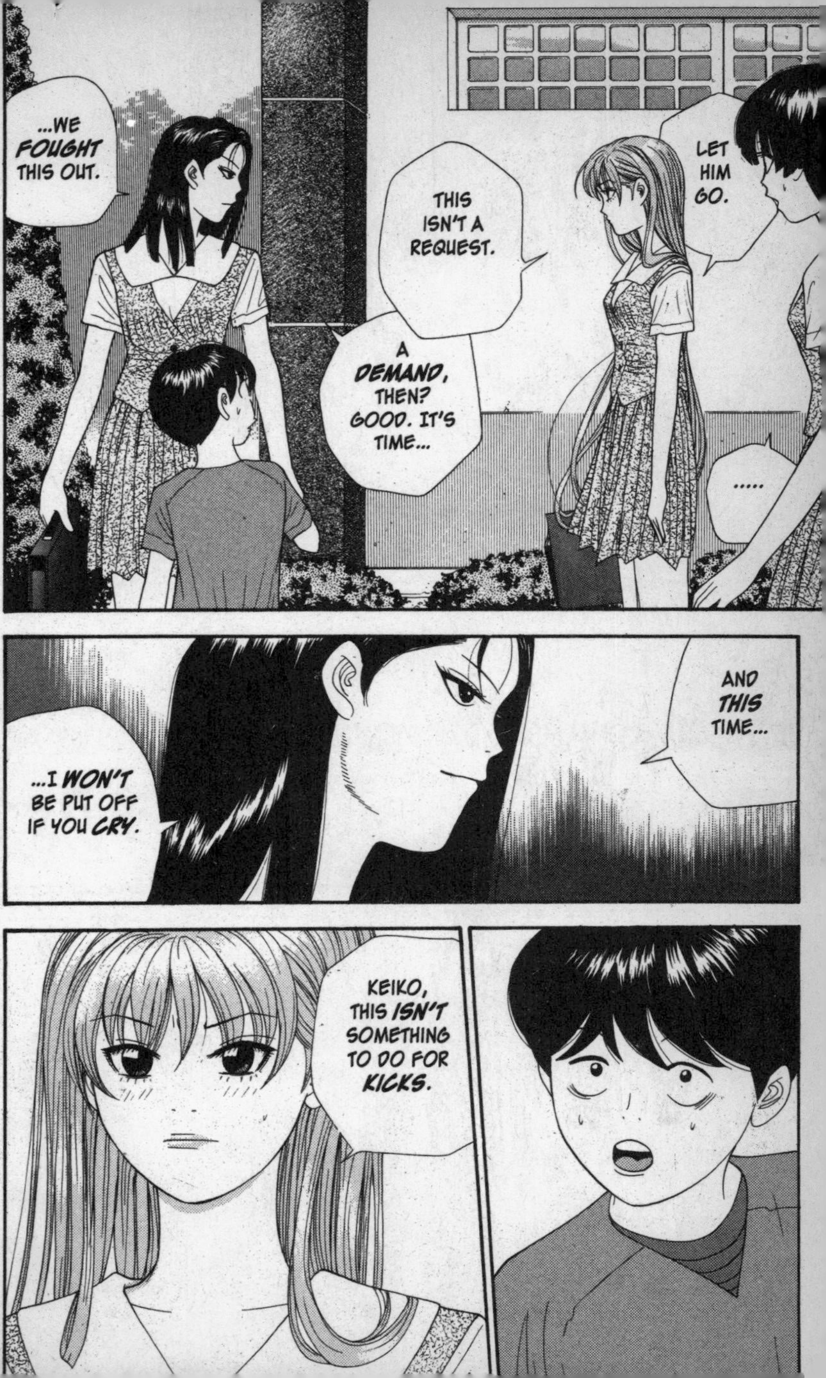
LET HIM GO.
.....
THIS ISN'T A REQUEST.
A DEMAND, THEN? GOOD. IT'S TIME...
...WE FOUGHT THIS OUT.
AND THIS TIME...
...I WON'T BE PUT OFF IF YOU CRY.
KEIKO, THIS ISN'T SOMETHING TO DO FOR KICKS.

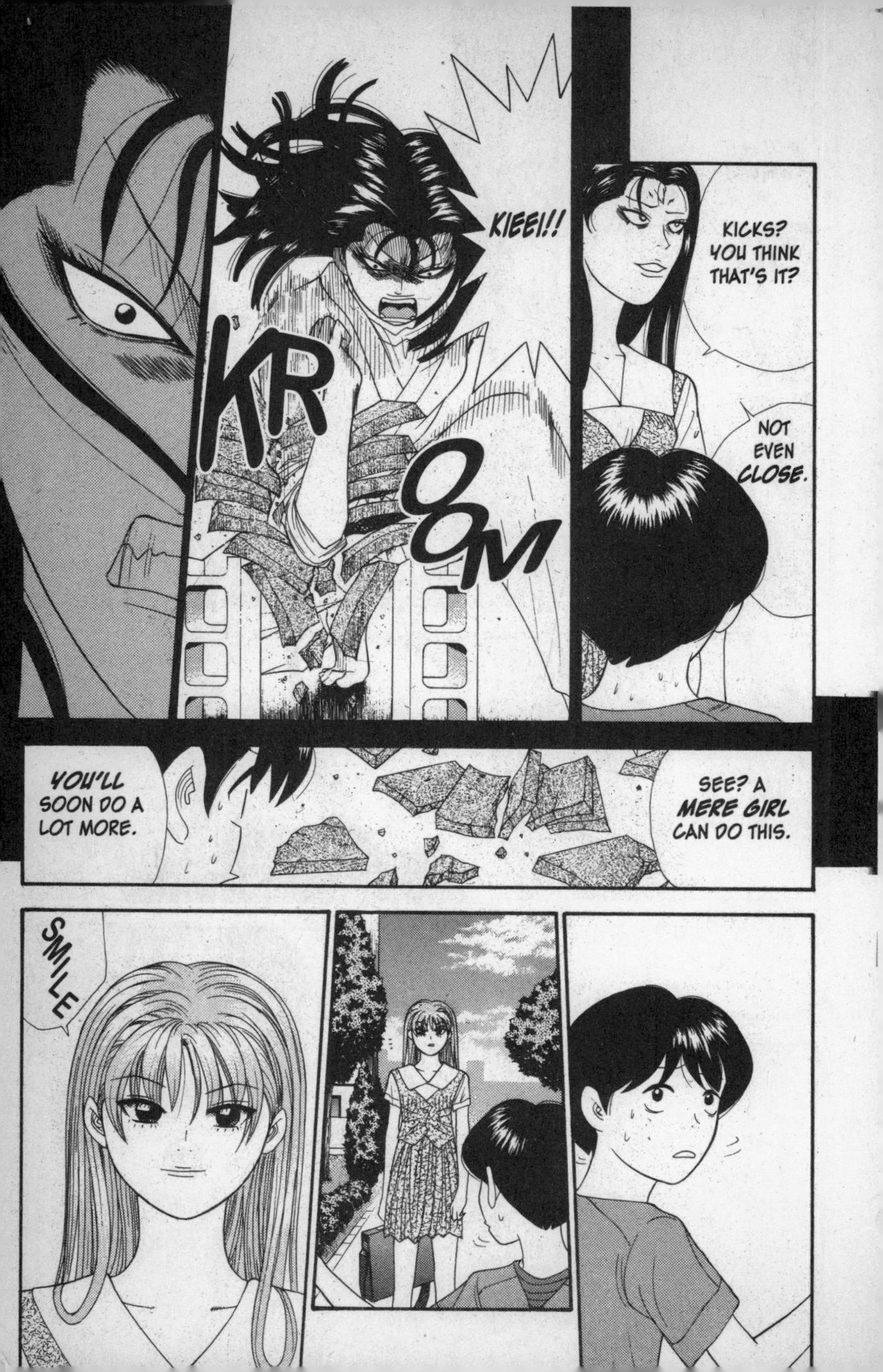
KICKS? YOU THINK THAT'S IT?
NOT EVEN CLOSE.
KIEEI!!
KR-OOM
SEE? A MERE GIRL CAN DO THIS.
YOU'LL SOON DO A LOT MORE.
SMILE

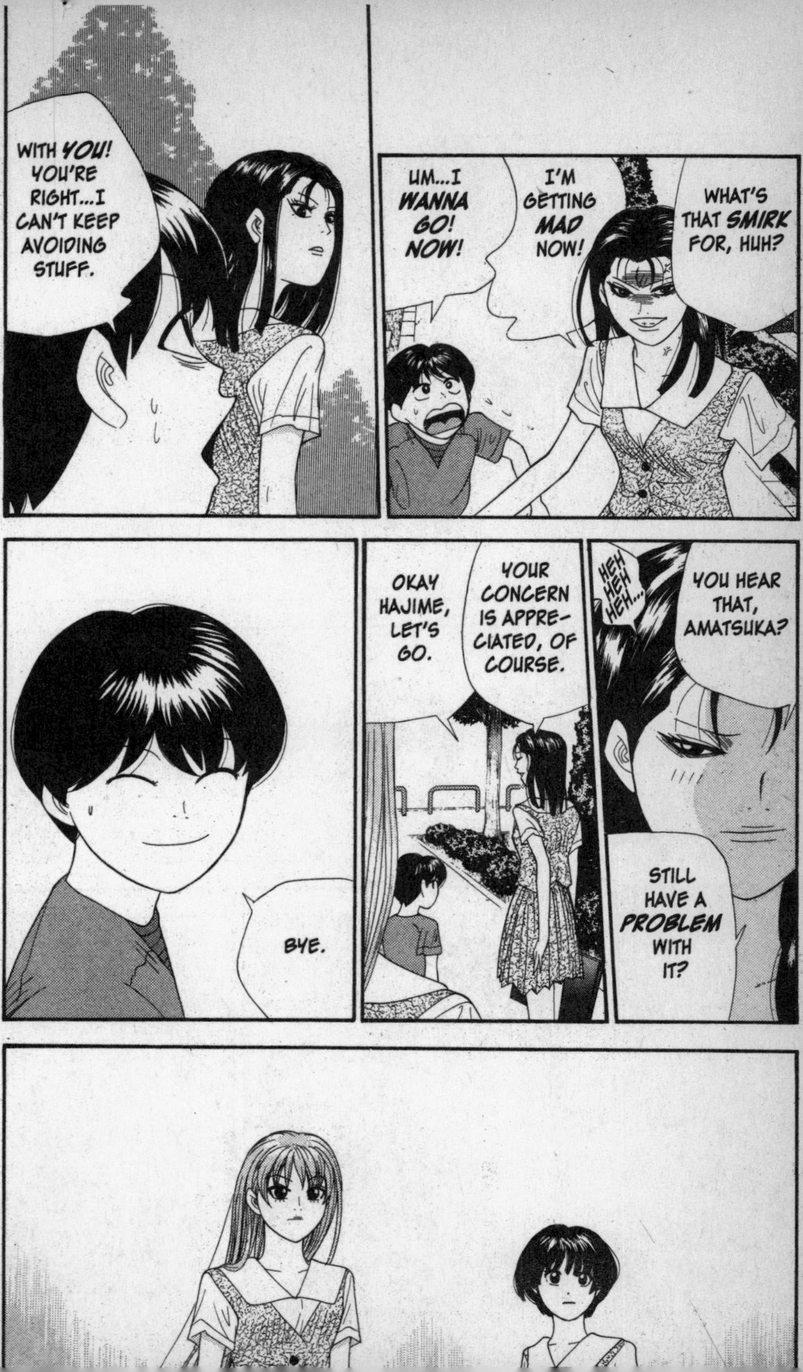
WHAT'S THAT SMIRK FOR, HUH?
I'M GETTING MAD NOW!
UM...I WANNA GO! NOW!
WITH YOU! YOU'RE RIGHT...I CAN'T KEEP AVOIDING STUFF.
YOU HEAR THAT, AMATSUKA?
HEH HEH HEH...
STILL HAVE A PROBLEM WITH IT?
YOUR CONCERN IS APPRECIATED, OF COURSE.
OKAY HAJIME, LET'S GO.
BYE.

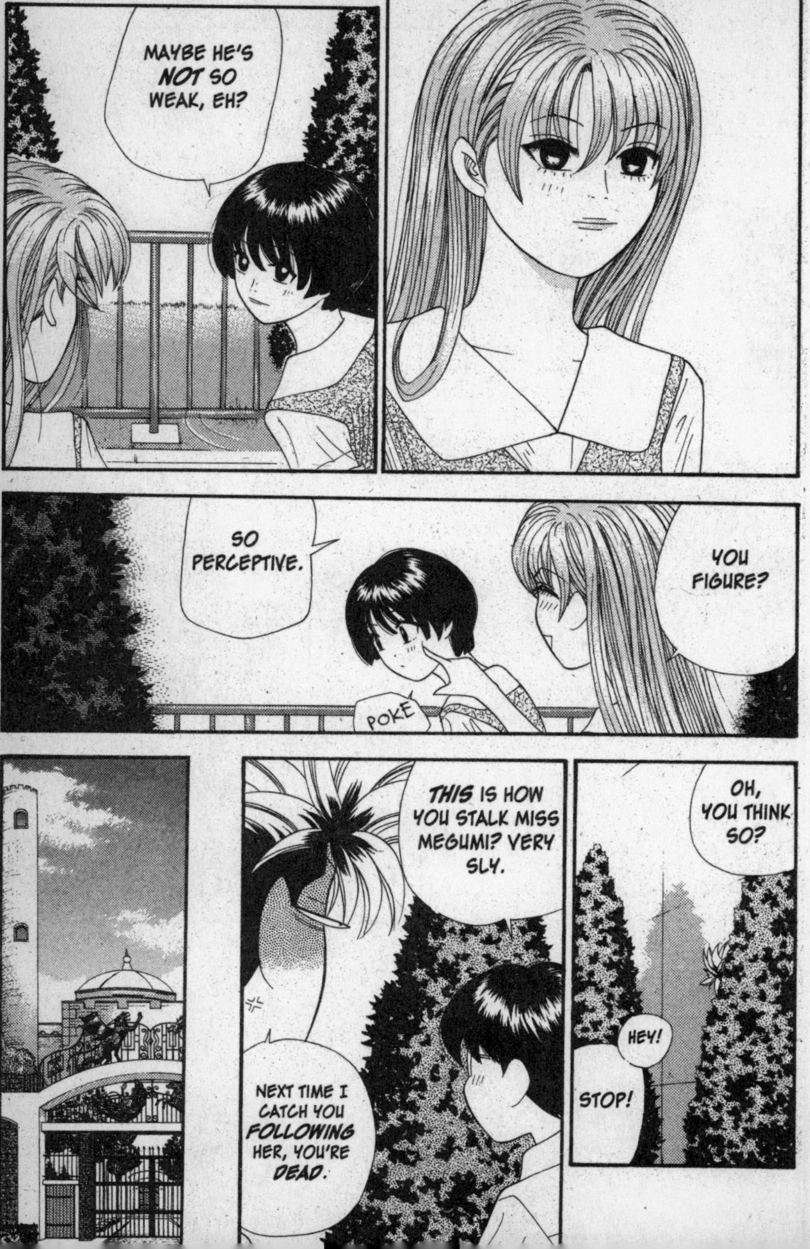
MAYBE HE'S *NOT* SO WEAK, EH?
YOU FIGURE?
SO PERCEPTIVE.
POKE
OH, YOU THINK SO?
HEY!
STOP!
THIS IS HOW YOU STALK MISS MEGUMI? VERY SLY.
NEXT TIME I CATCH YOU *FOLLOWING* HER, YOU'RE *DEAD*.

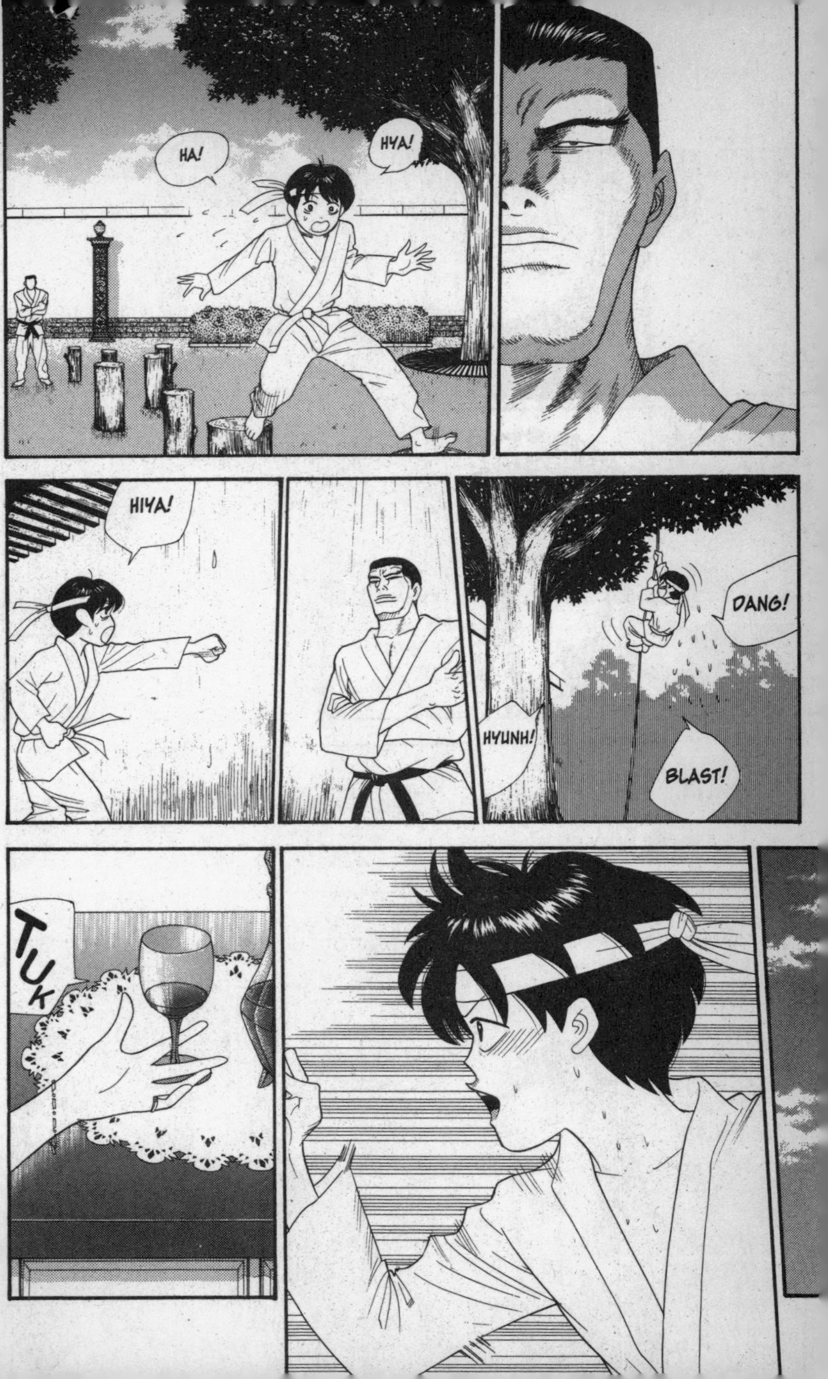
HYA!
HA!
DANG!
HYUNH!
BLAST!
HIYA!
TUK

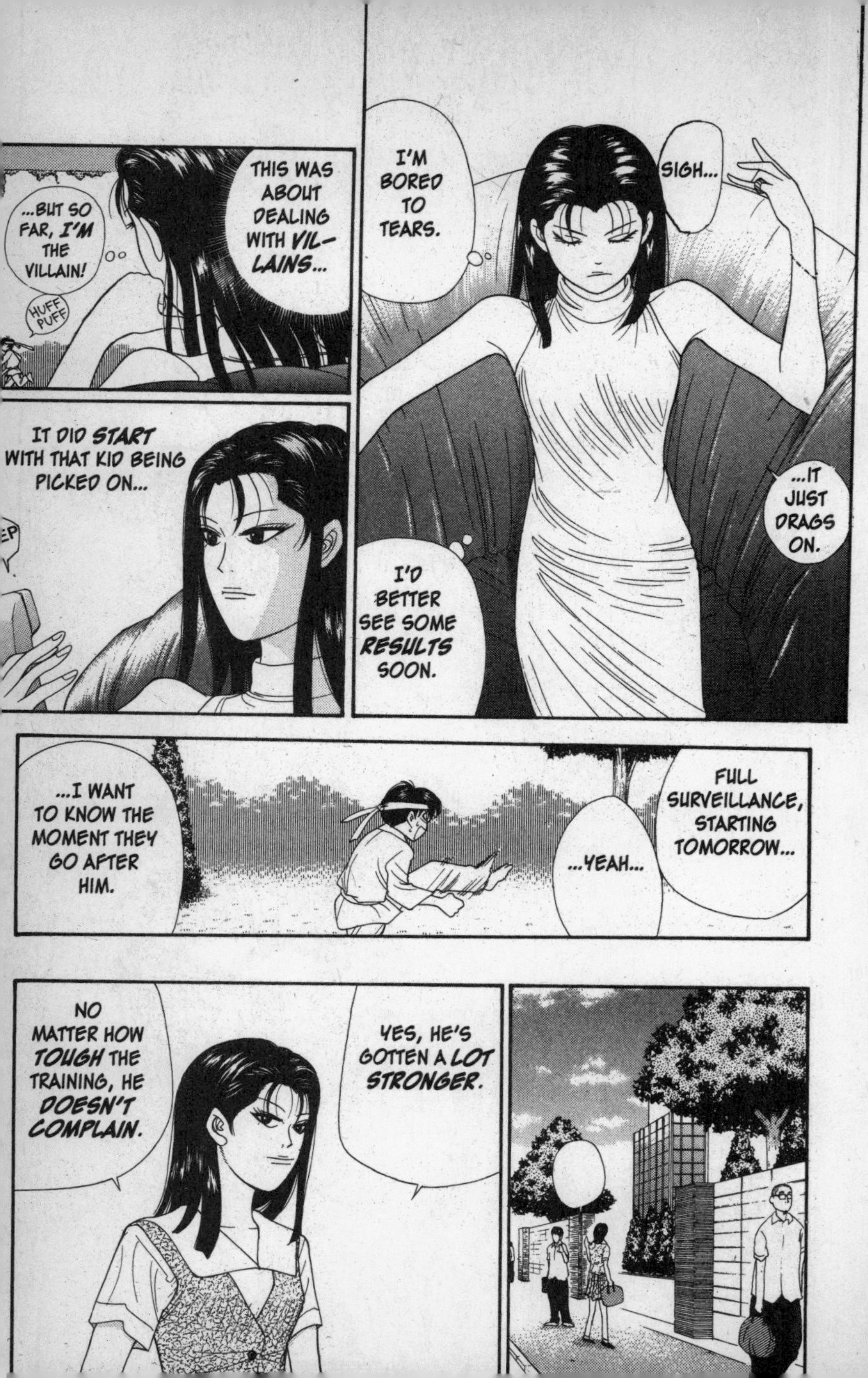
SIGH...
I'M BORED TO TEARS.
...IT JUST DRAGS ON.
I'D BETTER SEE SOME RESULTS SOON.
THIS WAS ABOUT DEALING WITH VIL-LAINS...
...BUT SO FAR, I'M THE VILLAIN!
HUFF PUFF
IT DID START WITH THAT KID BEING PICKED ON...
FULL SURVEILLANCE, STARTING TOMORROW...
...YEAH...
...I WANT TO KNOW THE MOMENT THEY GO AFTER HIM.
YES, HE'S GOTTEN A LOT STRONGER.
NO MATTER HOW TOUGH THE TRAINING, HE DOESN'T COMPLAIN.

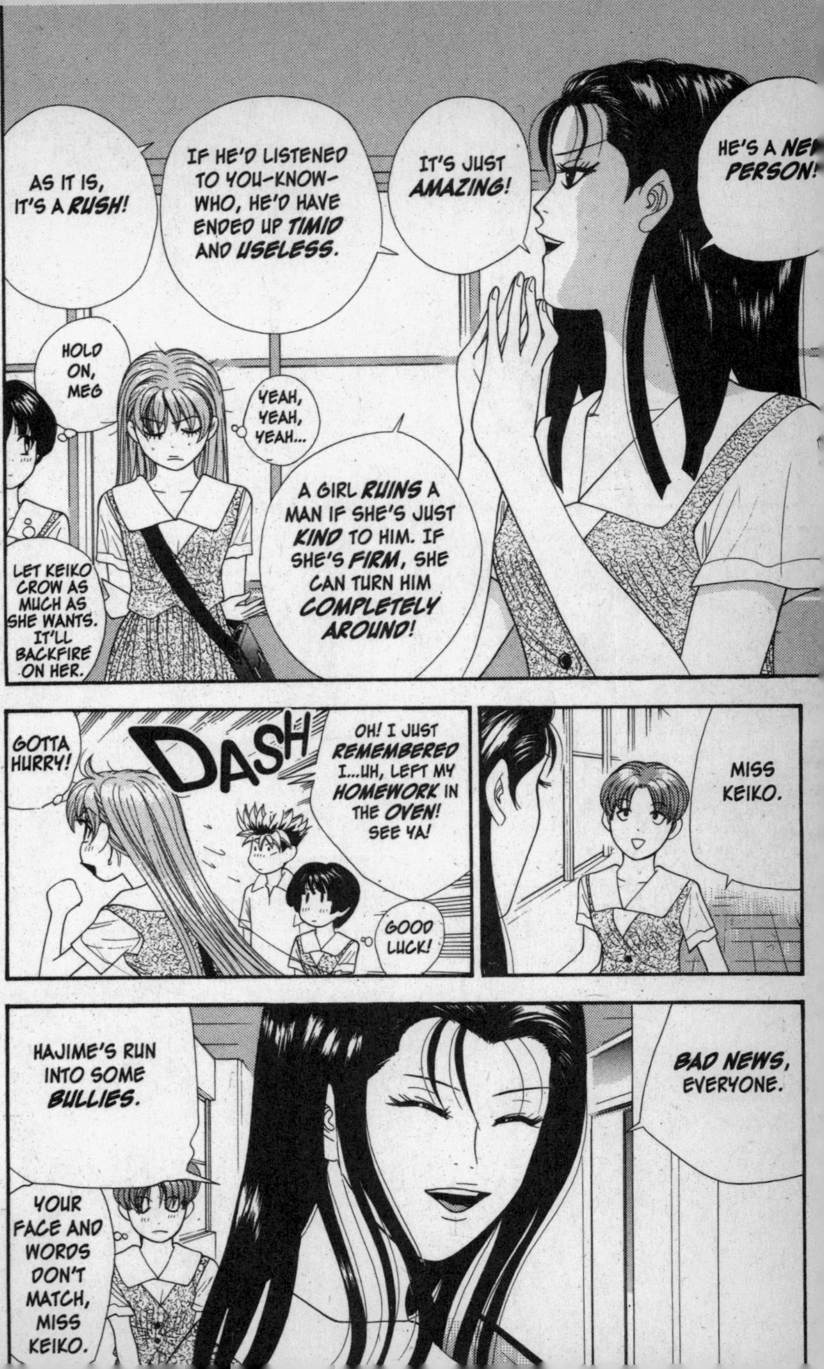
HE'S A NE PERSON!
IT'S JUST AMAZING!
IF HE'D LISTENED TO YOU-KNOW-WHO, HE'D HAVE ENDED UP TIMID AND USELESS.
AS IT IS, IT'S A RUSH!
A GIRL RUINS A MAN IF SHE'S JUST KIND TO HIM. IF SHE'S FIRM, SHE CAN TURN HIM COMPLETELY AROUND!
YEAH, YEAH, YEAH...
HOLD ON, MEG
LET KEIKO CROW AS MUCH AS SHE WANTS. IT'LL BACKFIRE ON HER.
MISS KEIKO.
OH! I JUST REMEMBERED I...UH, LEFT MY HOMEWORK IN THE OVEN! SEE YA!
DASH
GOTTA HURRY!
GOOD LUCK!
BAD NEWS, EVERYONE.
HAJIME'S RUN INTO SOME BULLIES.
YOUR FACE AND WORDS DON'T MATCH, MISS KEIKO.

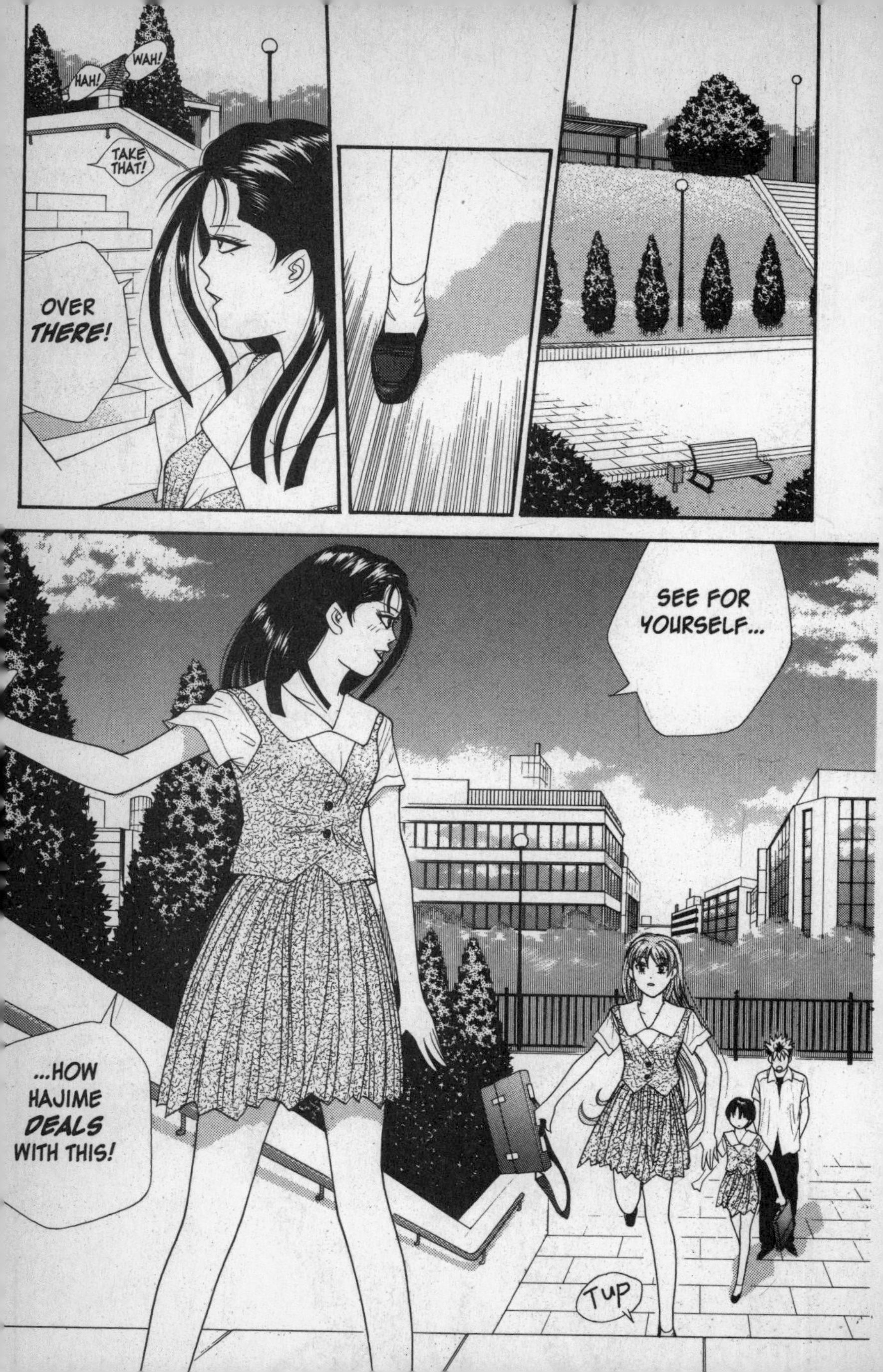
WAH!
HAH!
TAKE THAT!
OVER THERE!
SEE FOR YOURSELF...
...HOW HAJIME DEALS WITH THIS!
TUP

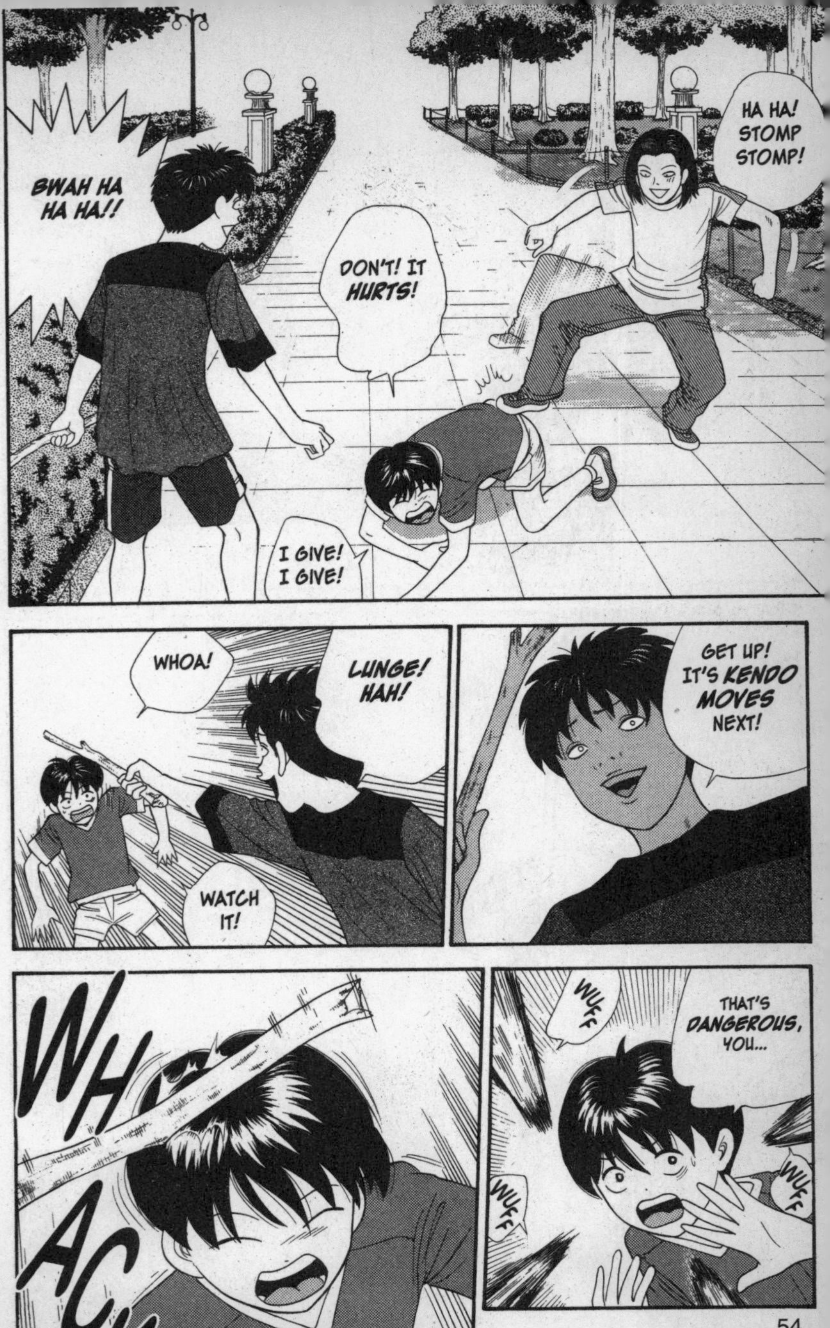
HA HA! STOMP STOMP!
DON'T! IT HURTS!
BWAH HA HA HA!!
I GIVE! I GIVE!
GET UP! IT'S KENDO MOVES NEXT!
LUNGE! HAH!
WHOA!
WATCH IT!
THAT'S DANGEROUS, YOU...
WUFF
WUFF
WUFF
WH
ACK

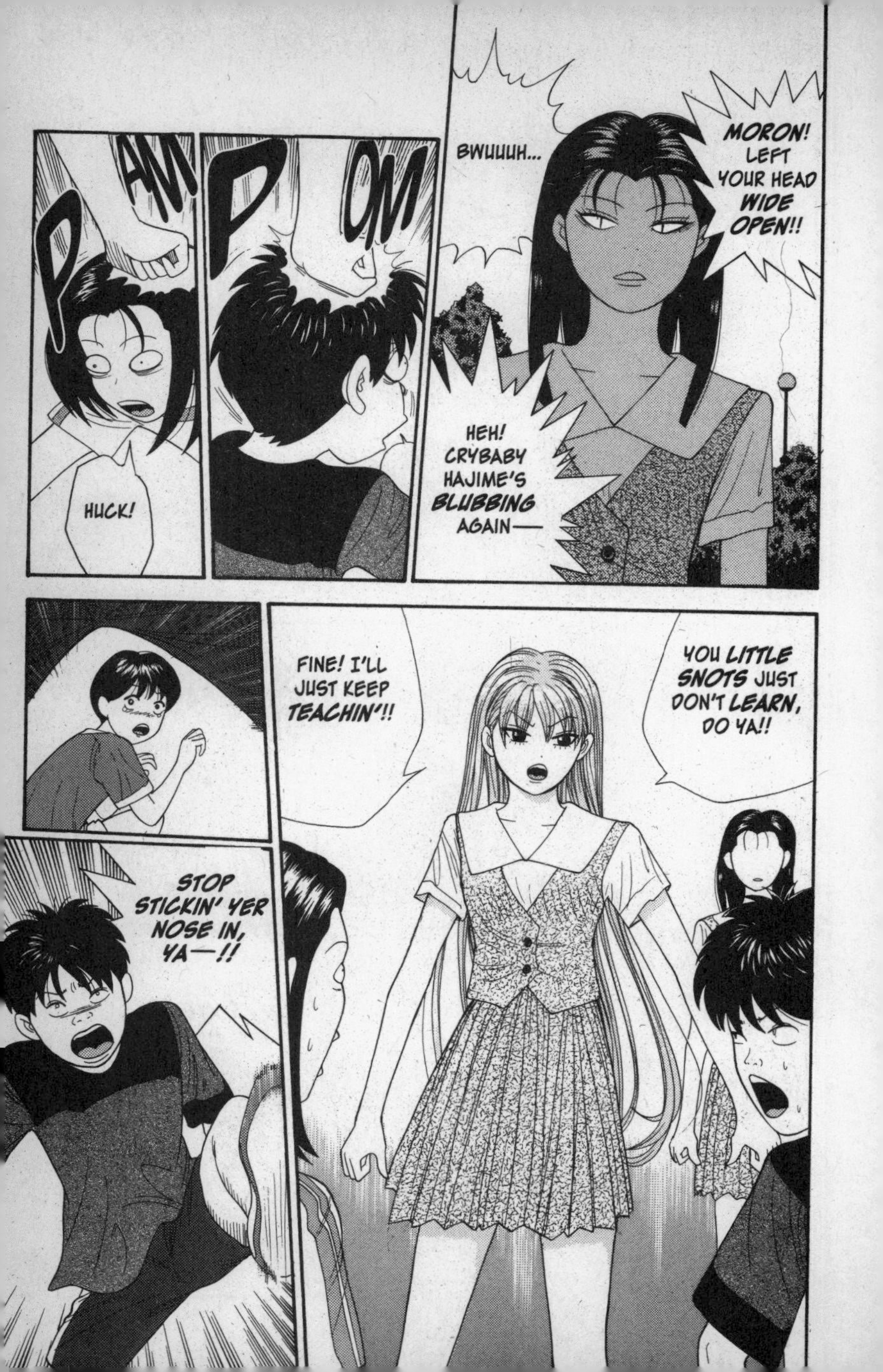
MORON! LEFT YOUR HEAD WIDE OPEN!!
BWUUUH...
HEH! CRYBABY HAJIME'S BLUBBING AGAIN—
POM
PAM
HUCK!
YOU LITTLE SNOTS JUST DON'T LEARN, DO YA!!
FINE! I'LL JUST KEEP TEACHIN'!!
STOP STICKIN' YER NOSE IN, YA—!!

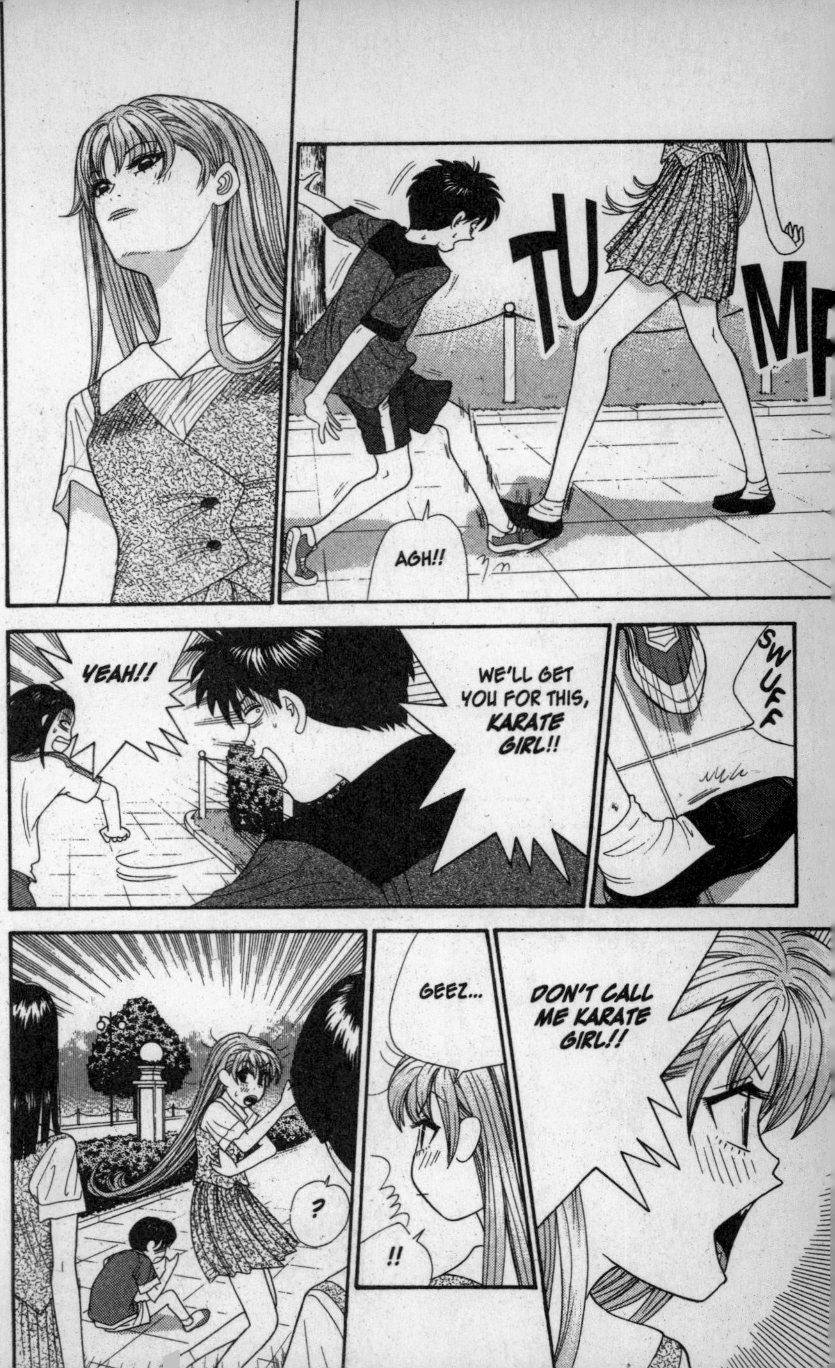
TUMP
AGH!!
SWUFF
WE'LL GET YOU FOR THIS, KARATE GIRL!!
YEAH!!
DON'T CALL ME KARATE GIRL!!
GEEZ...
!!
?

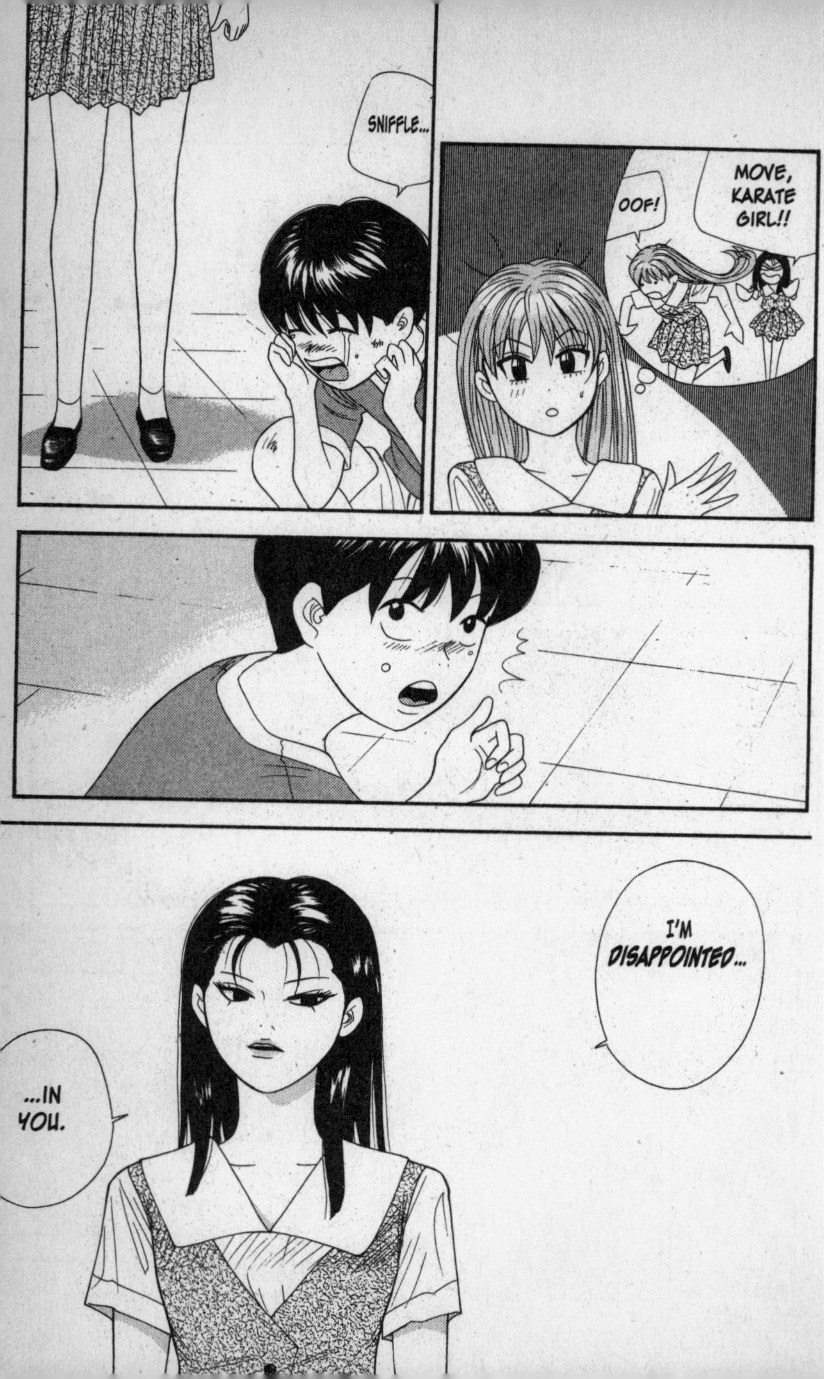
MOVE, KARATE GIRL!!
OOF!
SNIFFLE...
I'M DISAPPOINTED...
...IN YOU.

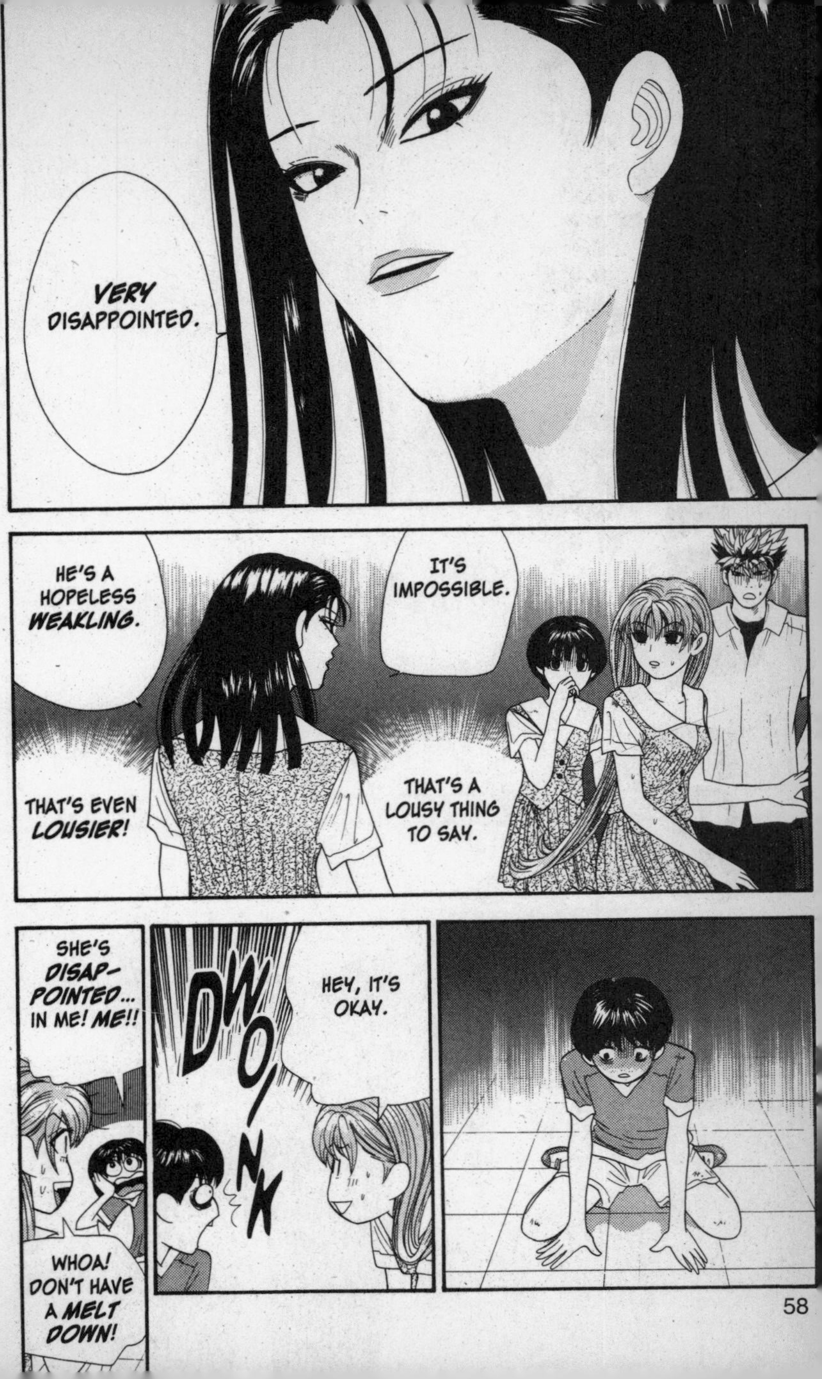
VERY DISAPPOINTED.
IT'S IMPOSSIBLE.
HE'S A HOPELESS WEAKLING.
THAT'S A LOUSY THING TO SAY.
THAT'S EVEN LOUSIER!
DWOINK
HEY, IT'S OKAY.
SHE'S DISAPPOINTED... IN ME! ME!!
WHOA! DON'T HAVE A MELT DOWN!

Chapter 63: Meg's Army Lecture

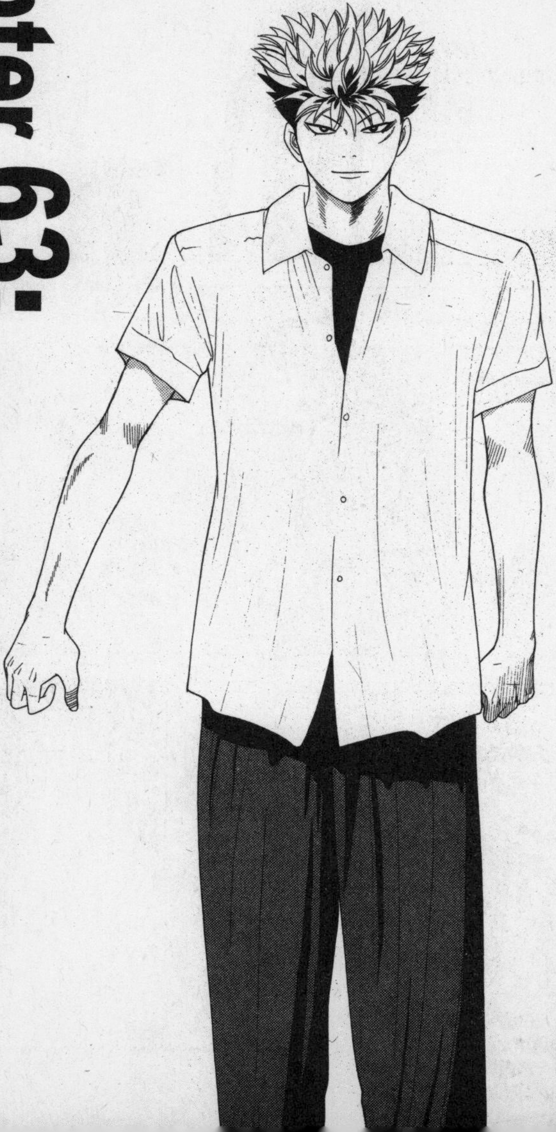

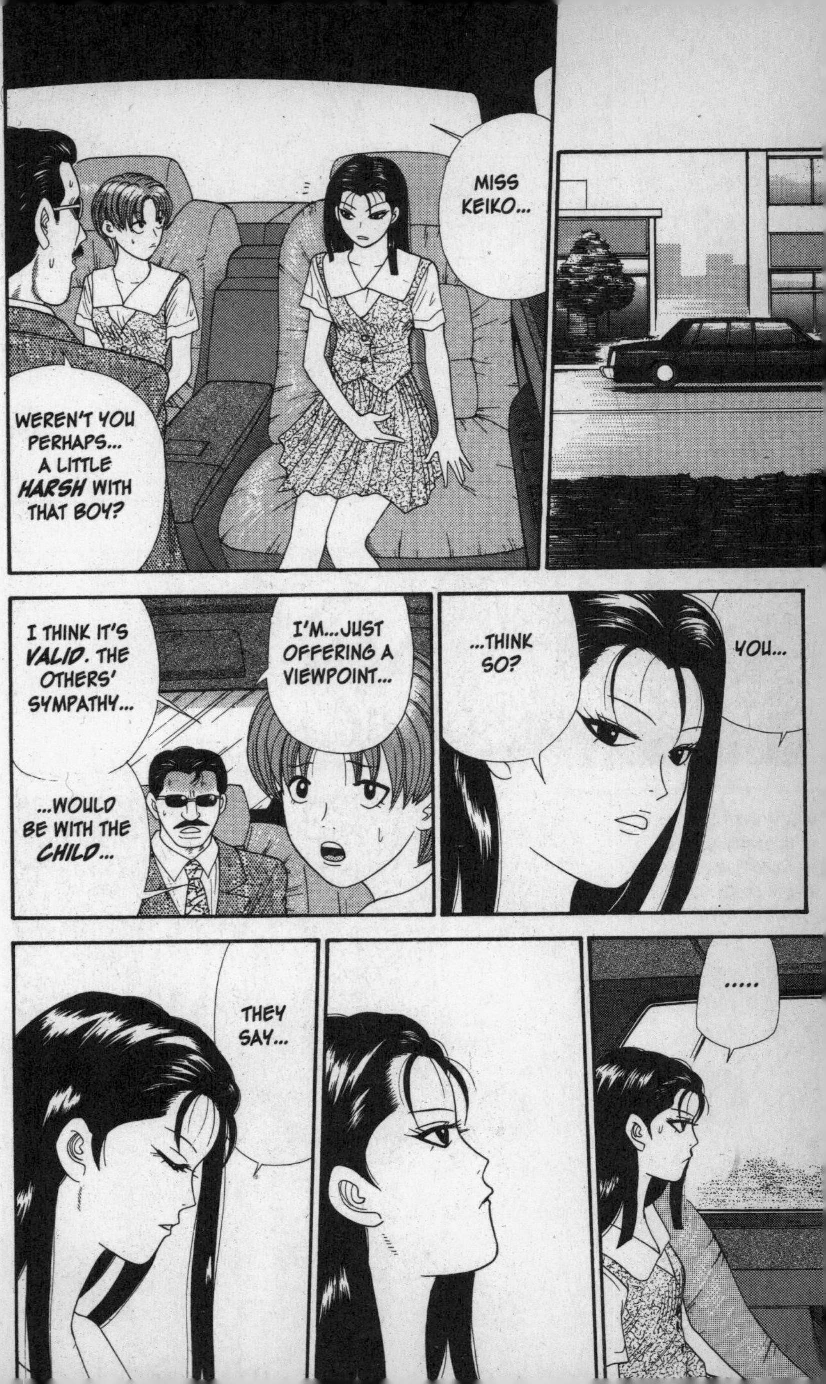
MISS KEIKO...
WEREN'T YOU PERHAPS... A LITTLE *HARSH* WITH THAT BOY?
YOU...
...THINK SO?
I'M...JUST OFFERING A VIEWPOINT...
I THINK IT'S *VALID*. THE OTHERS' SYMPATHY...
...WOULD BE WITH THE *CHILD*...
.....
THEY SAY...

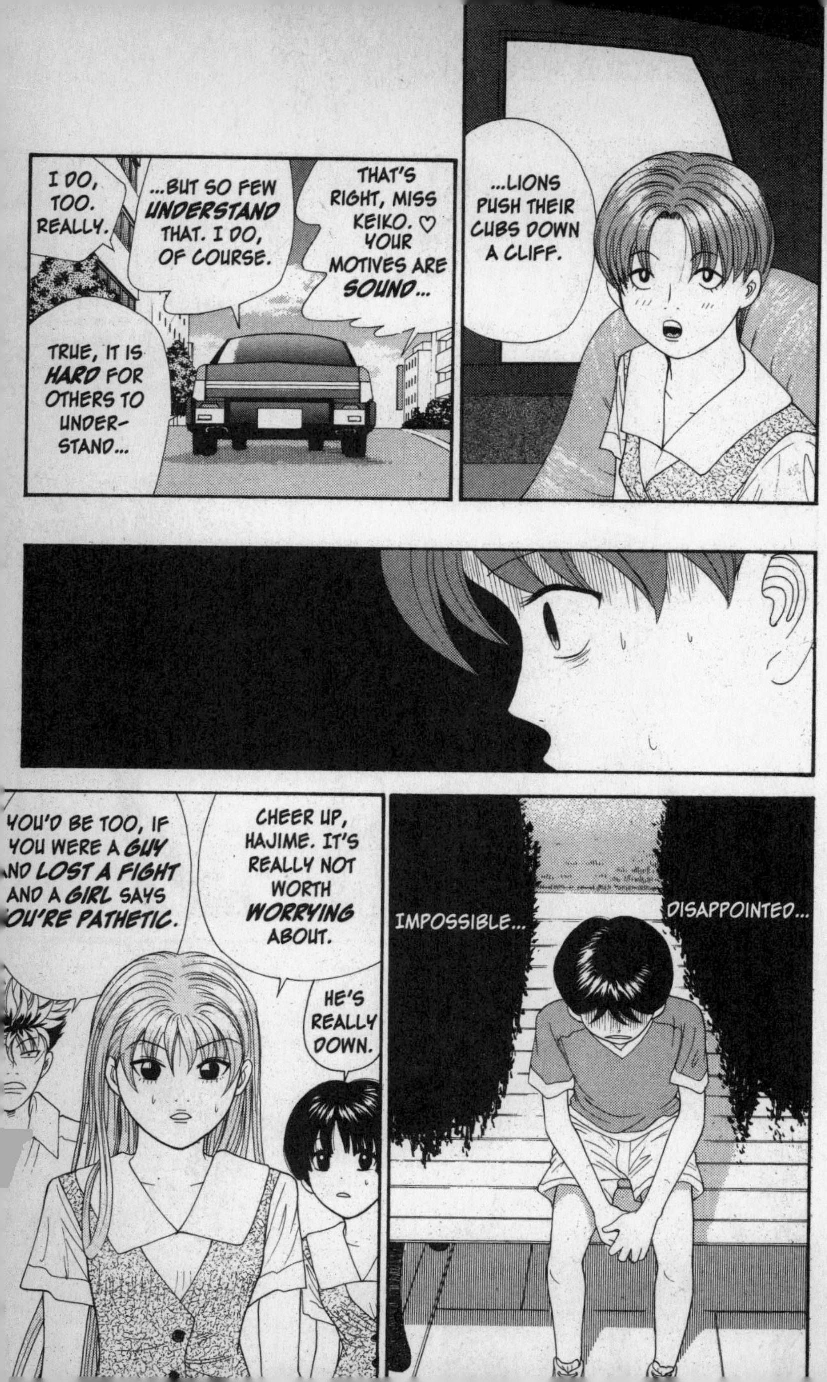
...LIONS PUSH THEIR CUBS DOWN A CLIFF.
THAT'S RIGHT, MISS KEIKO. ♡ YOUR MOTIVES ARE SOUND...
...BUT SO FEW UNDERSTAND THAT. I DO, OF COURSE.
I DO, TOO. REALLY.
TRUE, IT IS HARD FOR OTHERS TO UNDERSTAND...
DISAPPOINTED...
IMPOSSIBLE...
CHEER UP, HAJIME. IT'S REALLY NOT WORTH WORRYING ABOUT.
HE'S REALLY DOWN.
YOU'D BE TOO, IF YOU WERE A GUY ND LOST A FIGHT AND A GIRL SAYS OU'RE PATHETIC.

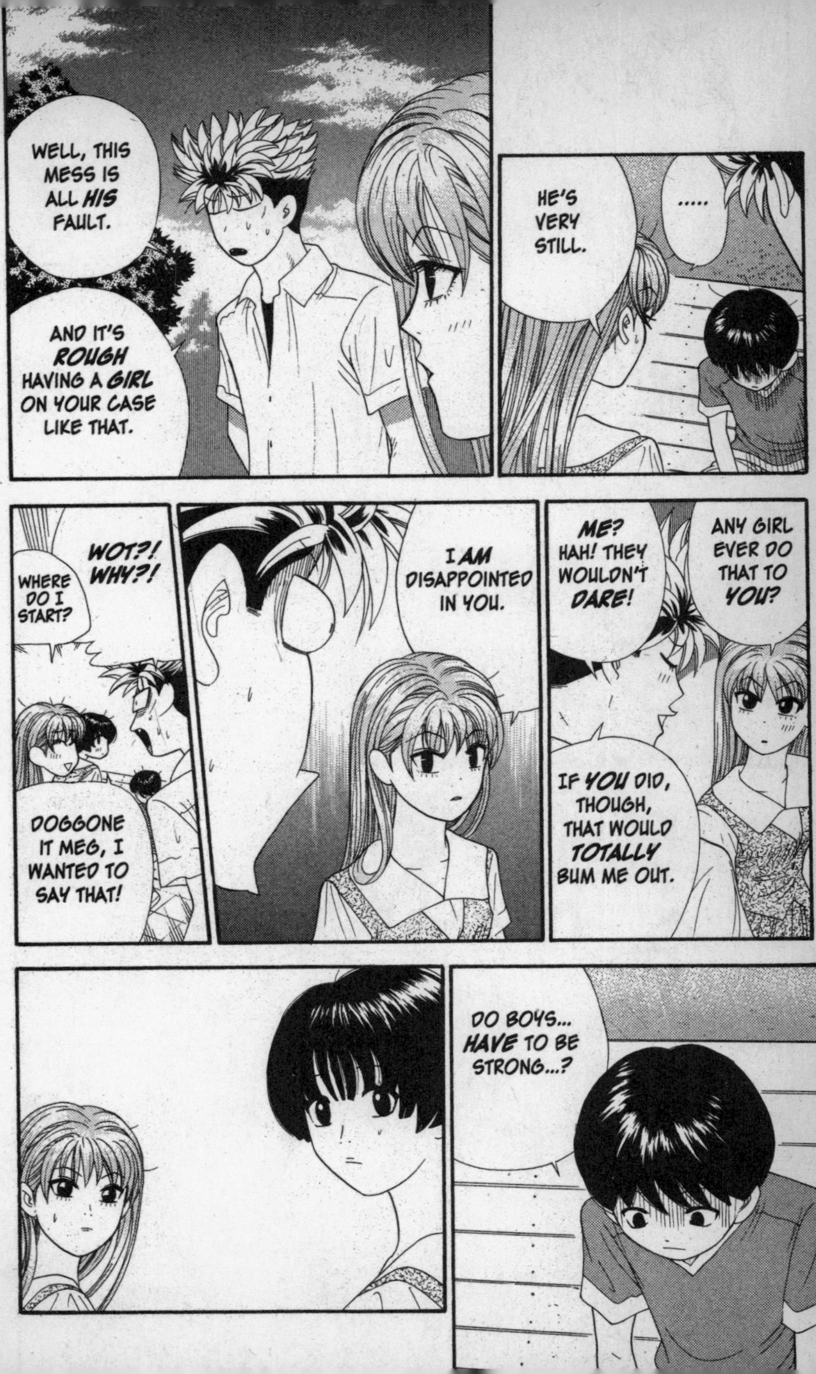
.....
HE'S VERY STILL.
WELL, THIS MESS IS ALL HIS FAULT.
AND IT'S ROUGH HAVING A GIRL ON YOUR CASE LIKE THAT.
ANY GIRL EVER DO THAT TO YOU?
ME? HAH! THEY WOULDN'T DARE!
IF YOU DID, THOUGH, THAT WOULD TOTALLY BUM ME OUT.
I AM DISAPPOINTED IN YOU.
WOT?! WHY?!
WHERE DO I START?
DOGGONE IT MEG, I WANTED TO SAY THAT!
DO BOYS... HAVE TO BE STRONG...?

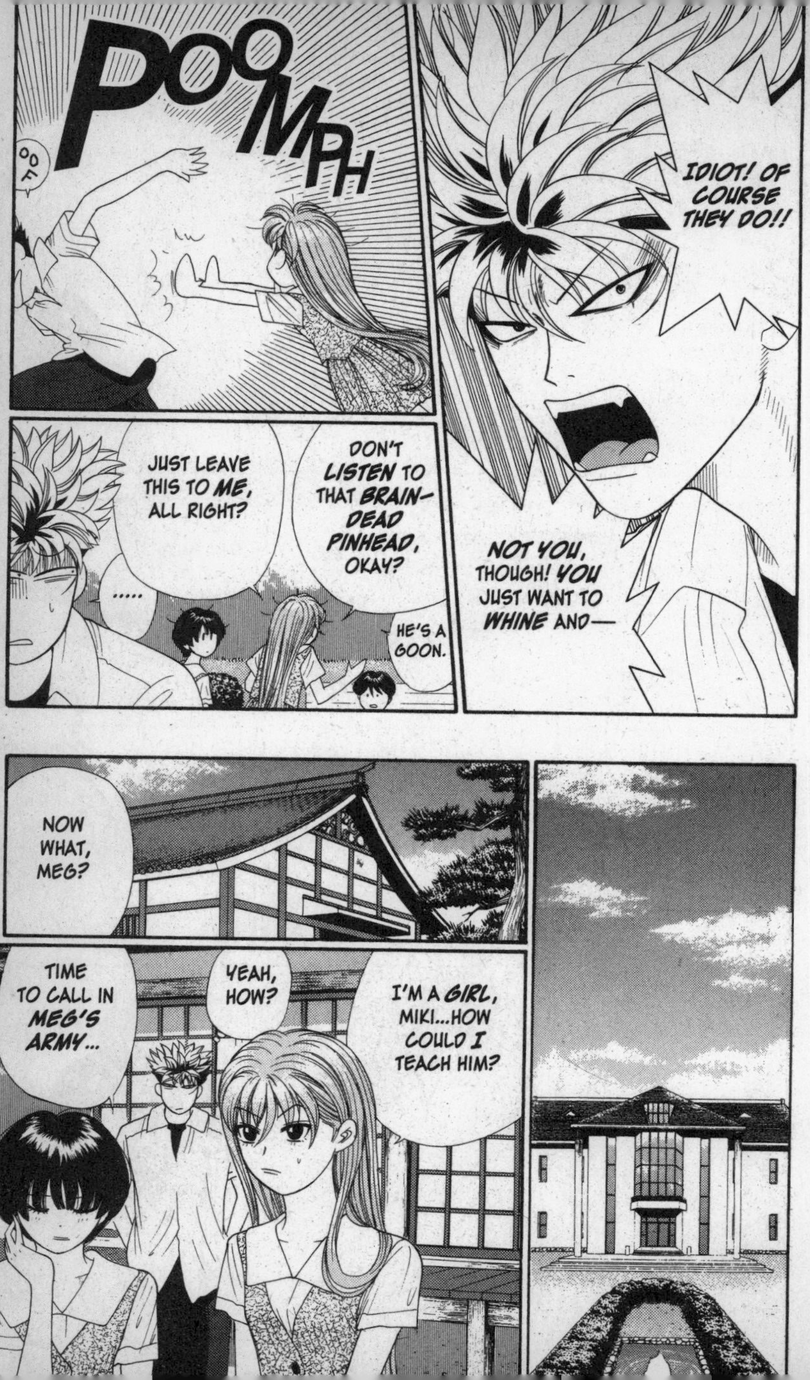
IDIOT! OF COURSE THEY DO!!
NOT YOU, THOUGH! YOU JUST WANT TO WHINE AND—
POOOMPH
OOF
DON'T LISTEN TO THAT BRAIN-DEAD PINHEAD, OKAY?
JUST LEAVE THIS TO ME, ALL RIGHT?
.....
HE'S A GOON.
NOW WHAT, MEG?
I'M A GIRL, MIKI...HOW COULD I TEACH HIM?
YEAH, HOW?
TIME TO CALL IN MEG'S ARMY...

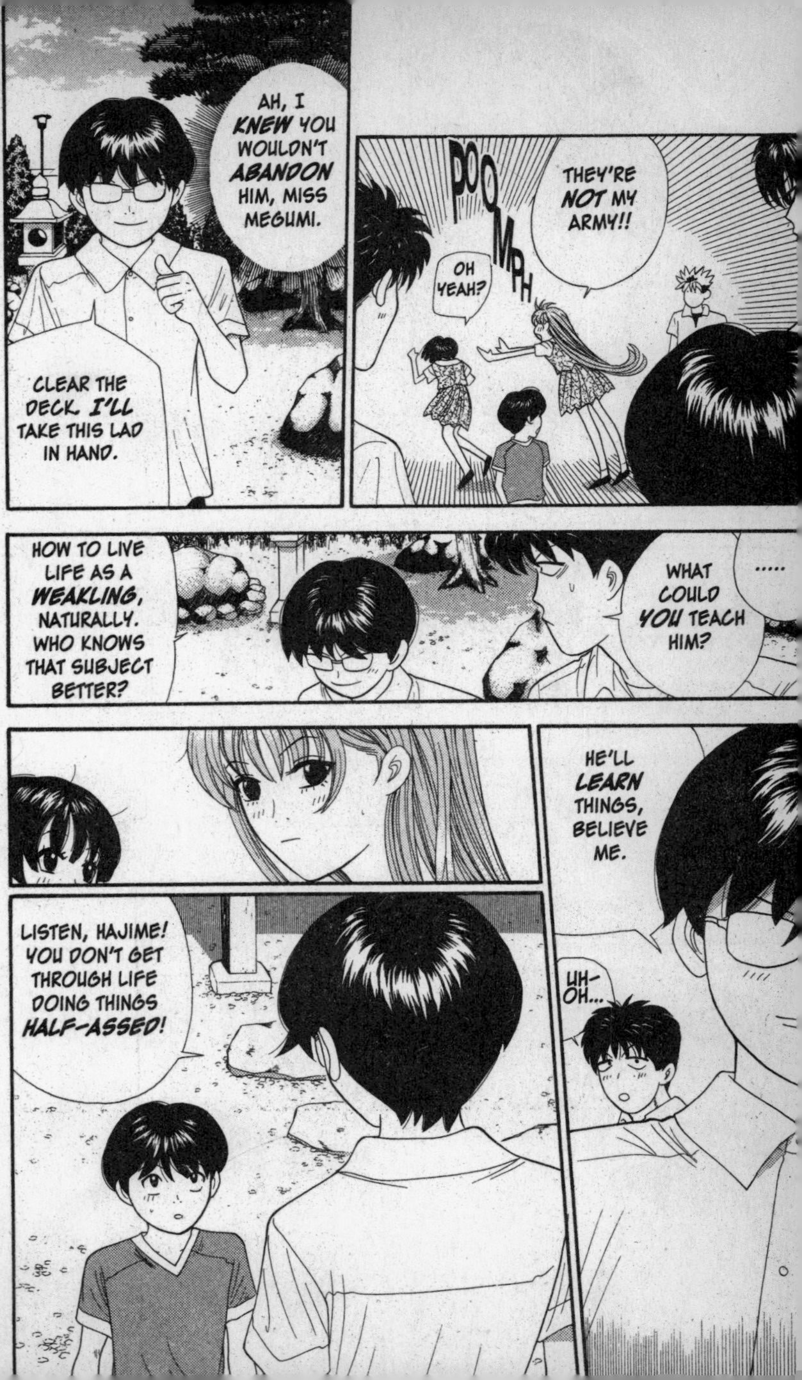
THEY'RE NOT MY ARMY!!
POOMPH
OH YEAH?
AH, I KNEW YOU WOULDN'T ABANDON HIM, MISS MEGUMI.
CLEAR THE DECK. I'LL TAKE THIS LAD IN HAND.
.....
WHAT COULD YOU TEACH HIM?
HOW TO LIVE LIFE AS A WEAKLING, NATURALLY. WHO KNOWS THAT SUBJECT BETTER?
HE'LL LEARN THINGS, BELIEVE ME.
UH-OH...
LISTEN, HAJIME! YOU DON'T GET THROUGH LIFE DOING THINGS HALF-ASSED!

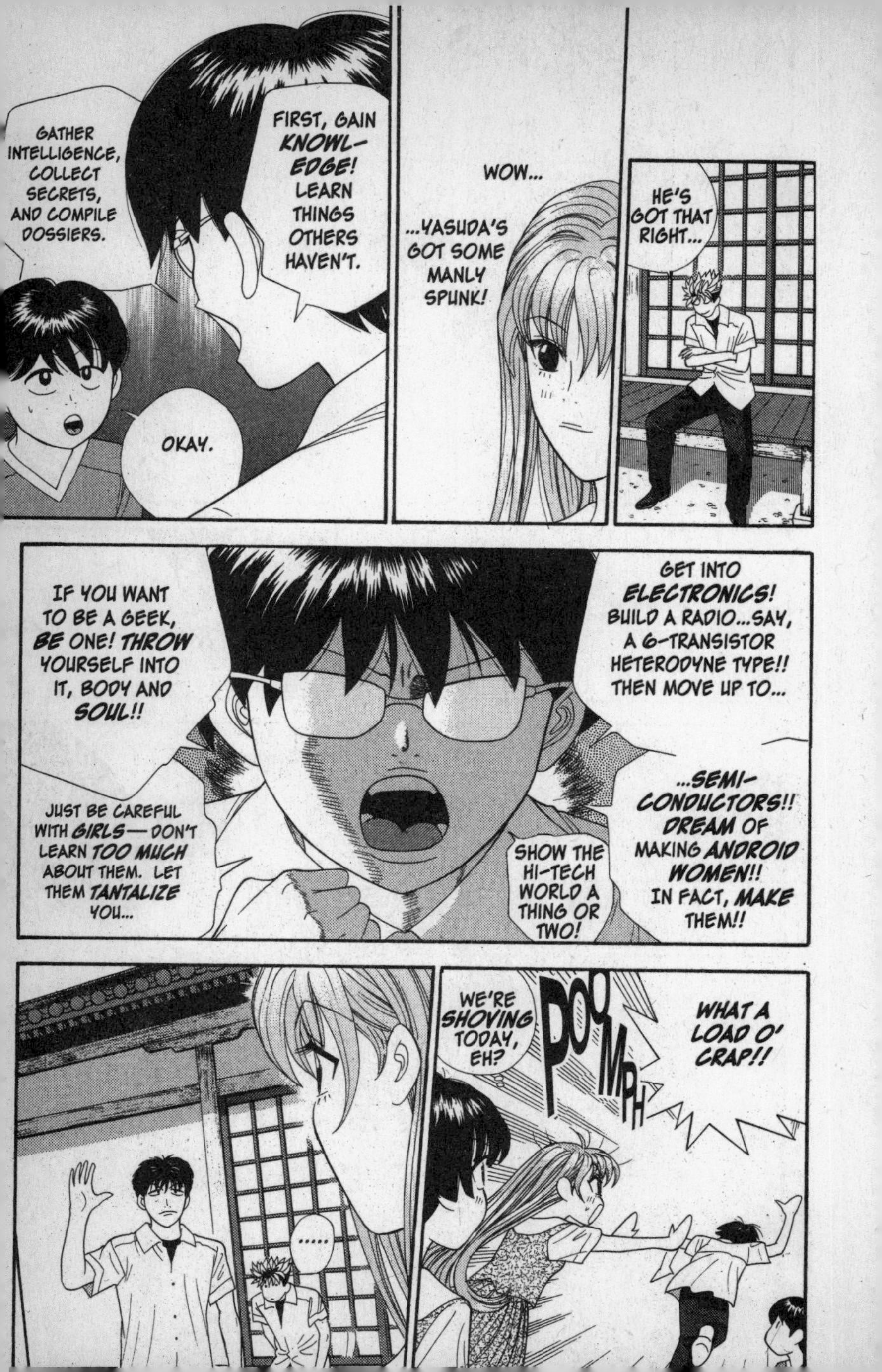
HE'S GOT THAT RIGHT...
WOW...
...YASUDA'S GOT SOME MANLY SPUNK!
FIRST, GAIN KNOWLEDGE! LEARN THINGS OTHERS HAVEN'T.
GATHER INTELLIGENCE, COLLECT SECRETS, AND COMPILE DOSSIERS.
OKAY.
GET INTO ELECTRONICS! BUILD A RADIO...SAY, A 6-TRANSISTOR HETERODYNE TYPE!! THEN MOVE UP TO...
IF YOU WANT TO BE A GEEK, BE ONE! THROW YOURSELF INTO IT, BODY AND SOUL!!
...SEMI-CONDUCTORS!! DREAM OF MAKING ANDROID WOMEN!! IN FACT, MAKE THEM!!
SHOW THE HI-TECH WORLD A THING OR TWO!
JUST BE CAREFUL WITH GIRLS— DON'T LEARN TOO MUCH ABOUT THEM. LET THEM TANTALIZE YOU...
WHAT A LOAD O' CRAP!!
POOMPH
WE'RE SHOVING TODAY, EH?
......

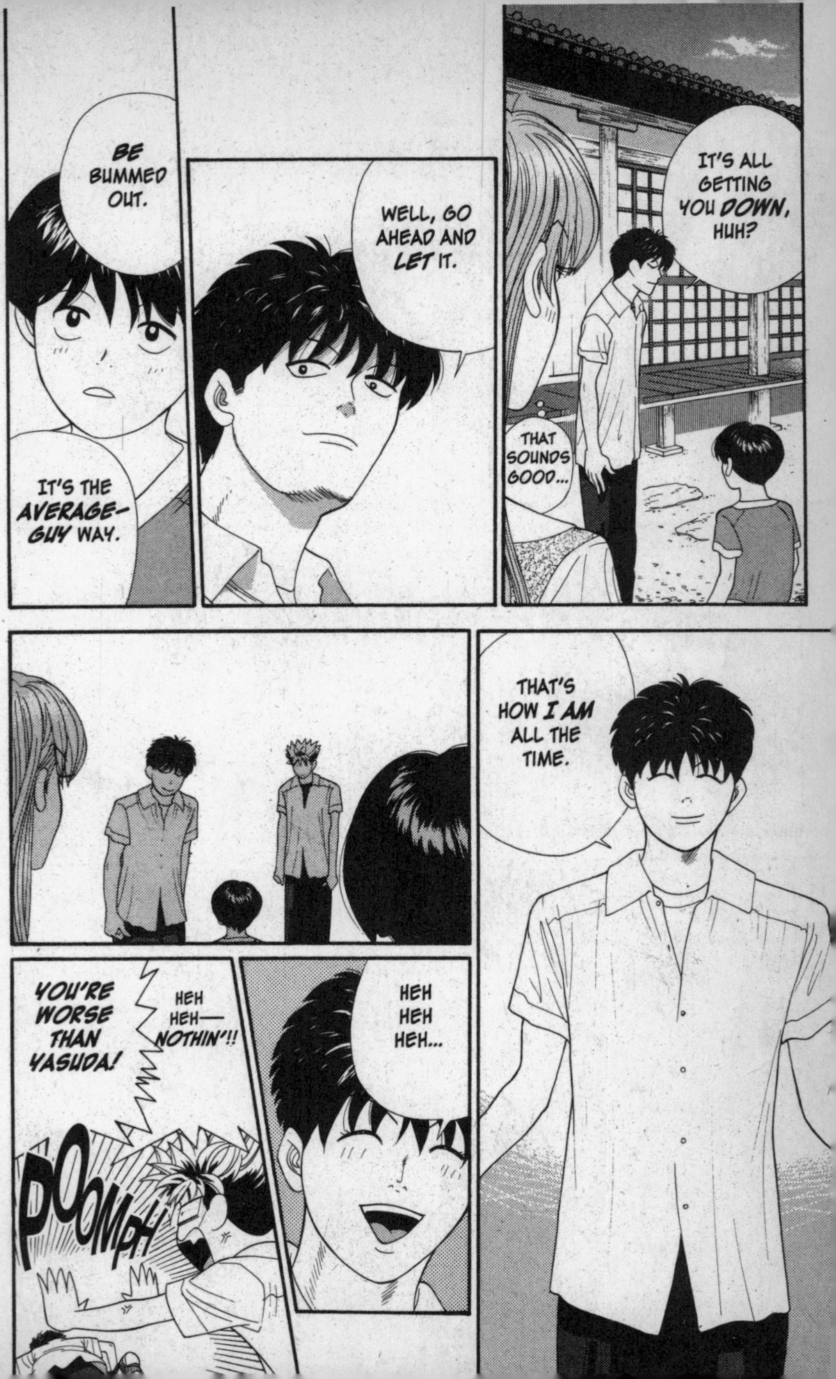
IT'S ALL GETTING YOU DOWN, HUH?
THAT SOUNDS GOOD...
WELL, GO AHEAD AND LET IT.
BE BUMMED OUT.
IT'S THE AVERAGE-GUY WAY.
THAT'S HOW I AM ALL THE TIME.
HEH HEH HEH...
HEH HEH— NOTHIN'!!
YOU'RE WORSE THAN YASUDA!
POOMPH!

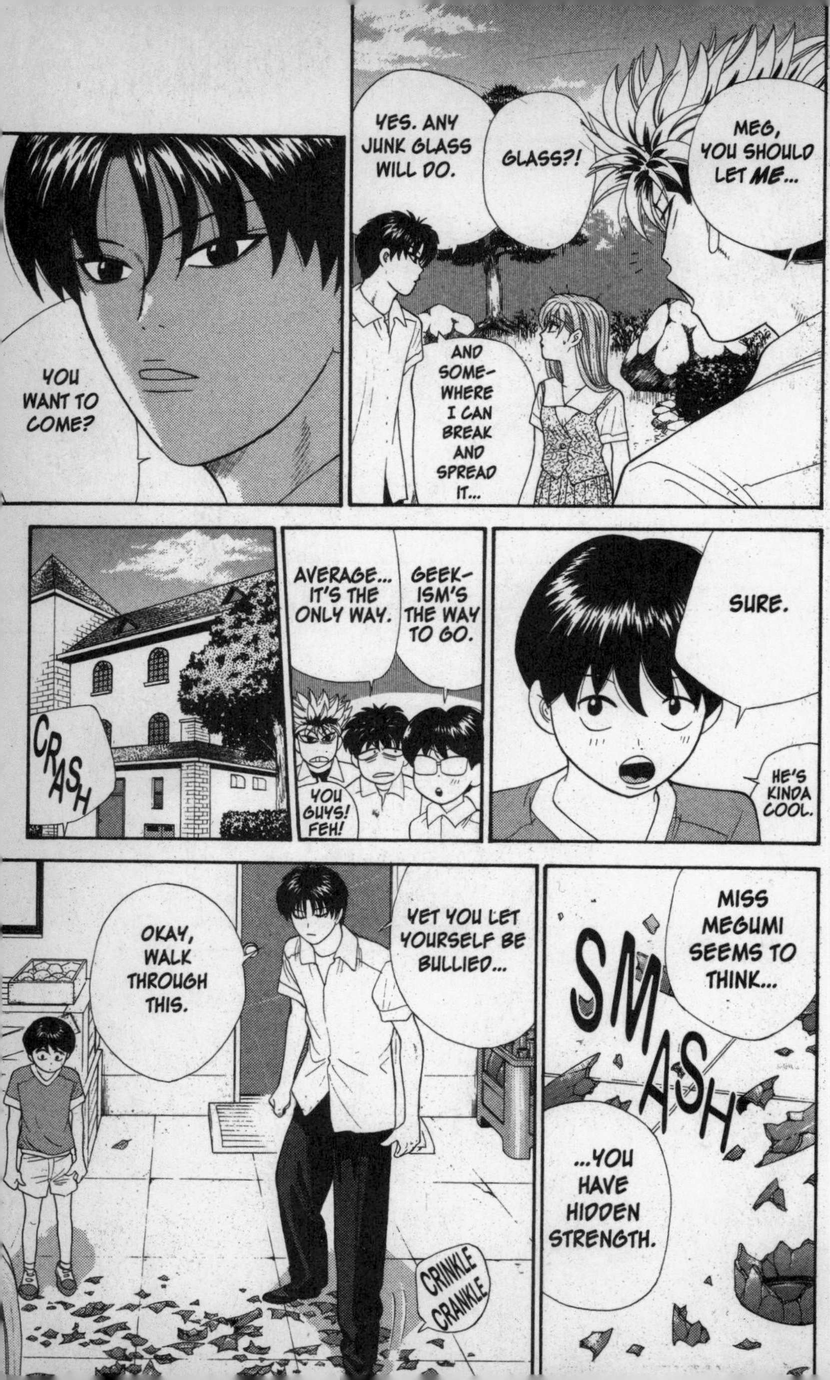
MEG, YOU SHOULD LET ME...
GLASS?!
YES. ANY JUNK GLASS WILL DO.
AND SOME-WHERE I CAN BREAK AND SPREAD IT...
YOU WANT TO COME?
SURE.
HE'S KINDA COOL.
GEEK-ISM'S THE WAY TO GO.
AVERAGE... IT'S THE ONLY WAY.
YOU GUYS! FEH!
CRASH
MISS MEGUMI SEEMS TO THINK...
SMASH
...YOU HAVE HIDDEN STRENGTH.
YET YOU LET YOURSELF BE BULLIED...
OKAY, WALK THROUGH THIS.
CRINKLE CRANKLE

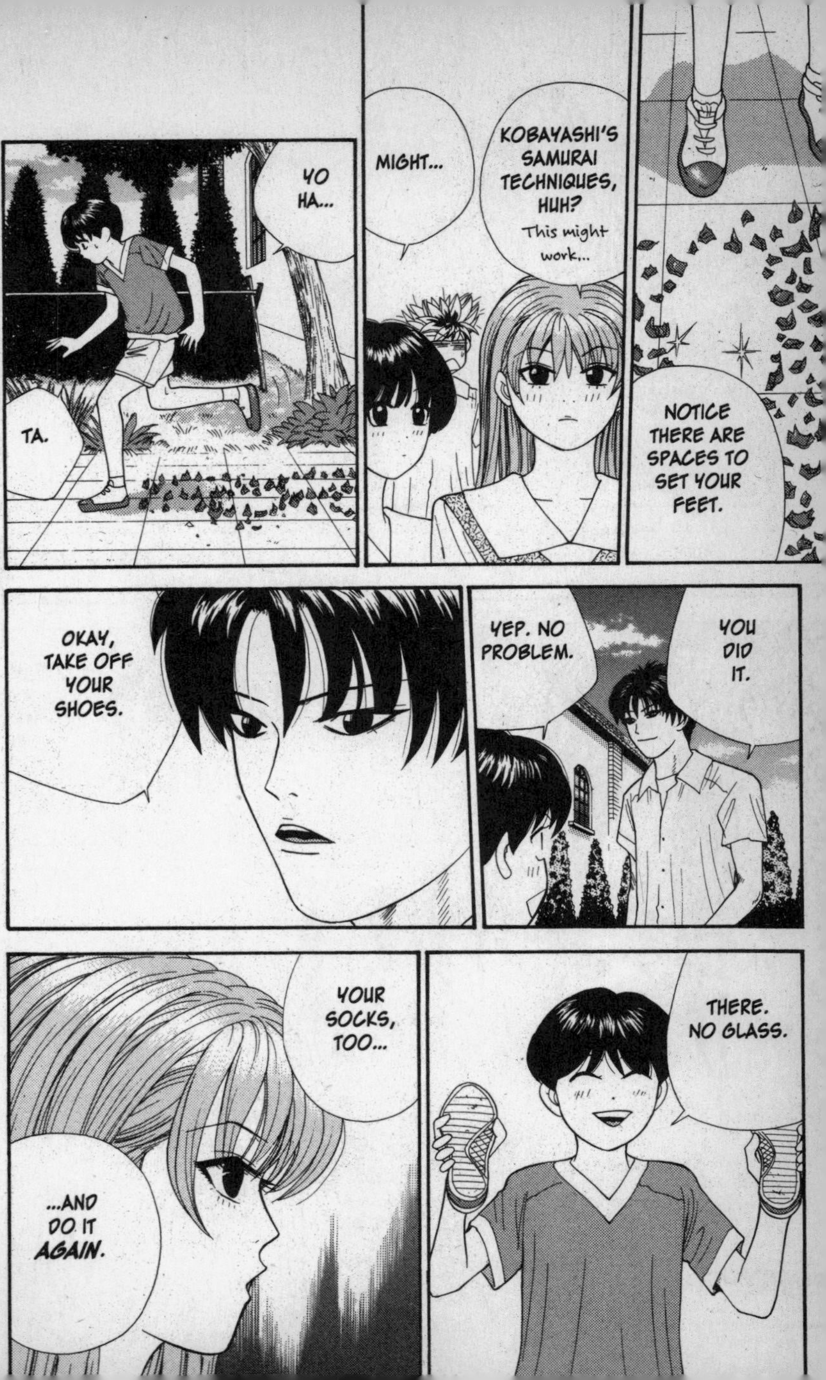
NOTICE THERE ARE SPACES TO SET YOUR FEET.
KOBAYASHI'S SAMURAI TECHNIQUES, HUH?
This might work...
MIGHT...
YO HA...
TA.
YOU DID IT.
YEP. NO PROBLEM.
OKAY, TAKE OFF YOUR SHOES.
THERE. NO GLASS.
YOUR SOCKS, TOO...
...AND DO IT AGAIN.

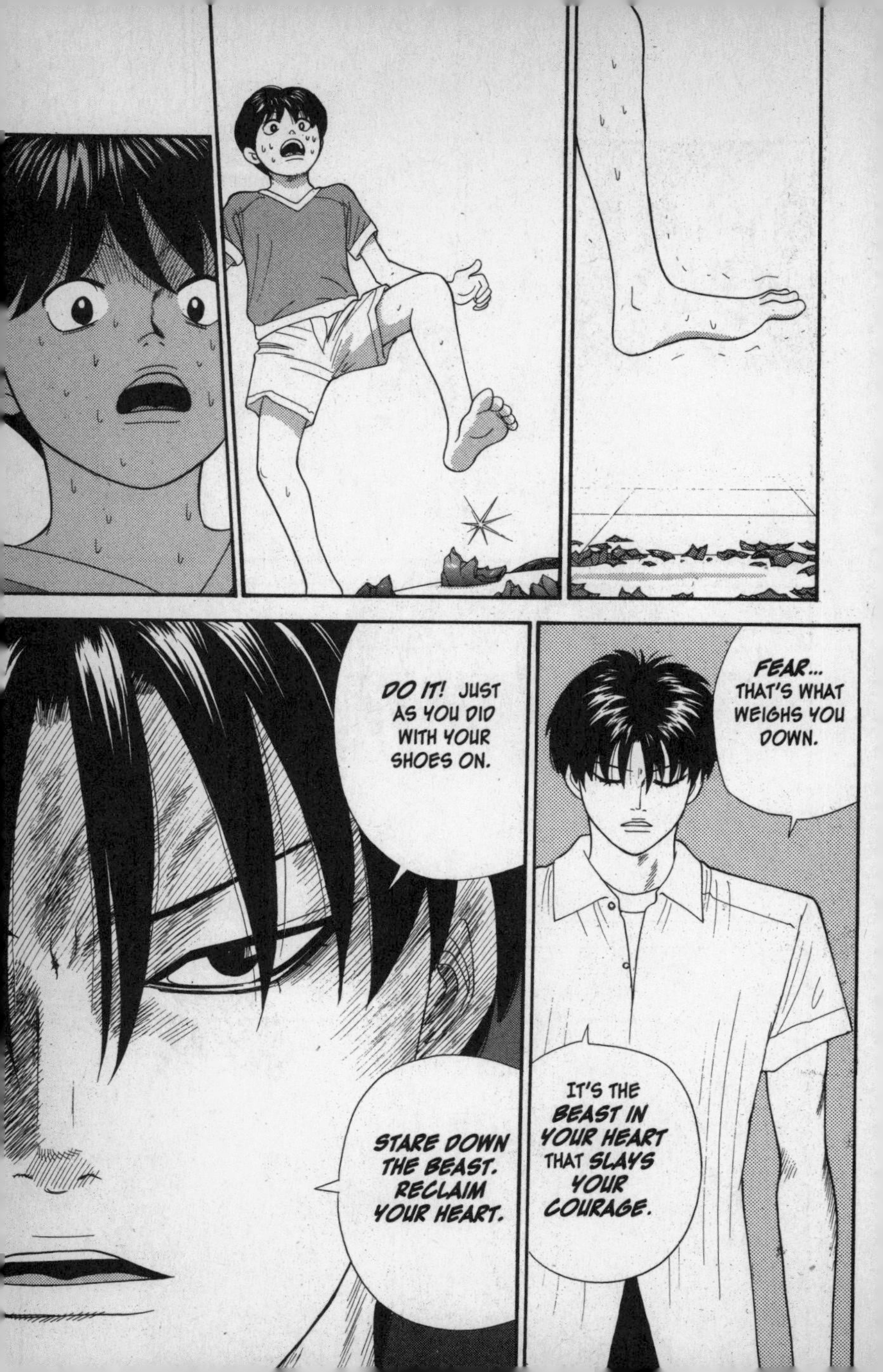
FEAR... THAT'S WHAT WEIGHS YOU DOWN.
IT'S THE BEAST IN YOUR HEART THAT SLAYS YOUR COURAGE.
DO IT! JUST AS YOU DID WITH YOUR SHOES ON.
STARE DOWN THE BEAST. RECLAIM YOUR HEART.

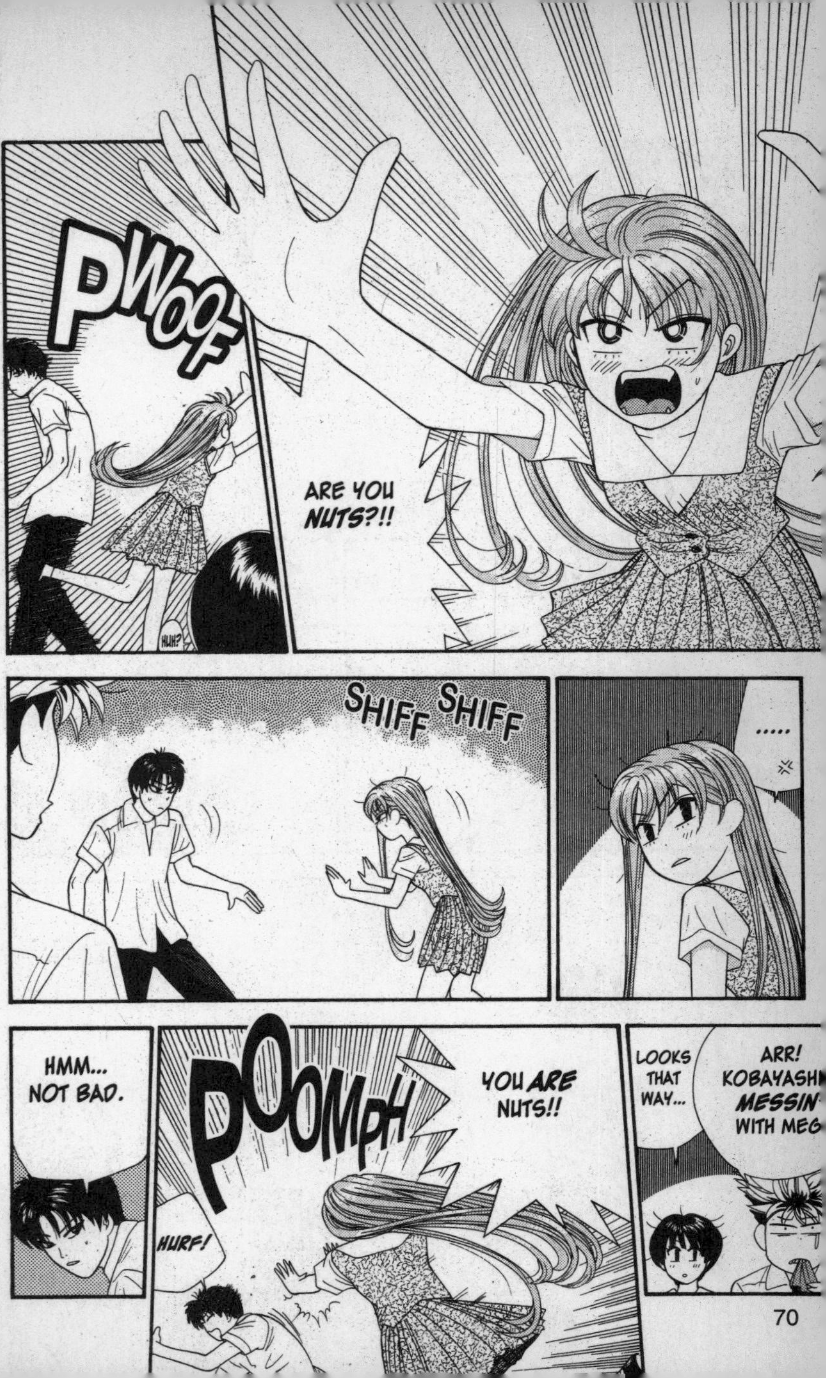
ARE YOU NUTS?!!
PWOOF
HUH?
.....
SHIFF SHIFF
ARR! KOBAYASHI MESSIN WITH MEG
LOOKS THAT WAY...
YOU ARE NUTS!!
POOMPH
HURF!
HMM... NOT BAD.

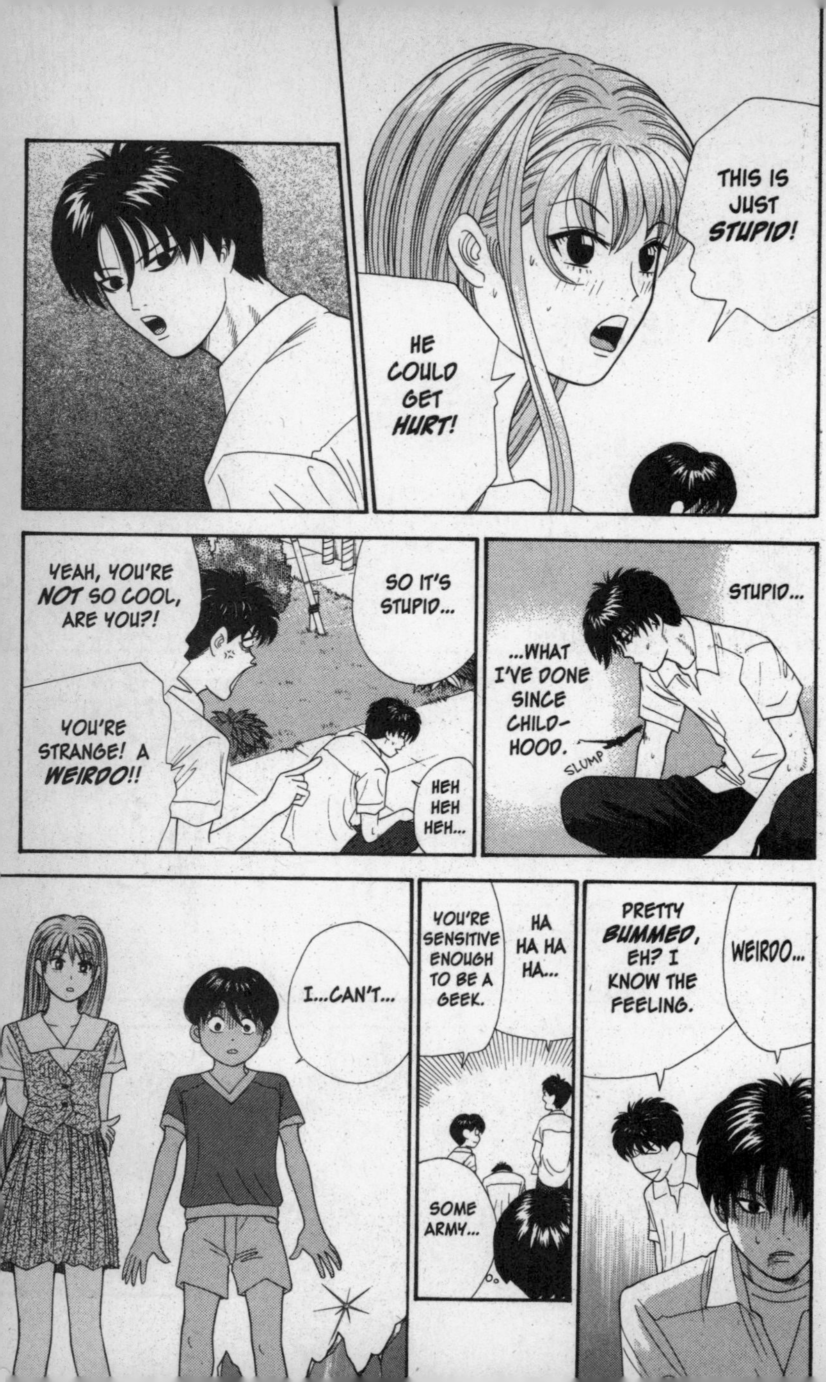
THIS IS JUST STUPID!
HE COULD GET HURT!
STUPID...
...WHAT I'VE DONE SINCE CHILDHOOD.
SLUMP
SO IT'S STUPID...
YEAH, YOU'RE NOT SO COOL, ARE YOU?!
YOU'RE STRANGE! A WEIRDO!!
HEH HEH HEH...
WEIRDO...
PRETTY BUMMED, EH? I KNOW THE FEELING.
HA HA HA HA...
YOU'RE SENSITIVE ENOUGH TO BE A GEEK.
SOME ARMY...
I...CAN'T...

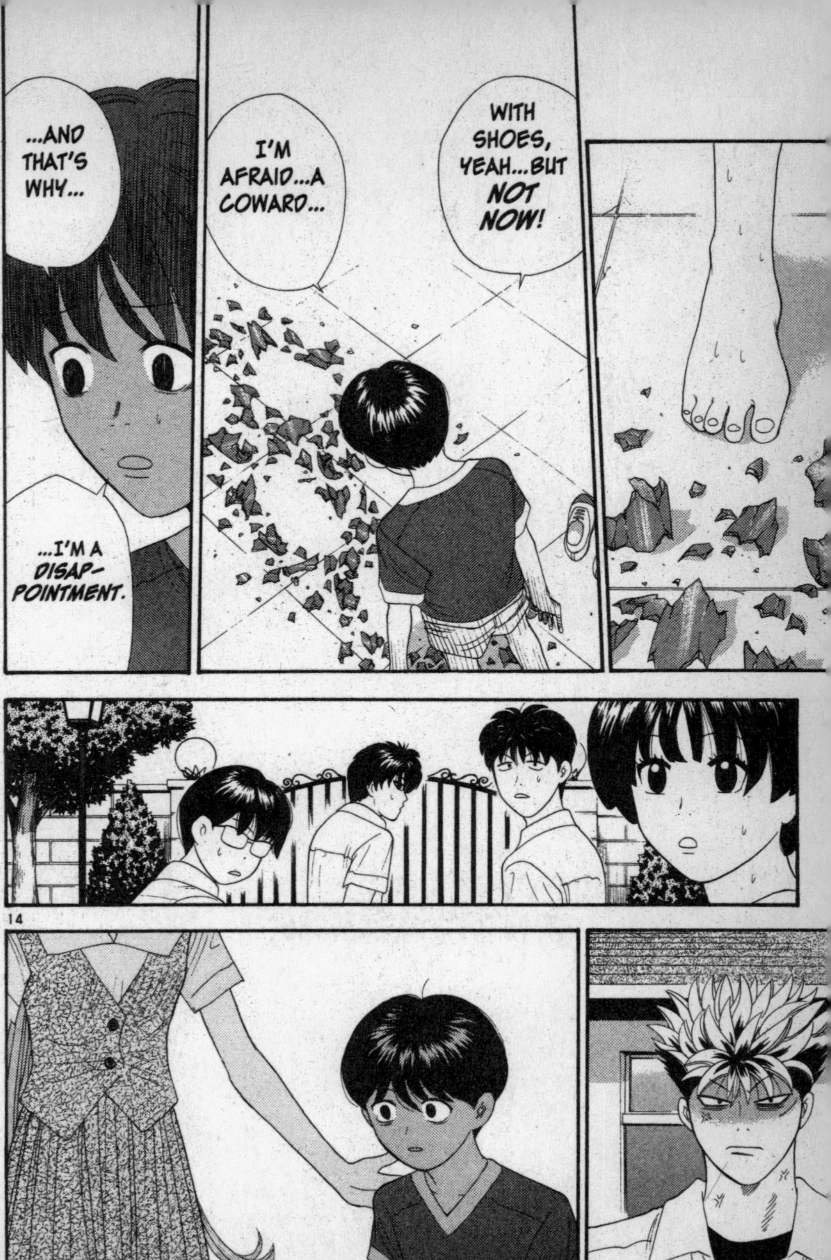
WITH SHOES, YEAH...BUT NOT NOW!
I'M AFRAID...A COWARD...
...AND THAT'S WHY...
...I'M A DISAPPOINTMENT.

14

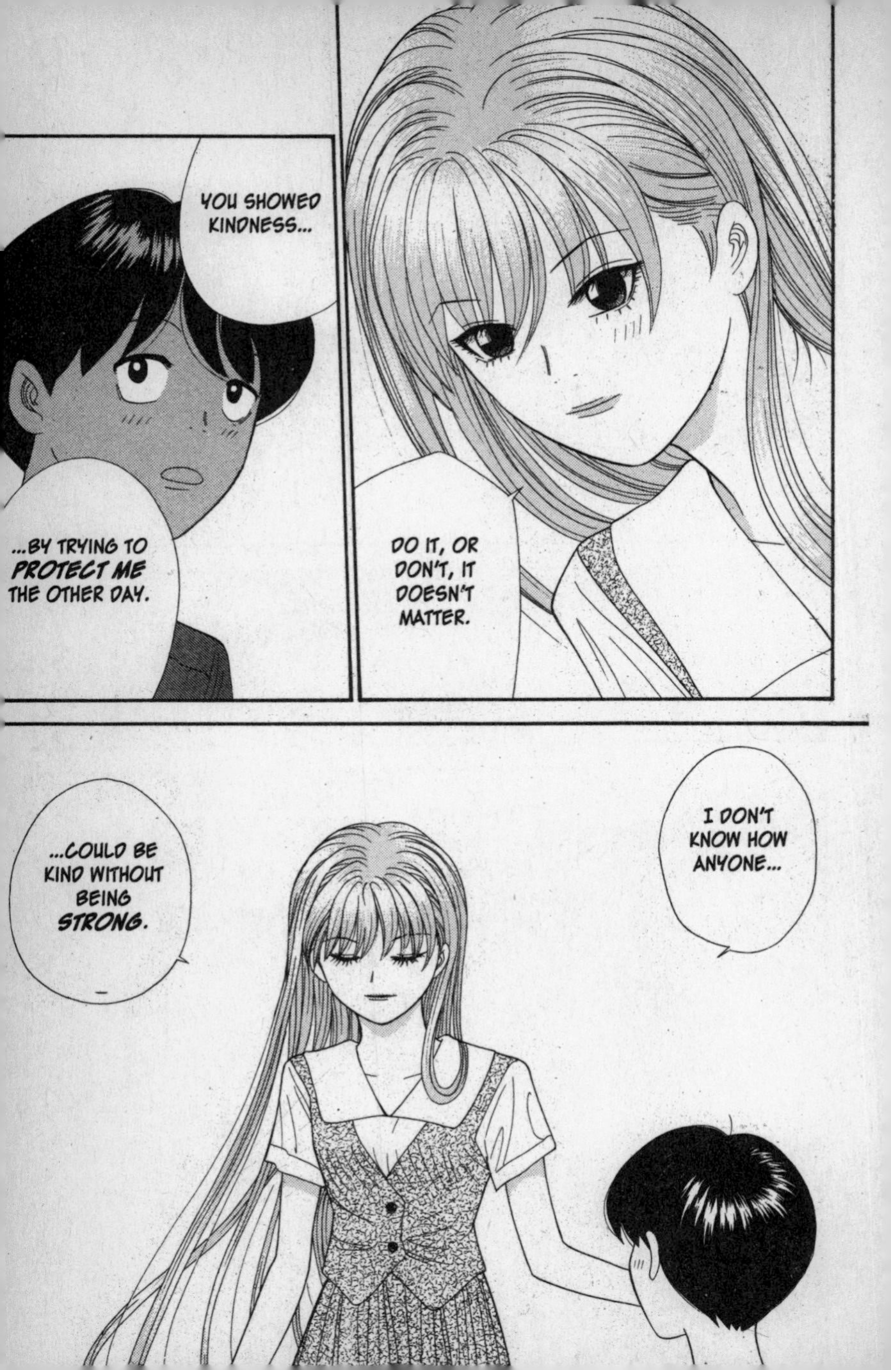
DO IT, OR DON'T, IT DOESN'T MATTER.
YOU SHOWED KINDNESS...
...BY TRYING TO *PROTECT ME* THE OTHER DAY.
I DON'T KNOW HOW ANYONE...
...COULD BE KIND WITHOUT BEING *STRONG*.

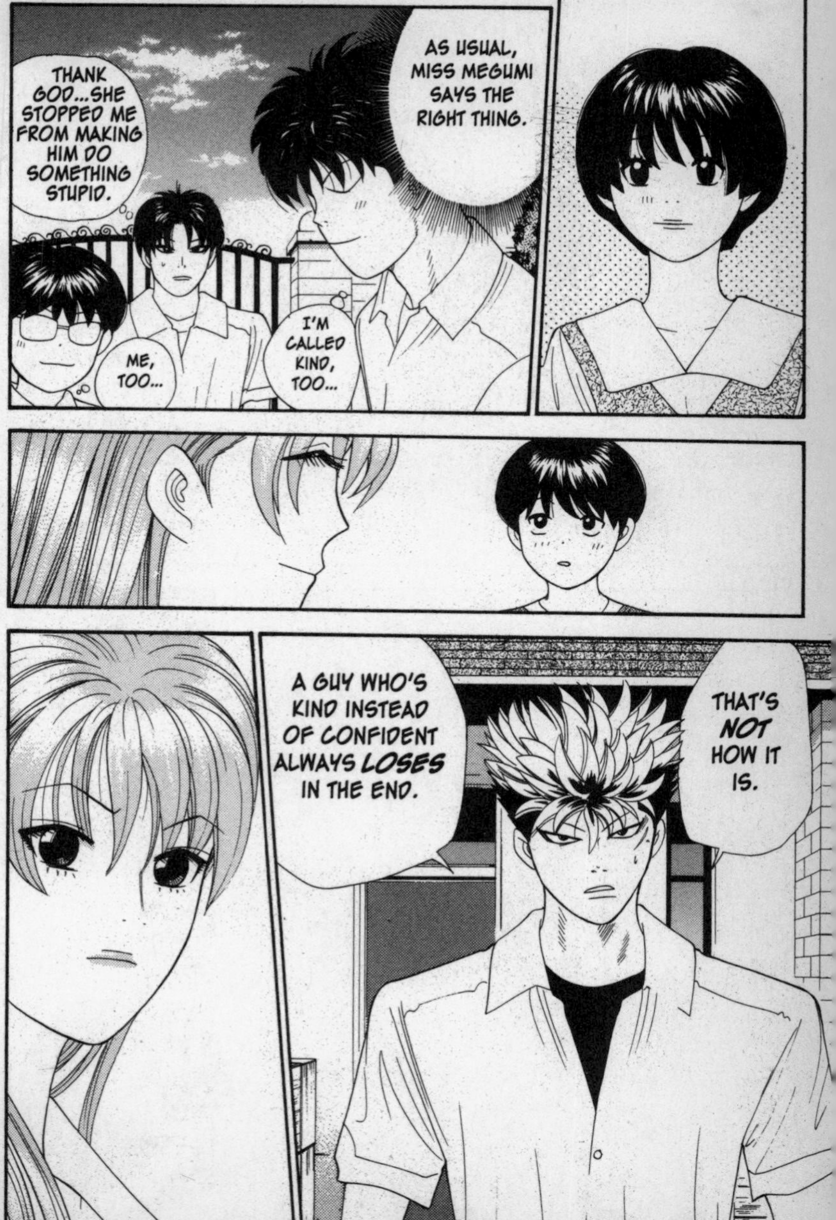
AS USUAL, MISS MEGUMI SAYS THE RIGHT THING.
THANK GOD...SHE STOPPED ME FROM MAKING HIM DO SOMETHING STUPID.
I'M CALLED KIND, TOO...
ME, TOO...
THAT'S *NOT* HOW IT IS.
A GUY WHO'S KIND INSTEAD OF CONFIDENT ALWAYS *LOSES* IN THE END.

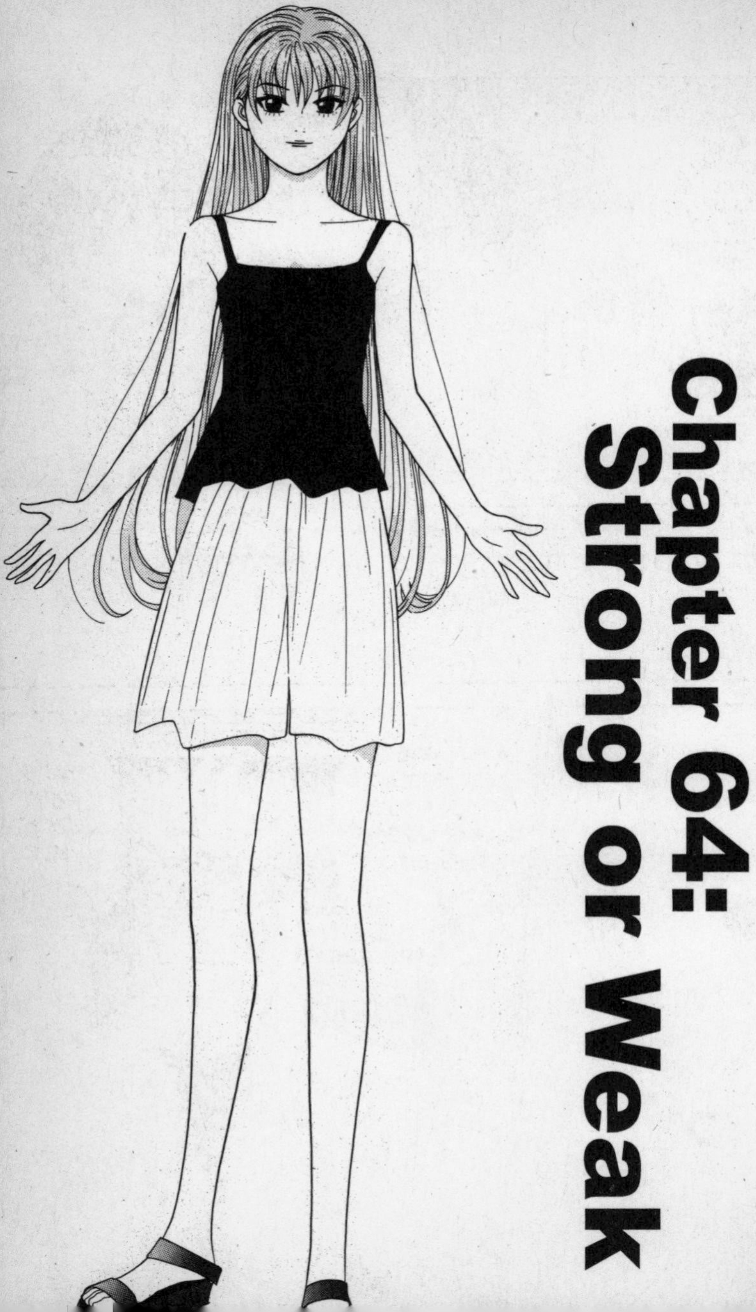

Chapter 64: Strong or Weak

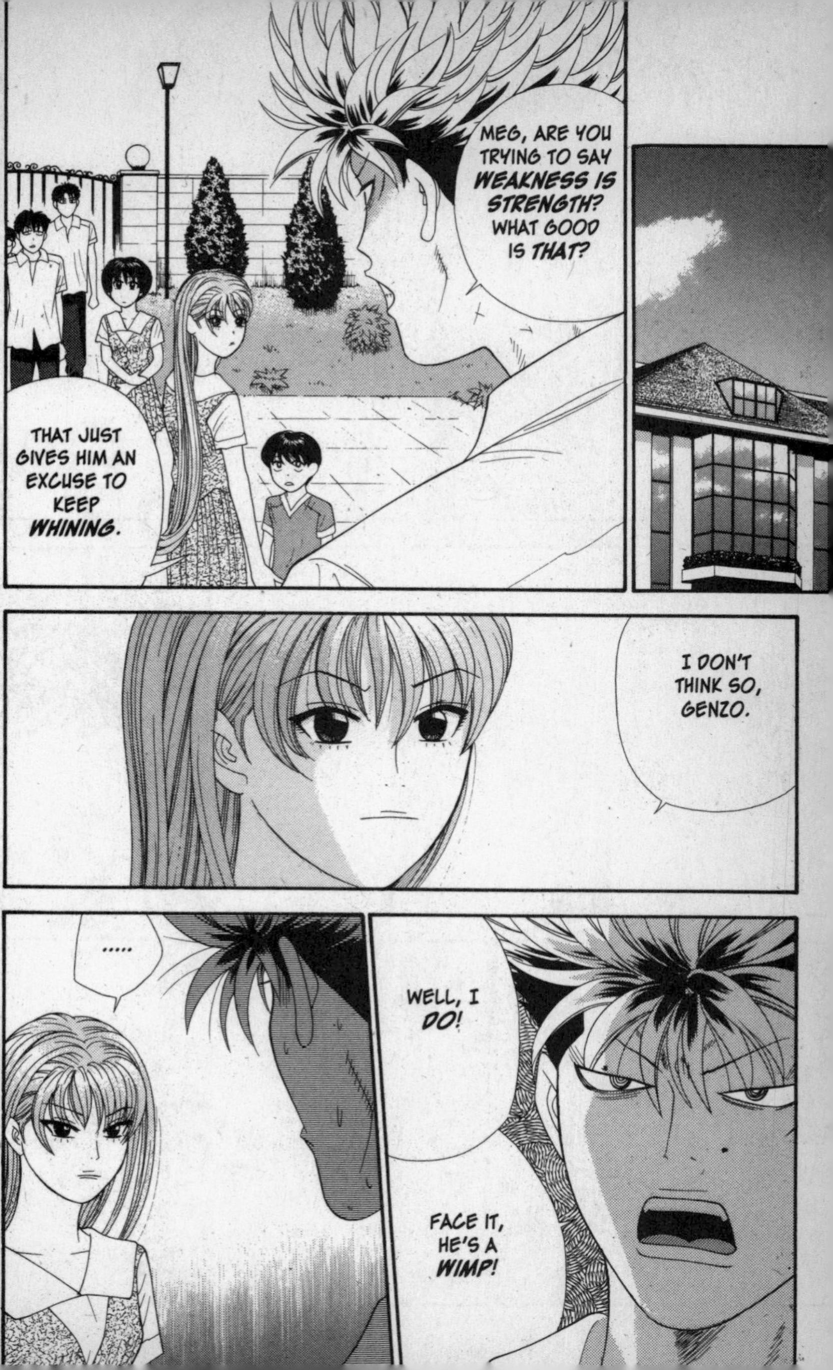
MEG, ARE YOU TRYING TO SAY WEAKNESS IS STRENGTH? WHAT GOOD IS THAT?
THAT JUST GIVES HIM AN EXCUSE TO KEEP WHINING.
I DON'T THINK SO, GENZO.
WELL, I DO!
FACE IT, HE'S A WIMP!
.....

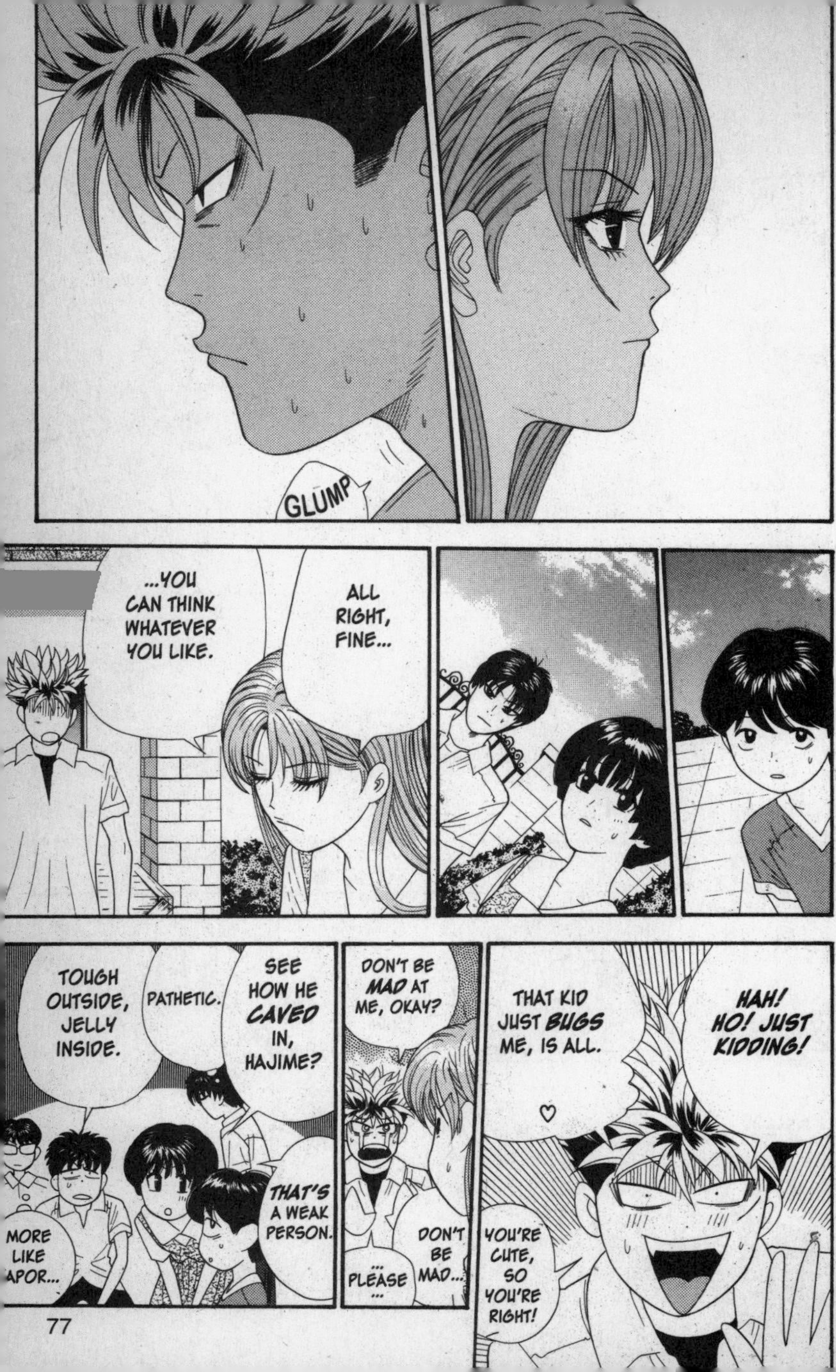
GLUMP
ALL RIGHT, FINE...
...YOU CAN THINK WHATEVER YOU LIKE.
HAH! HO! JUST KIDDING!
THAT KID JUST BUGS ME, IS ALL.
YOU'RE CUTE, SO YOU'RE RIGHT!
DON'T BE MAD AT ME, OKAY?
DON'T BE MAD...
...PLEASE...
SEE HOW HE CAVED IN, HAJIME?
PATHETIC.
TOUGH OUTSIDE, JELLY INSIDE.
THAT'S A WEAK PERSON.
MORE LIKE APOR...

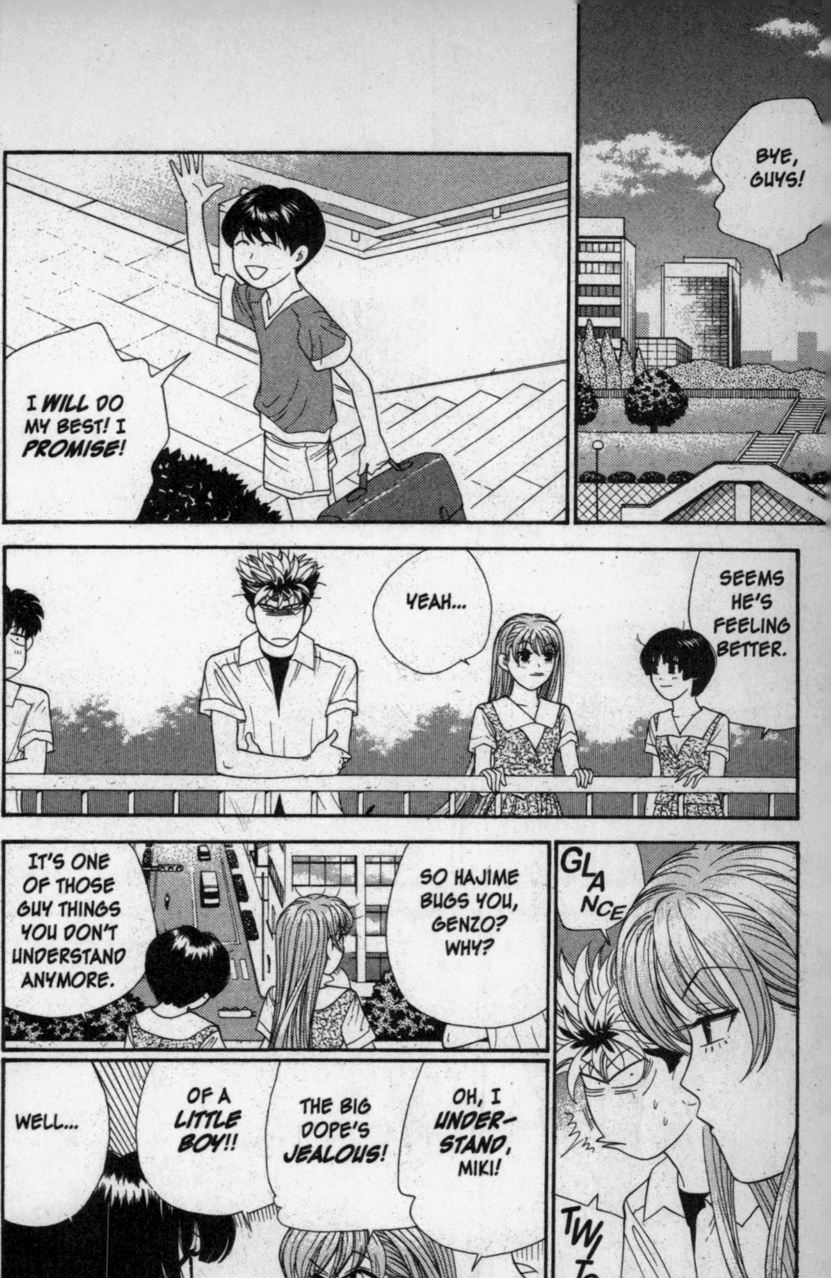
BYE, GUYS!
I WILL DO MY BEST! I PROMISE!
SEEMS HE'S FEELING BETTER.
YEAH...
GLANCE
TWITCH
SO HAJIME BUGS YOU, GENZO? WHY?
IT'S ONE OF THOSE GUY THINGS YOU DON'T UNDERSTAND ANYMORE.
OH, I UNDERSTAND, MIKI!
THE BIG DOPE'S JEALOUS!
OF A LITTLE BOY!!
WELL...

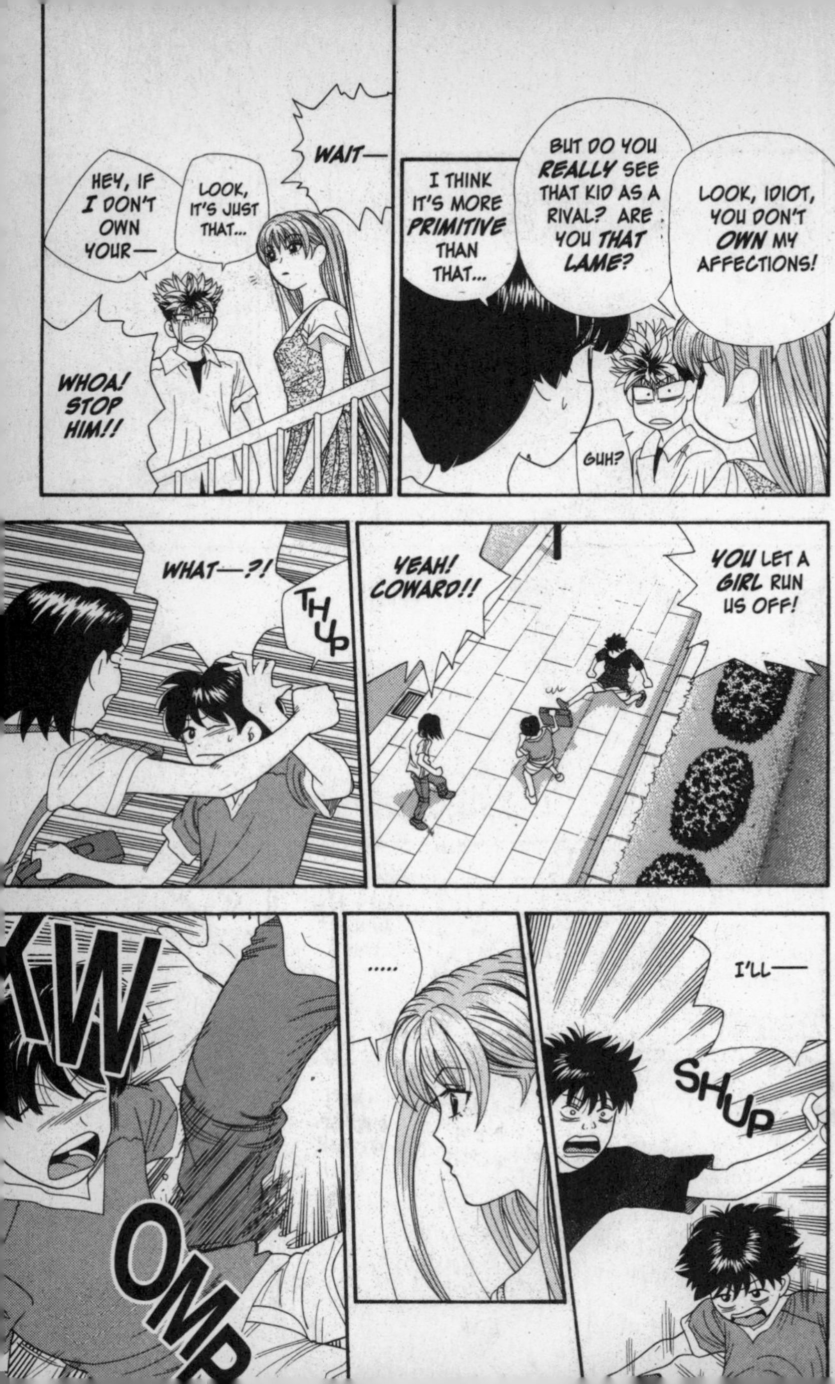
LOOK, IDIOT, YOU DON'T OWN MY AFFECTIONS!
BUT DO YOU REALLY SEE THAT KID AS A RIVAL? ARE YOU THAT LAME?
I THINK IT'S MORE PRIMITIVE THAN THAT...
GUH?
WAIT—
LOOK, IT'S JUST THAT...
HEY, IF I DON'T OWN YOUR—
WHOA! STOP HIM!!
YOU LET A GIRL RUN US OFF!
YEAH! COWARD!!
THUP
WHAT—?!
I'LL—
SHUP
.....
KW
OMP

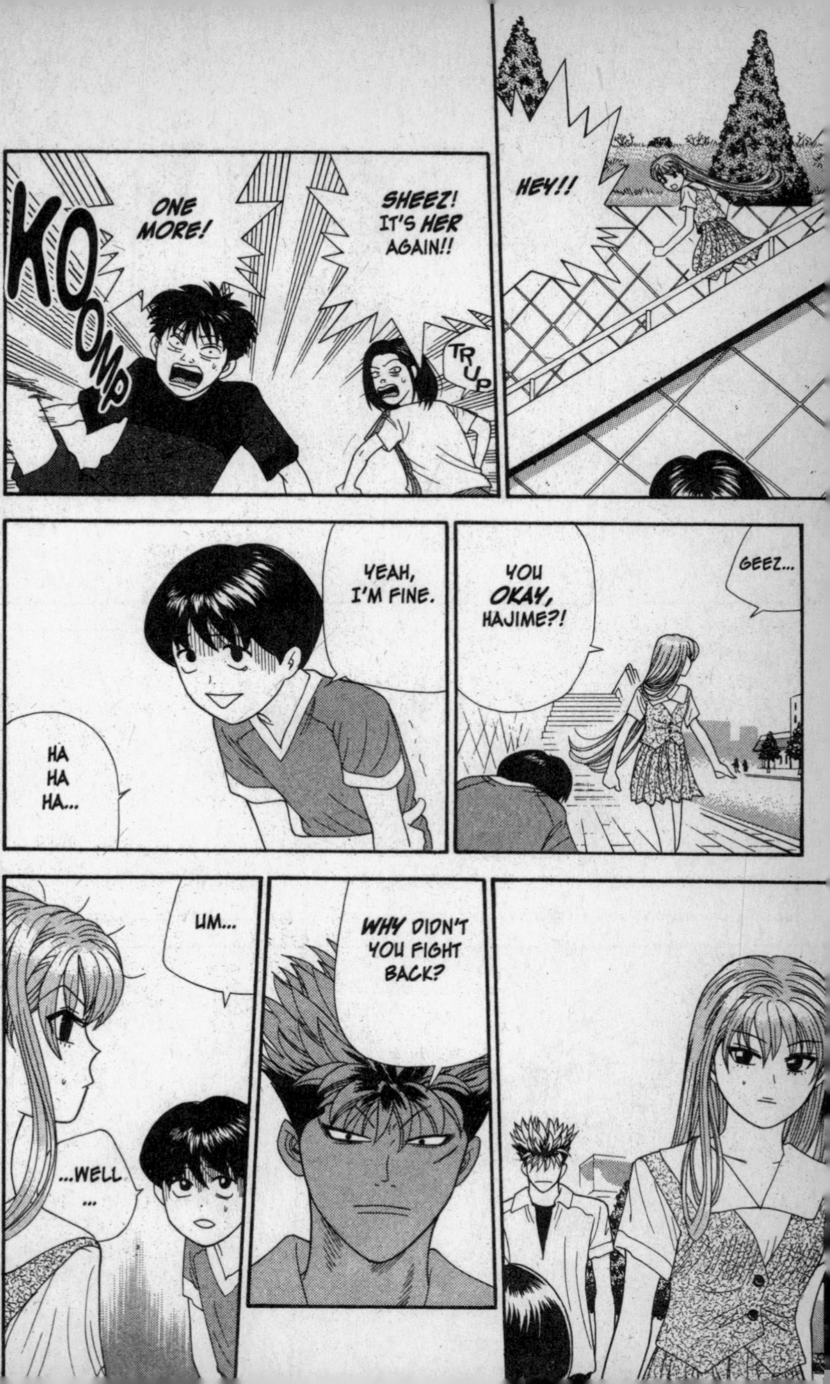
HEY!!
SHEEZ! IT'S HER AGAIN!!
TRUP
ONE MORE!
KOOOMP
GEEZ...
YOU OKAY, HAJIME?!
YEAH, I'M FINE.
HA HA HA...
WHY DIDN'T YOU FIGHT BACK?
UM...
...WELL ...

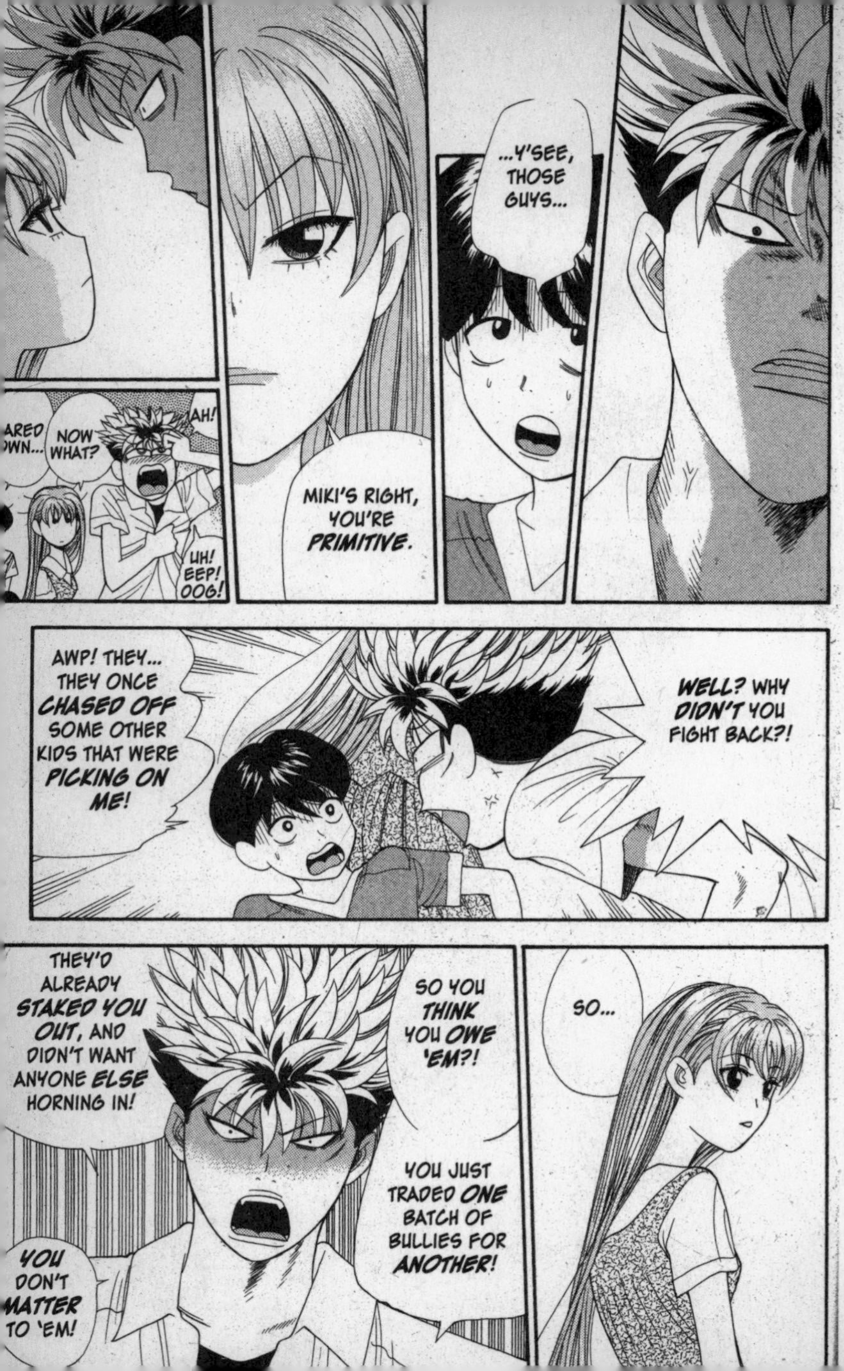
...Y'SEE, THOSE GUYS...
MIKI'S RIGHT, YOU'RE *PRIMITIVE*.
AH!
NOW WHAT?
ARED OWN...
UH! EEP! OOG!
WELL? WHY *DIDN'T* YOU FIGHT BACK?!
AWP! THEY... THEY ONCE *CHASED OFF* SOME OTHER KIDS THAT WERE *PICKING ON ME!*
SO...
SO YOU *THINK* YOU *OWE 'EM*?!
THEY'D ALREADY *STAKED YOU OUT*, AND DIDN'T WANT ANYONE *ELSE* HORNING IN!
YOU JUST TRADED *ONE* BATCH OF BULLIES FOR *ANOTHER*!
YOU DON'T *MATTER* TO 'EM!

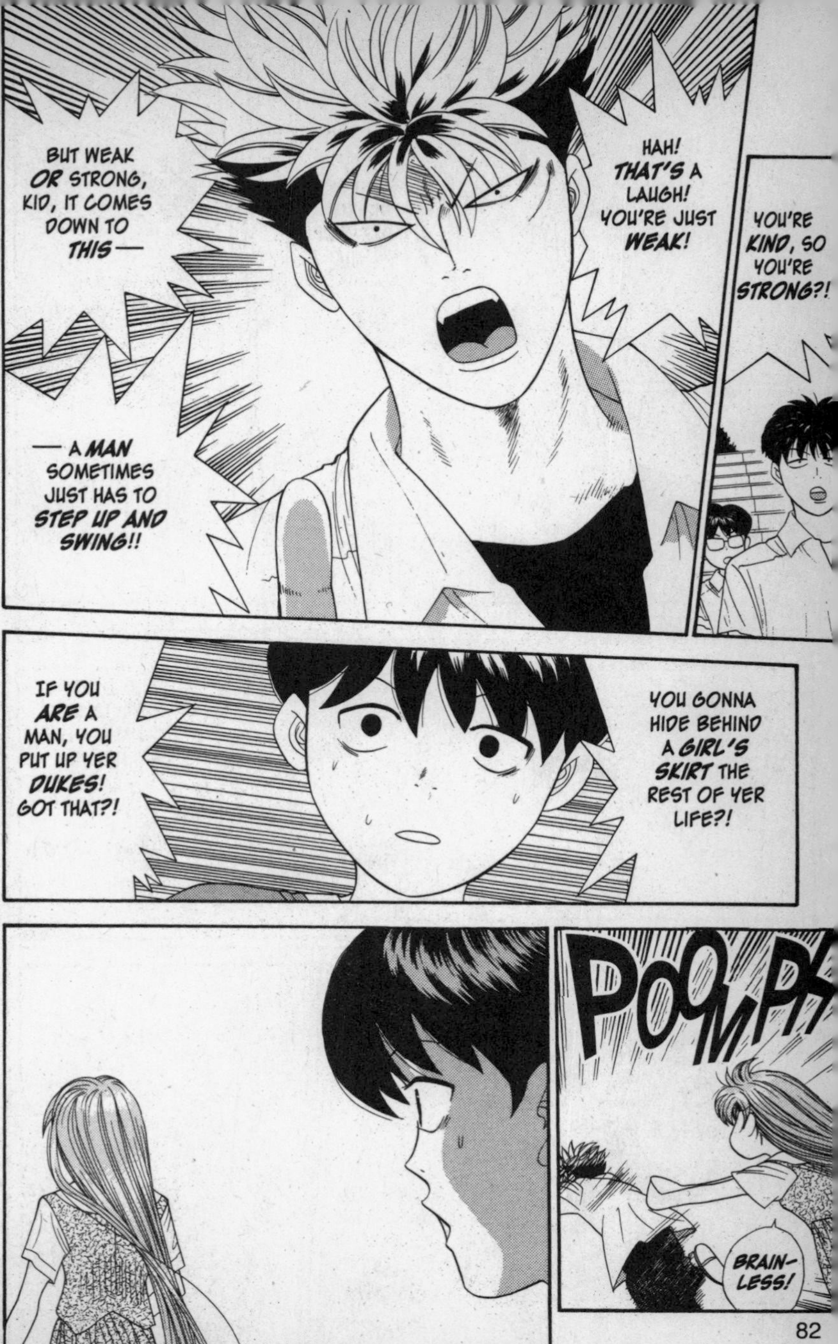
YOU'RE KIND, SO YOU'RE STRONG?!
HAH! THAT'S A LAUGH! YOU'RE JUST WEAK!
BUT WEAK OR STRONG, KID, IT COMES DOWN TO THIS—
—A MAN SOMETIMES JUST HAS TO STEP UP AND SWING!!
YOU GONNA HIDE BEHIND A GIRL'S SKIRT THE REST OF YER LIFE?!
IF YOU ARE A MAN, YOU PUT UP YER DUKES! GOT THAT?!
POOMPH
BRAIN-LESS!

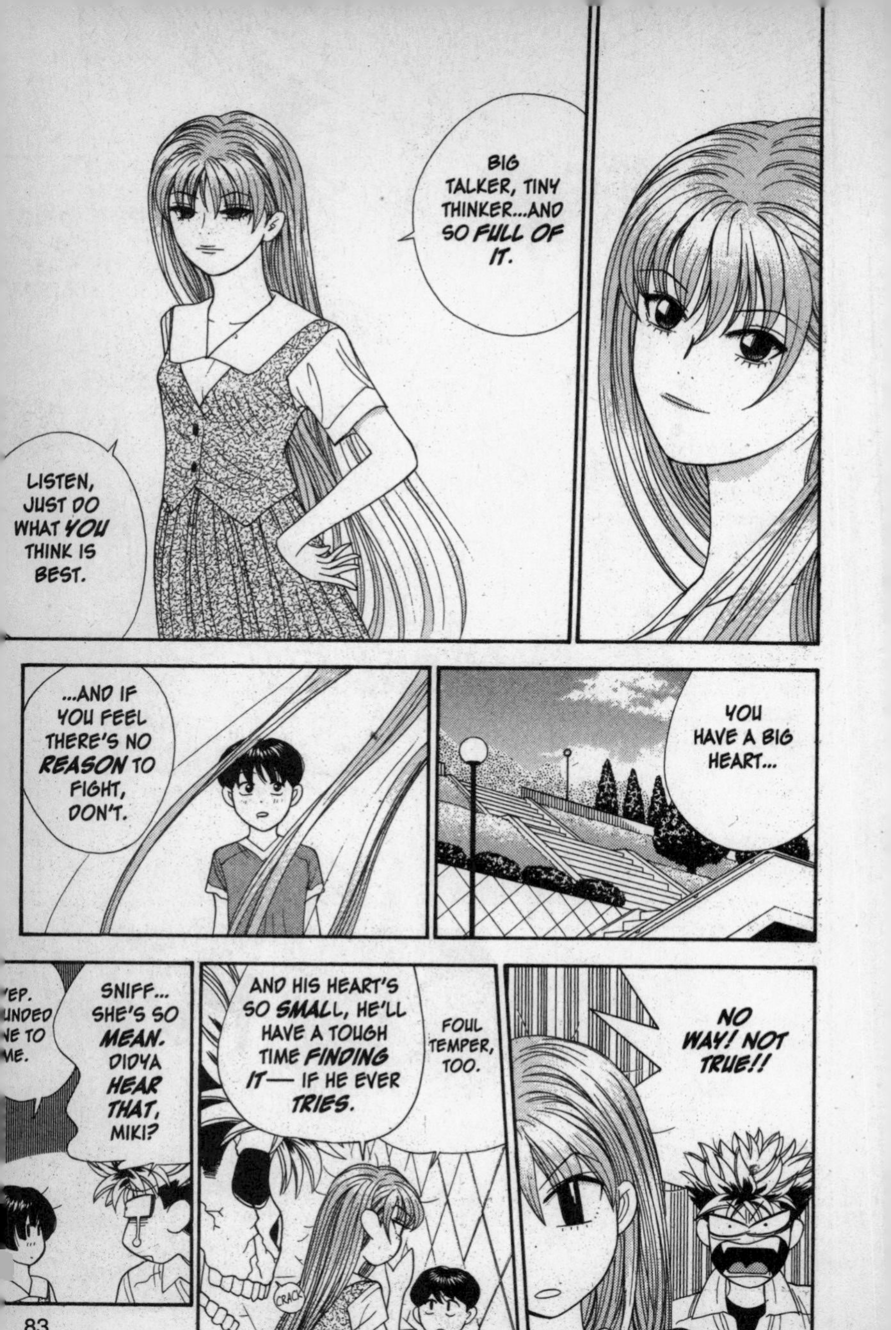
BIG TALKER, TINY THINKER...AND SO FULL OF IT.
LISTEN, JUST DO WHAT YOU THINK IS BEST.
YOU HAVE A BIG HEART...
...AND IF YOU FEEL THERE'S NO REASON TO FIGHT, DON'T.
NO WAY! NOT TRUE!!
FOUL TEMPER, TOO.
AND HIS HEART'S SO SMALL, HE'LL HAVE A TOUGH TIME FINDING IT— IF HE EVER TRIES.
CRACK
SNIFF... SHE'S SO MEAN. DIDYA HEAR THAT, MIKI?

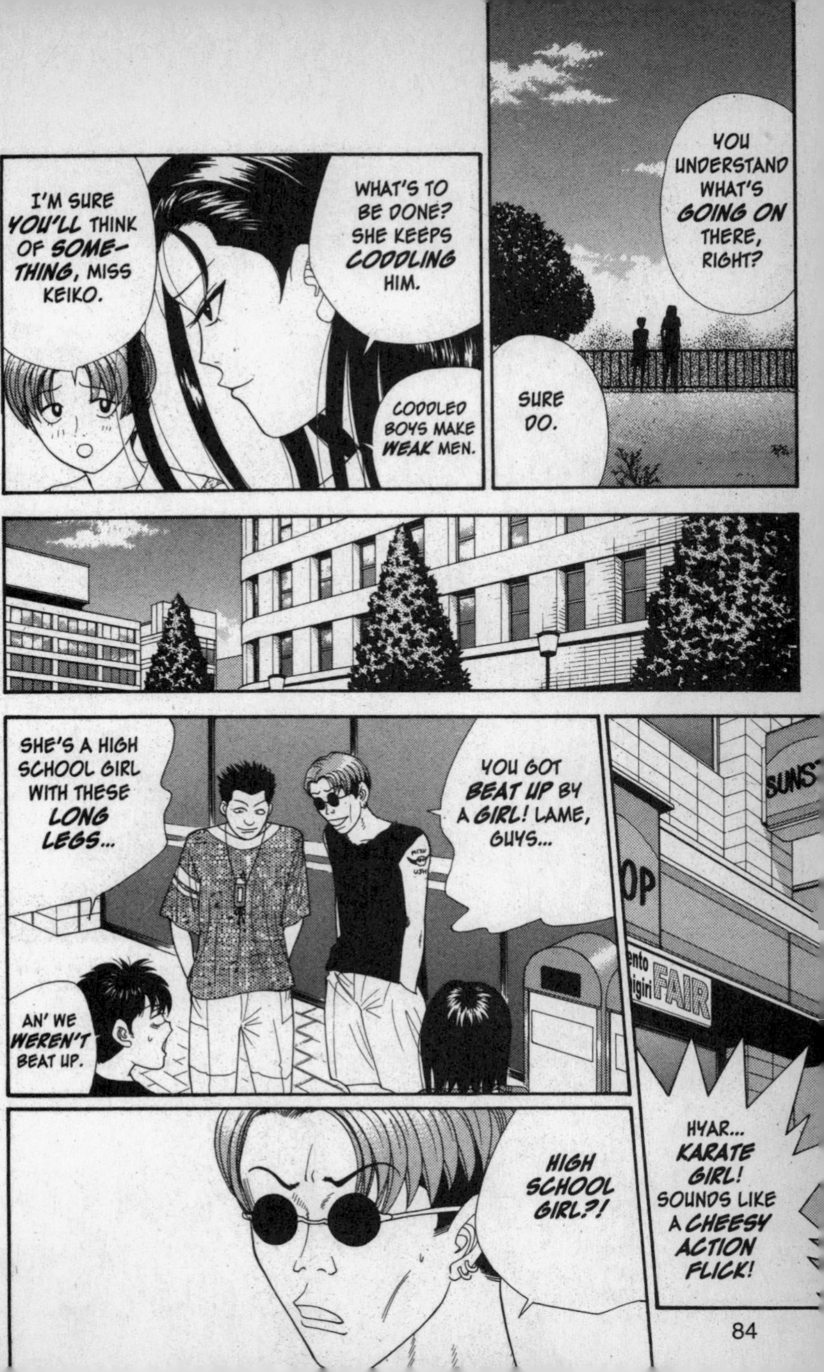
YOU UNDERSTAND WHAT'S *GOING ON* THERE, RIGHT?
SURE DO.
WHAT'S TO BE DONE? SHE KEEPS *CODDLING* HIM.
CODDLED BOYS MAKE *WEAK* MEN.
I'M SURE *YOU'LL* THINK OF *SOME-THING*, MISS KEIKO.
FAIR
HYAR... *KARATE GIRL!* SOUNDS LIKE A *CHEESY ACTION FLICK!*
YOU GOT *BEAT UP* BY A *GIRL!* LAME, GUYS...
SHE'S A HIGH SCHOOL GIRL WITH THESE *LONG LEGS*...
AN' WE *WEREN'T* BEAT UP.
HIGH SCHOOL GIRL?!

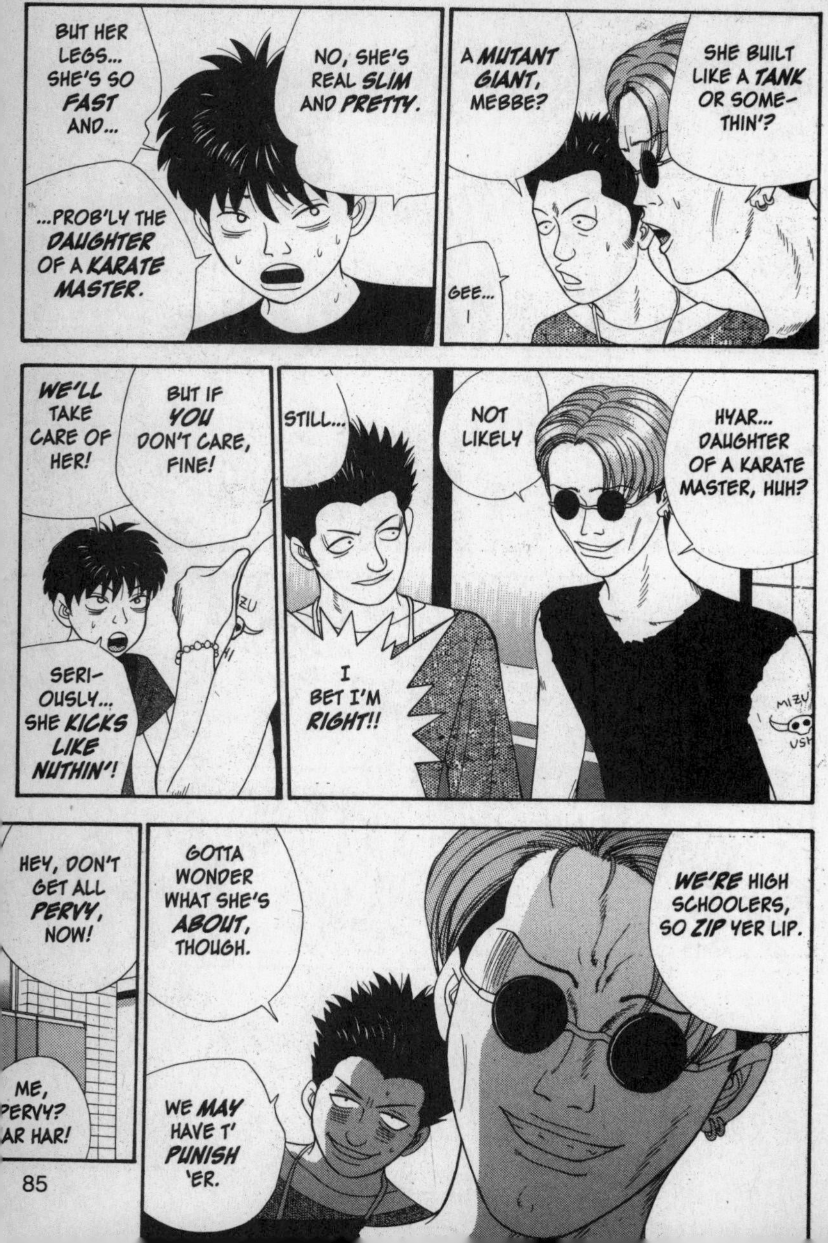

SHE BUILT LIKE A *TANK* OR SOME-THIN'?
A *MUTANT GIANT*, MEBBE?
GEE... I
NO, SHE'S REAL *SLIM* AND *PRETTY*.
BUT HER LEGS... SHE'S SO *FAST* AND...
...PROB'LY THE *DAUGHTER* OF A *KARATE MASTER*.
HYAR... DAUGHTER OF A KARATE MASTER, HUH?
NOT LIKELY
STILL...
I BET I'M *RIGHT*!!
BUT IF *YOU* DON'T CARE, FINE!
WE'LL TAKE CARE OF HER!
SERI-OUSLY... SHE *KICKS LIKE NUTHIN'*!
WE'RE HIGH SCHOOLERS, SO *ZIP* YER LIP.
GOTTA WONDER WHAT SHE'S *ABOUT*, THOUGH.
WE *MAY* HAVE T' *PUNISH* 'ER.
HEY, DON'T GET ALL *PERVY*, NOW!
ME, PERVY? AR HAR!

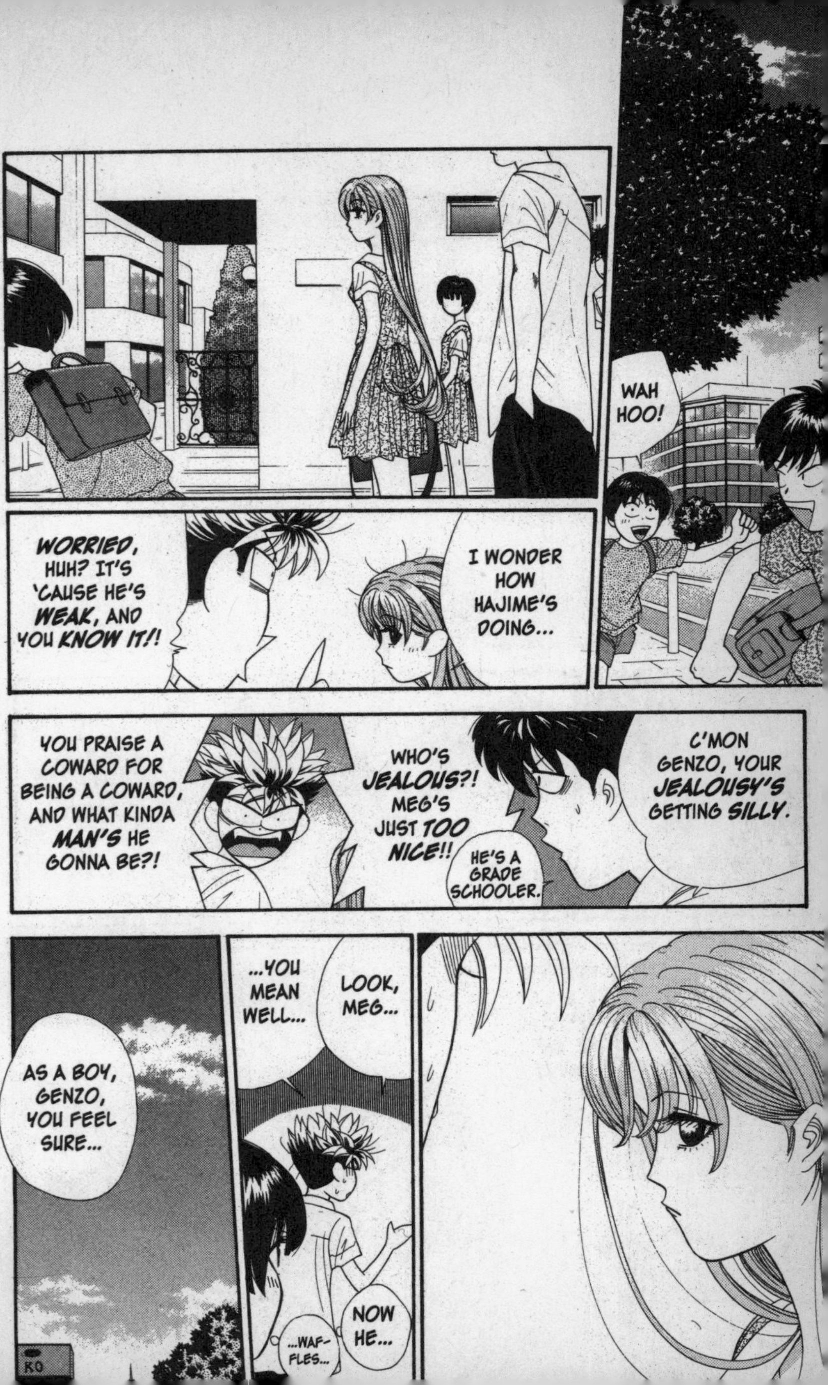
WAH HOO!
I WONDER HOW HAJIME'S DOING...
WORRIED, HUH? IT'S 'CAUSE HE'S WEAK, AND YOU KNOW IT!!
C'MON GENZO, YOUR JEALOUSY'S GETTING SILLY.
WHO'S JEALOUS?! MEG'S JUST TOO NICE!!
HE'S A GRADE SCHOOLER.
YOU PRAISE A COWARD FOR BEING A COWARD, AND WHAT KINDA MAN'S HE GONNA BE?!
LOOK, MEG...
...YOU MEAN WELL...
NOW HE...
...WAF-FLES...
AS A BOY, GENZO, YOU FEEL SURE...

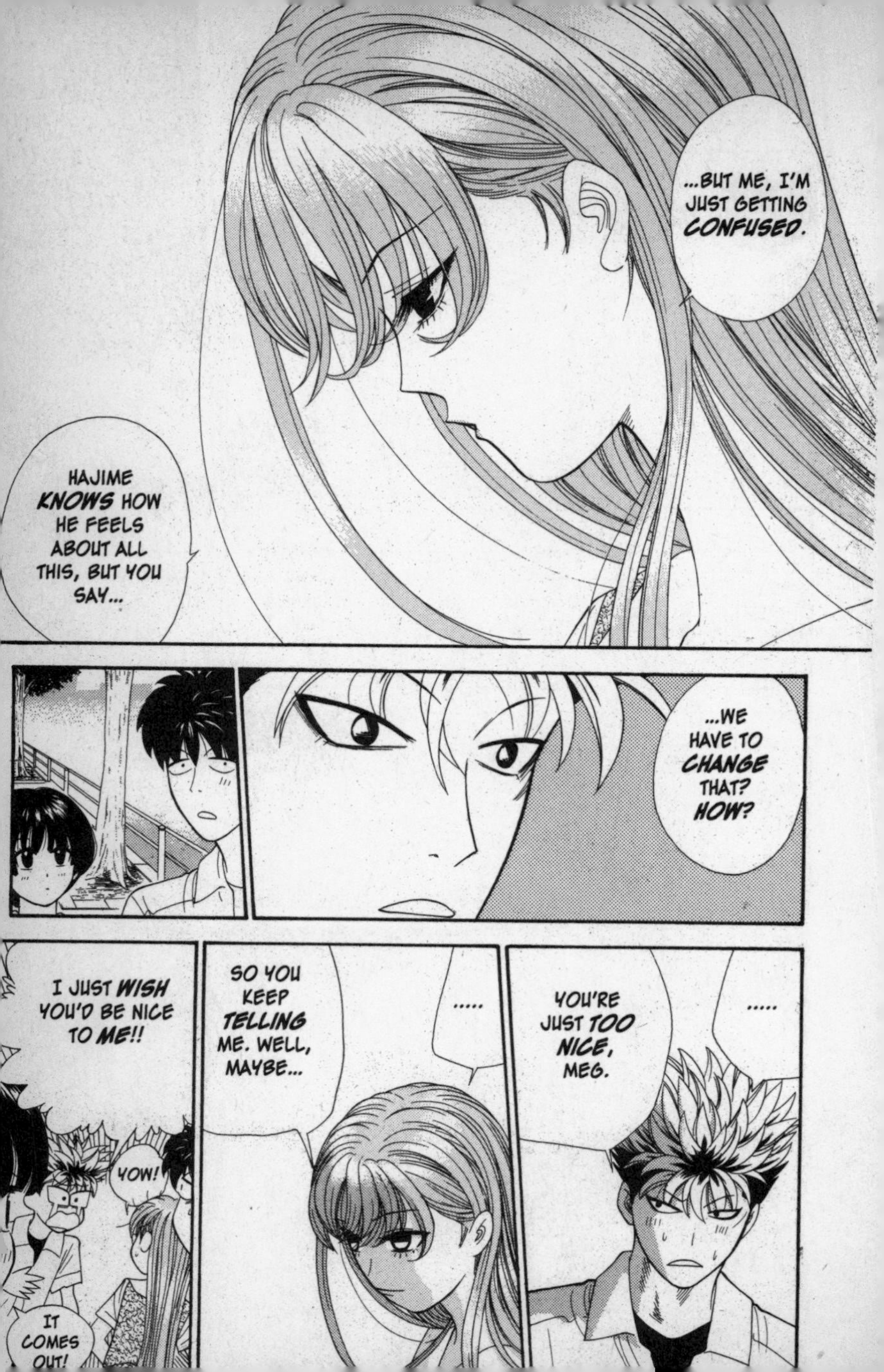
...BUT ME, I'M JUST GETTING CONFUSED.
HAJIME KNOWS HOW HE FEELS ABOUT ALL THIS, BUT YOU SAY...
...WE HAVE TO CHANGE THAT? HOW?
.....
YOU'RE JUST TOO NICE, MEG.
.....
SO YOU KEEP TELLING ME. WELL, MAYBE...
I JUST WISH YOU'D BE NICE TO ME!!
YOW!
IT COMES OUT!

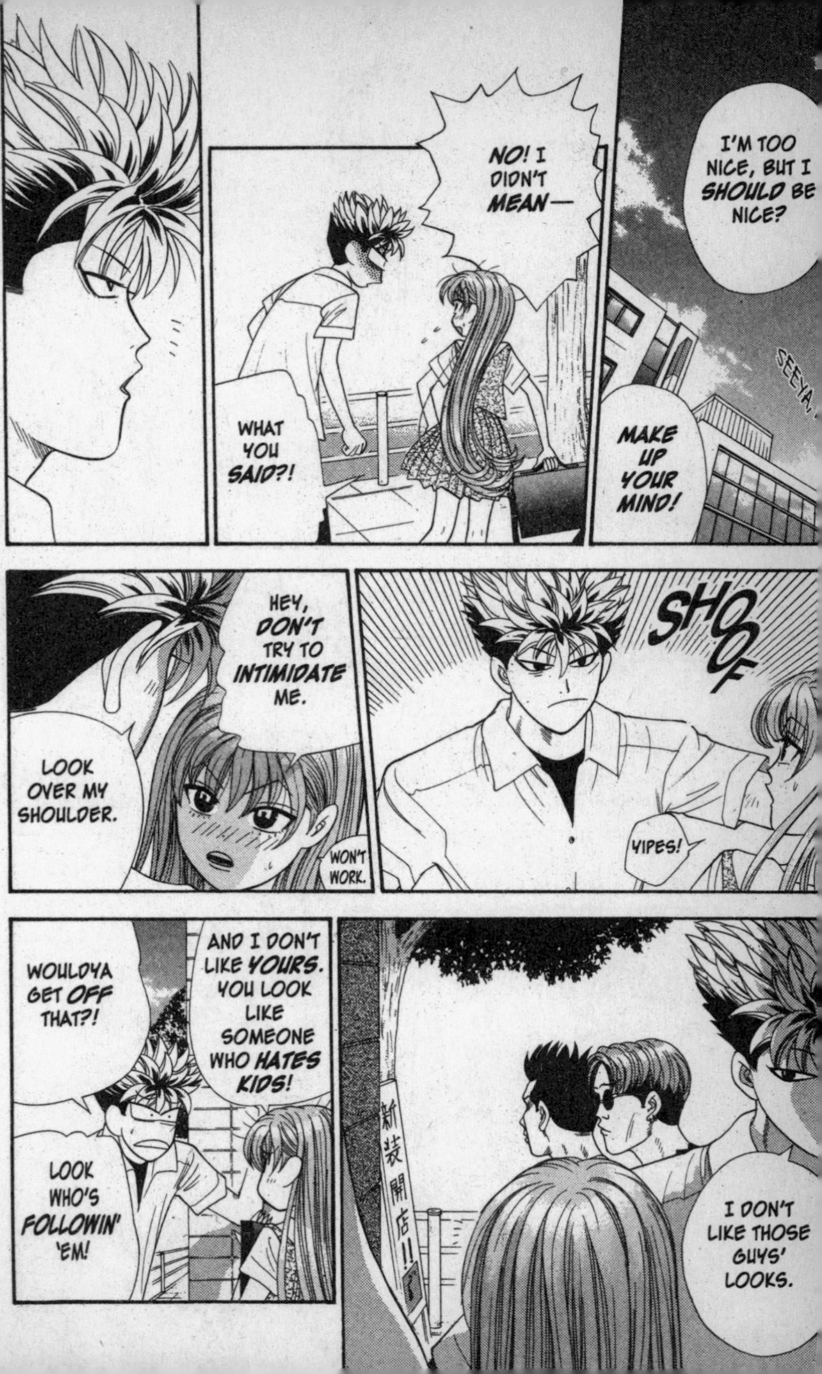
I'M TOO NICE, BUT I SHOULD BE NICE?
SEEYA.
MAKE UP YOUR MIND!
NO! I DIDN'T MEAN—
WHAT YOU SAID?!
SHOOF
YIPES!
HEY, DON'T TRY TO INTIMIDATE ME.
LOOK OVER MY SHOULDER.
WON'T WORK.
新装開店!!
I DON'T LIKE THOSE GUYS' LOOKS.
AND I DON'T LIKE YOURS. YOU LOOK LIKE SOMEONE WHO HATES KIDS!
WOULDYA GET OFF THAT?!
LOOK WHO'S FOLLOWIN' 'EM!

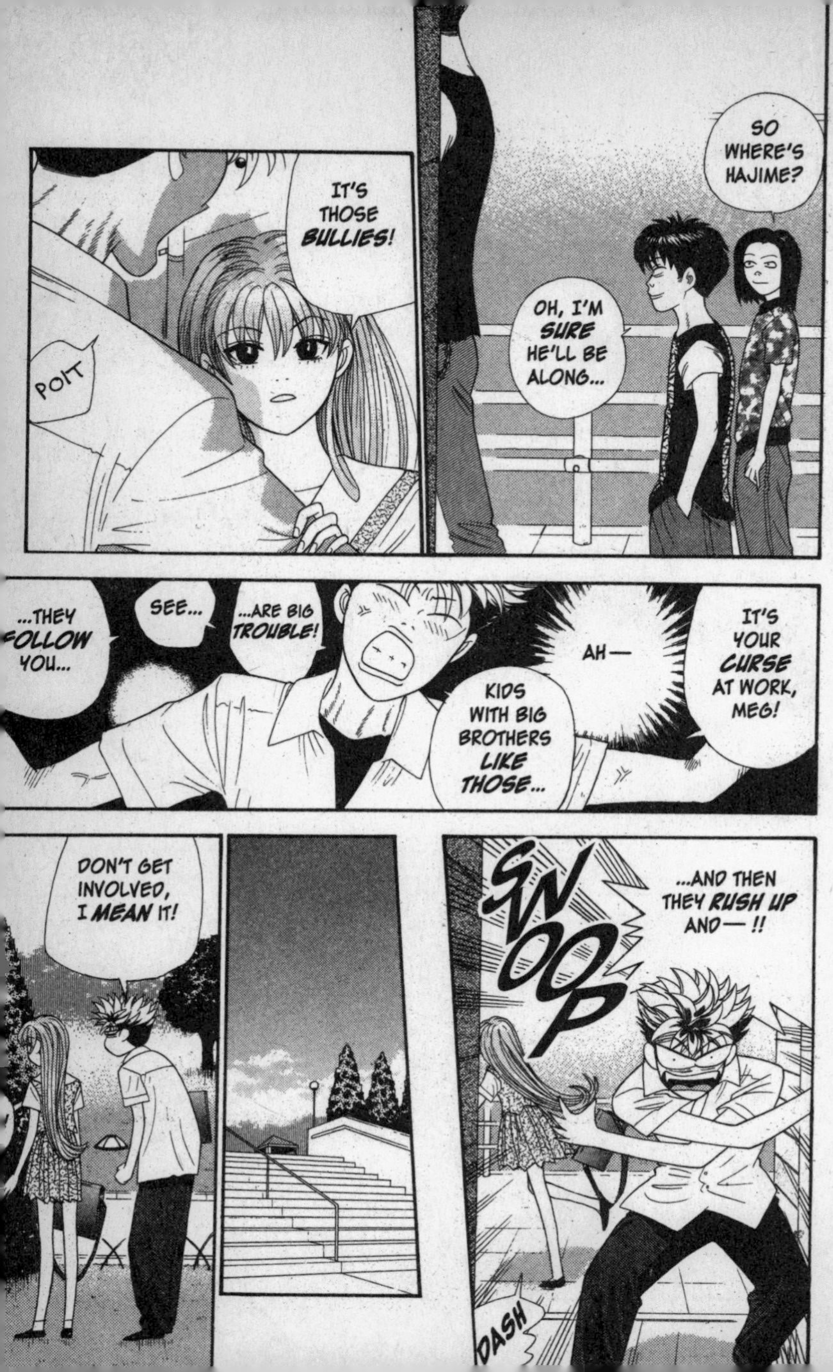
SO WHERE'S HAJIME?
OH, I'M SURE HE'LL BE ALONG...
IT'S THOSE BULLIES!
POIT
IT'S YOUR CURSE AT WORK, MEG!
AH—
KIDS WITH BIG BROTHERS LIKE THOSE...
...ARE BIG TROUBLE!
SEE...
...THEY FOLLOW YOU...
SWOOP
...AND THEN THEY RUSH UP AND— !!
DASH
DON'T GET INVOLVED, I MEAN IT!

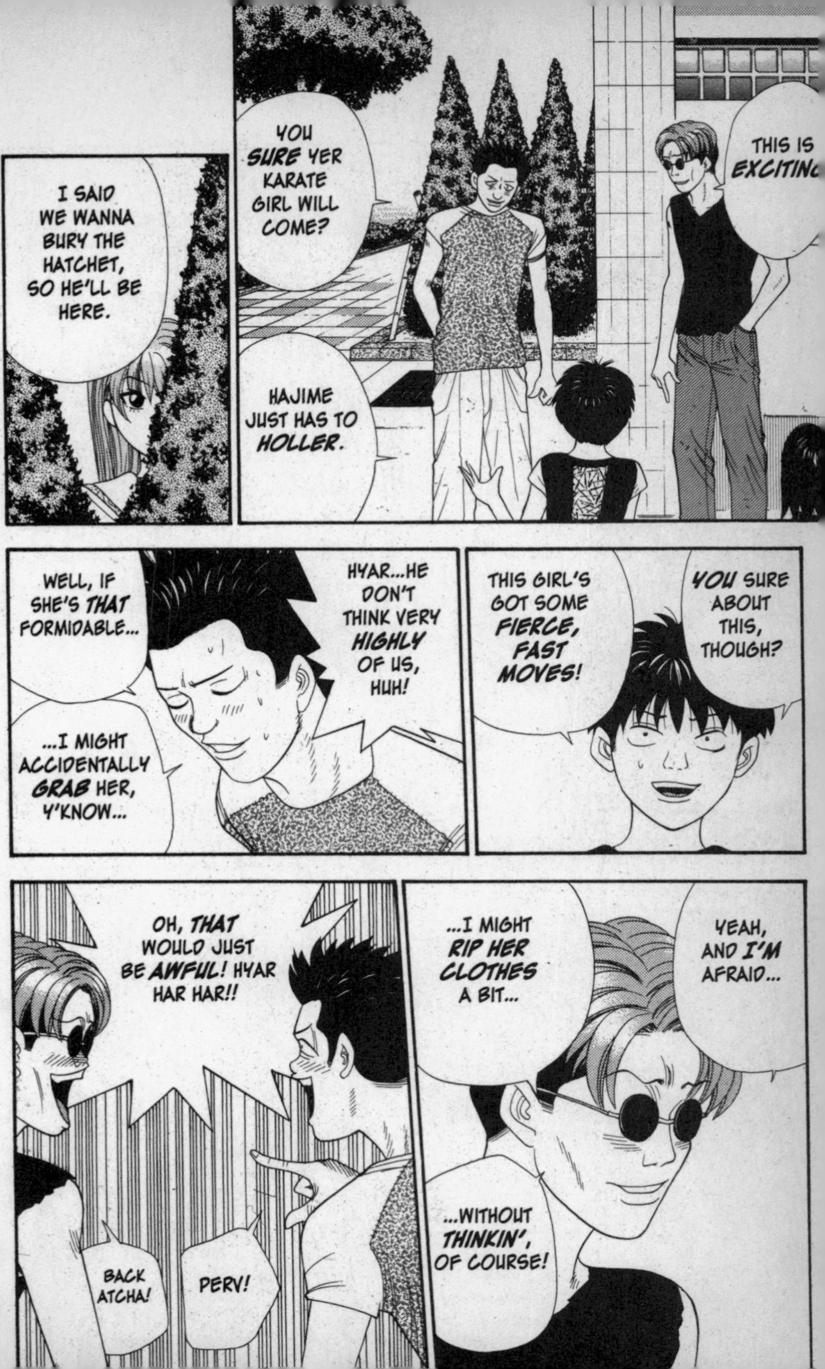
THIS IS EXCITIN
YOU SURE YER KARATE GIRL WILL COME?
HAJIME JUST HAS TO HOLLER.
I SAID WE WANNA BURY THE HATCHET, SO HE'LL BE HERE.
YOU SURE ABOUT THIS, THOUGH?
THIS GIRL'S GOT SOME FIERCE, FAST MOVES!
HYAR...HE DON'T THINK VERY HIGHLY OF US, HUH!
WELL, IF SHE'S THAT FORMIDABLE...
...I MIGHT ACCIDENTALLY GRAB HER, Y'KNOW...
YEAH, AND I'M AFRAID...
...I MIGHT RIP HER CLOTHES A BIT...
...WITHOUT THINKIN', OF COURSE!
OH, THAT WOULD JUST BE AWFUL! HYAR HAR HAR!!
PERV!
BACK ATCHA!

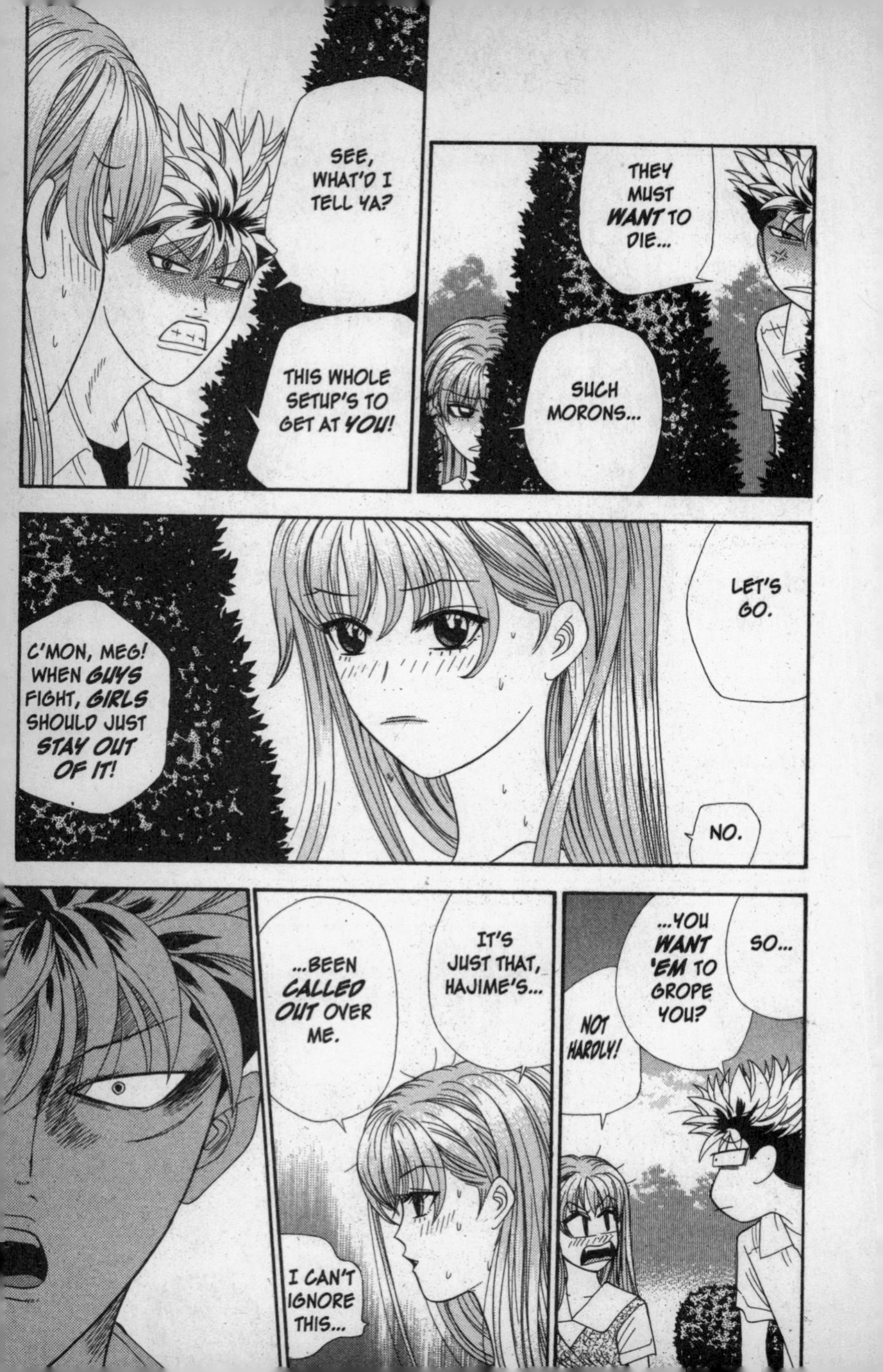
THEY MUST *WANT* TO DIE...
SUCH MORONS...
SEE, WHAT'D I TELL YA?
THIS WHOLE SETUP'S TO GET AT *YOU*!
LET'S GO.
C'MON, MEG! WHEN *GUYS* FIGHT, *GIRLS* SHOULD JUST *STAY OUT OF IT*!
NO.
SO...
...YOU *WANT 'EM* TO GROPE YOU?
NOT HARDLY!
IT'S JUST THAT, HAJIME'S...
...BEEN *CALLED OUT* OVER ME.
I CAN'T IGNORE THIS...

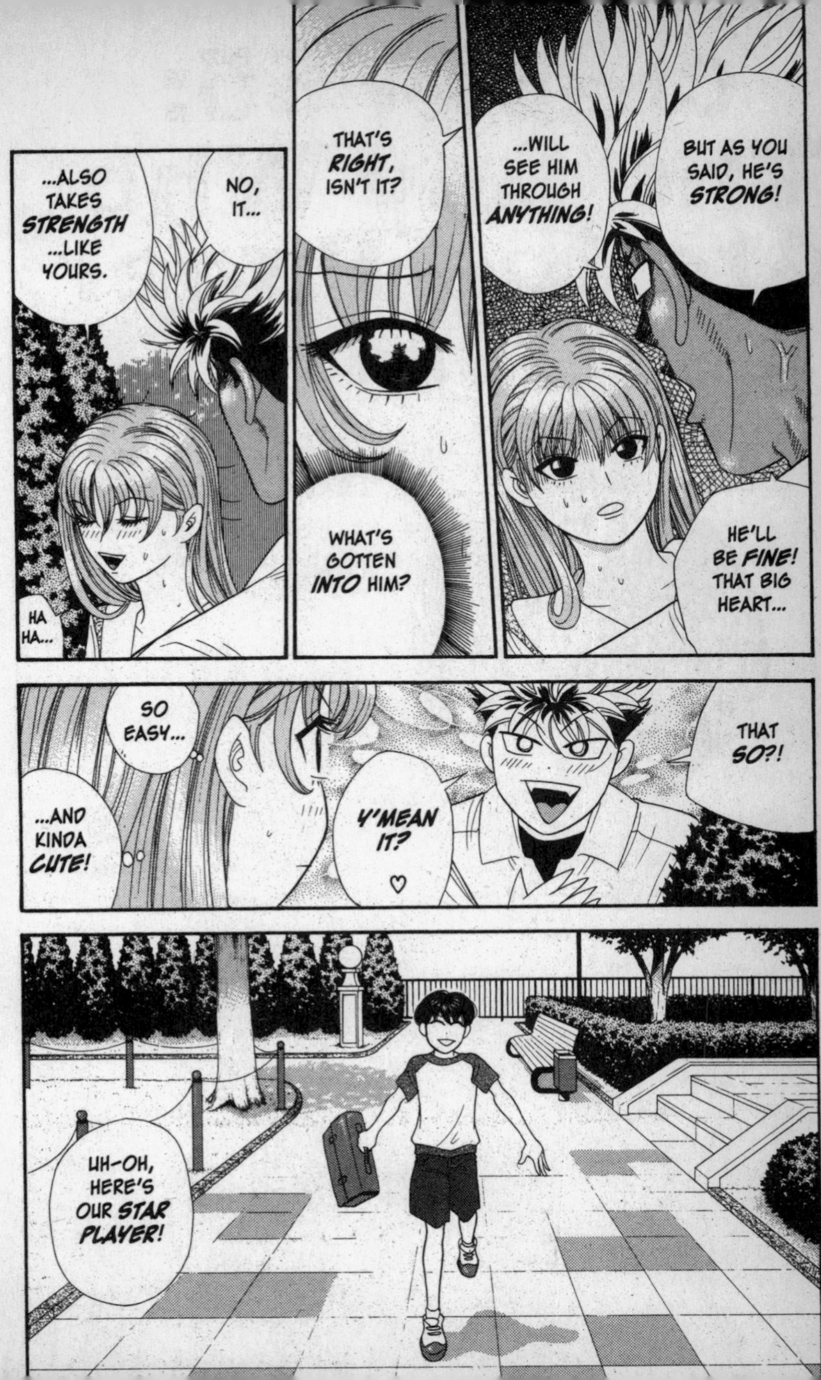
BUT AS YOU SAID, HE'S STRONG!
HE'LL BE FINE! THAT BIG HEART...
...WILL SEE HIM THROUGH ANYTHING!
THAT'S RIGHT, ISN'T IT?
WHAT'S GOTTEN INTO HIM?
NO, IT...
...ALSO TAKES STRENGTH ...LIKE YOURS.
HA HA...
THAT SO?!
Y'MEAN IT? ♡
SO EASY...
...AND KINDA CUTE!
UH-OH, HERE'S OUR STAR PLAYER!

Chapter 65: The Boy Who Ate the Paper Is...

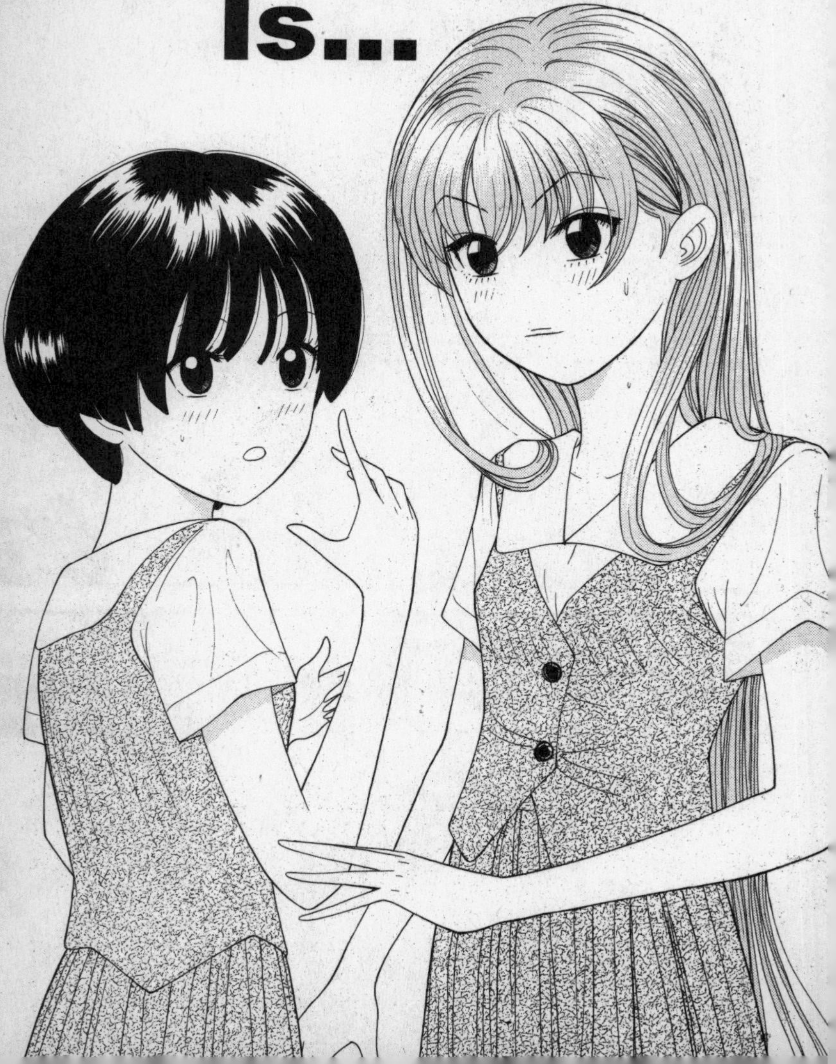

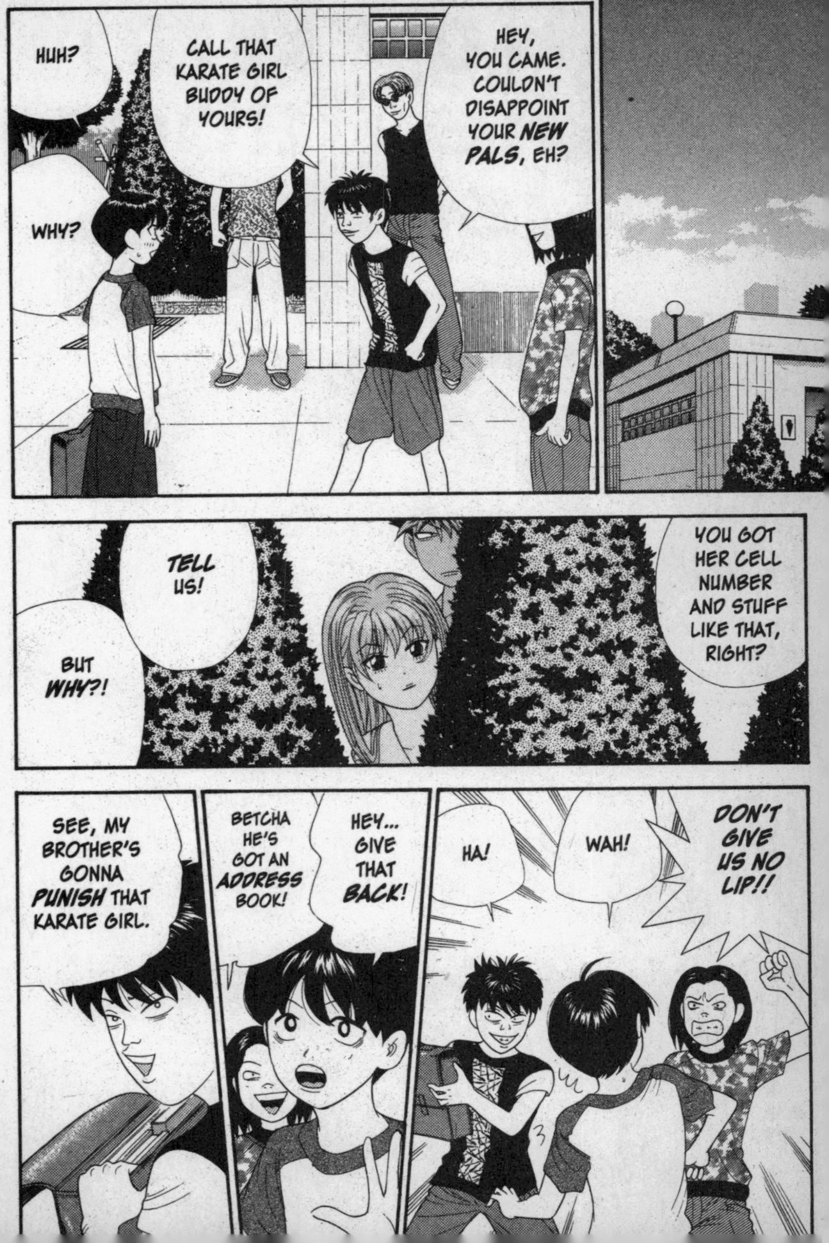
HEY, YOU CAME. COULDN'T DISAPPOINT YOUR *NEW PALS*, EH?
CALL THAT KARATE GIRL BUDDY OF YOURS!
HUH?
WHY?
YOU GOT HER CELL NUMBER AND STUFF LIKE THAT, RIGHT?
TELL US!
BUT *WHY?!*
DON'T GIVE US NO LIP!!
WAH!
HA!
HEY... GIVE THAT *BACK!*
BETCHA HE'S GOT AN *ADDRESS* BOOK!
SEE, MY BROTHER'S GONNA *PUNISH* THAT KARATE GIRL.

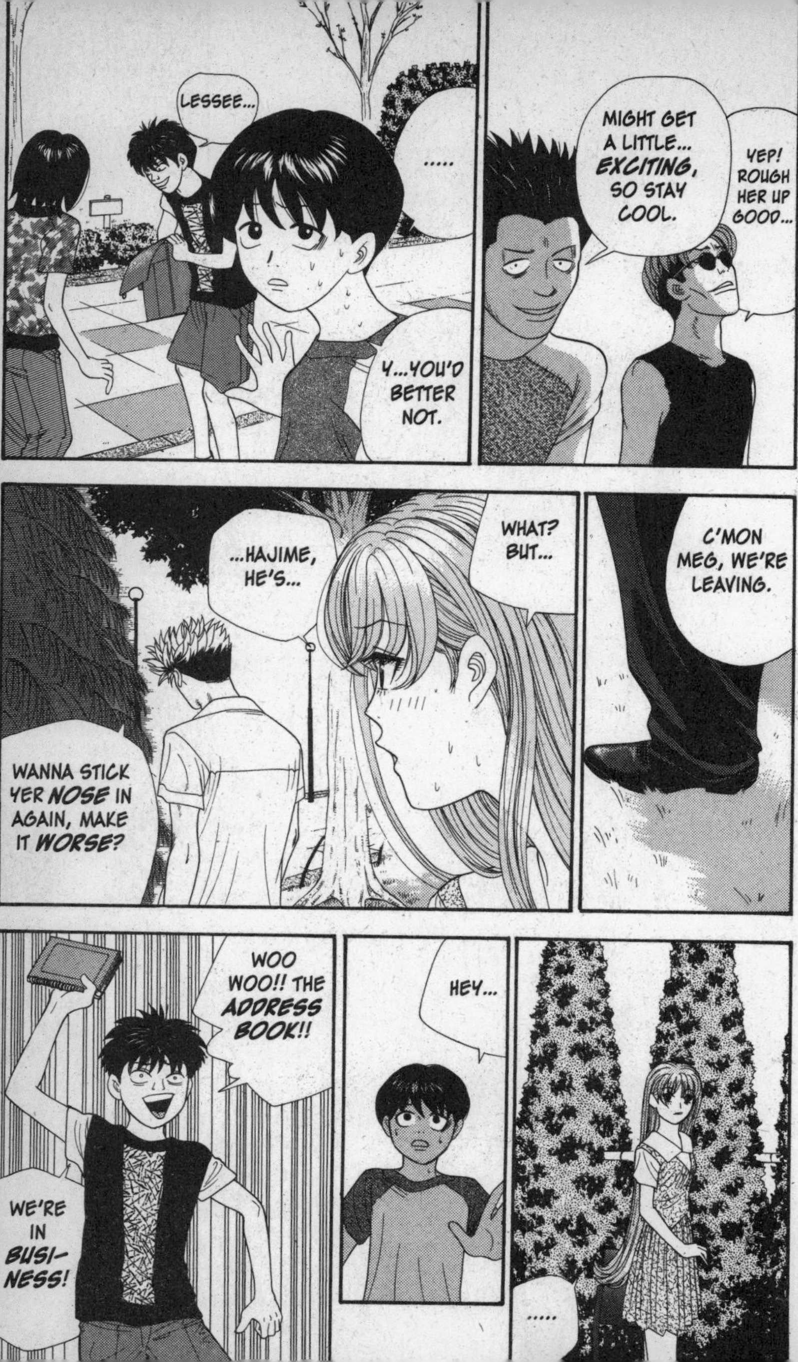
LESSEE...
.....
Y...YOU'D BETTER NOT.
MIGHT GET A LITTLE... EXCITING, SO STAY COOL.
YEP! ROUGH HER UP GOOD...
...HAJIME, HE'S...
WHAT? BUT...
WANNA STICK YER NOSE IN AGAIN, MAKE IT WORSE?
C'MON MEG, WE'RE LEAVING.
WOO WOO!! THE ADDRESS BOOK!!
WE'RE IN BUSINESS!
HEY...
.....

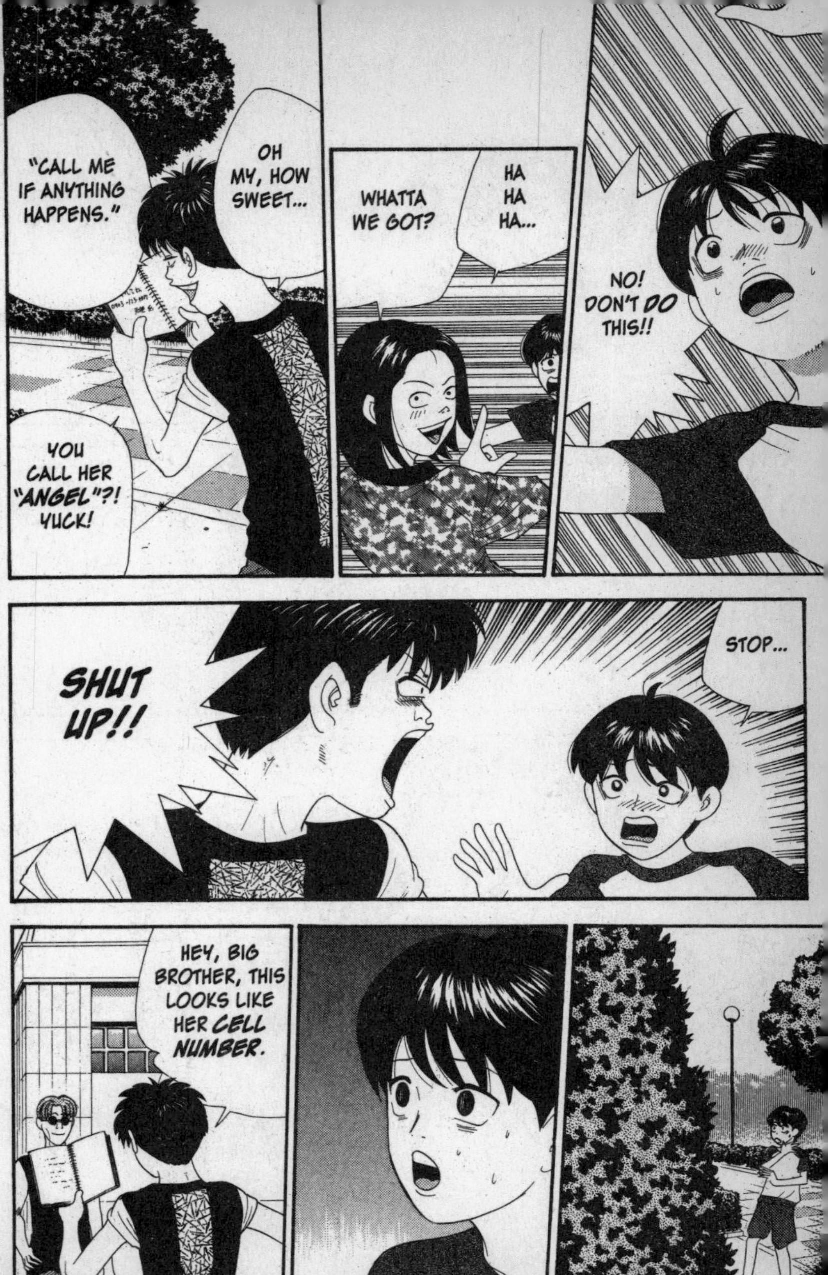
NO! DON'T DO THIS!!
HA HA HA...
WHATTA WE GOT?
OH MY, HOW SWEET...
"CALL ME IF ANYTHING HAPPENS."
YOU CALL HER "ANGEL"?! YUCK!
STOP...
SHUT UP!!
HEY, BIG BROTHER, THIS LOOKS LIKE HER CELL NUMBER.

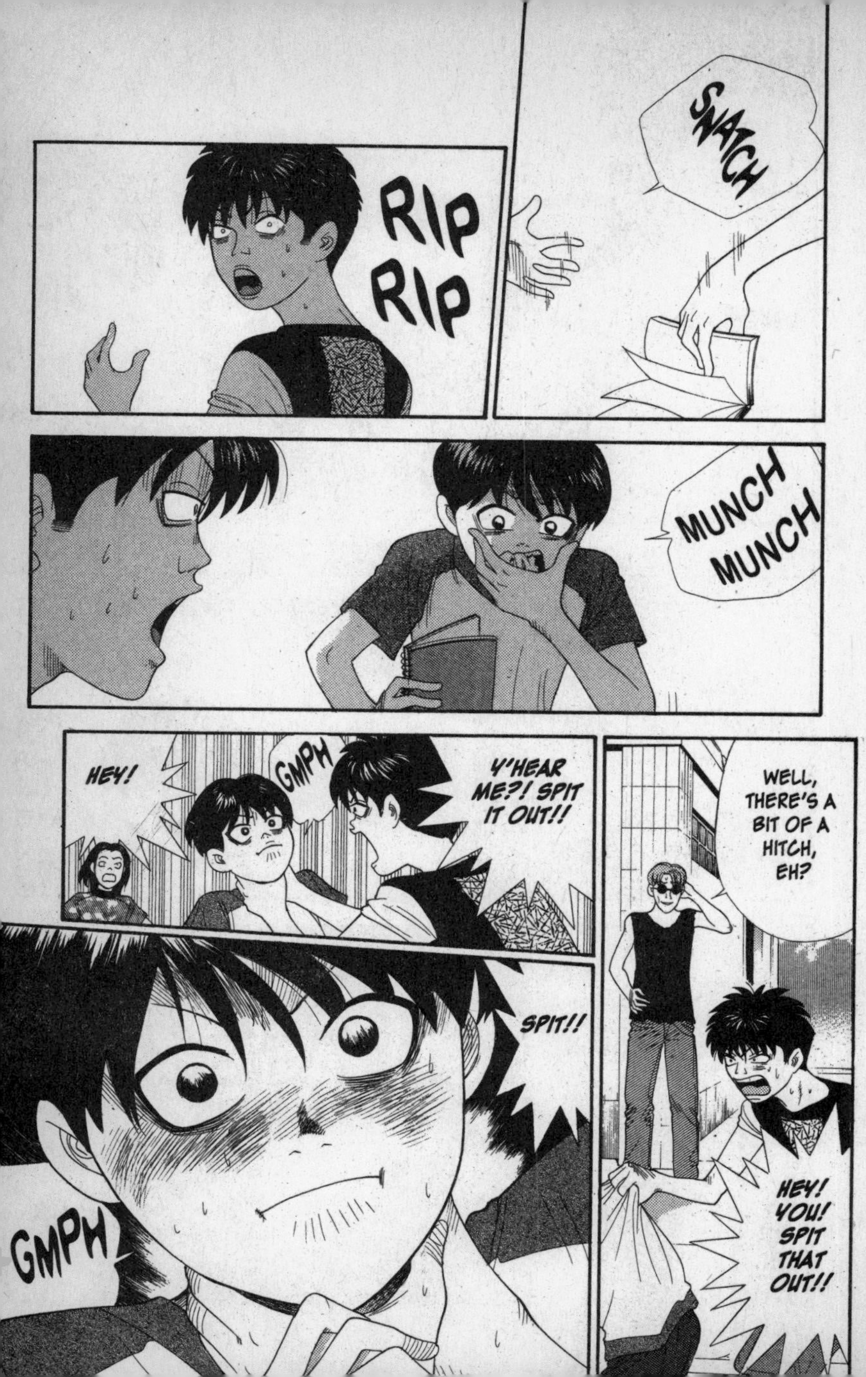
SNATCH
RIP RIP
MUNCH MUNCH
WELL, THERE'S A BIT OF A HITCH, EH?
HEY! YOU! SPIT THAT OUT!!
Y'HEAR ME?! SPIT IT OUT!!
GMPH
HEY!
SPIT!!
GMPH

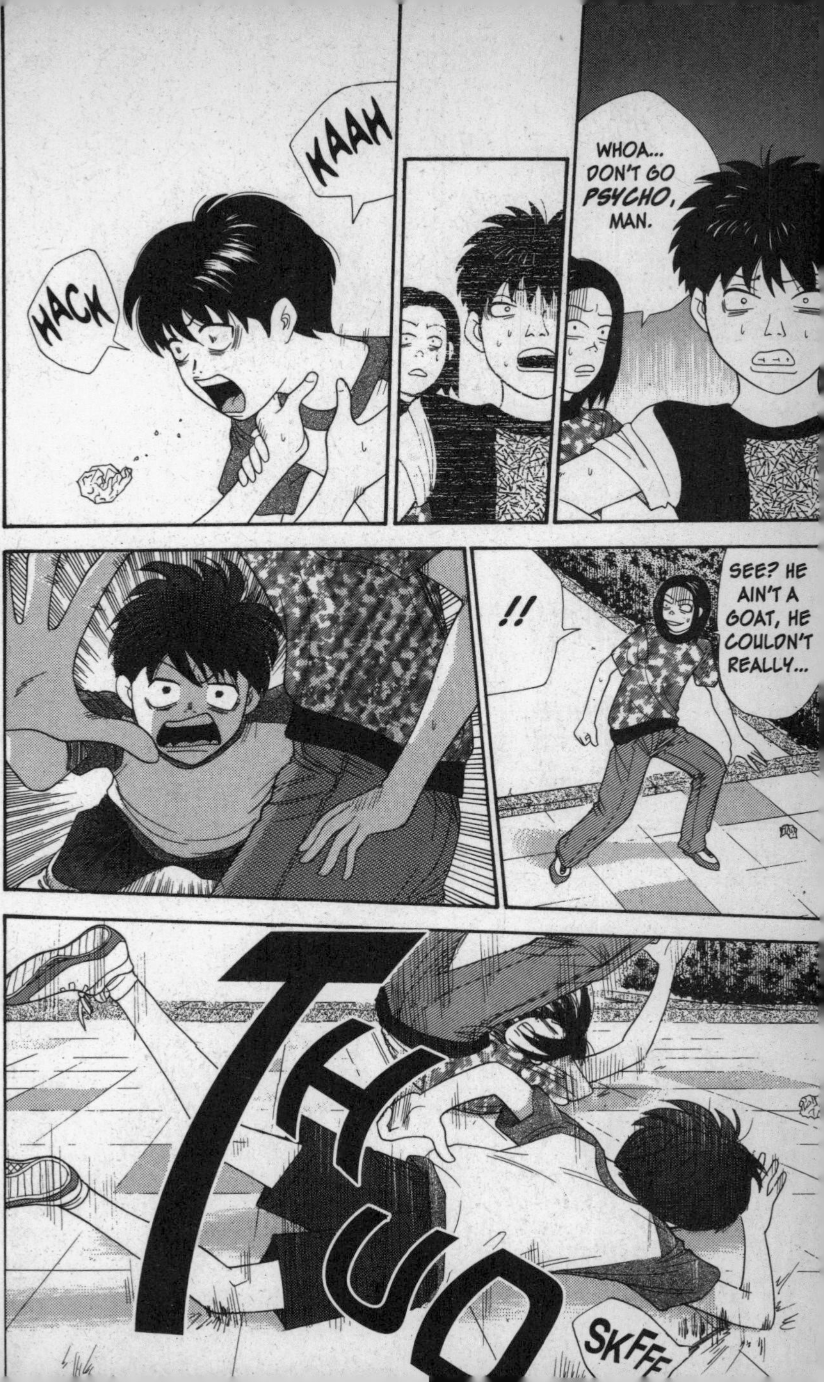
WHOA... DON'T GO PSYCHO, MAN.
KAAH
HACK
SEE? HE AIN'T A GOAT, HE COULDN'T REALLY...
!!
THUD
SKFFF

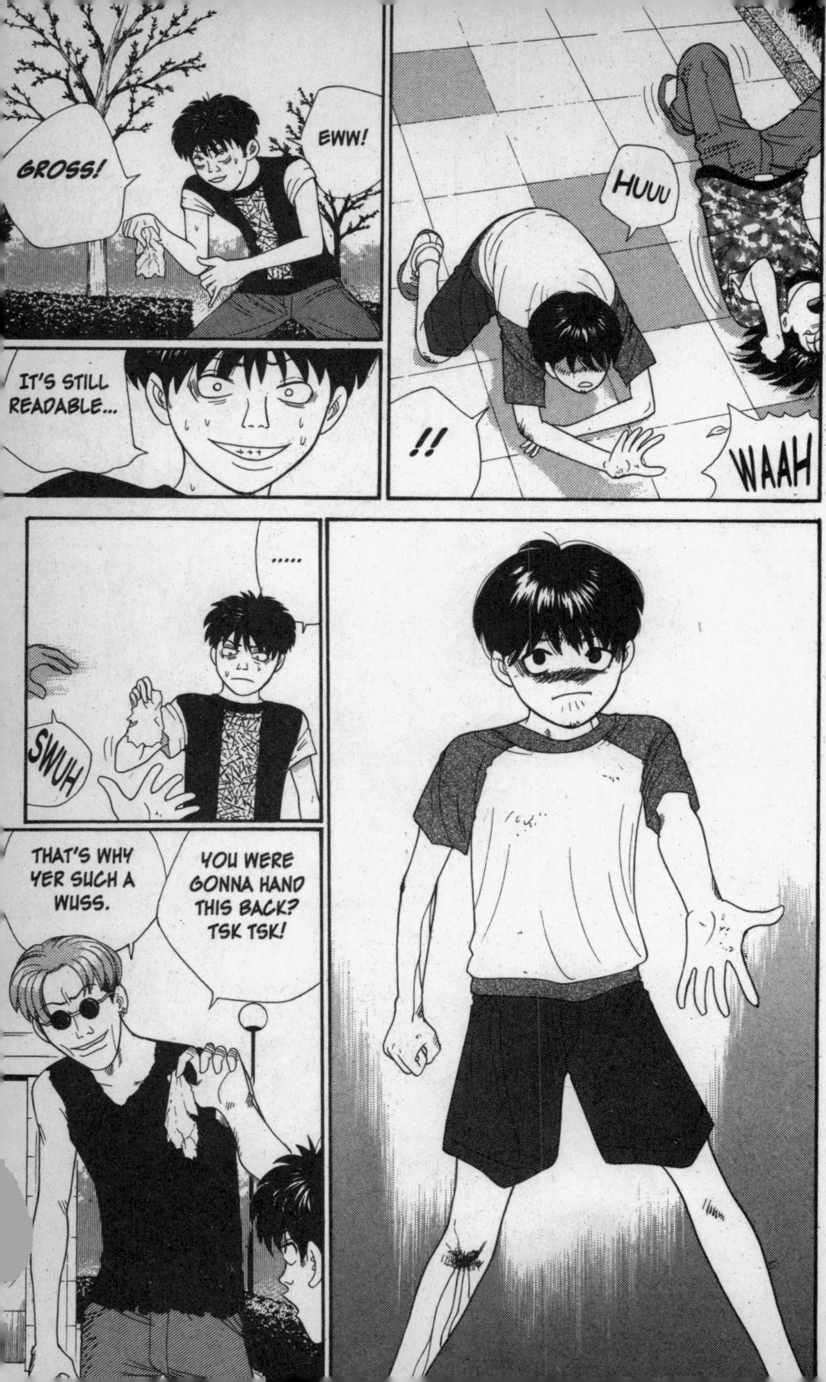
HUUU
WAAH
!!
EWW!
GROSS!
IT'S STILL READABLE...
.....
SWUH
YOU WERE GONNA HAND THIS BACK? TSK TSK!
THAT'S WHY YER SUCH A WUSS.

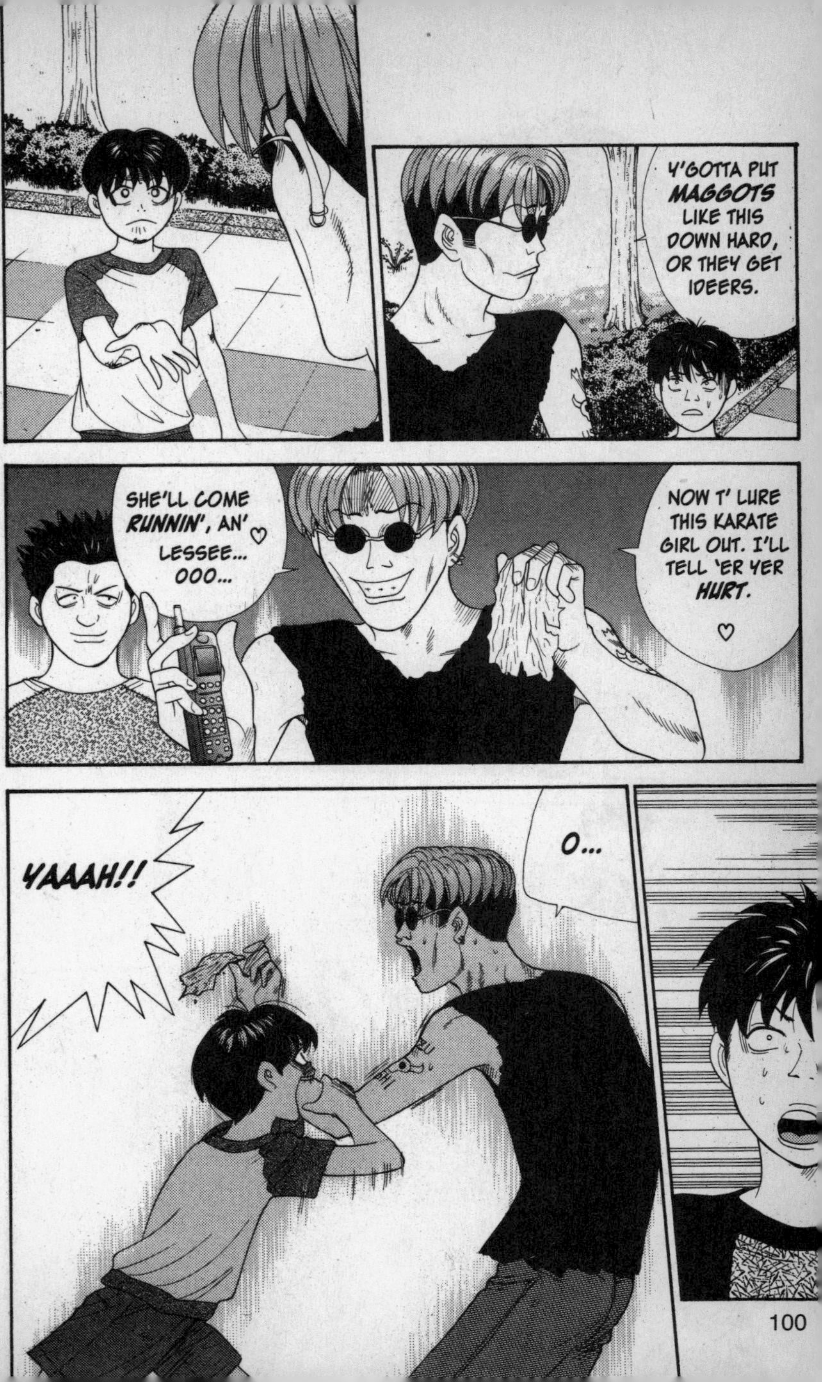
Y'GOTTA PUT MAGGOTS LIKE THIS DOWN HARD, OR THEY GET IDEERS.
NOW T' LURE THIS KARATE GIRL OUT. I'LL TELL 'ER YER HURT. ♡
SHE'LL COME RUNNIN', AN' LESSEE... OOO... ♡
O...
YAAAH!!

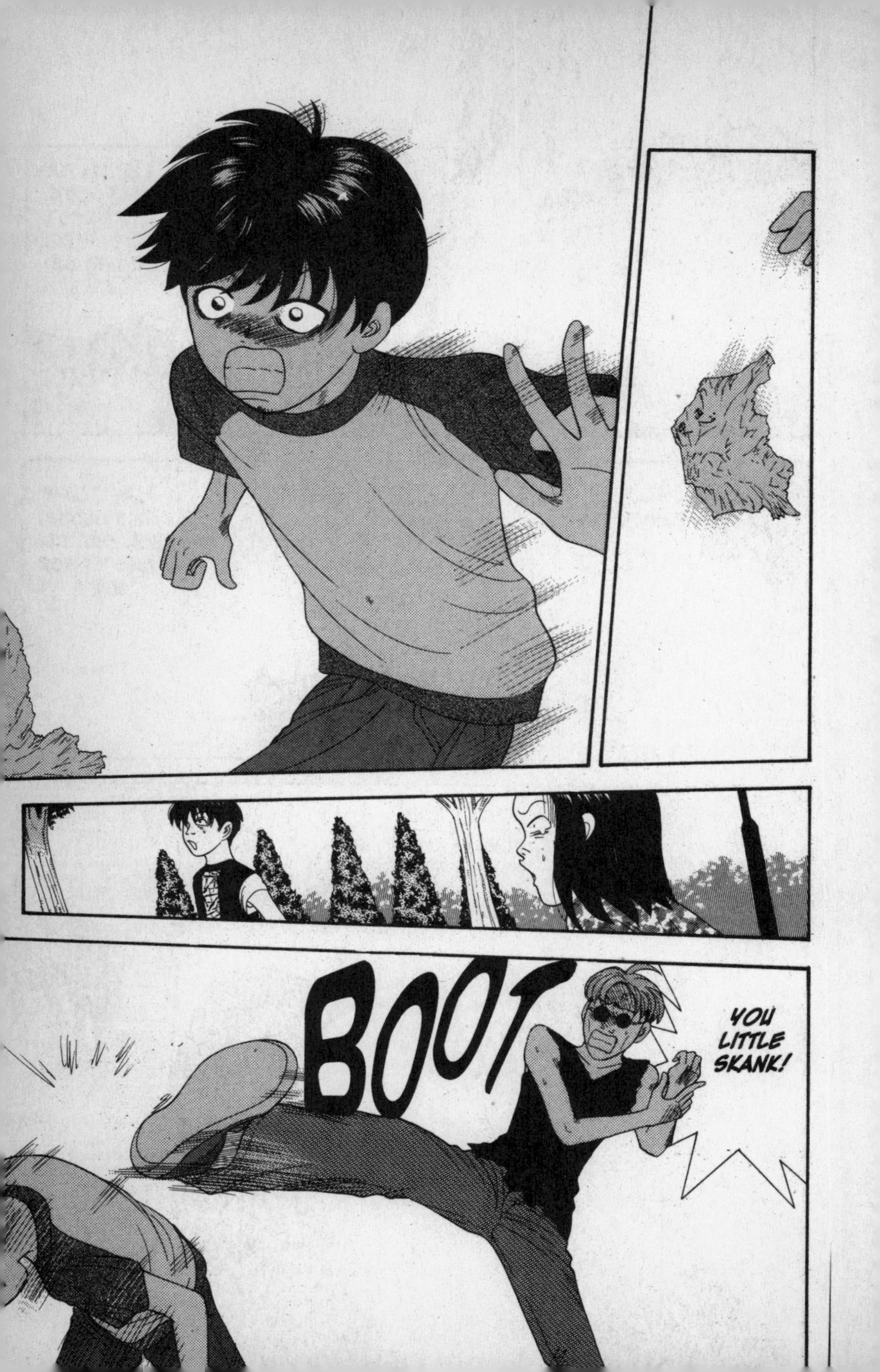
BOOT
YOU LITTLE SKANK!

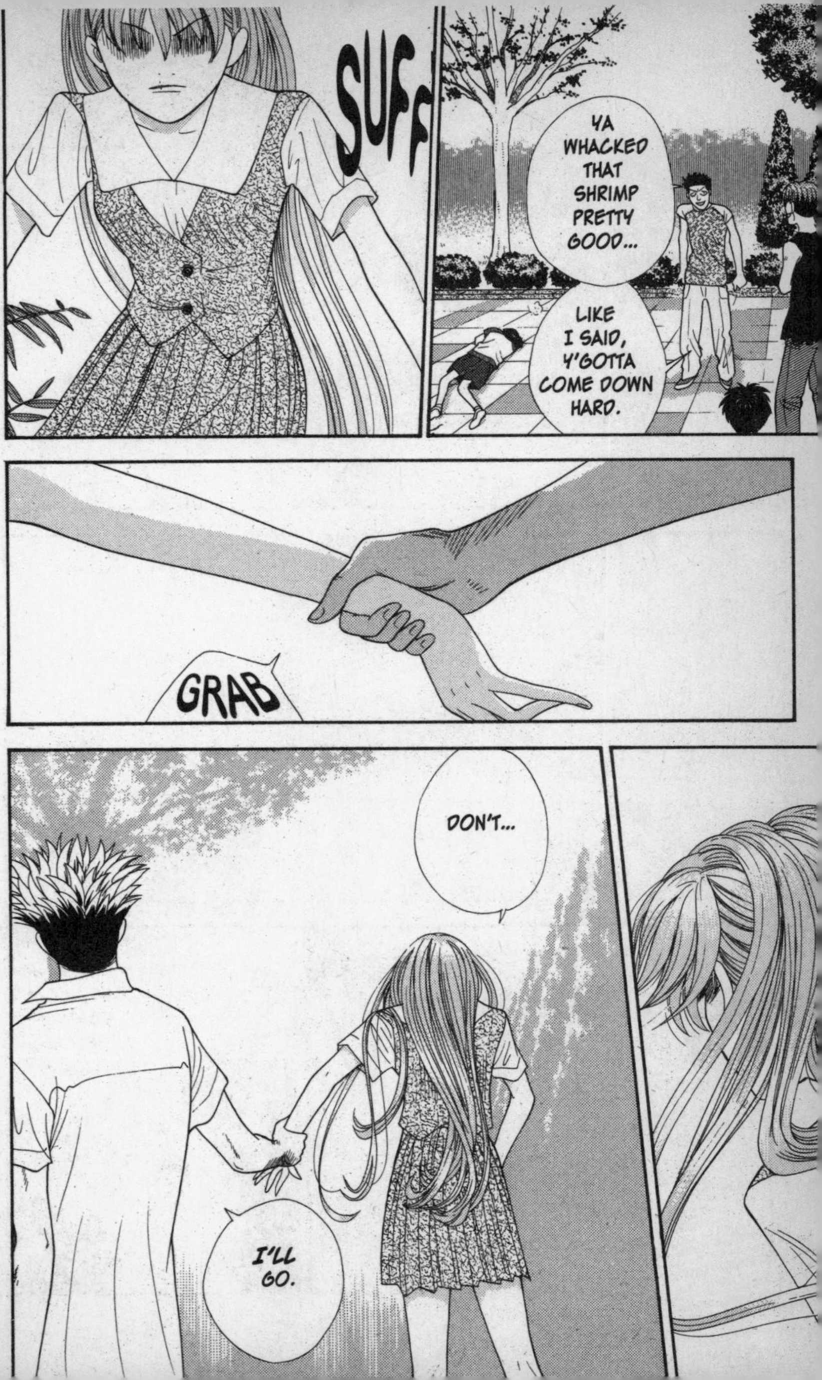
YA WHACKED THAT SHRIMP PRETTY GOOD...
LIKE I SAID, Y'GOTTA COME DOWN HARD.
SUFF
GRAB
DON'T...
I'LL GO.

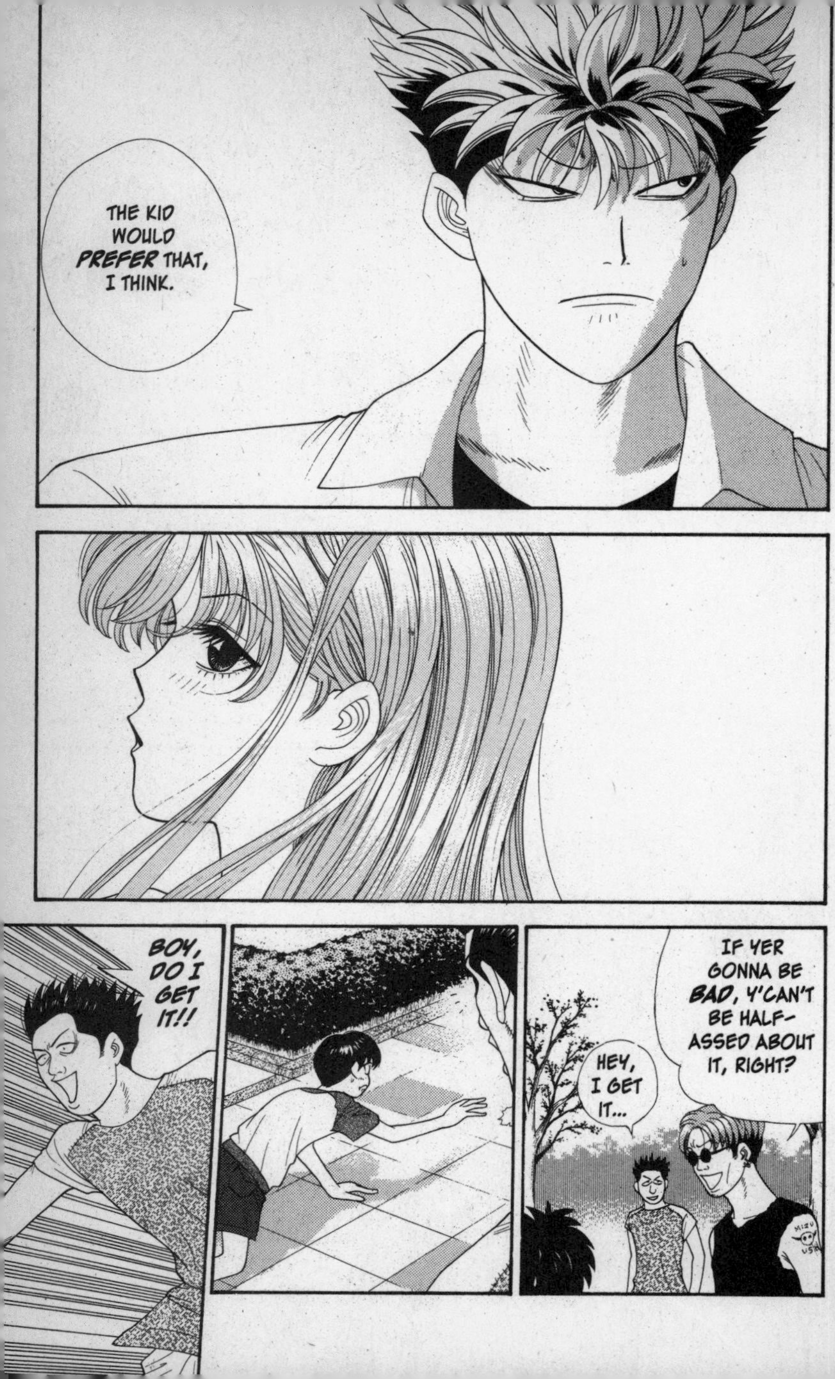
THE KID WOULD PREFER THAT, I THINK.
IF YER GONNA BE BAD, Y'CAN'T BE HALF-ASSED ABOUT IT, RIGHT?
HEY, I GET IT...
BOY, DO I GET IT!!

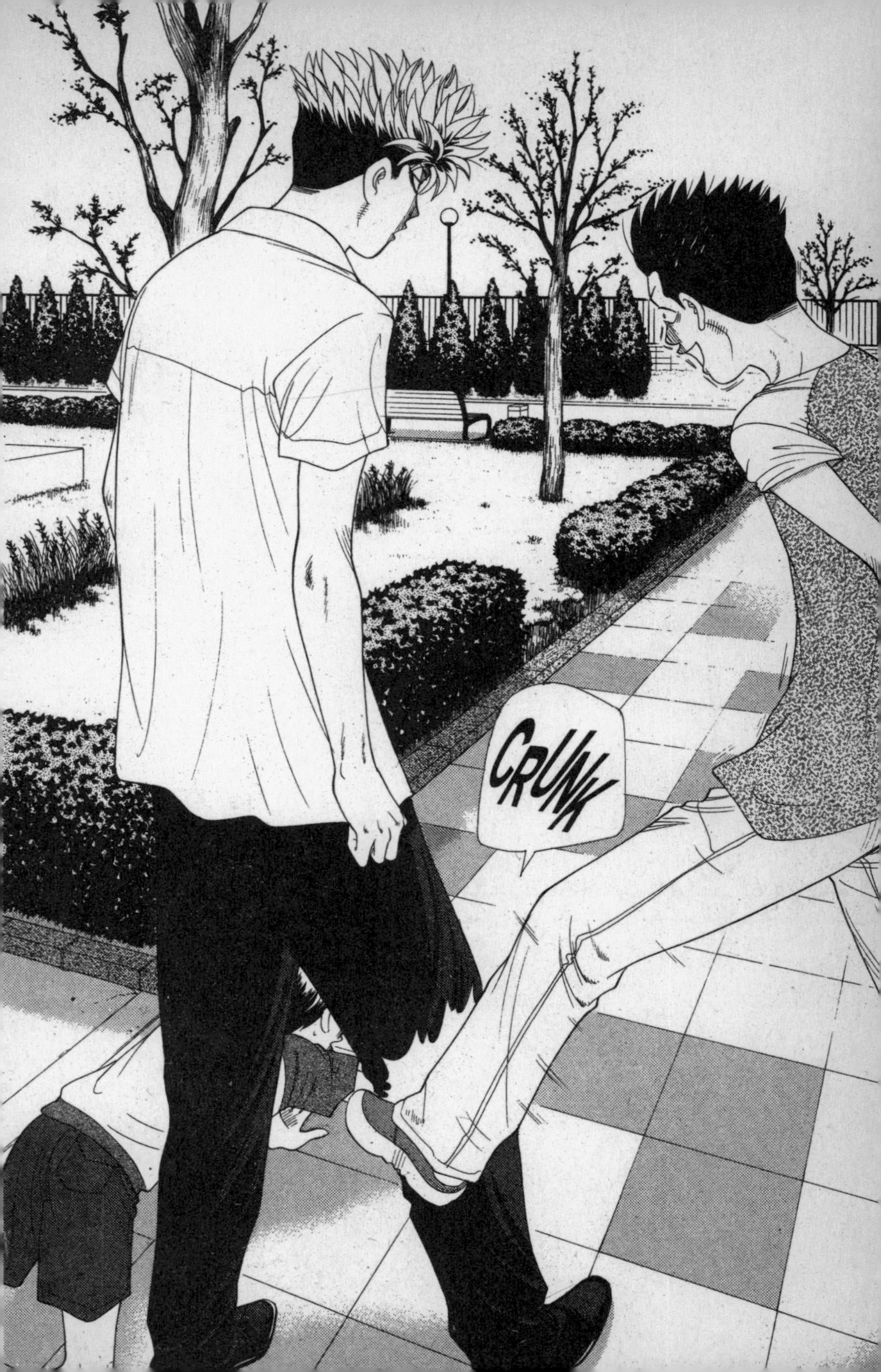
CRUNK

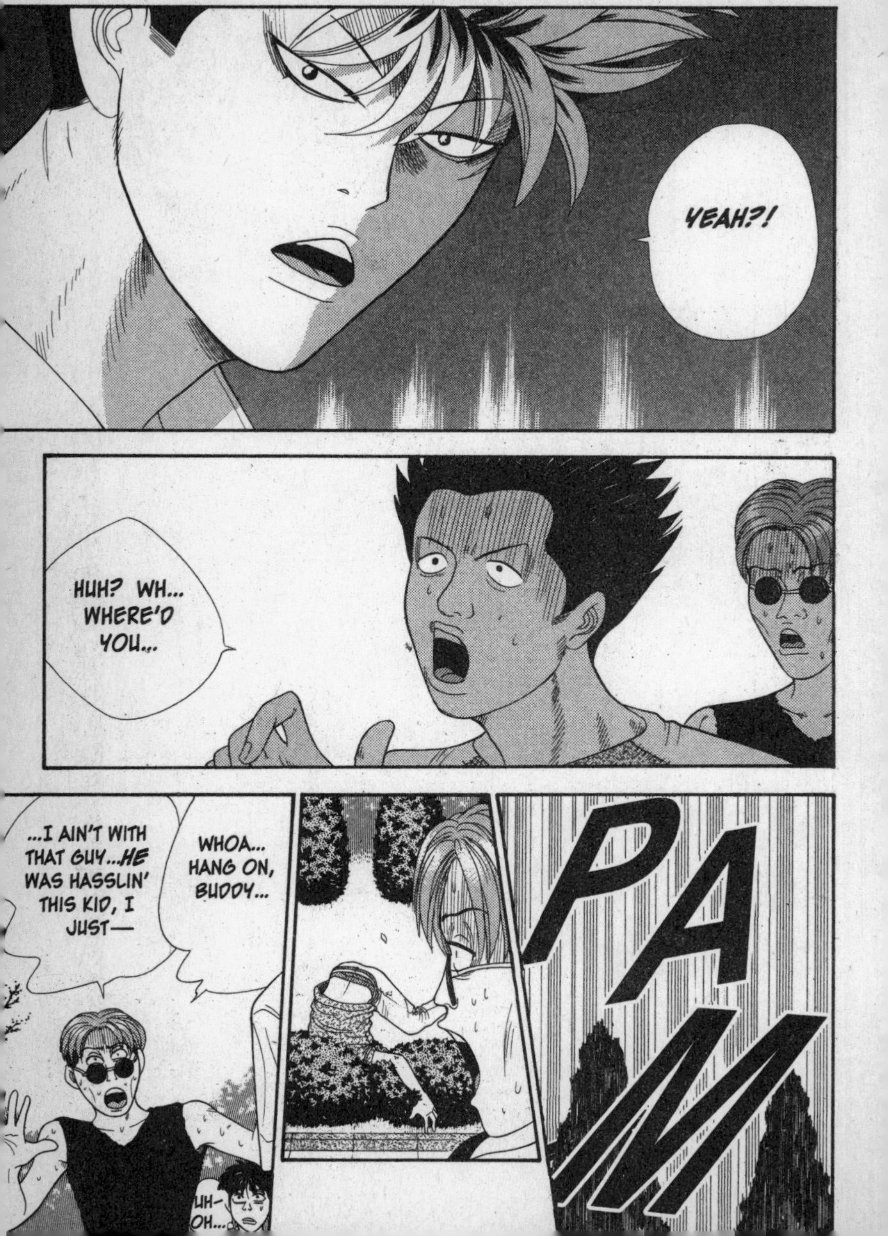
YEAH?!
HUH? WH... WHERE'D YOU...
PAM
WHOA... HANG ON, BUDDY...
...I AIN'T WITH THAT GUY...HE WAS HASSLIN' THIS KID, I JUST—
UH-OH...

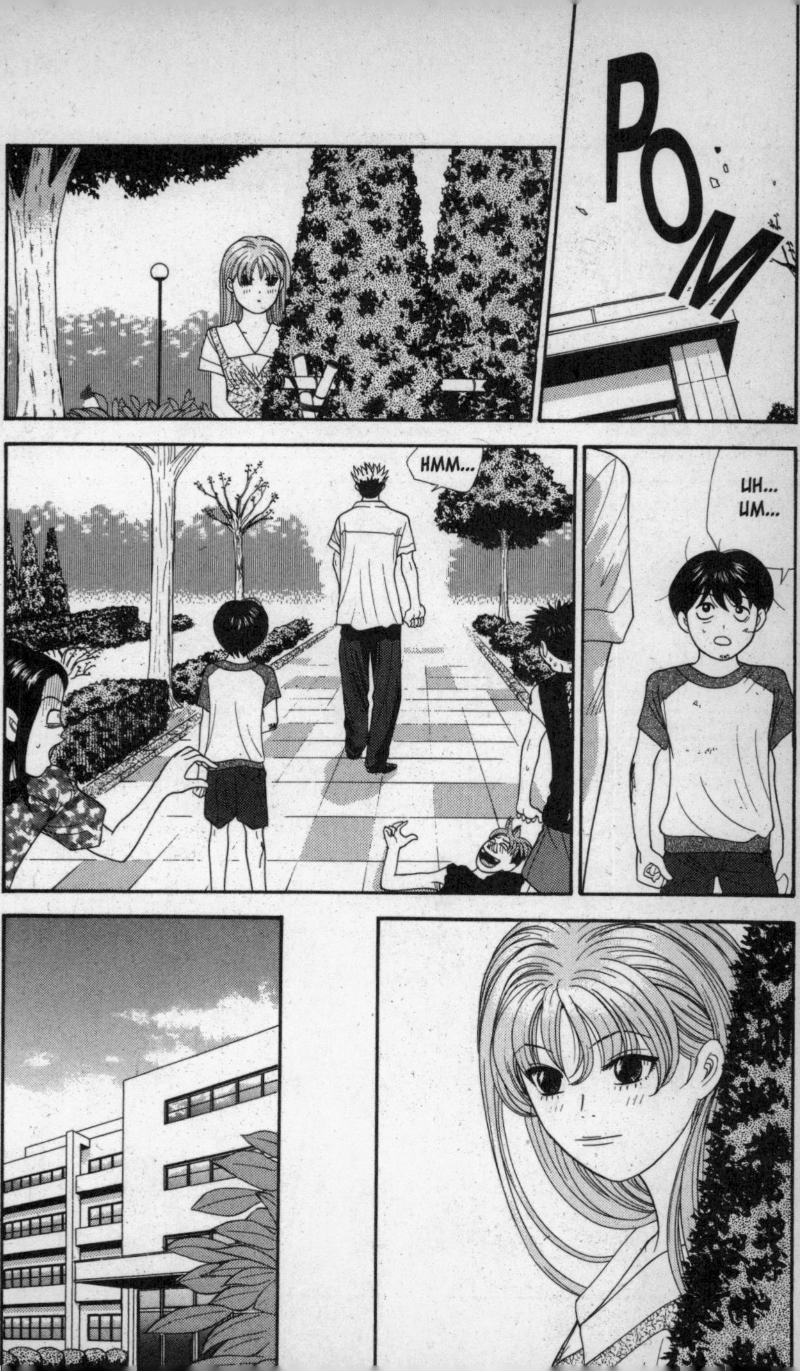
POM
UH... UM...
HMM...

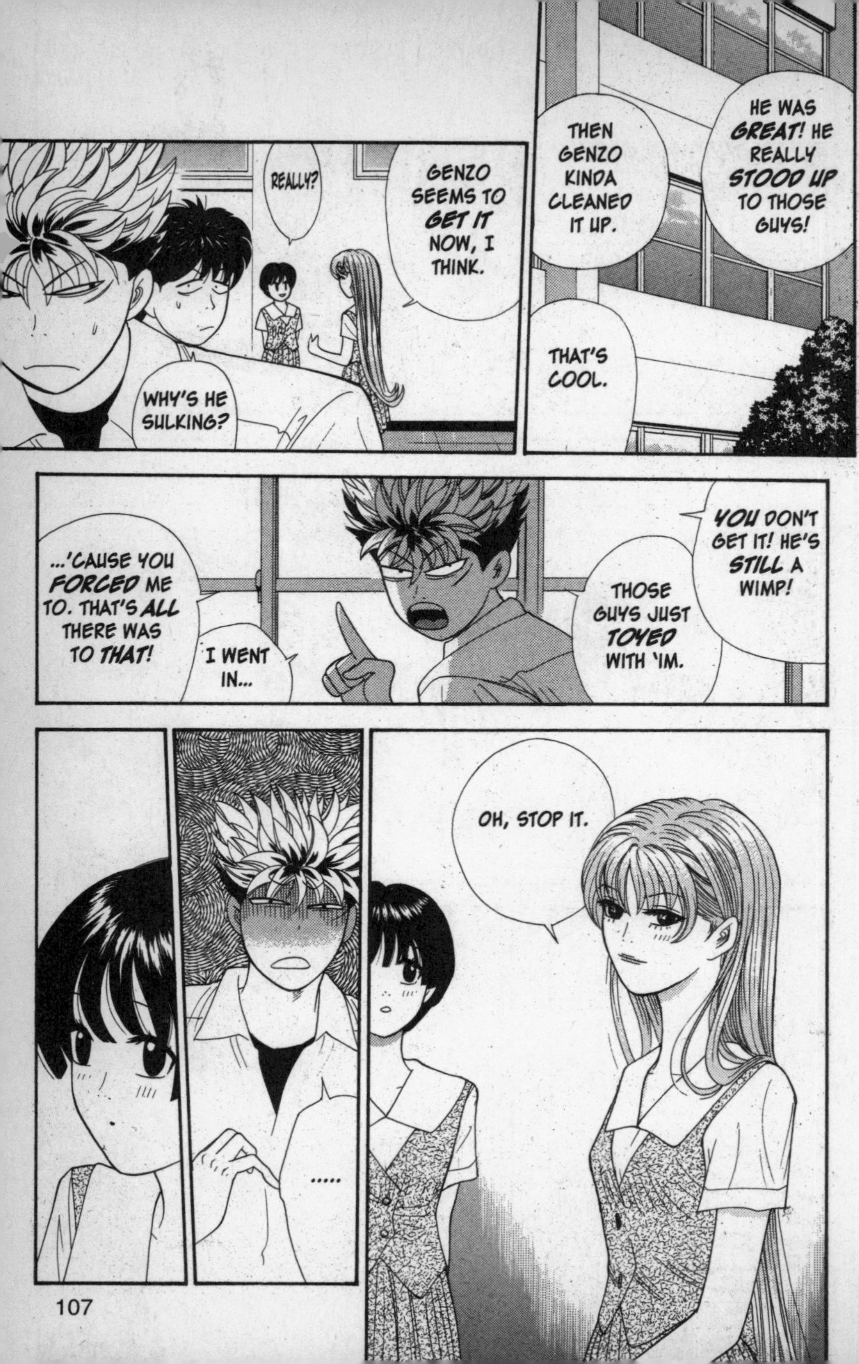
HE WAS GREAT! HE REALLY STOOD UP TO THOSE GUYS!
THEN GENZO KINDA CLEANED IT UP.
THAT'S COOL.
GENZO SEEMS TO GET IT NOW, I THINK.
REALLY?
WHY'S HE SULKING?
YOU DON'T GET IT! HE'S STILL A WIMP!
THOSE GUYS JUST TOYED WITH 'IM.
I WENT IN...
...'CAUSE YOU FORCED ME TO. THAT'S ALL THERE WAS TO THAT!
OH, STOP IT.
.....

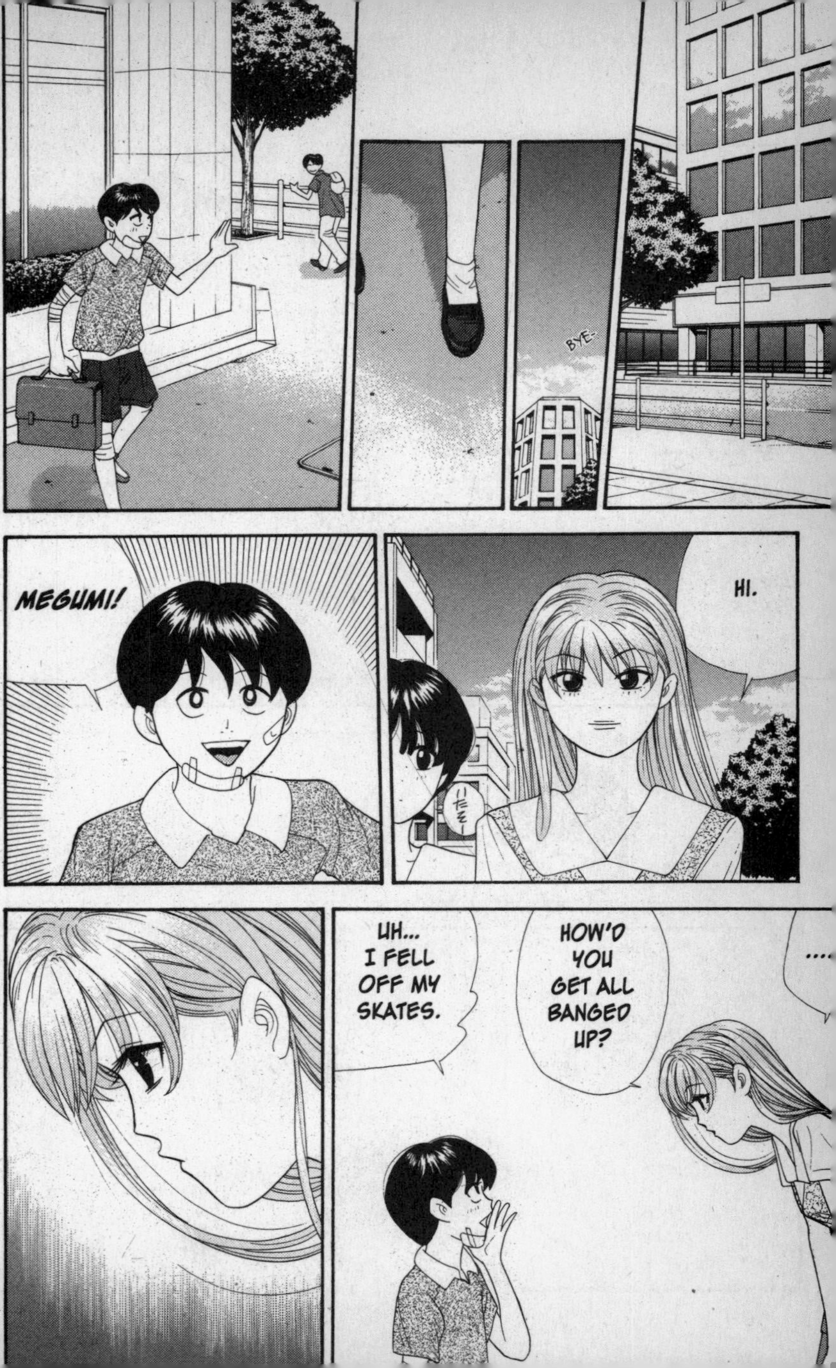
BYE-
HI.
いたぞー
MEGUMI!
....
HOW'D YOU GET ALL BANGED UP?
UH... I FELL OFF MY SKATES.

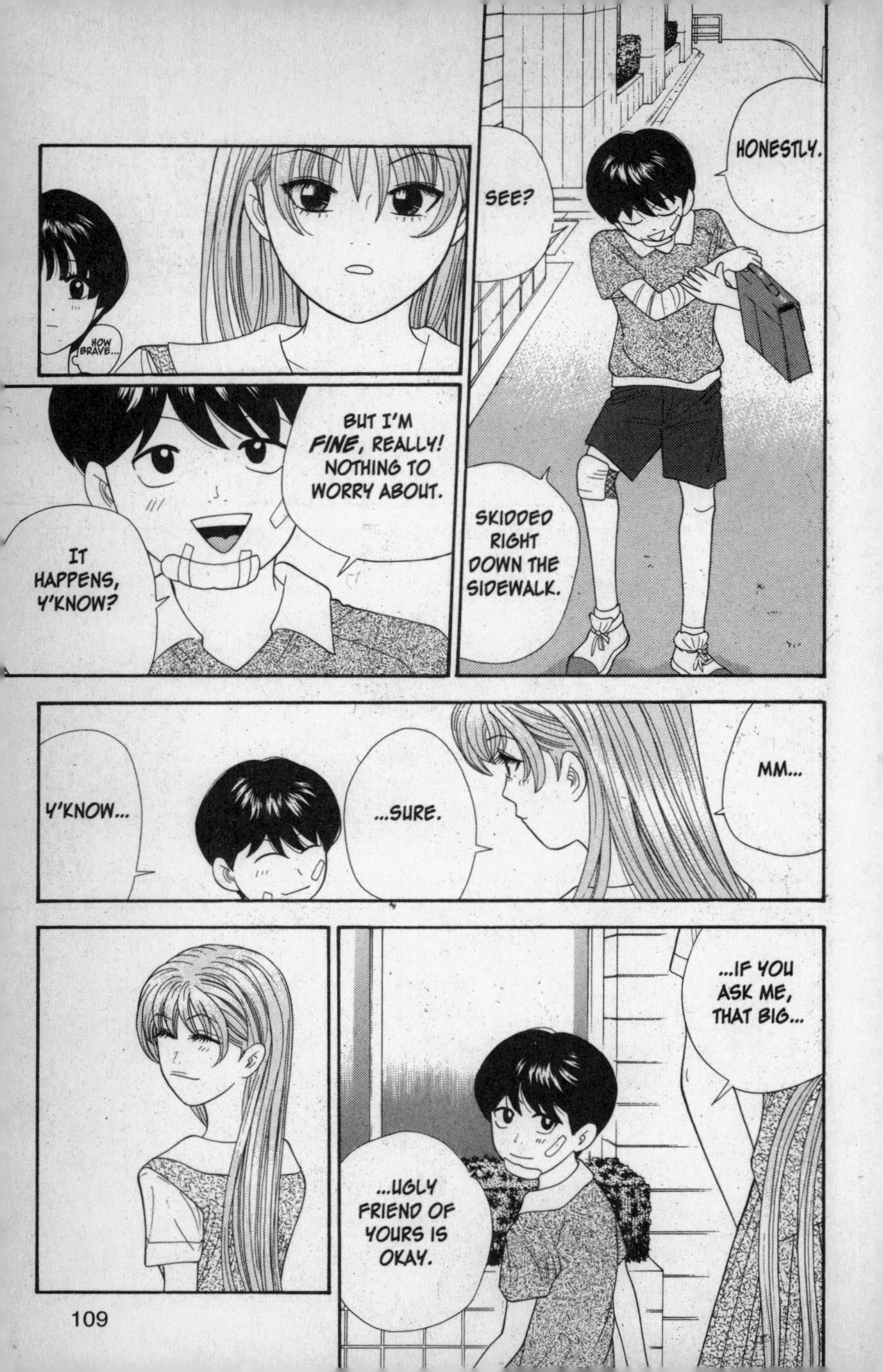
HONESTLY.
SEE?
SKIDDED RIGHT DOWN THE SIDEWALK.
HOW BRAVE...
BUT I'M *FINE*, REALLY! NOTHING TO WORRY ABOUT.
IT HAPPENS, Y'KNOW?
MM...
...SURE.
Y'KNOW...
...IF YOU ASK ME, THAT BIG...
...UGLY FRIEND OF YOURS IS OKAY.

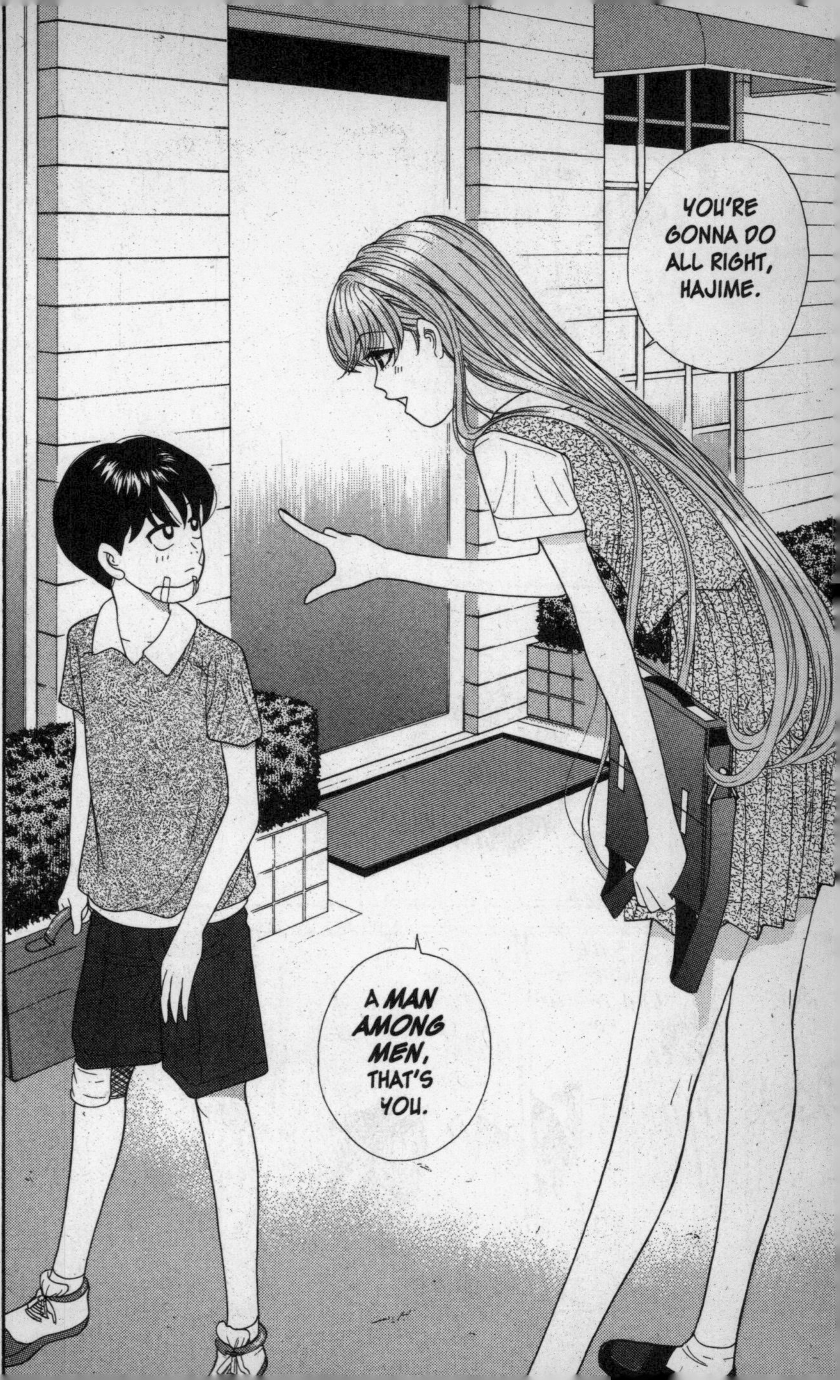
YOU'RE GONNA DO ALL RIGHT, HAJIME.
A MAN AMONG MEN, THAT'S YOU.

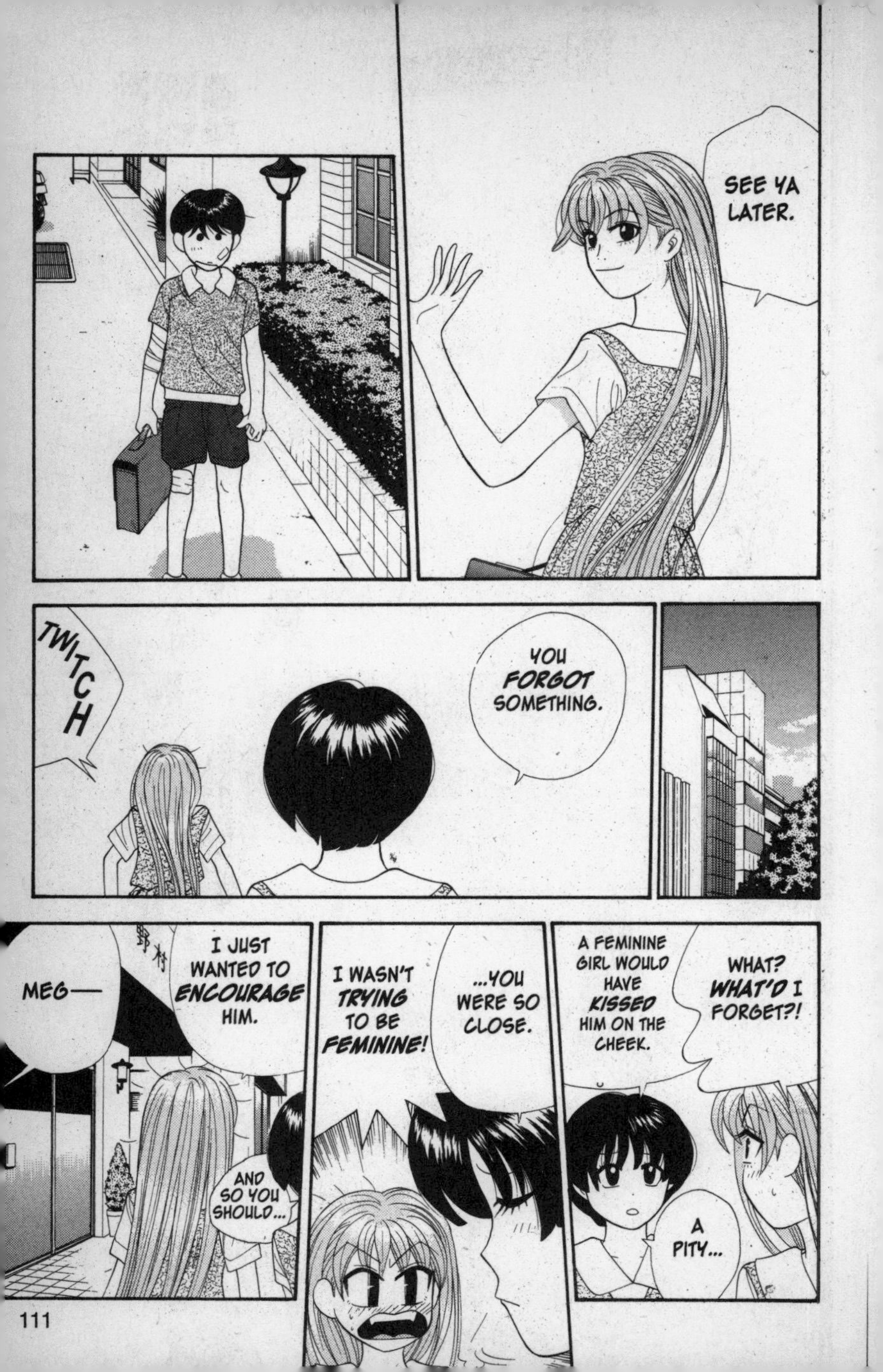
SEE YA LATER.
YOU FORGOT SOMETHING.
TWITCH
WHAT? WHAT'D I FORGET?!
A FEMININE GIRL WOULD HAVE KISSED HIM ON THE CHEEK.
A PITY...
...YOU WERE SO CLOSE.
I WASN'T TRYING TO BE FEMININE!
I JUST WANTED TO ENCOURAGE HIM.
AND SO YOU SHOULD...
MEG—

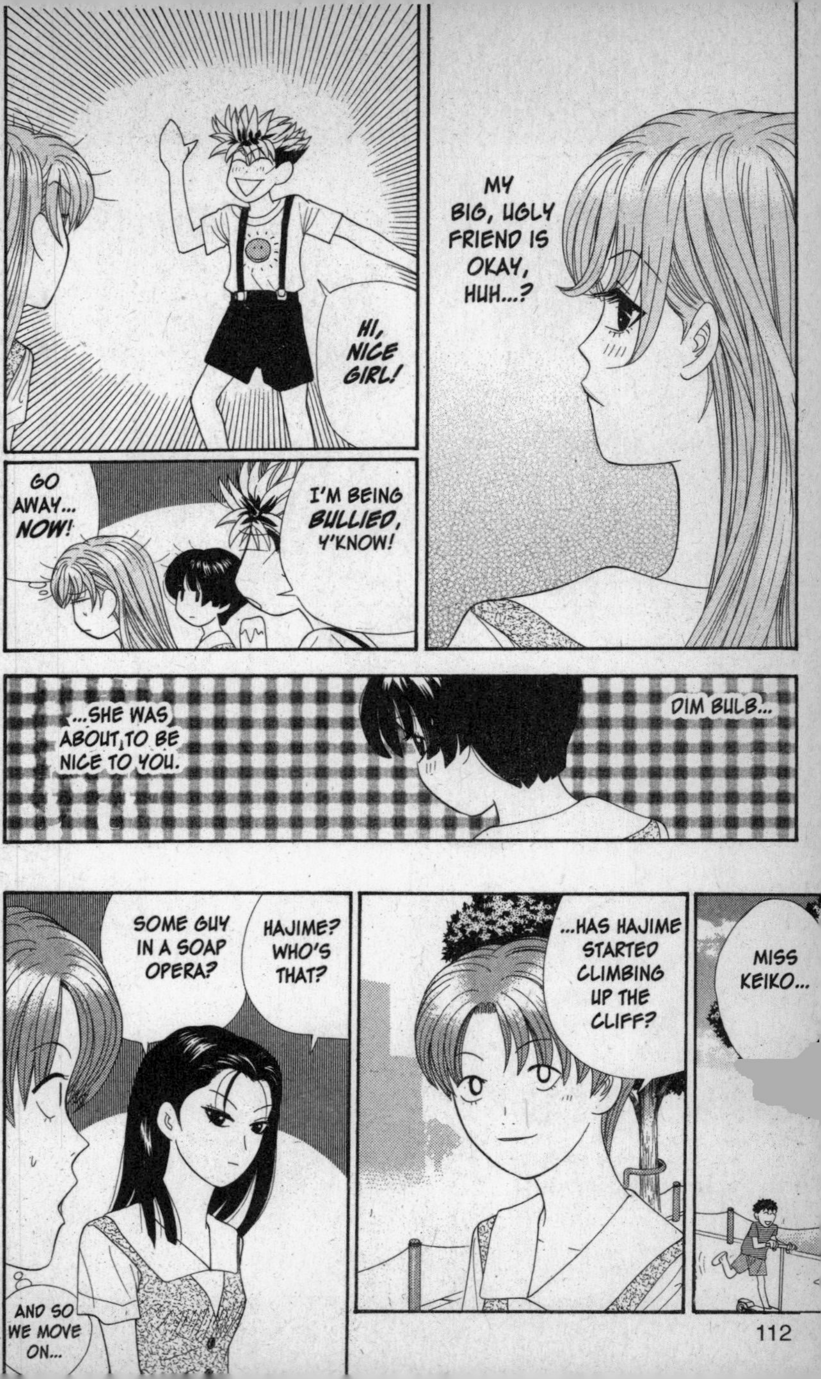
MY BIG, UGLY FRIEND IS OKAY, HUH...?
HI, NICE GIRL!
I'M BEING BULLIED, Y'KNOW!
GO AWAY... NOW!
DIM BULB...
...SHE WAS ABOUT TO BE NICE TO YOU.
MISS KEIKO...
...HAS HAJIME STARTED CLIMBING UP THE CLIFF?
HAJIME? WHO'S THAT?
SOME GUY IN A SOAP OPERA?
AND SO WE MOVE ON...

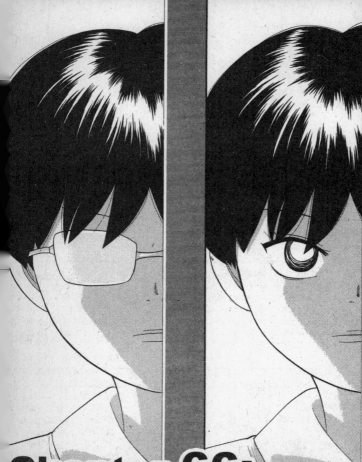

Chapter 66: Secret

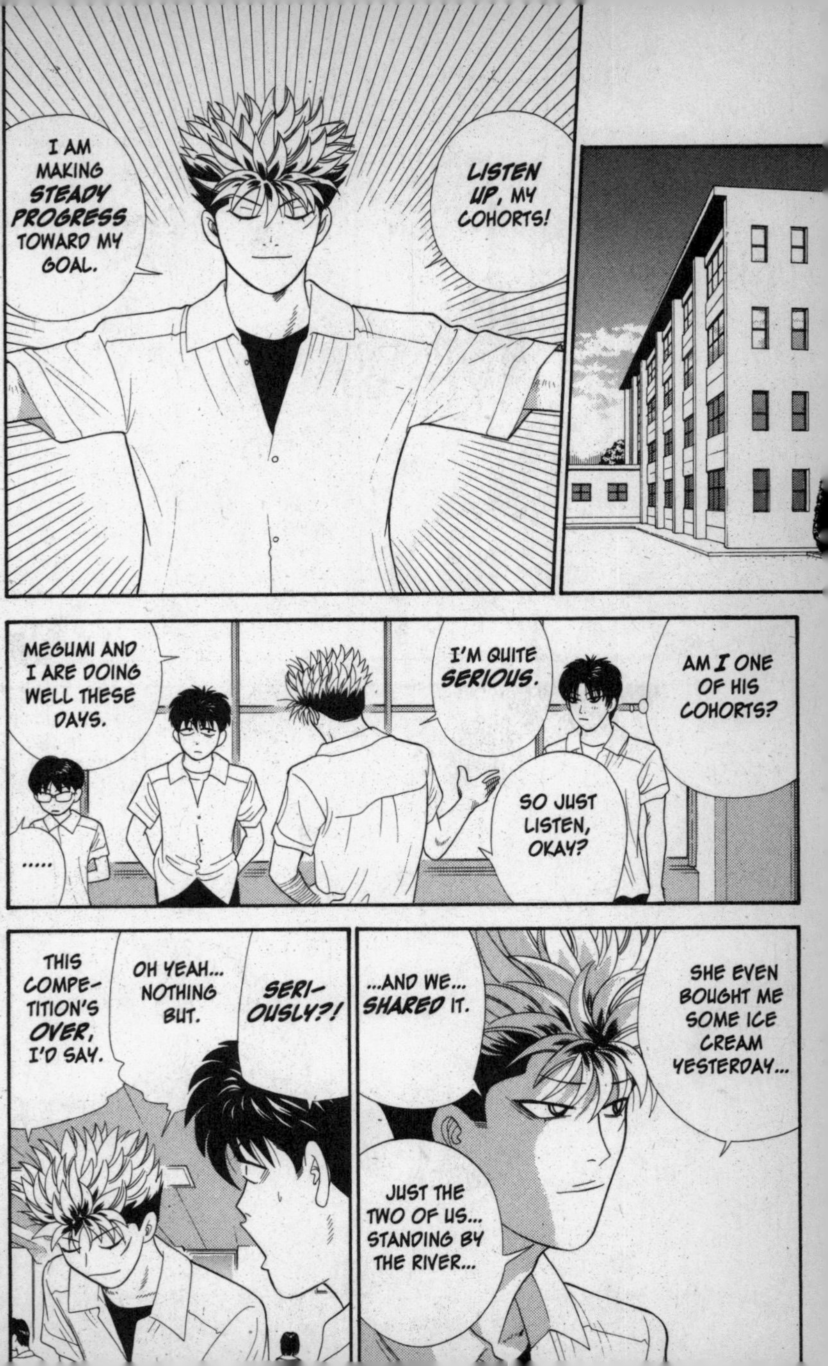
LISTEN UP, MY COHORTS!
I AM MAKING STEADY PROGRESS TOWARD MY GOAL.
AM I ONE OF HIS COHORTS?
I'M QUITE SERIOUS.
SO JUST LISTEN, OKAY?
MEGUMI AND I ARE DOING WELL THESE DAYS.
.....
SHE EVEN BOUGHT ME SOME ICE CREAM YESTERDAY...
...AND WE... SHARED IT.
JUST THE TWO OF US... STANDING BY THE RIVER...
SERI-OUSLY?!
OH YEAH... NOTHING BUT.
THIS COMPE-TITION'S OVER, I'D SAY.

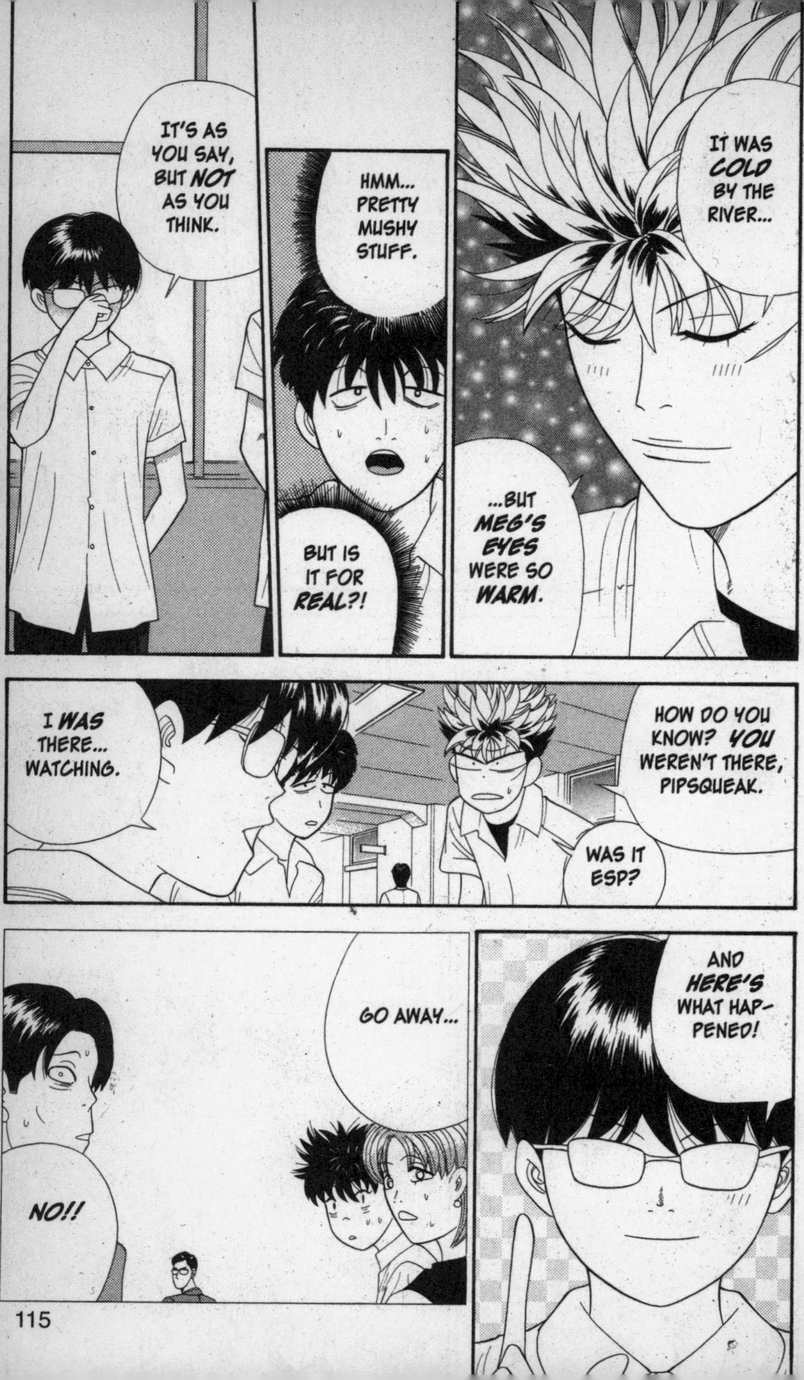
IT WAS COLD BY THE RIVER...
...BUT MEG'S EYES WERE SO WARM.
HMM... PRETTY MUSHY STUFF.
BUT IS IT FOR REAL?!
IT'S AS YOU SAY, BUT NOT AS YOU THINK.
HOW DO YOU KNOW? YOU WEREN'T THERE, PIPSQUEAK.
WAS IT ESP?
I WAS THERE... WATCHING.
AND HERE'S WHAT HAP-PENED!
GO AWAY...
NO!!

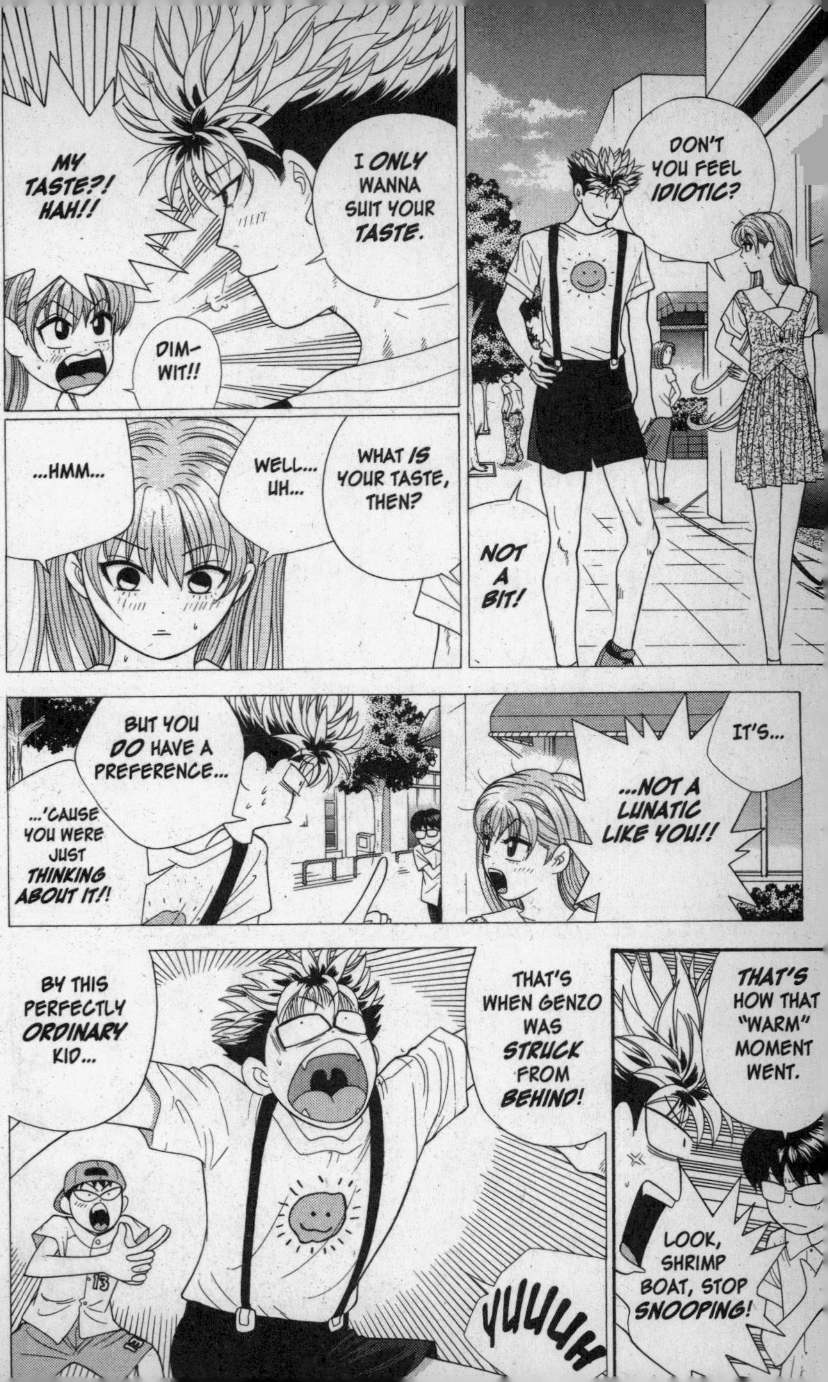
DON'T YOU FEEL IDIOTIC?
NOT A BIT!
I ONLY WANNA SUIT YOUR TASTE.
MY TASTE?! HAH!!
DIM-WIT!!
WHAT IS YOUR TASTE, THEN?
WELL... UH...
...HMM...
IT'S...
...NOT A LUNATIC LIKE YOU!!
BUT YOU DO HAVE A PREFERENCE...
...'CAUSE YOU WERE JUST THINKING ABOUT IT!!
THAT'S HOW THAT "WARM" MOMENT WENT.
LOOK, SHRIMP BOAT, STOP SNOOPING!
THAT'S WHEN GENZO WAS STRUCK FROM BEHIND!
BY THIS PERFECTLY ORDINARY KID...
YUUUH

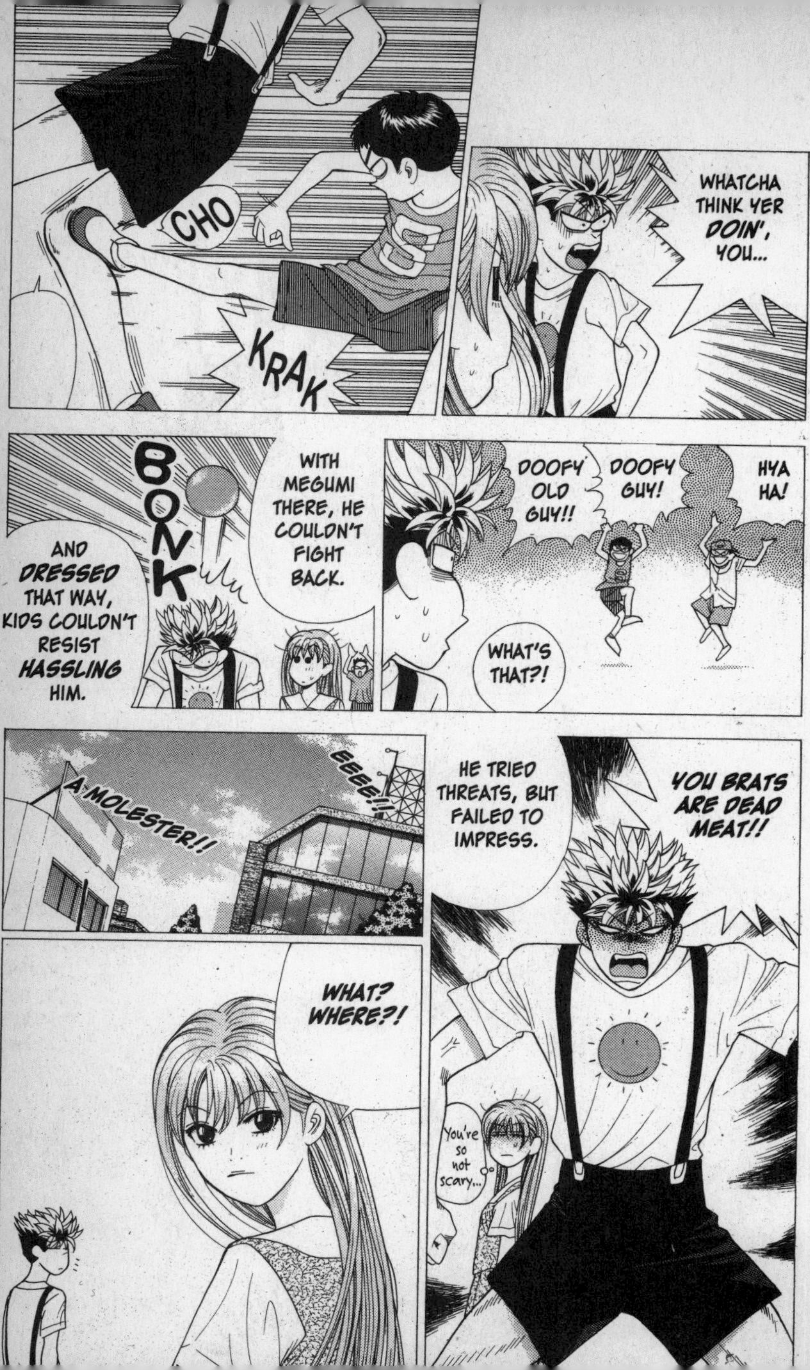
WHATCHA THINK YER DOIN', YOU...
CHO
KRAK
HYA HA!
DOOFY GUY!
DOOFY OLD GUY!!
WHAT'S THAT?!
WITH MEGUMI THERE, HE COULDN'T FIGHT BACK.
BONK
AND DRESSED THAT WAY, KIDS COULDN'T RESIST HASSLING HIM.
YOU BRATS ARE DEAD MEAT!!
HE TRIED THREATS, BUT FAILED TO IMPRESS.
You're so not scary...
EEEE!!!
A MOLESTER!!
WHAT? WHERE?!

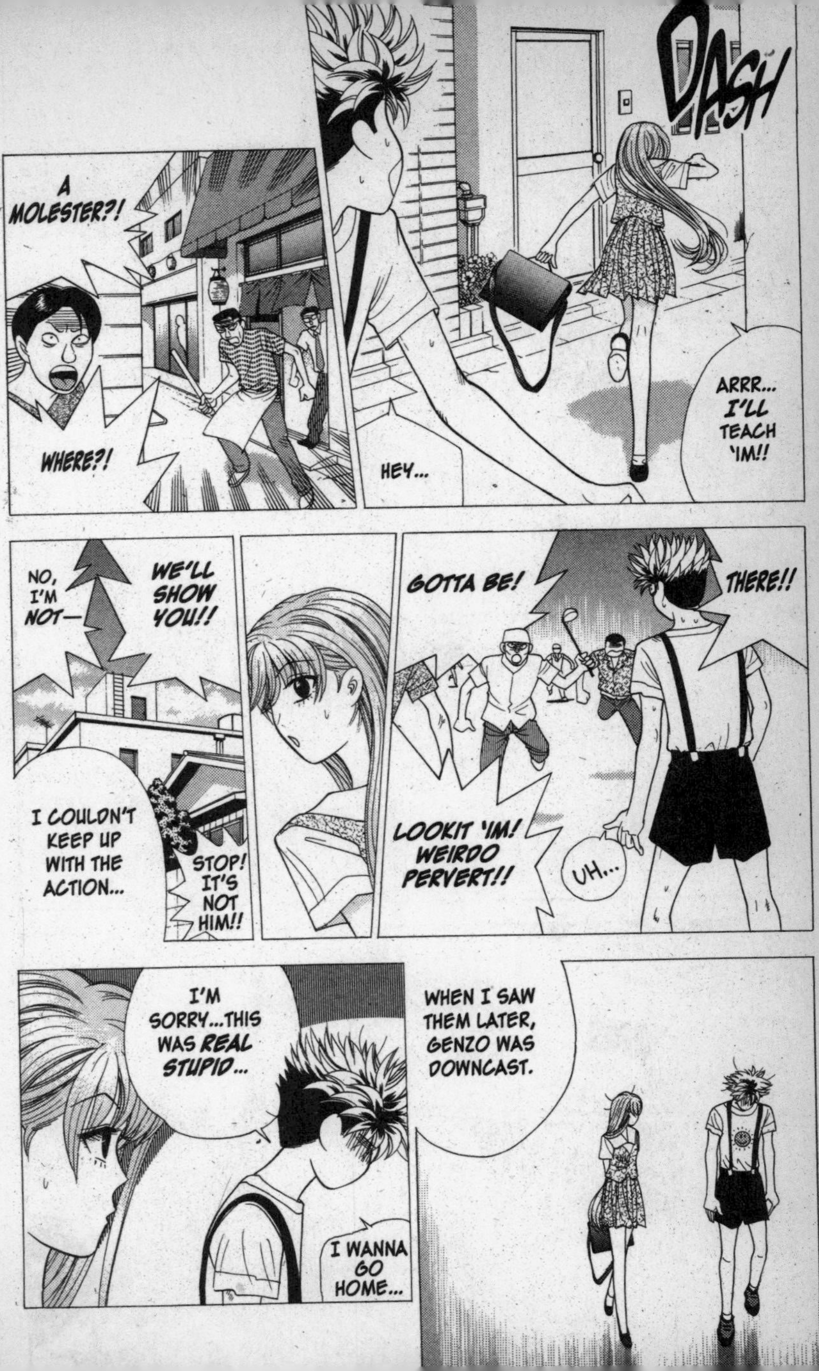
DASH
ARRR... I'LL TEACH 'IM!!
HEY...
A MOLESTER?!
WHERE?!
THERE!!
GOTTA BE!
UH...
LOOKIT 'IM! WEIRDO PERVERT!!
STOP! IT'S NOT HIM!!
WE'LL SHOW YOU!!
NO, I'M NOT—
I COULDN'T KEEP UP WITH THE ACTION...
WHEN I SAW THEM LATER, GENZO WAS DOWNCAST.
I'M SORRY...THIS WAS REAL STUPID...
I WANNA GO HOME...

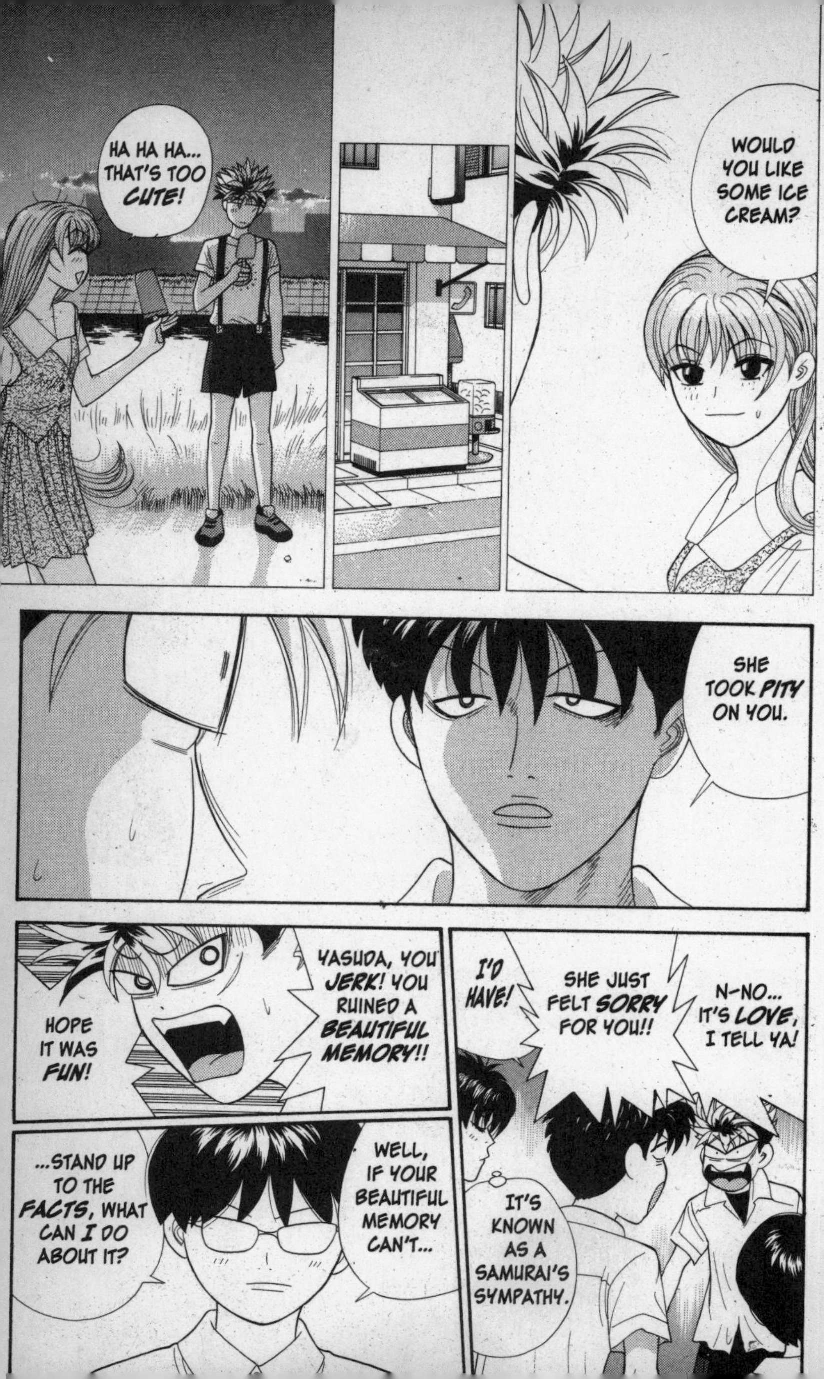
WOULD YOU LIKE SOME ICE CREAM?
HA HA HA... THAT'S TOO CUTE!
SHE TOOK PITY ON YOU.
N-NO... IT'S LOVE, I TELL YA!
SHE JUST FELT SORRY FOR YOU!!
I'D HAVE!
IT'S KNOWN AS A SAMURAI'S SYMPATHY.
YASUDA, YOU JERK! YOU RUINED A BEAUTIFUL MEMORY!!
HOPE IT WAS FUN!
WELL, IF YOUR BEAUTIFUL MEMORY CAN'T...
...STAND UP TO THE FACTS, WHAT CAN I DO ABOUT IT?

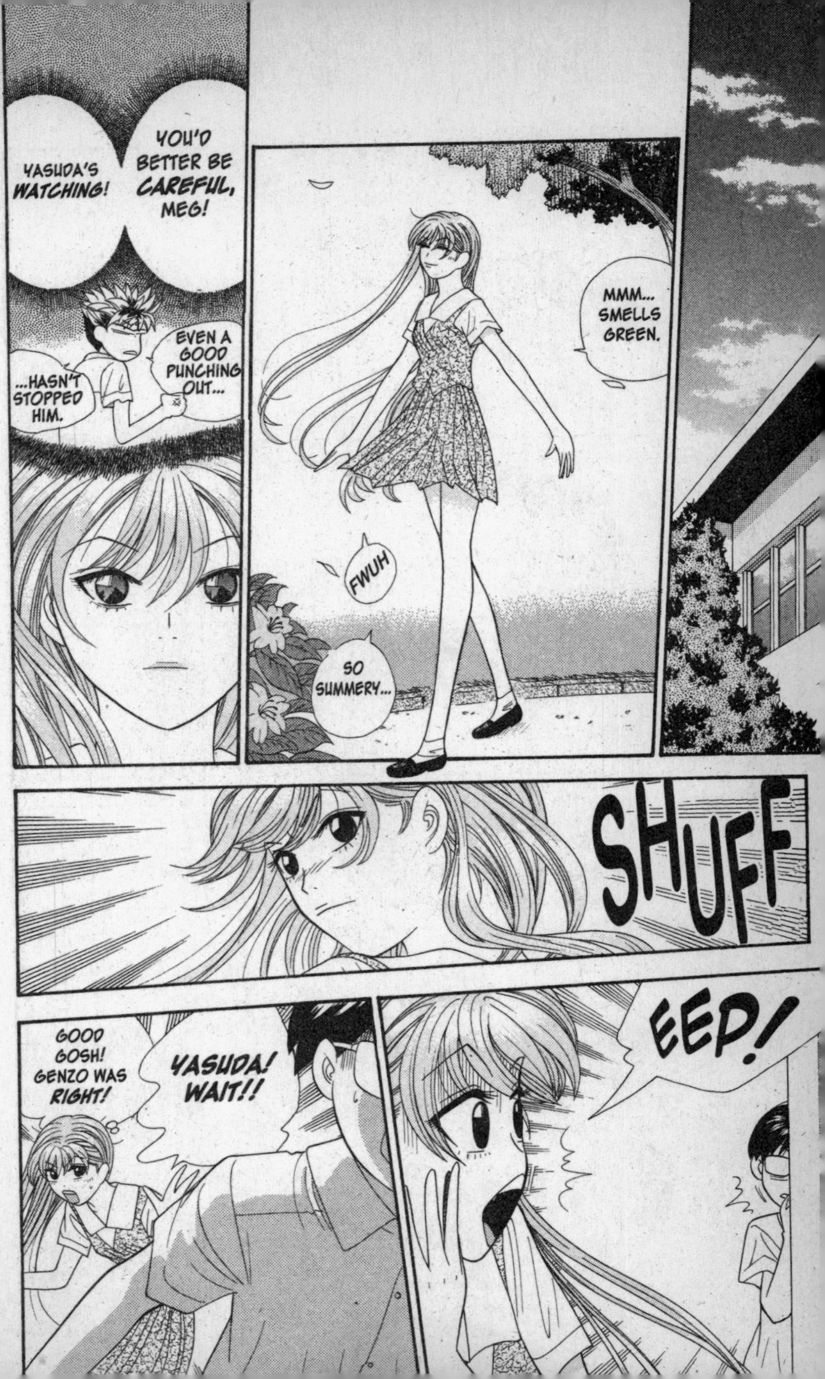
MMM... SMELLS GREEN.
FWUH
SO SUMMERY...
YOU'D BETTER BE CAREFUL, MEG!
YASUDA'S WATCHING!
EVEN A GOOD PUNCHING OUT...
...HASN'T STOPPED HIM.
SHUFF
EEP!
YASUDA! WAIT!!
GOOD GOSH! GENZO WAS RIGHT!

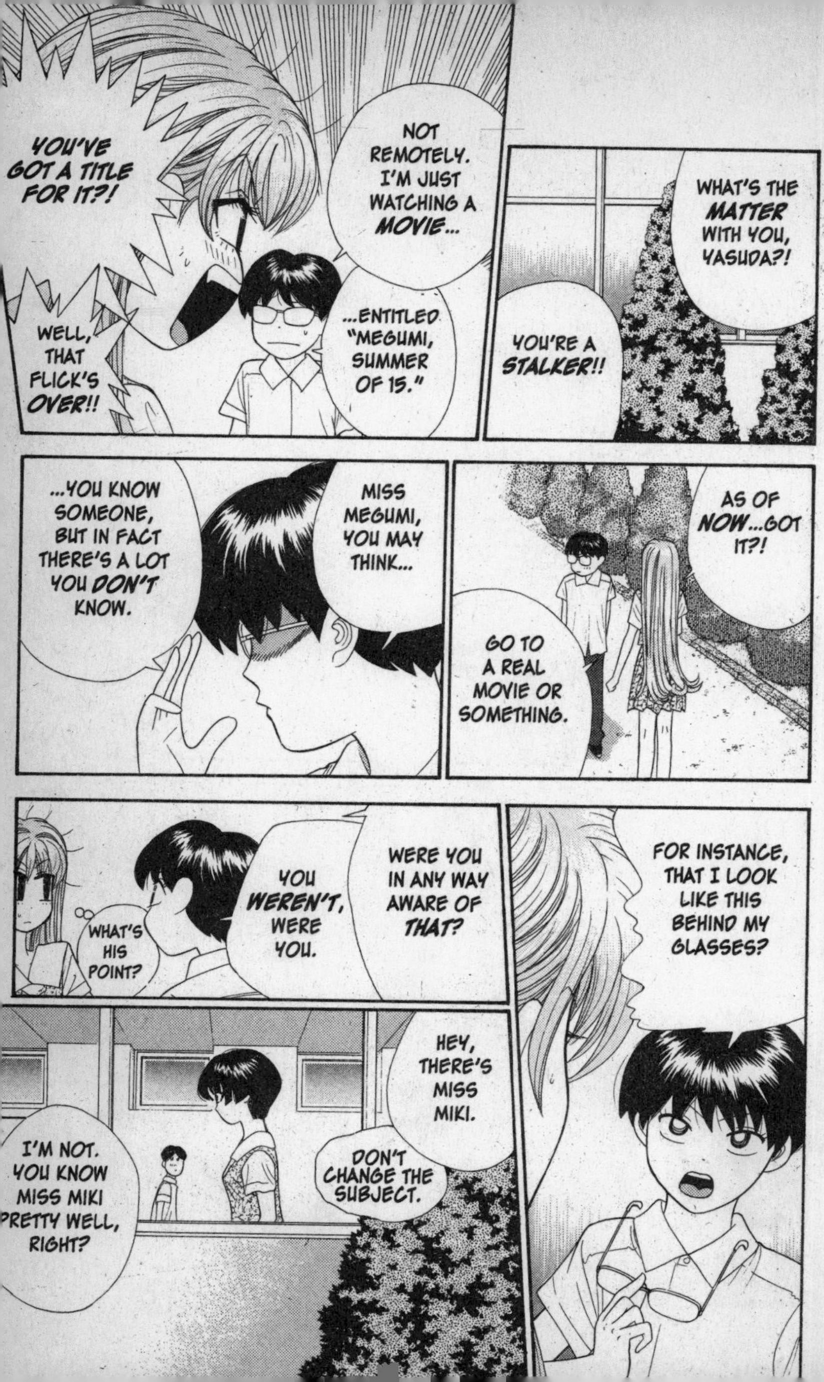
WHAT'S THE MATTER WITH YOU, YASUDA?!
YOU'RE A STALKER!!
NOT REMOTELY. I'M JUST WATCHING A MOVIE...
...ENTITLED "MEGUMI, SUMMER OF 15."
YOU'VE GOT A TITLE FOR IT?!
WELL, THAT FLICK'S OVER!!
AS OF NOW...GOT IT?!
GO TO A REAL MOVIE OR SOMETHING.
MISS MEGUMI, YOU MAY THINK...
...YOU KNOW SOMEONE, BUT IN FACT THERE'S A LOT YOU DON'T KNOW.
FOR INSTANCE, THAT I LOOK LIKE THIS BEHIND MY GLASSES?
WERE YOU IN ANY WAY AWARE OF THAT?
YOU WEREN'T, WERE YOU.
WHAT'S HIS POINT?
HEY, THERE'S MISS MIKI.
DON'T CHANGE THE SUBJECT.
I'M NOT. YOU KNOW MISS MIKI PRETTY WELL, RIGHT?

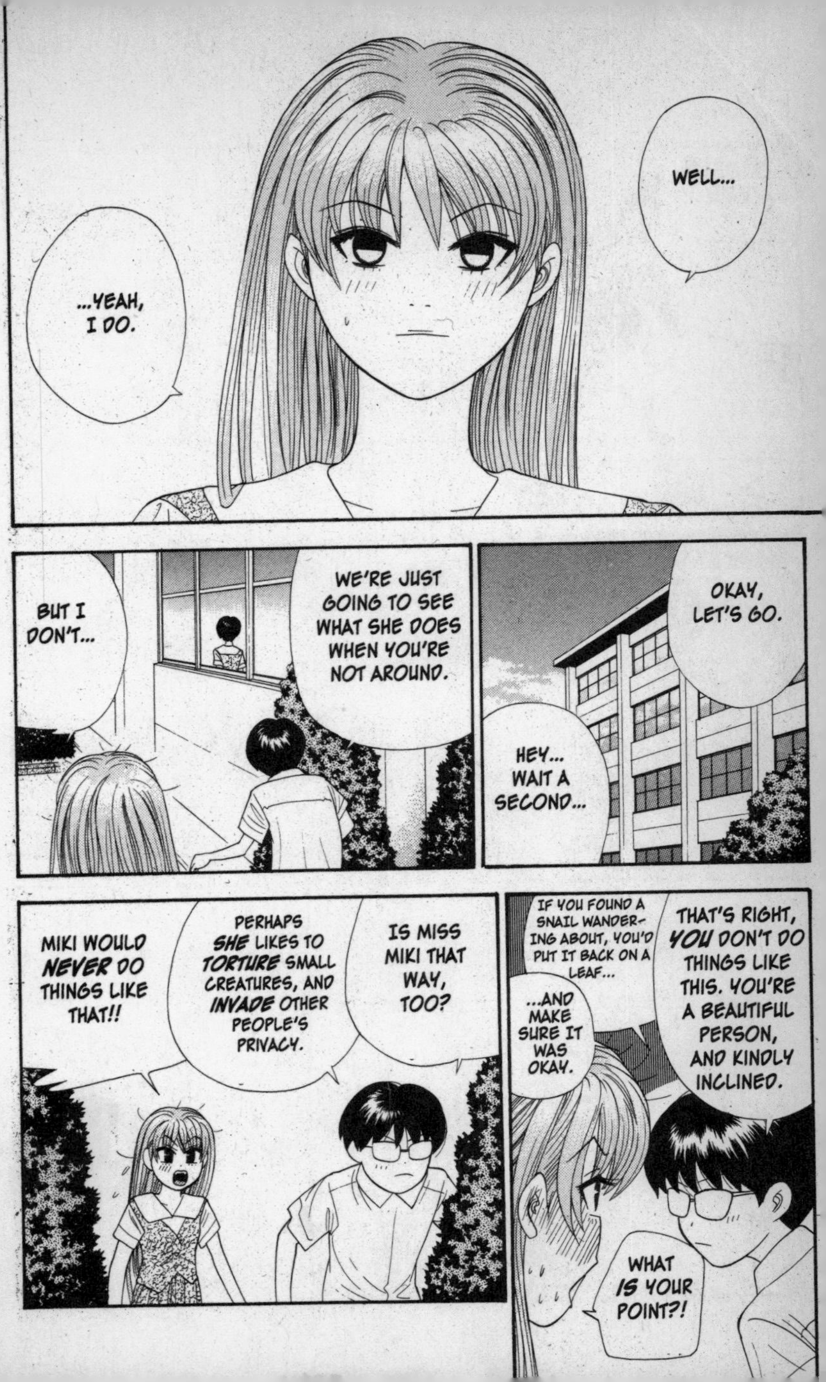
WELL...
...YEAH, I DO.
OKAY, LET'S GO.
HEY... WAIT A SECOND...
WE'RE JUST GOING TO SEE WHAT SHE DOES WHEN YOU'RE NOT AROUND.
BUT I DON'T...
THAT'S RIGHT, YOU DON'T DO THINGS LIKE THIS. YOU'RE A BEAUTIFUL PERSON, AND KINDLY INCLINED.
IF YOU FOUND A SNAIL WANDERING ABOUT, YOU'D PUT IT BACK ON A LEAF...
...AND MAKE SURE IT WAS OKAY.
WHAT IS YOUR POINT?!
IS MISS MIKI THAT WAY, TOO?
PERHAPS SHE LIKES TO TORTURE SMALL CREATURES, AND INVADE OTHER PEOPLE'S PRIVACY.
MIKI WOULD NEVER DO THINGS LIKE THAT!!

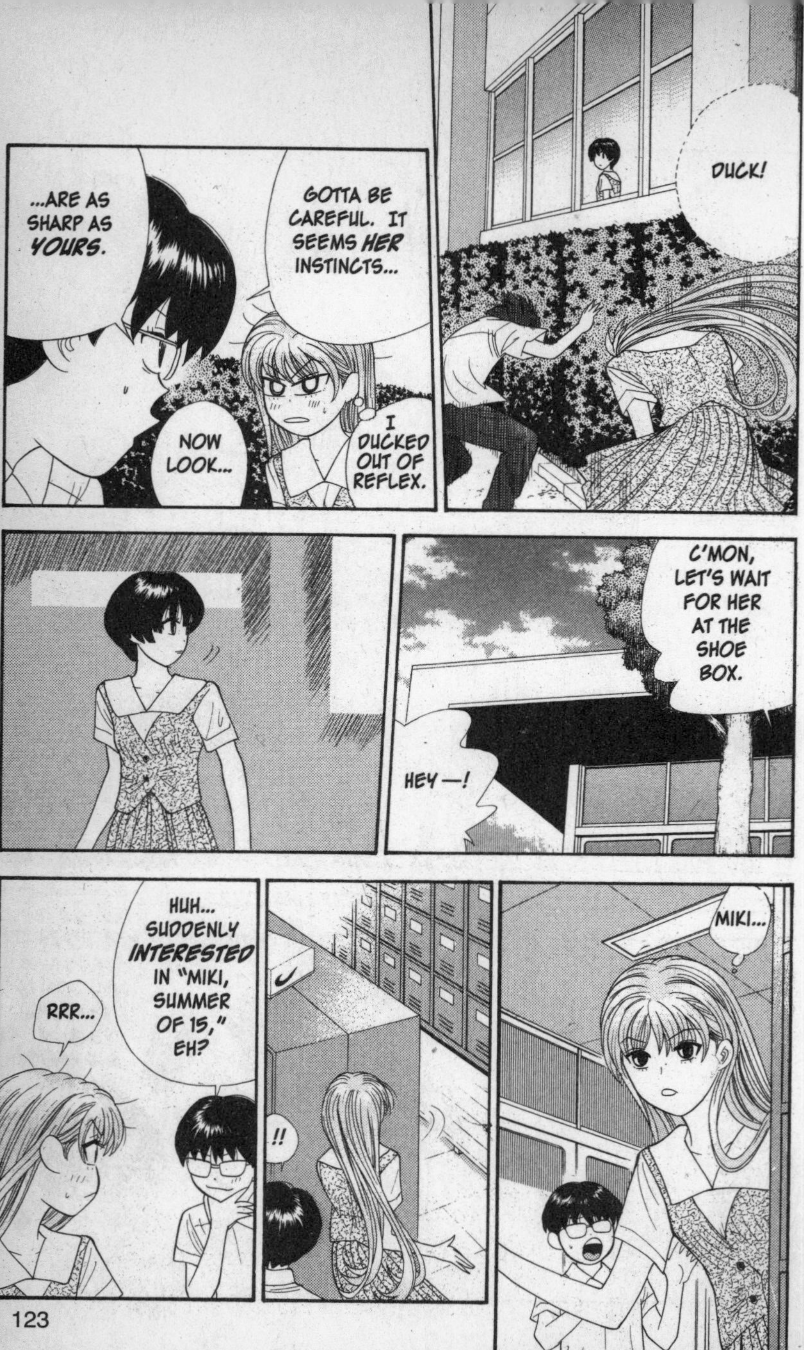
DUCK!
GOTTA BE CAREFUL. IT SEEMS *HER* INSTINCTS...
...ARE AS SHARP AS *YOURS*.
I DUCKED OUT OF REFLEX.
NOW LOOK...
C'MON, LET'S WAIT FOR HER AT THE SHOE BOX.
HEY—!
MIKI...
!!
HUH... SUDDENLY *INTERESTED* IN "MIKI, SUMMER OF 15," EH?
RRR...

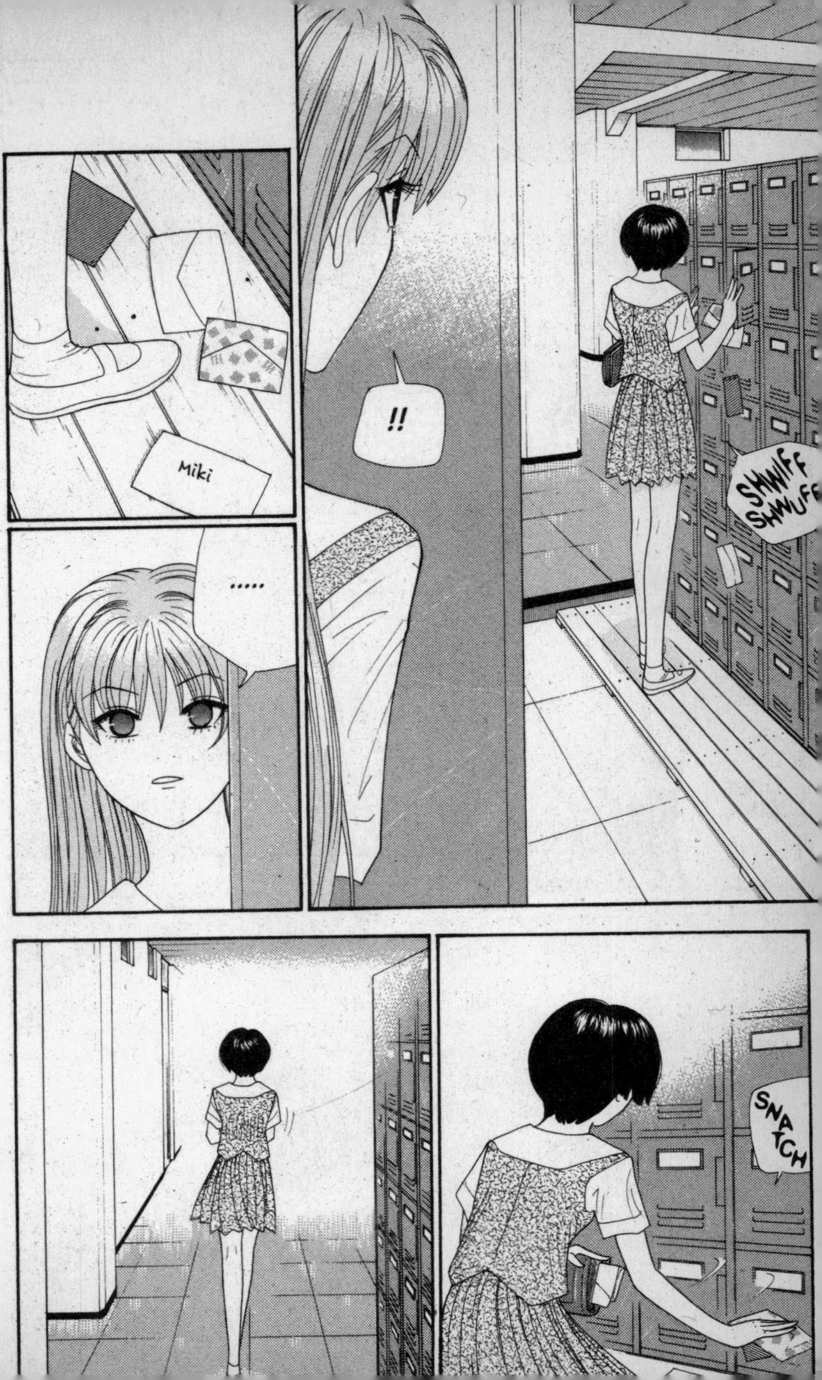
SHWUFF SHWUFF
!!
Miki
.....
SNATCH

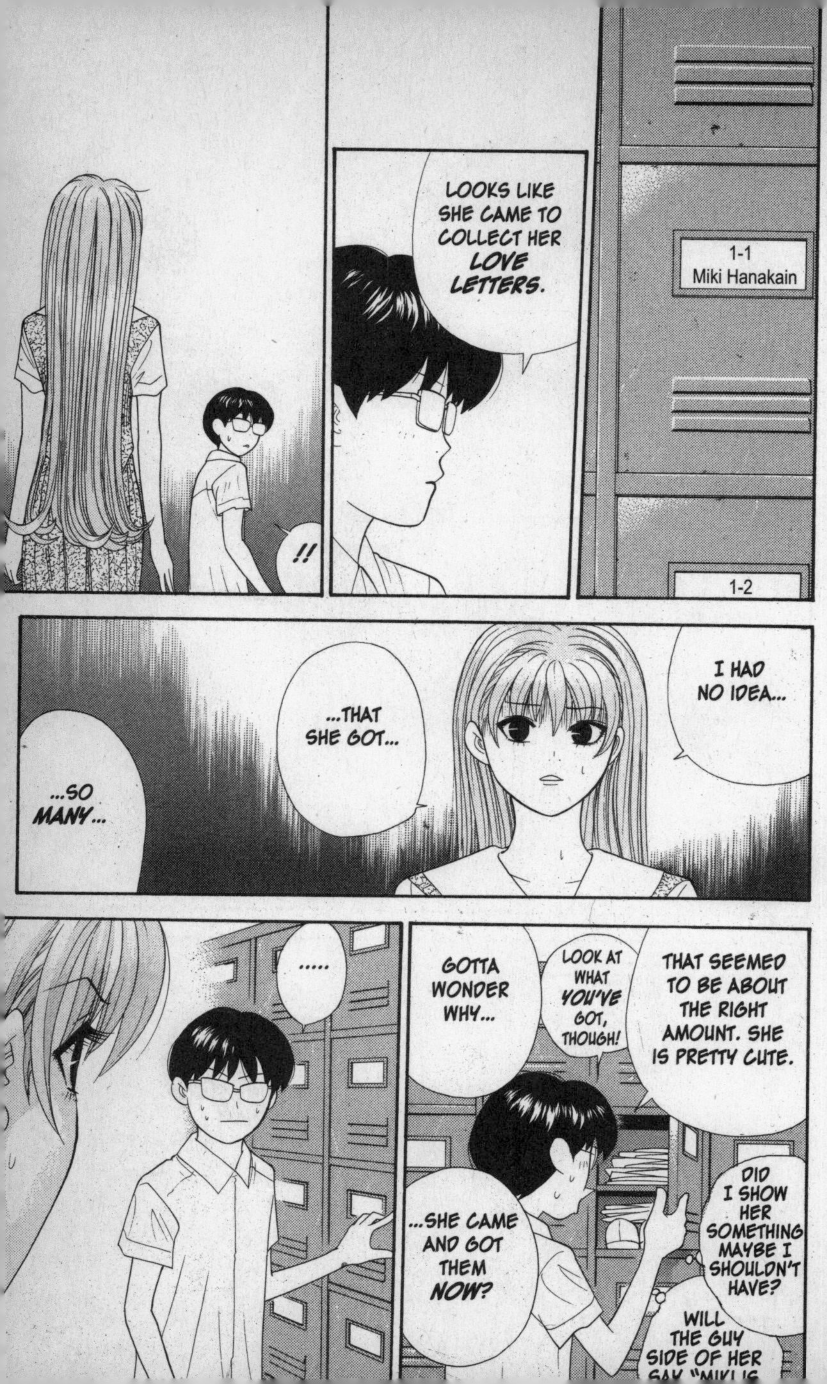
1-1
Miki Hanakain
1-2
LOOKS LIKE SHE CAME TO COLLECT HER LOVE LETTERS.
!!
I HAD NO IDEA...
...THAT SHE GOT...
...SO MANY...
THAT SEEMED TO BE ABOUT THE RIGHT AMOUNT. SHE IS PRETTY CUTE.
LOOK AT WHAT YOU'VE GOT, THOUGH!
GOTTA WONDER WHY...
...SHE CAME AND GOT THEM NOW?
DID I SHOW HER SOMETHING MAYBE I SHOULDN'T HAVE?
WILL THE GUY SIDE OF HER
.....

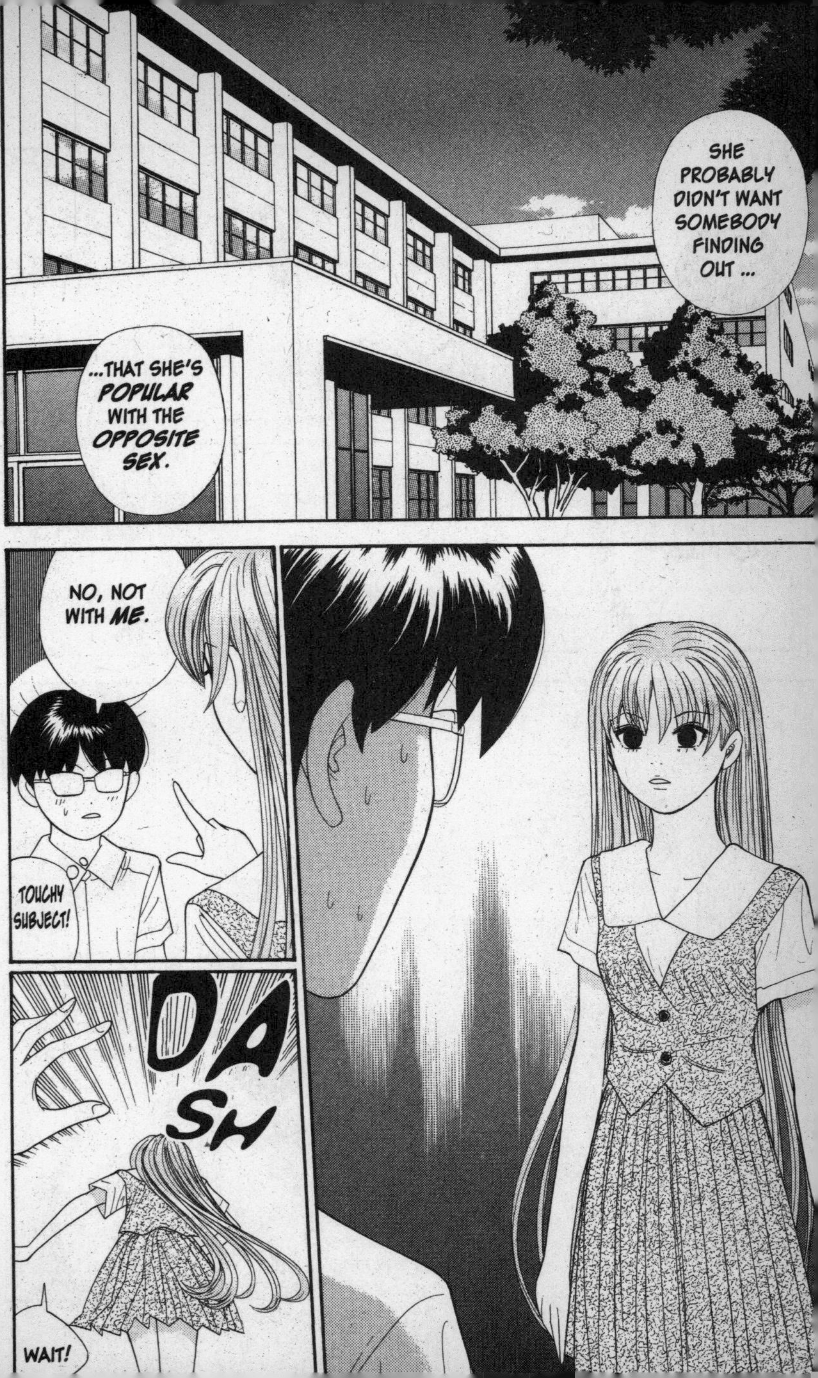
SHE PROBABLY DIDN'T WANT SOMEBODY FINDING OUT ...
...THAT SHE'S *POPULAR* WITH THE *OPPOSITE SEX*.
NO, NOT WITH *ME*.
TOUCHY SUBJECT!
DASH
WAIT!

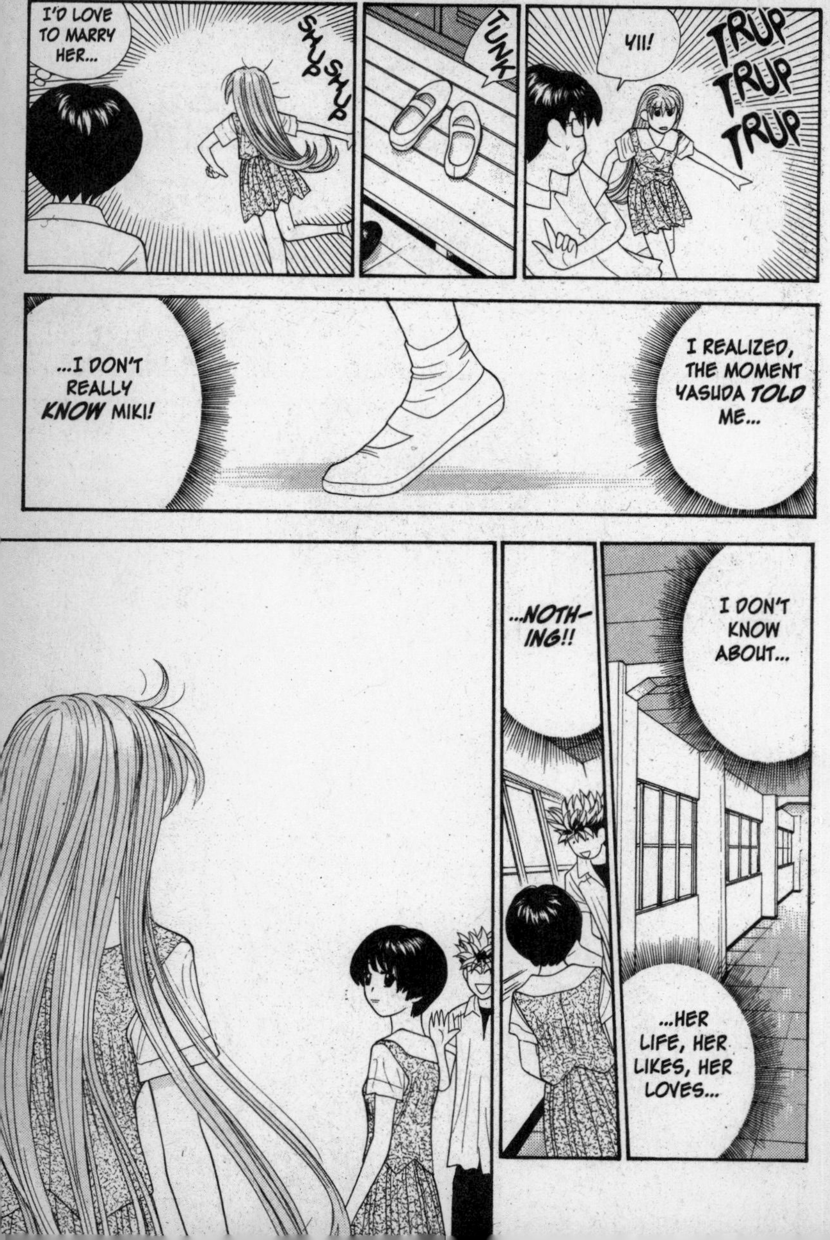
YII!
TRUP TRUP TRUP
TUNK
I'D LOVE TO MARRY HER...
SKUP SKUP
I REALIZED, THE MOMENT YASUDA *TOLD* ME...
...I DON'T REALLY *KNOW* MIKI!
I DON'T KNOW ABOUT...
...HER LIFE, HER LIKES, HER LOVES...
...*NOTHING!!*

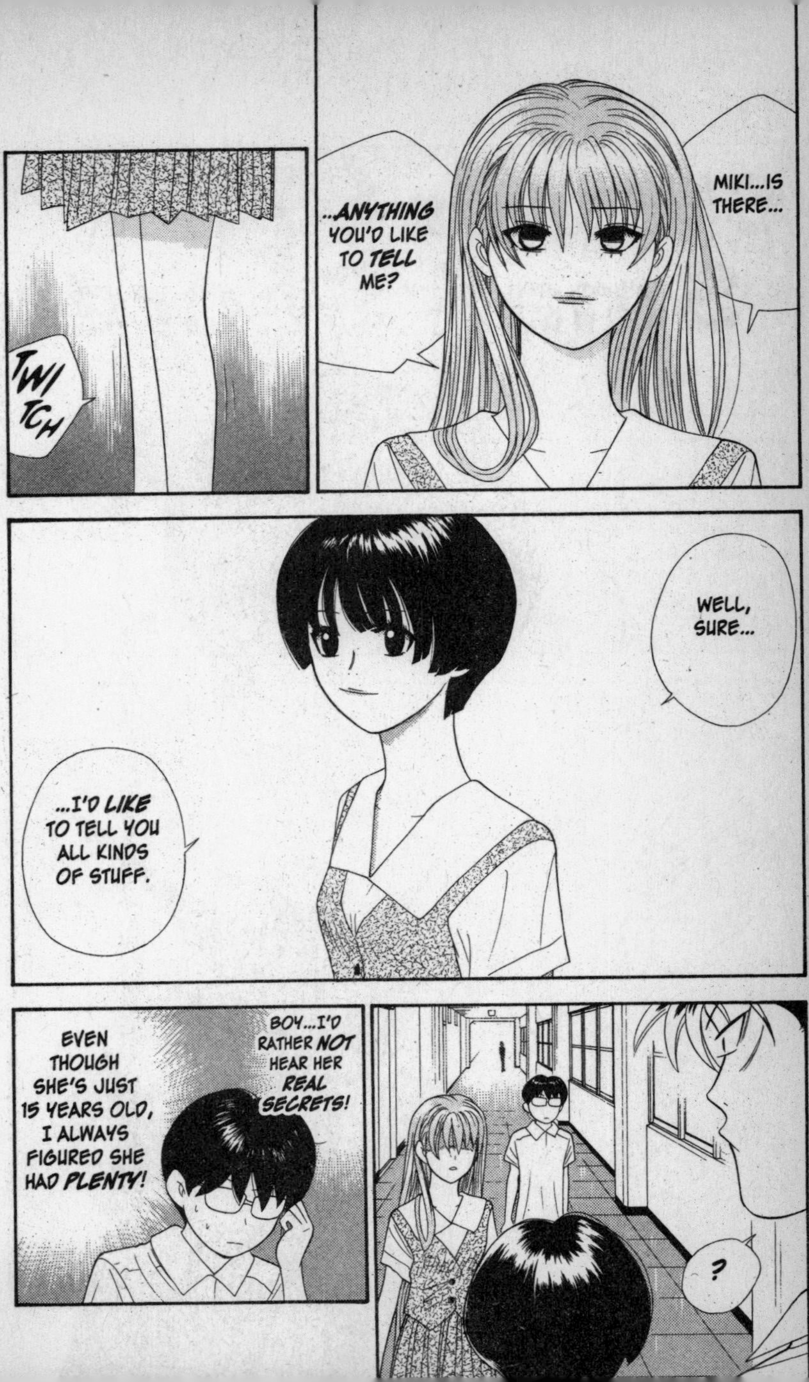
MIKI...IS THERE...
...ANYTHING YOU'D LIKE TO TELL ME?
TWITCH
WELL, SURE...
...I'D LIKE TO TELL YOU ALL KINDS OF STUFF.
?
BOY...I'D RATHER NOT HEAR HER REAL SECRETS!
EVEN THOUGH SHE'S JUST 15 YEARS OLD, I ALWAYS FIGURED SHE HAD PLENTY!

Chapter 67: Small Secret

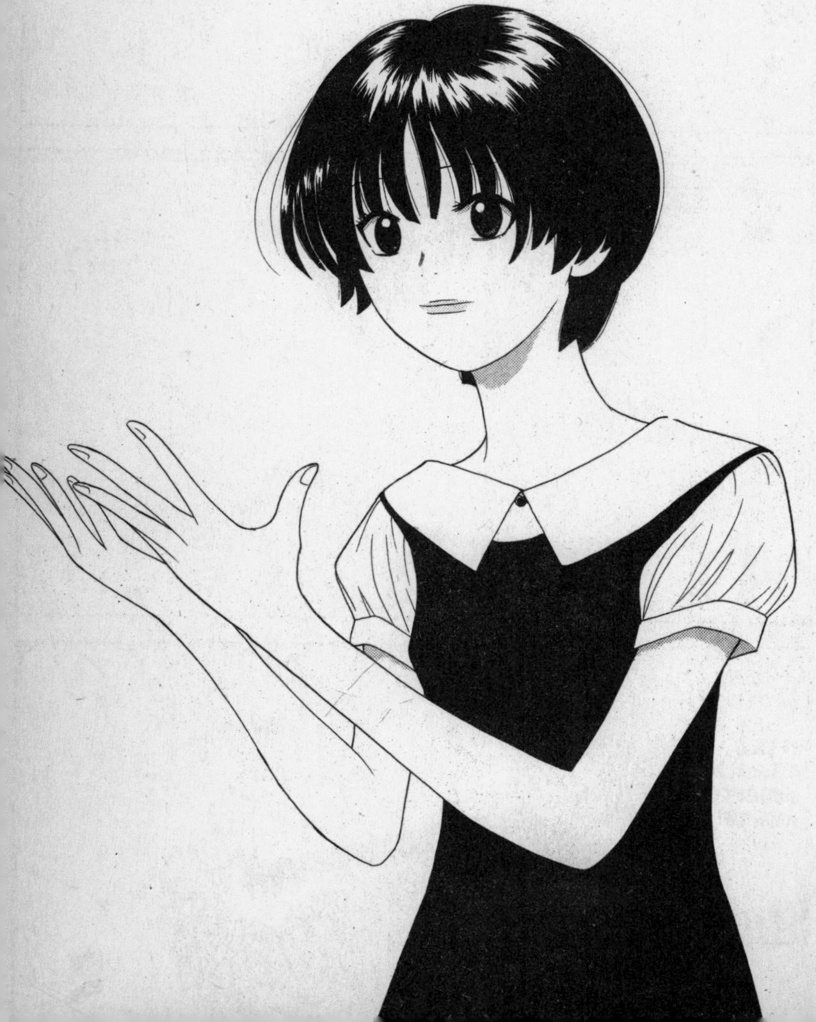

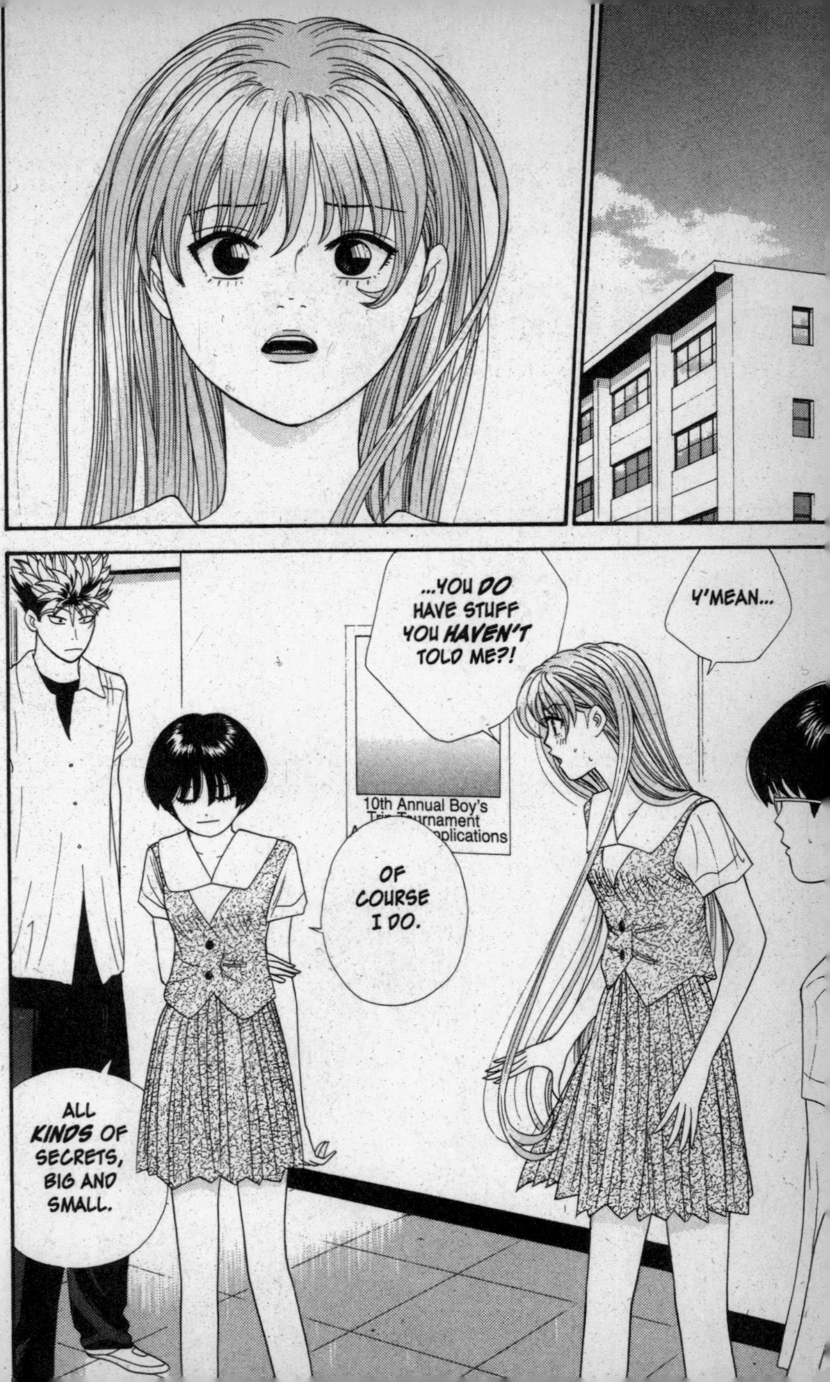
Y'MEAN...
...YOU DO HAVE STUFF YOU HAVEN'T TOLD ME?!
10th Annual Boy's
OF COURSE I DO.
ALL KINDS OF SECRETS, BIG AND SMALL.

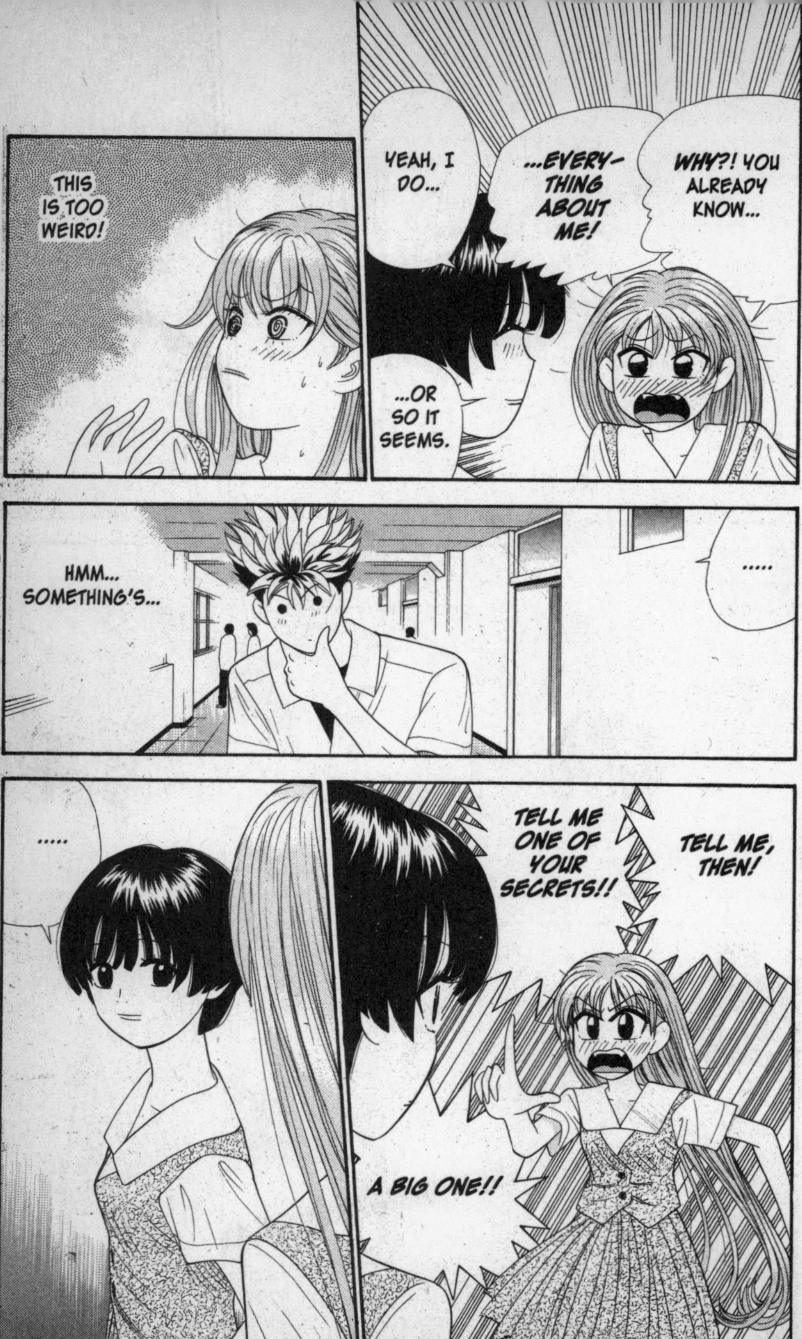
WHY?! YOU ALREADY KNOW...
...EVERY-THING ABOUT ME!
YEAH, I DO...
...OR SO IT SEEMS.
THIS IS TOO WEIRD!
.....
HMM... SOMETHING'S...
TELL ME, THEN!
TELL ME ONE OF YOUR SECRETS!!
A BIG ONE!!
.....

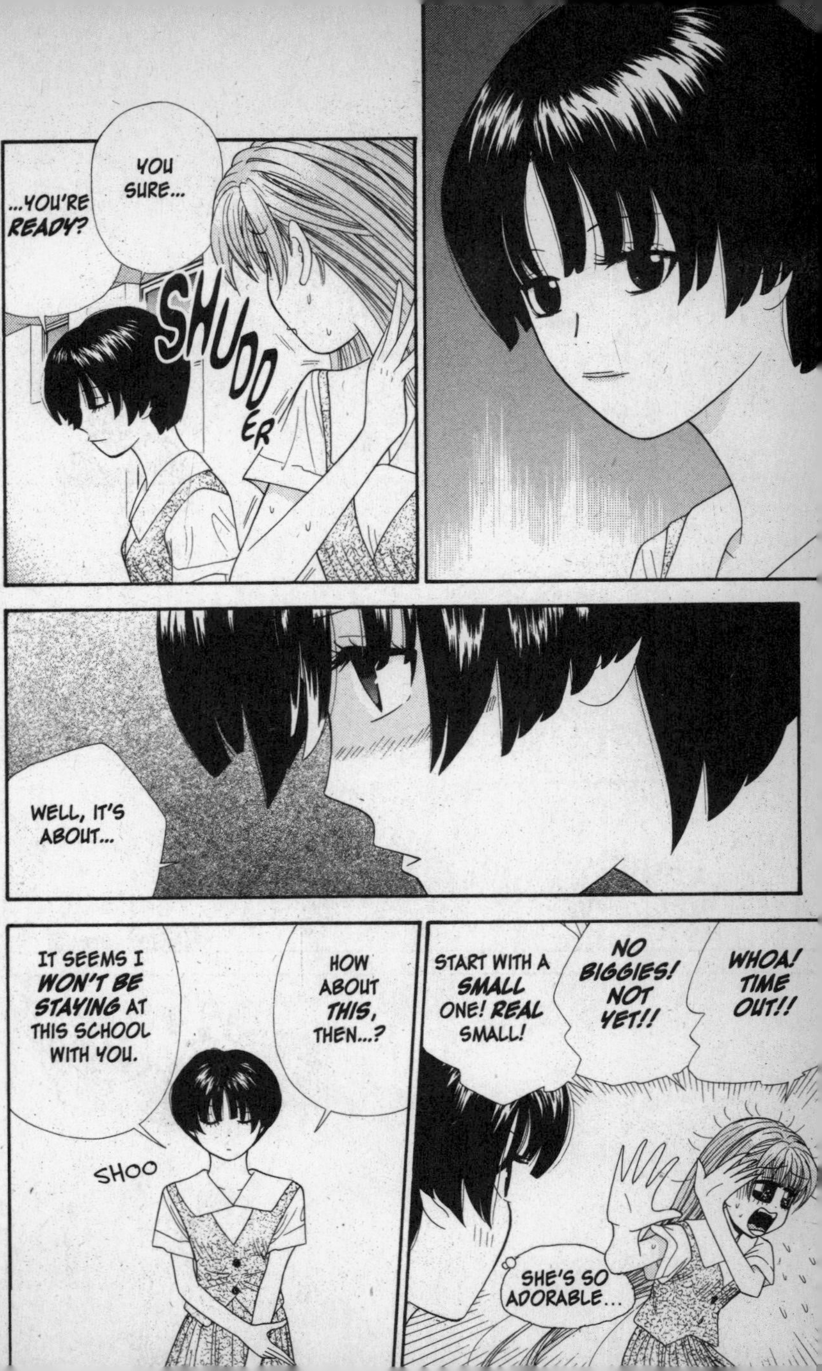
YOU SURE...
...YOU'RE READY?
SHUDDER
WELL, IT'S ABOUT...
WHOA! TIME OUT!!
NO BIGGIES! NOT YET!!
START WITH A SMALL ONE! REAL SMALL!
SHE'S SO ADORABLE...
HOW ABOUT THIS, THEN...?
IT SEEMS I WON'T BE STAYING AT THIS SCHOOL WITH YOU.
SHOO

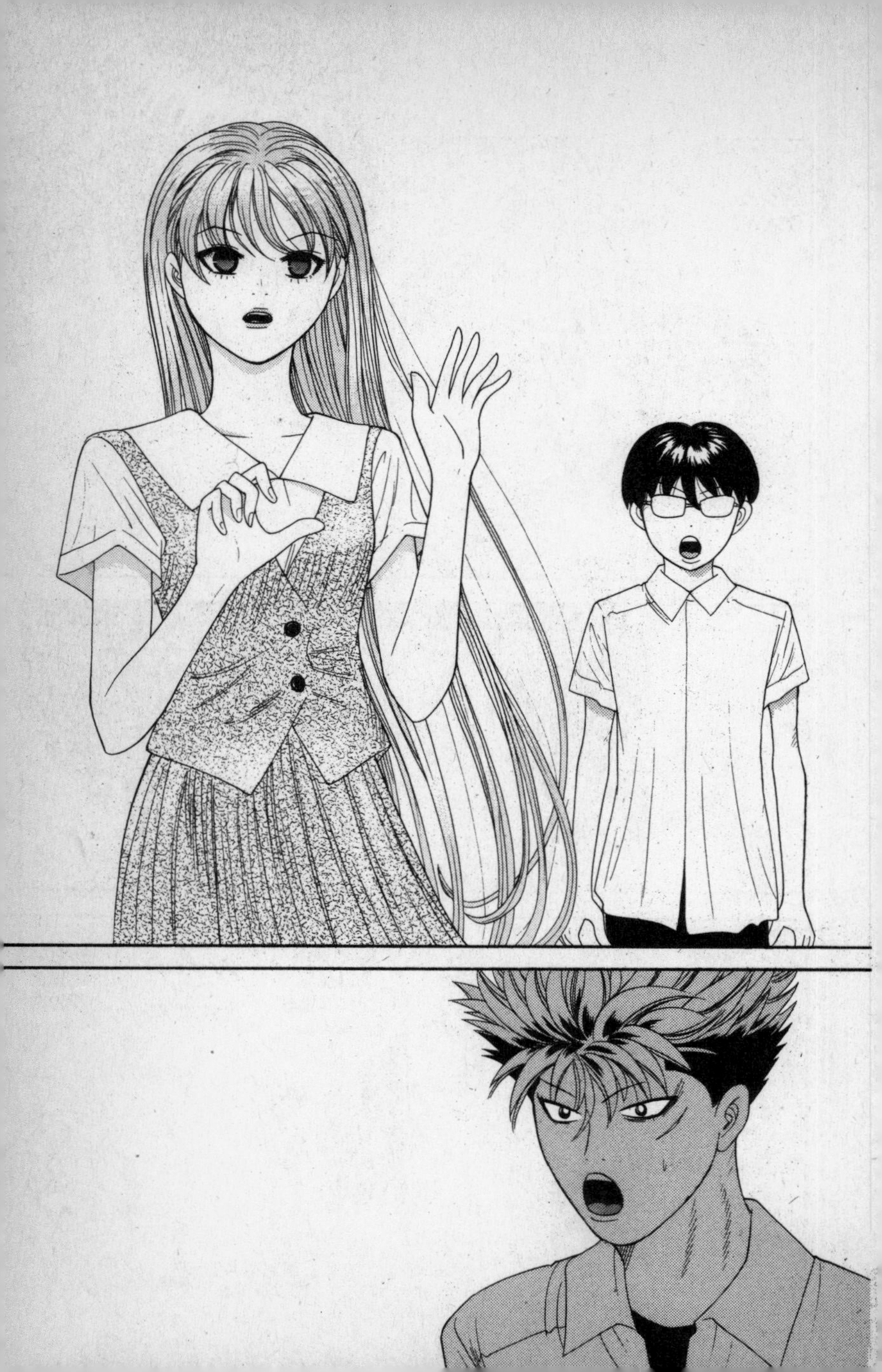

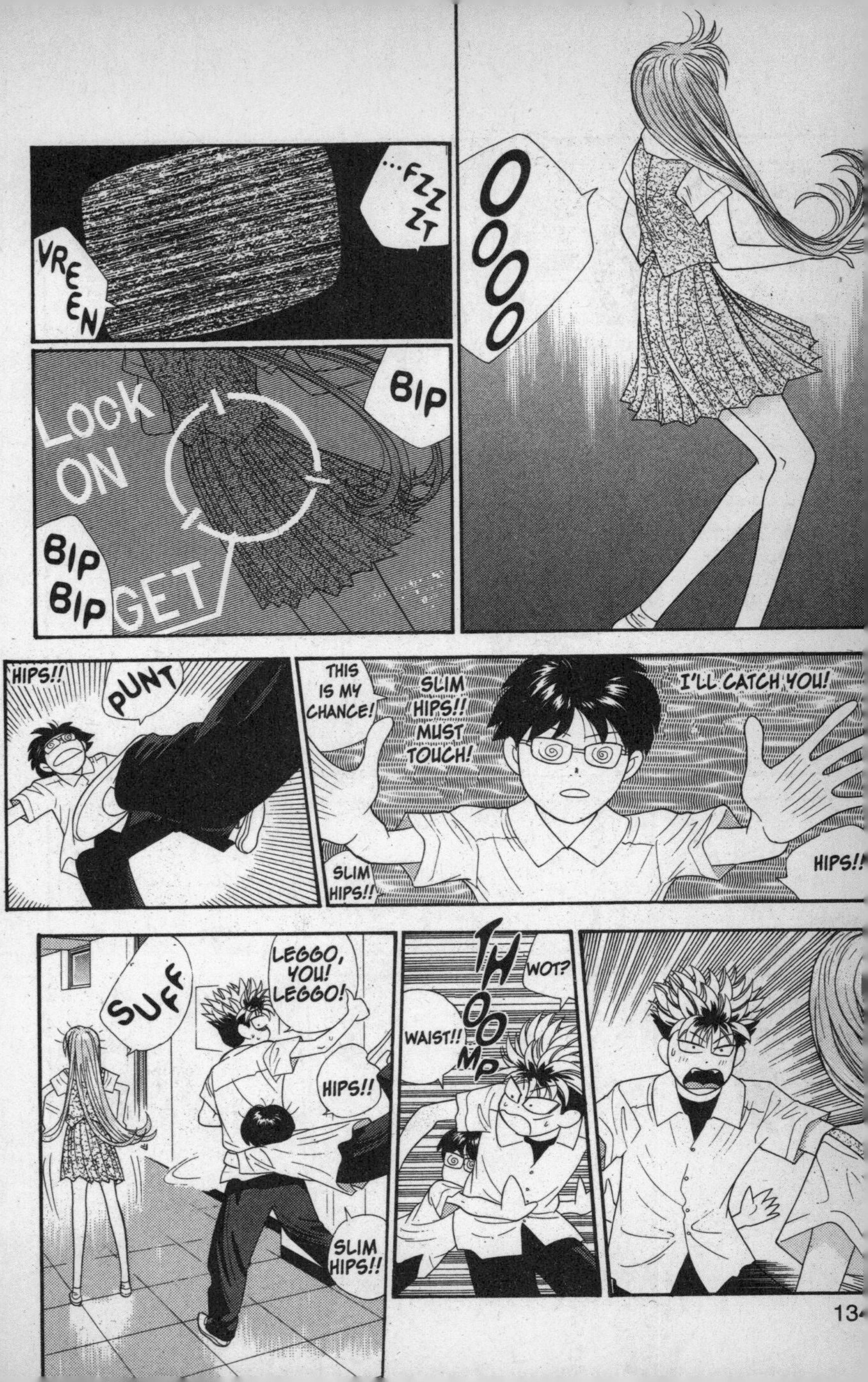
OOOO
...FZZZZT
VREEN
BIP
LOCK ON
BIP BIP
GET
I'LL CATCH YOU!
SLIM HIPS!! MUST TOUCH!
THIS IS MY CHANCE!
HIPS!!
SLIM HIPS!!
PUNT
HIPS!!
WOT?
THOOOMP
WAIST!!
LEGGO, YOU! LEGGO!
SUFF
HIPS!!
SLIM HIPS!!

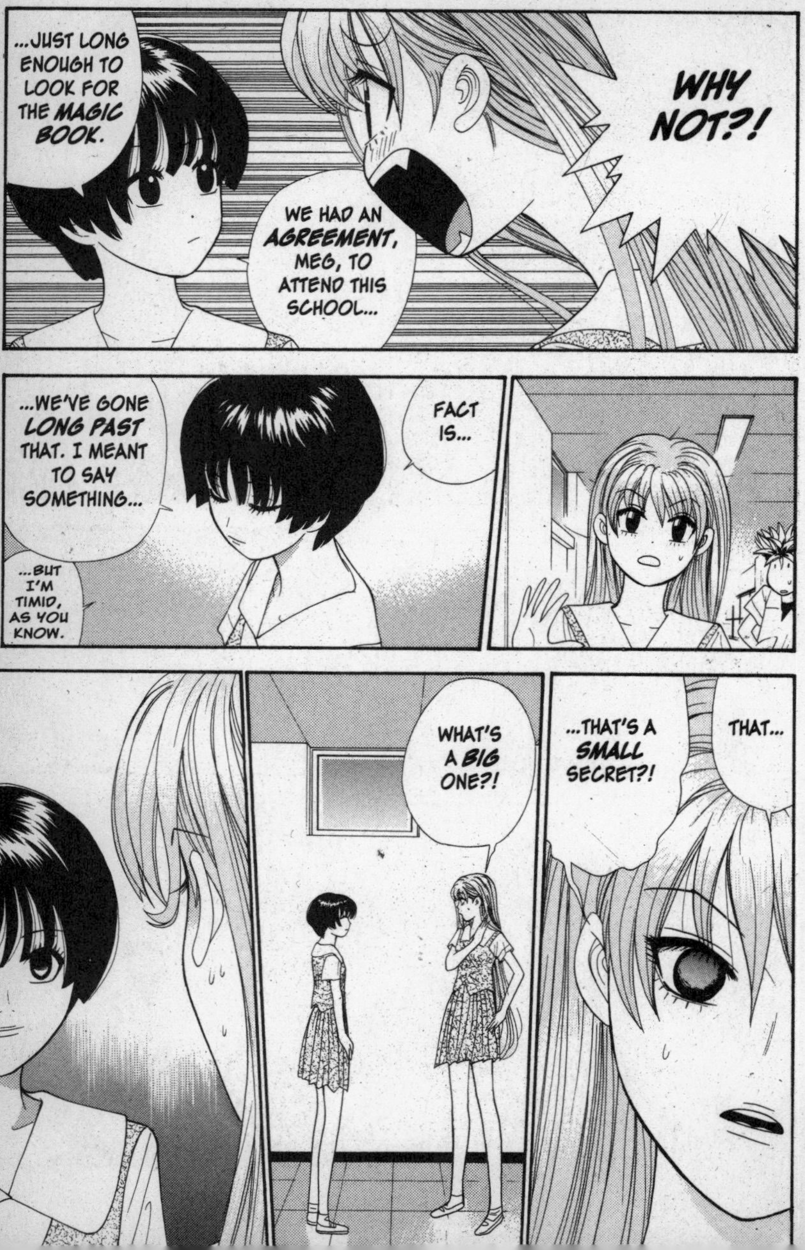
WHY NOT?!
WE HAD AN AGREEMENT, MEG, TO ATTEND THIS SCHOOL...
...JUST LONG ENOUGH TO LOOK FOR THE MAGIC BOOK.
FACT IS...
...WE'VE GONE LONG PAST THAT. I MEANT TO SAY SOMETHING...
...BUT I'M TIMID, AS YOU KNOW.
THAT...
...THAT'S A SMALL SECRET?!
WHAT'S A BIG ONE?!

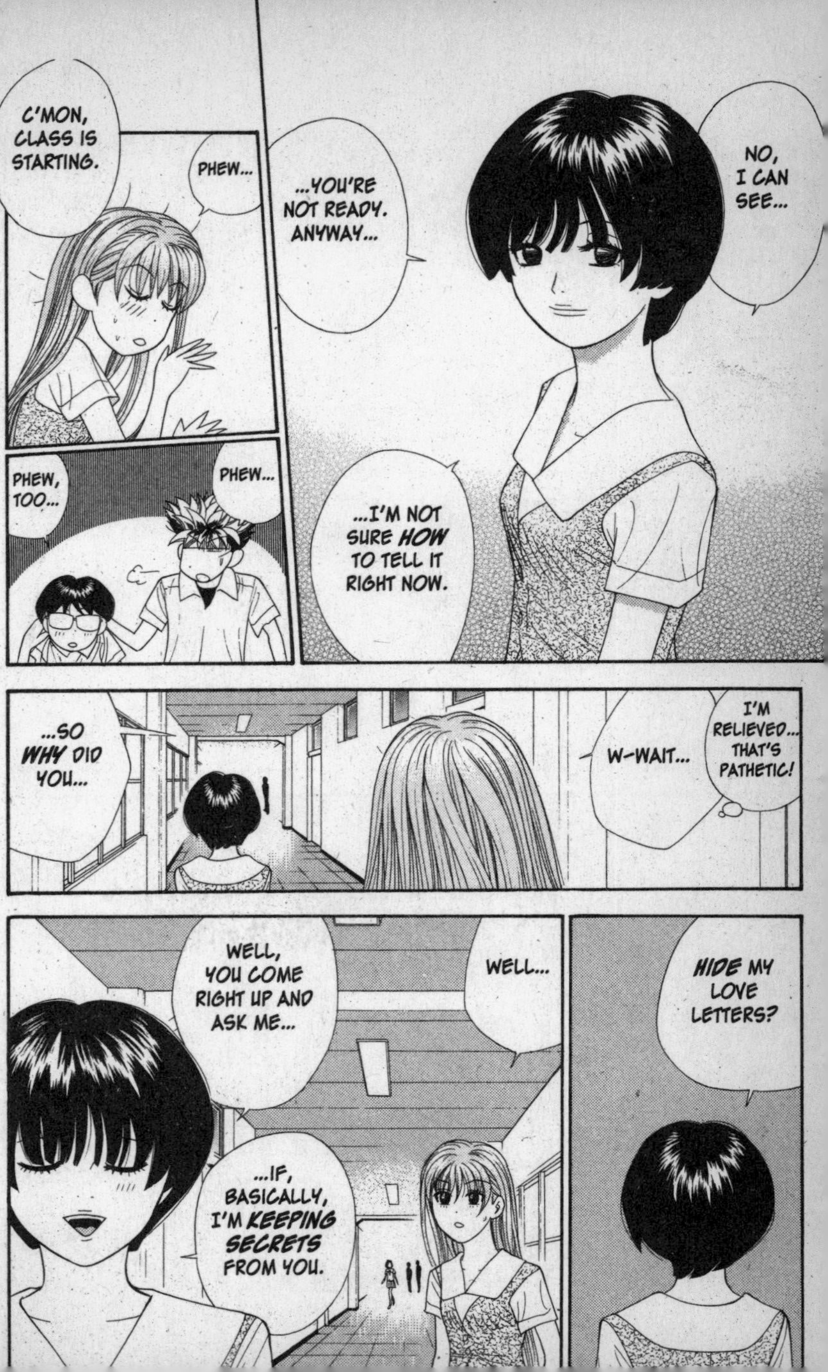
NO, I CAN SEE...
...YOU'RE NOT READY. ANYWAY...
...I'M NOT SURE *HOW* TO TELL IT RIGHT NOW.
PHEW...
C'MON, CLASS IS STARTING.
PHEW...
PHEW, TOO...
I'M RELIEVED... THAT'S PATHETIC!
W-WAIT...
...SO *WHY* DID YOU...
HIDE MY LOVE LETTERS?
WELL...
WELL, YOU COME RIGHT UP AND ASK ME...
...IF, BASICALLY, I'M *KEEPING SECRETS* FROM YOU.

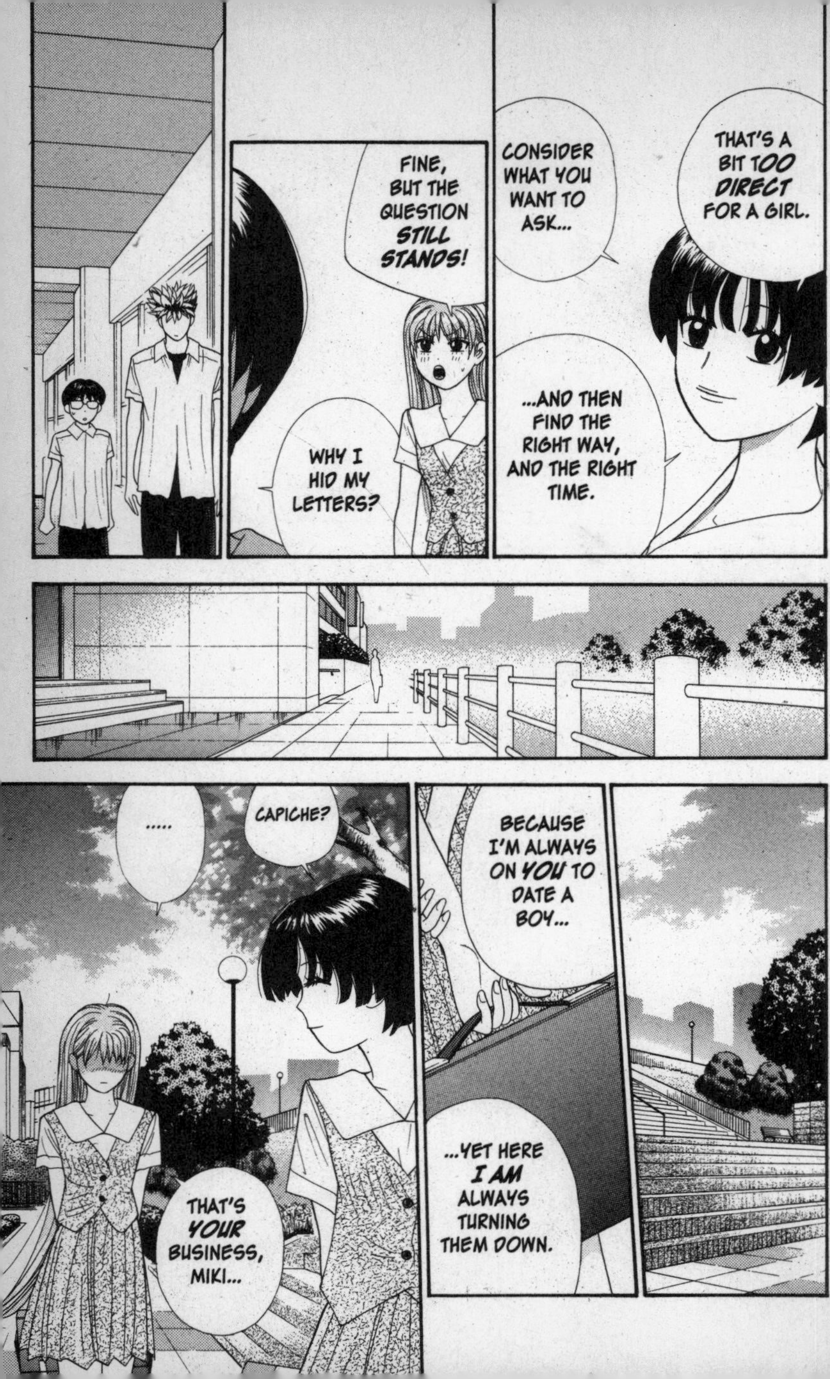
THAT'S A BIT TOO DIRECT FOR A GIRL.
CONSIDER WHAT YOU WANT TO ASK...
...AND THEN FIND THE RIGHT WAY, AND THE RIGHT TIME.
FINE, BUT THE QUESTION STILL STANDS!
WHY I HID MY LETTERS?
BECAUSE I'M ALWAYS ON YOU TO DATE A BOY...
...YET HERE I AM ALWAYS TURNING THEM DOWN.
CAPICHE?
.....
THAT'S YOUR BUSINESS, MIKI...

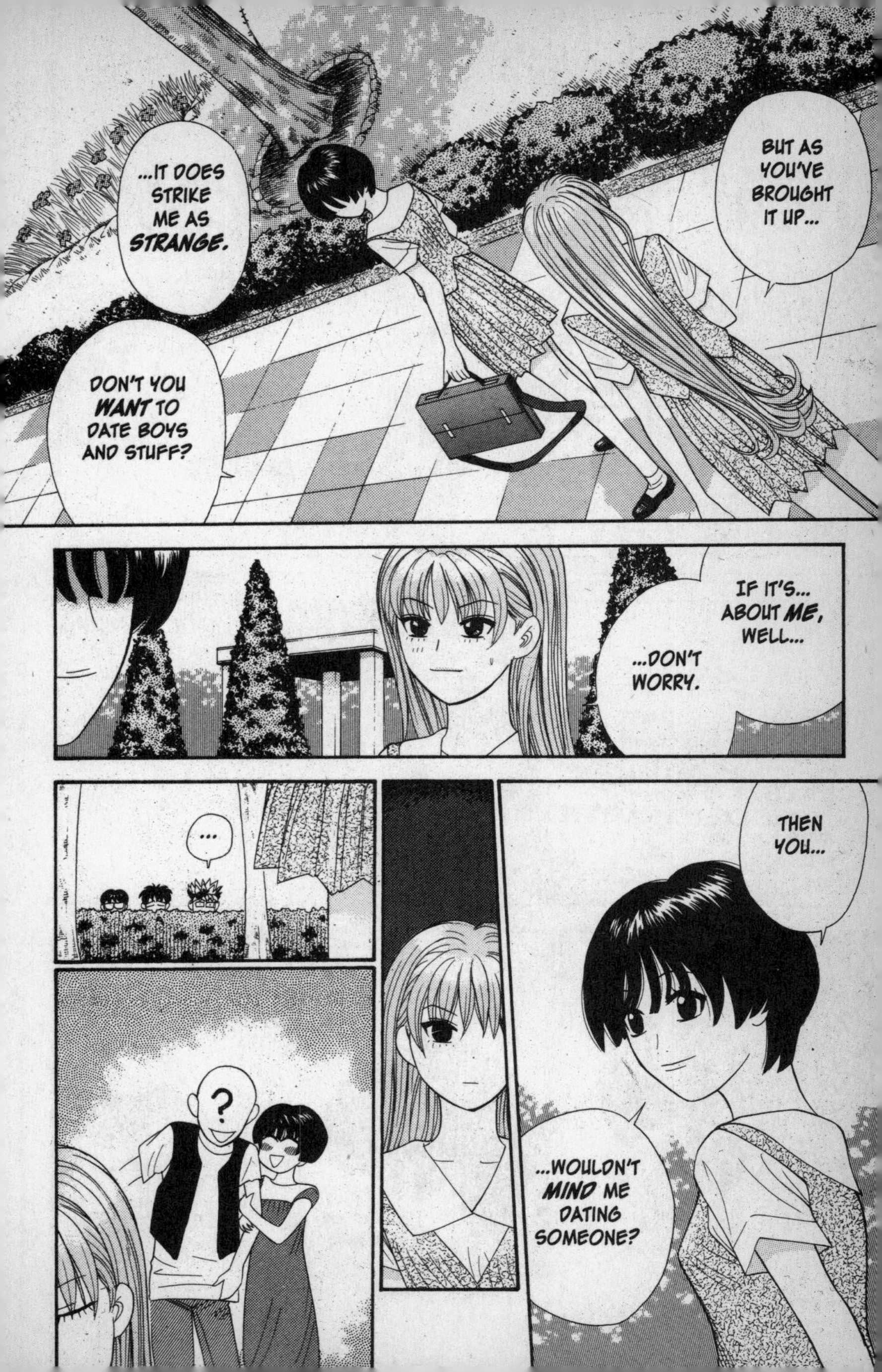
BUT AS YOU'VE BROUGHT IT UP...
...IT DOES STRIKE ME AS STRANGE.
DON'T YOU WANT TO DATE BOYS AND STUFF?
IF IT'S... ABOUT ME, WELL...
...DON'T WORRY.
THEN YOU...
...WOULDN'T MIND ME DATING SOMEONE?
...
?

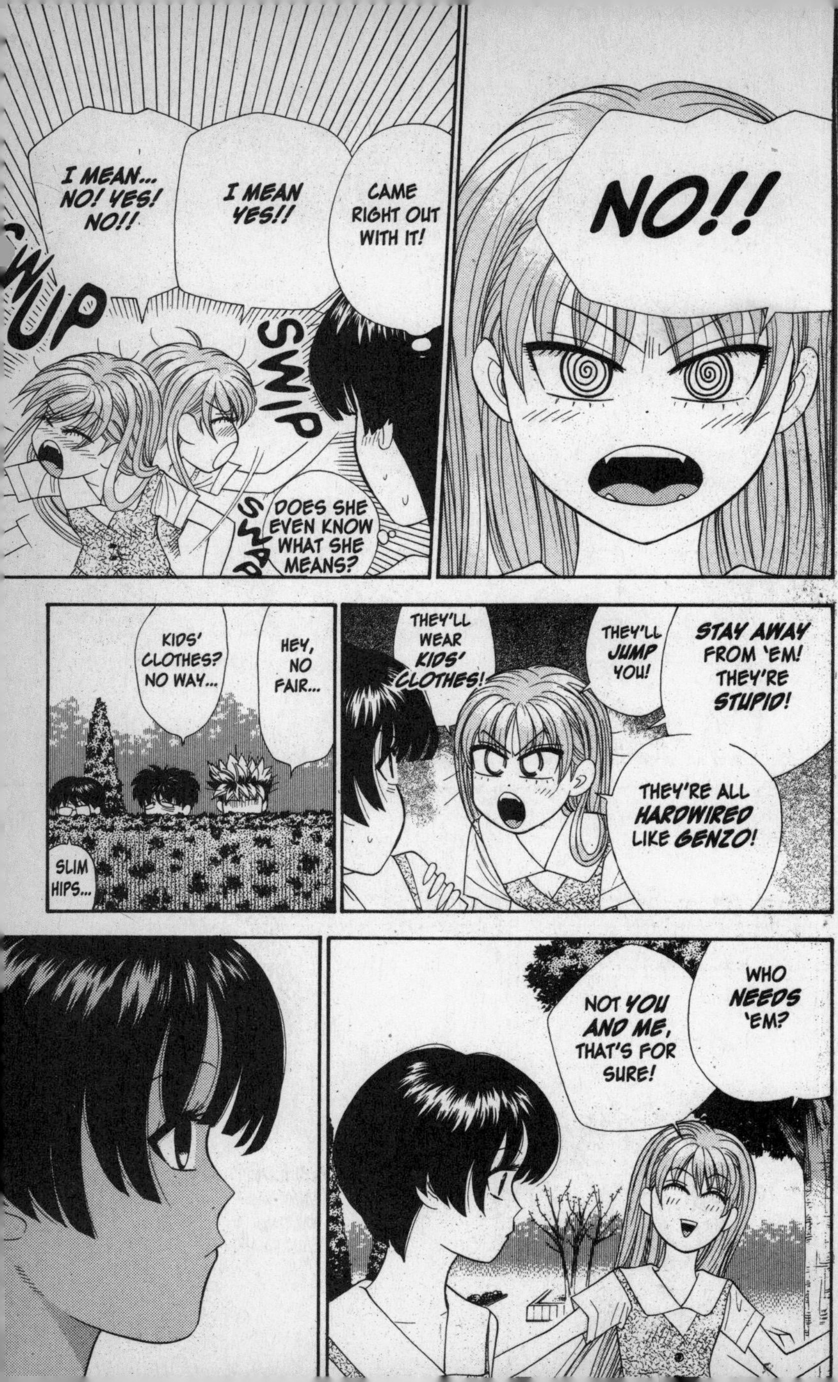
NO!!
CAME RIGHT OUT WITH IT!
I MEAN YES!!
I MEAN... NO! YES! NO!!
SWUP
SWIP
DOES SHE EVEN KNOW WHAT SHE MEANS?
STAY AWAY FROM 'EM! THEY'RE STUPID!
THEY'LL JUMP YOU!
THEY'LL WEAR KIDS' CLOTHES!
THEY'RE ALL HARDWIRED LIKE GENZO!
HEY, NO FAIR...
KIDS' CLOTHES? NO WAY...
SLIM HIPS...
WHO NEEDS 'EM?
NOT YOU AND ME, THAT'S FOR SURE!

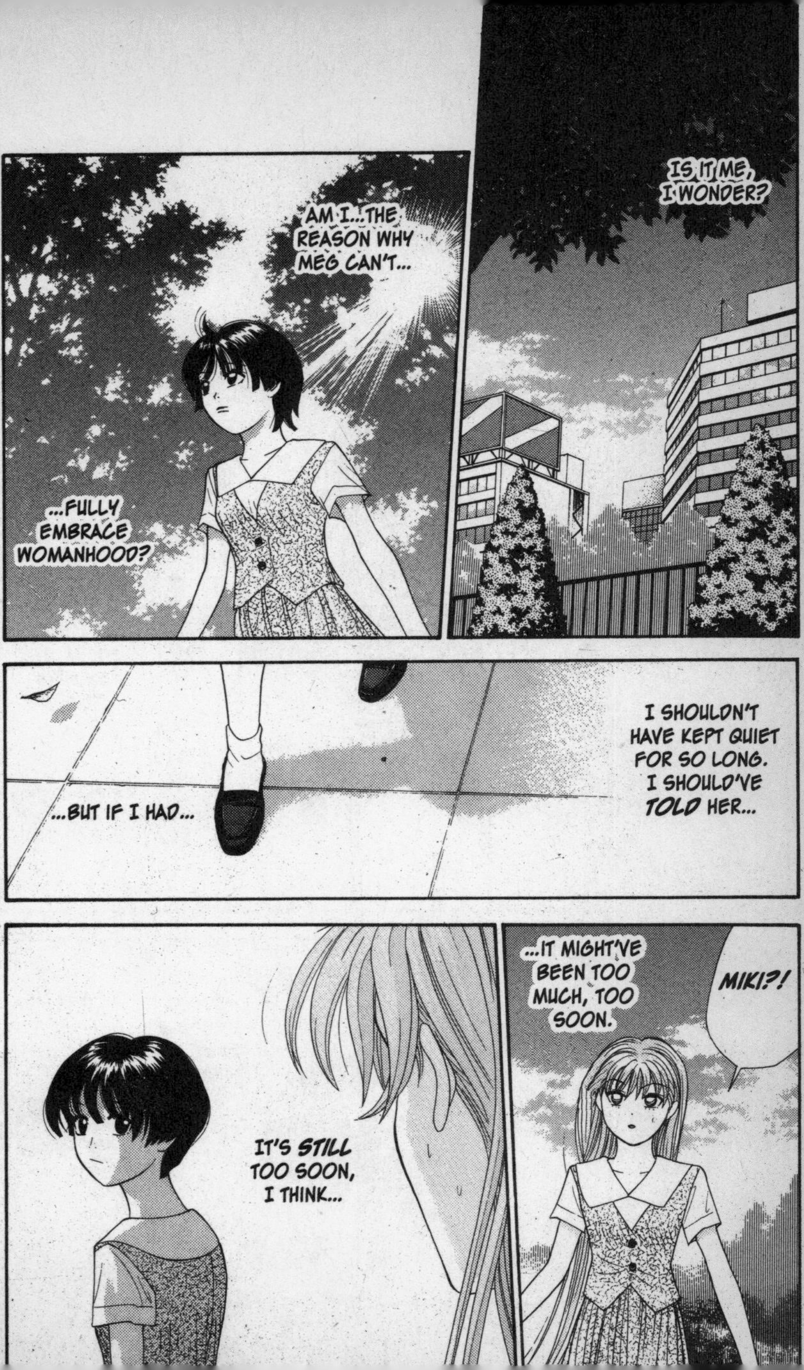
IS IT ME, I WONDER?
AM I...THE REASON WHY MEG CAN'T...
...FULLY EMBRACE WOMANHOOD?
I SHOULDN'T HAVE KEPT QUIET FOR SO LONG. I SHOULD'VE *TOLD* HER...
...BUT IF I HAD...
MIKI?!
...IT MIGHT'VE BEEN TOO MUCH, TOO SOON.
IT'S *STILL* TOO SOON, I THINK...

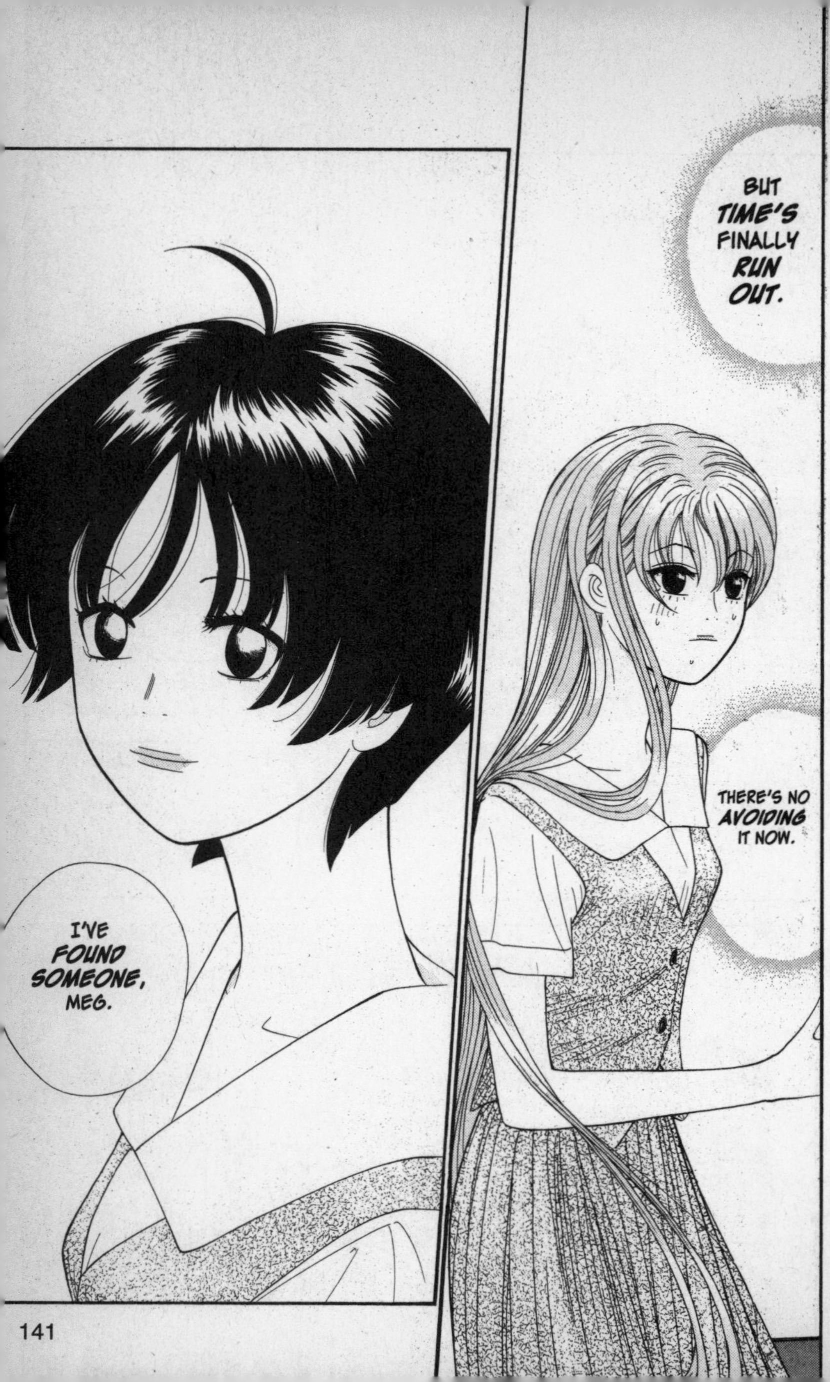
BUT TIME'S FINALLY RUN OUT.
THERE'S NO AVOIDING IT NOW.
I'VE FOUND SOMEONE, MEG.

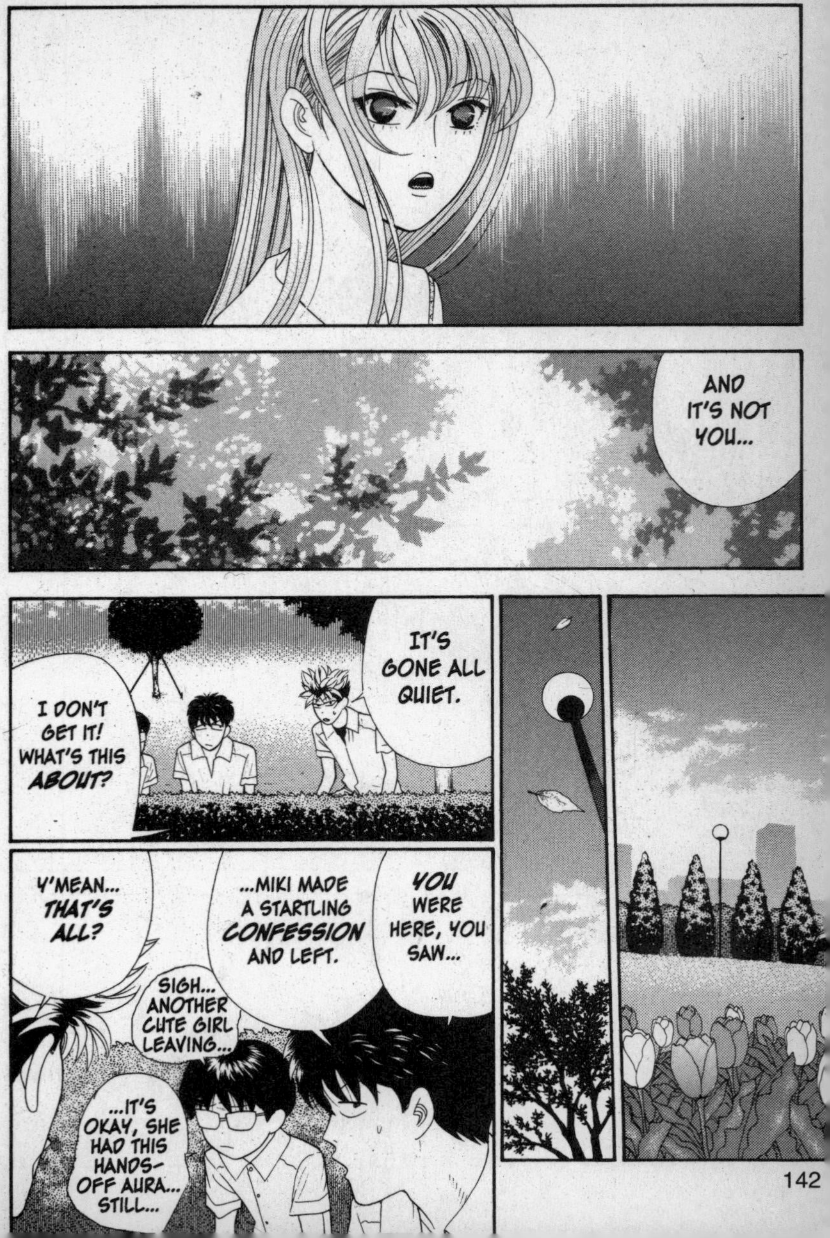
AND IT'S NOT YOU...
IT'S GONE ALL QUIET.
I DON'T GET IT! WHAT'S THIS *ABOUT?*
YOU WERE HERE, YOU SAW...
...MIKI MADE A STARTLING *CONFESSION* AND LEFT.
Y'MEAN... *THAT'S ALL?*
SIGH... ANOTHER CUTE GIRL LEAVING...
...IT'S OKAY, SHE HAD THIS HANDS-OFF AURA... STILL...

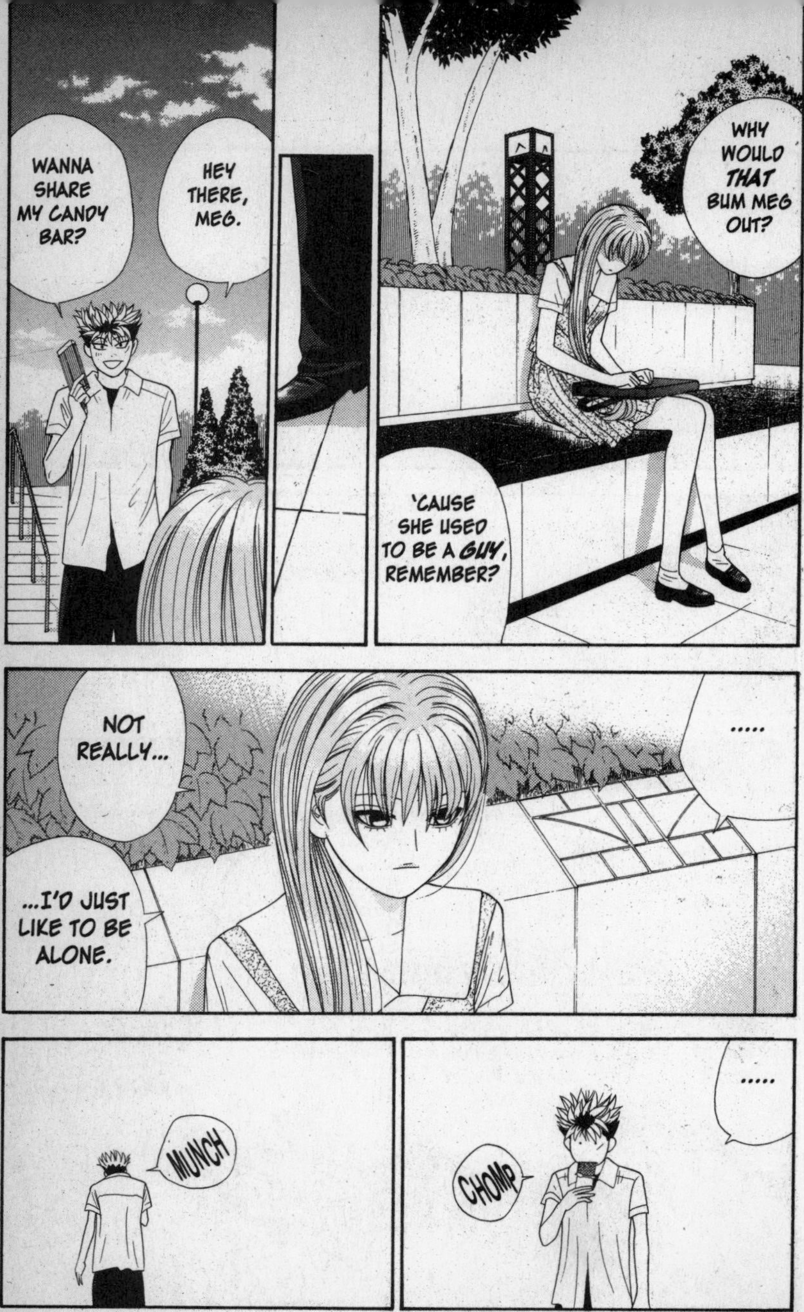
WHY WOULD *THAT* BUM MEG OUT?
'CAUSE SHE USED TO BE A *GUY*, REMEMBER?
HEY THERE, MEG.
WANNA SHARE MY CANDY BAR?
.....
NOT REALLY...
...I'D JUST LIKE TO BE ALONE.
.....
CHOMP
MUNCH

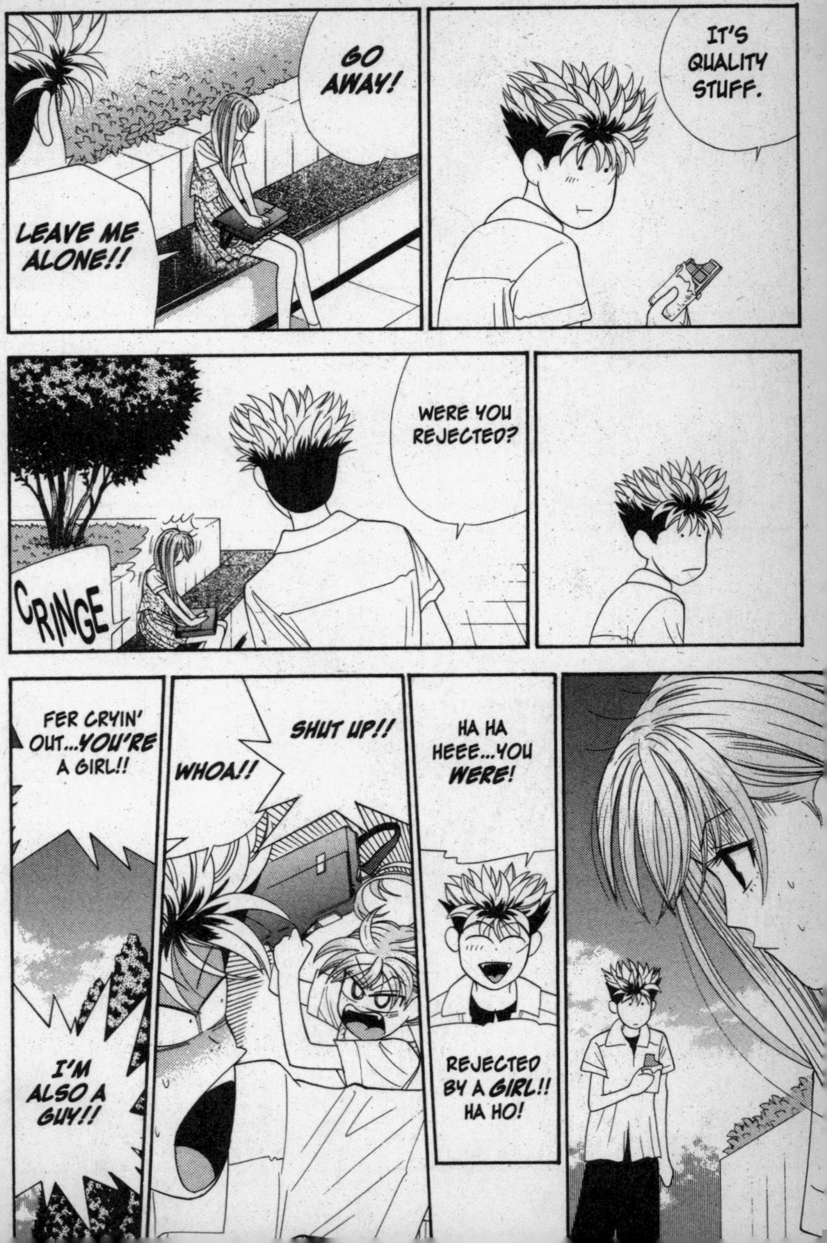
IT'S QUALITY STUFF.
GO AWAY!
LEAVE ME ALONE!!
WERE YOU REJECTED?
CRINGE
HA HA HEEE...YOU WERE!
REJECTED BY A GIRL!! HA HO!
SHUT UP!!
WHOA!!
FER CRYIN' OUT...YOU'RE A GIRL!!
I'M ALSO A GUY!!

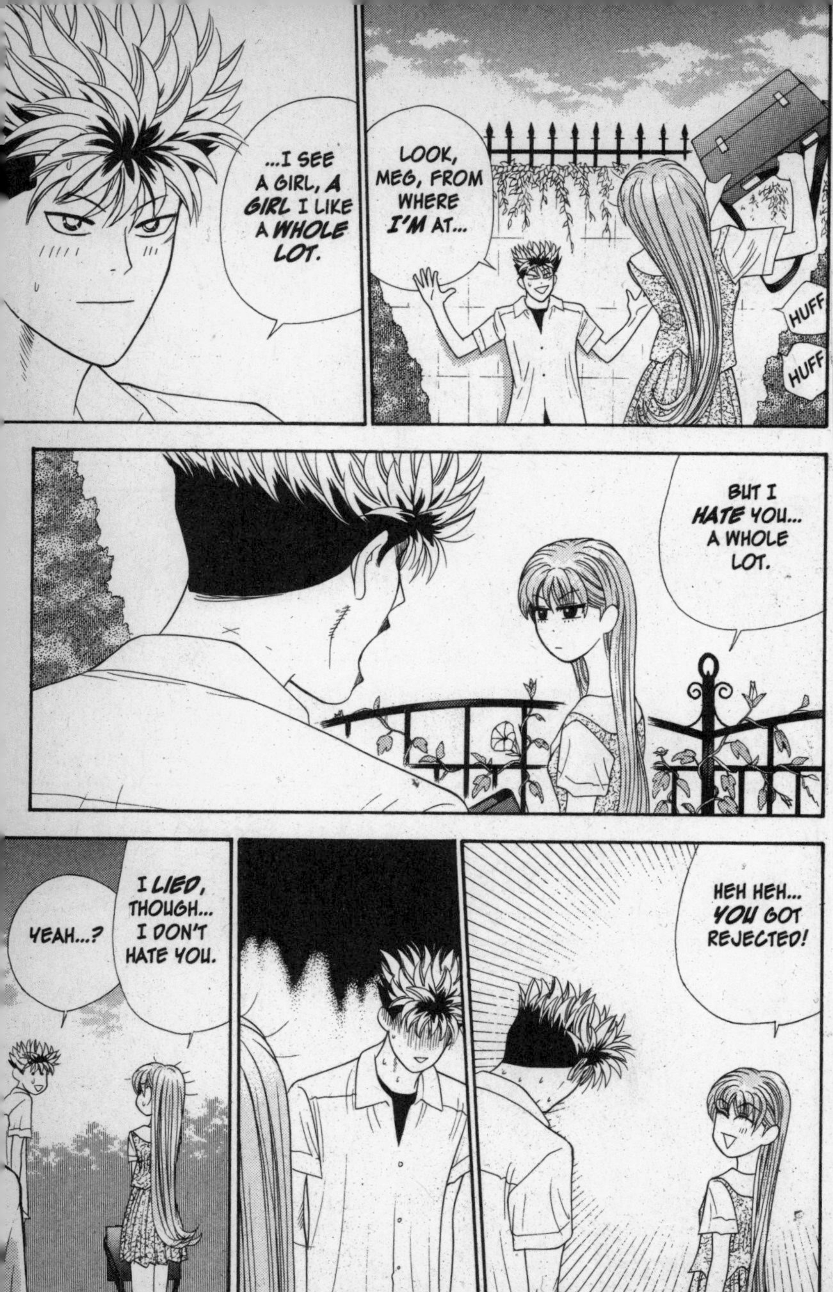
LOOK, MEG, FROM WHERE I'M AT...
HUFF
HUFF
...I SEE A GIRL, A GIRL I LIKE A WHOLE LOT.
BUT I HATE YOU... A WHOLE LOT.
HEH HEH... YOU GOT REJECTED!
I LIED, THOUGH... I DON'T HATE YOU.
YEAH...?

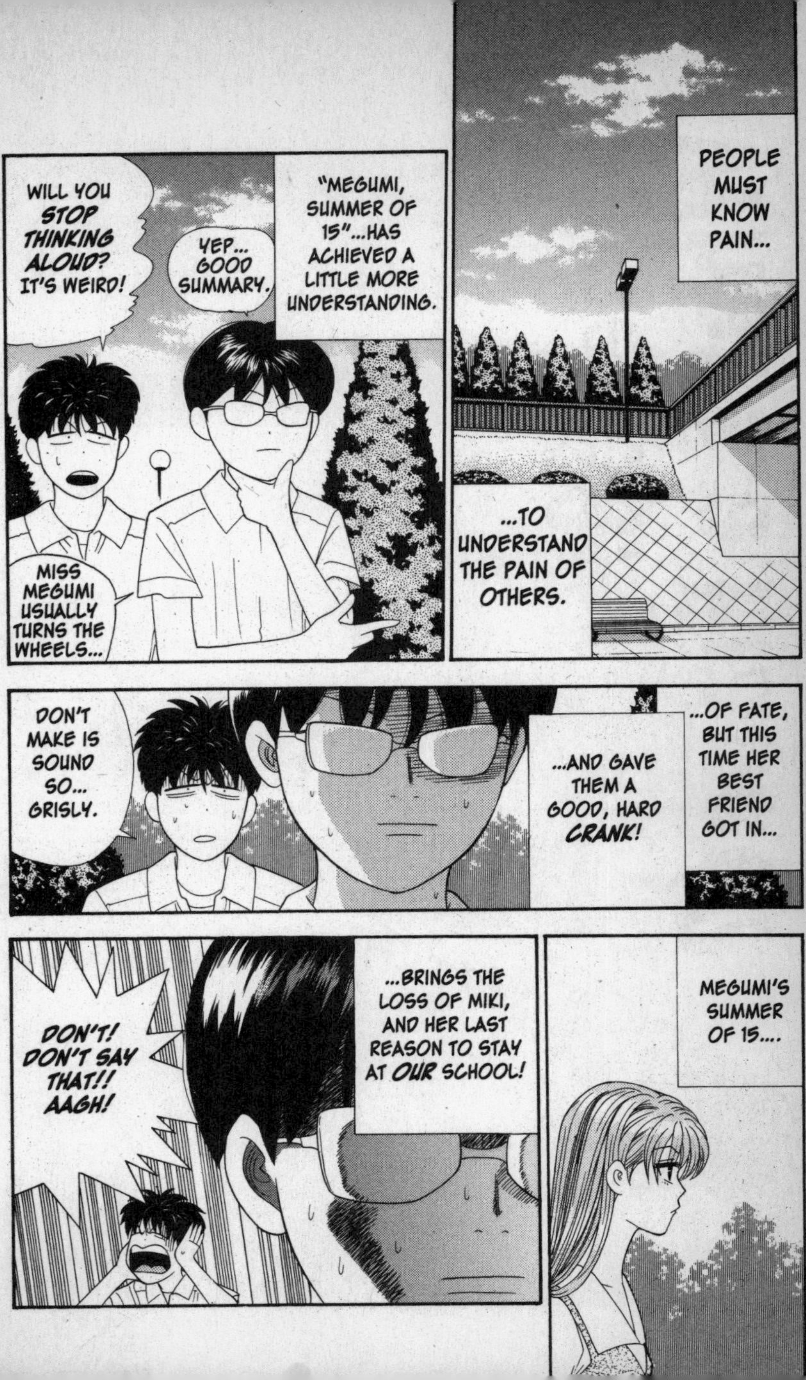
PEOPLE MUST KNOW PAIN...
...TO UNDERSTAND THE PAIN OF OTHERS.
"MEGUMI, SUMMER OF 15"...HAS ACHIEVED A LITTLE MORE UNDERSTANDING.
YEP... GOOD SUMMARY.
WILL YOU STOP THINKING ALOUD? IT'S WEIRD!
MISS MEGUMI USUALLY TURNS THE WHEELS...
...OF FATE, BUT THIS TIME HER BEST FRIEND GOT IN...
...AND GAVE THEM A GOOD, HARD CRANK!
DON'T MAKE IS SOUND SO... GRISLY.
MEGUMI'S SUMMER OF 15....
...BRINGS THE LOSS OF MIKI, AND HER LAST REASON TO STAY AT OUR SCHOOL!
DON'T! DON'T SAY THAT!! AAGH!

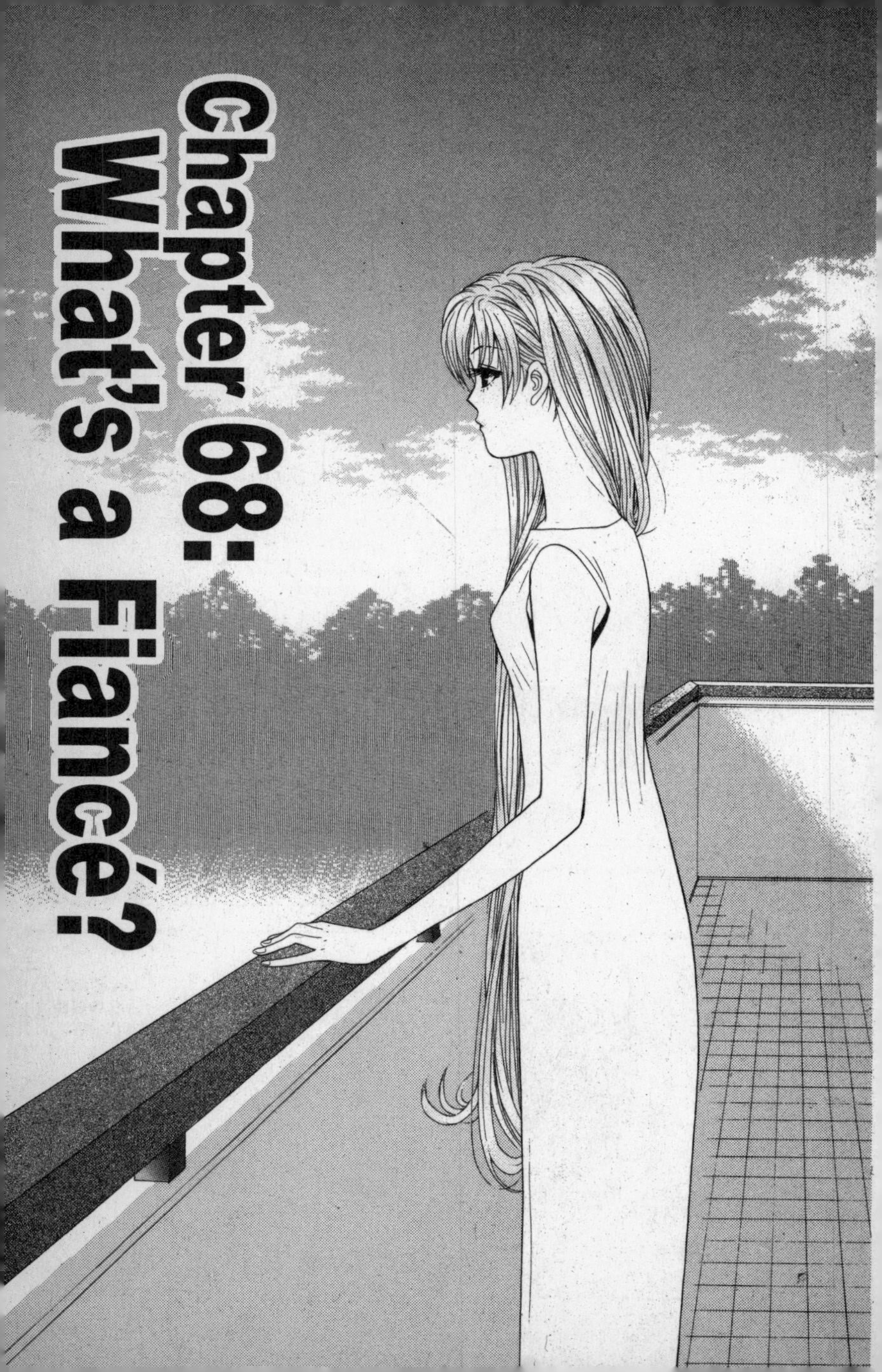
Chapter 68:
What's a Fiancé?

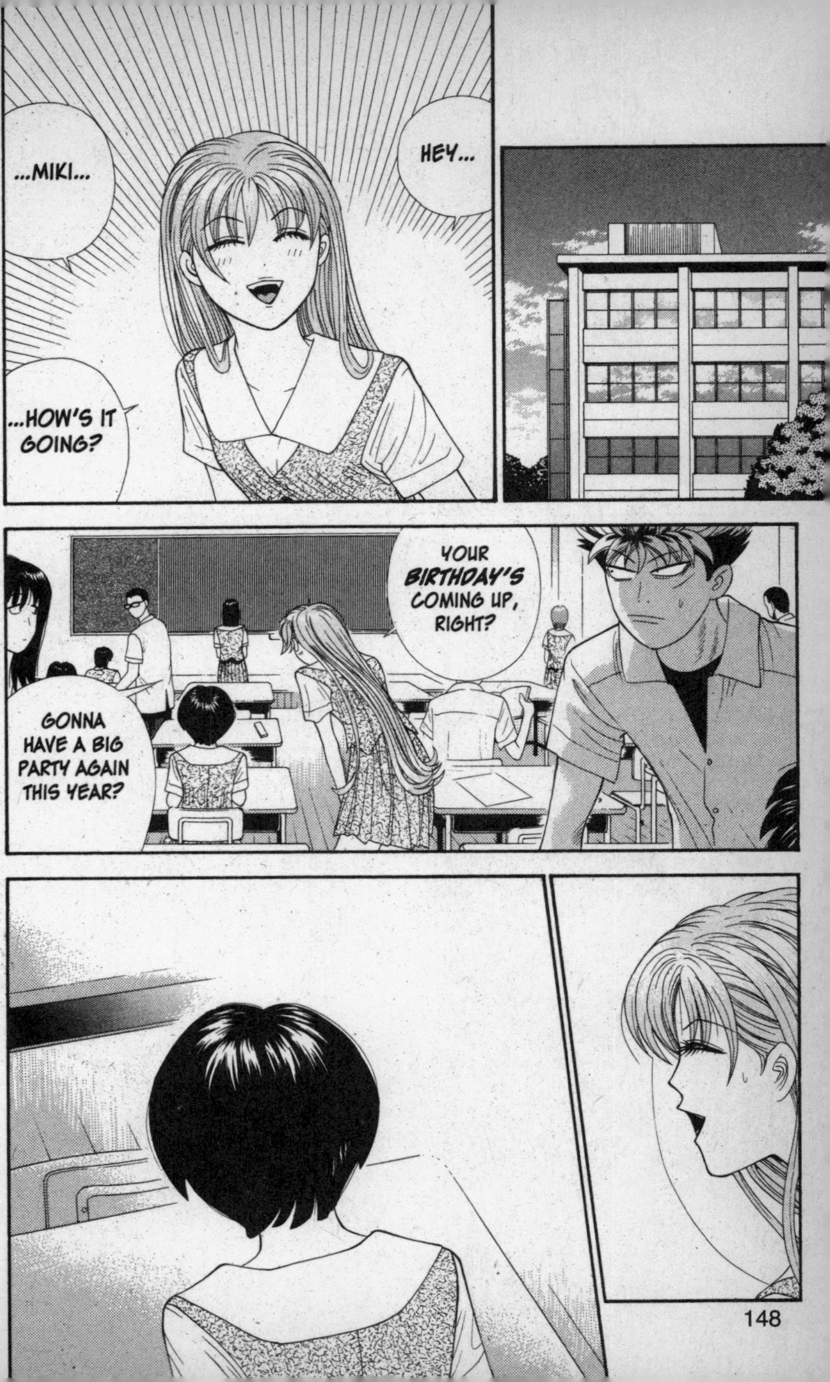
HEY...
...MIKI...
...HOW'S IT GOING?
YOUR BIRTHDAY'S COMING UP, RIGHT?
GONNA HAVE A BIG PARTY AGAIN THIS YEAR?

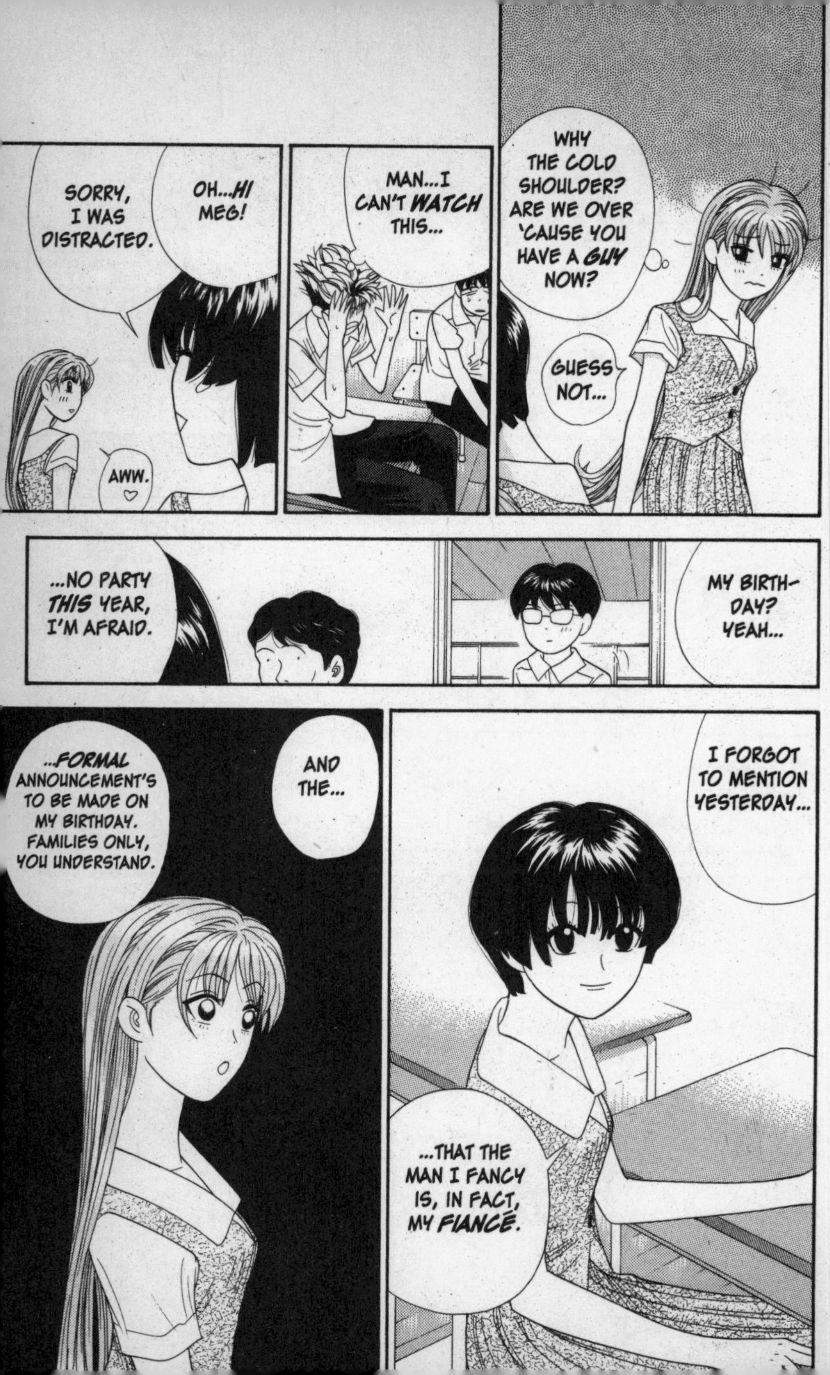
WHY THE COLD SHOULDER? ARE WE OVER 'CAUSE YOU HAVE A GUY NOW?
GUESS NOT...
MAN...I CAN'T WATCH THIS...
OH...HI MEG!
SORRY, I WAS DISTRACTED.
AWW. ♡
MY BIRTH-DAY? YEAH...
...NO PARTY THIS YEAR, I'M AFRAID.
I FORGOT TO MENTION YESTERDAY...
...THAT THE MAN I FANCY IS, IN FACT, MY FIANCÉ.
AND THE...
...FORMAL ANNOUNCEMENT'S TO BE MADE ON MY BIRTHDAY. FAMILIES ONLY, YOU UNDERSTAND.

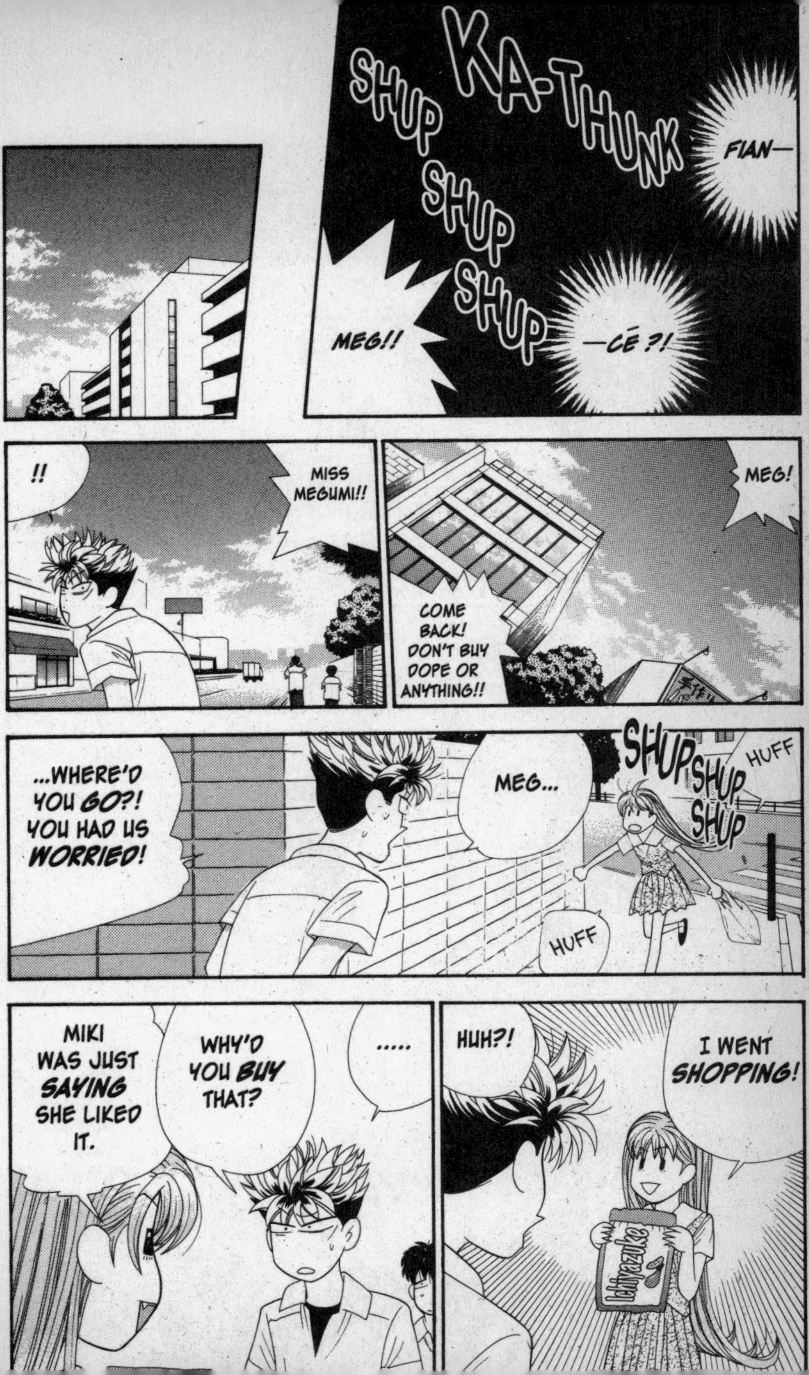
KA-THUNK
FIAN—
SHUP SHUP SHUP SHUP
—CÉ ?!
MEG!!
MEG!
COME BACK! DON'T BUY DOPE OR ANYTHING!!
MISS MEGUMI!!
!!
HUFF
SHUP SHUP SHUP
MEG...
HUFF
...WHERE'D YOU GO?! YOU HAD US WORRIED!
I WENT SHOPPING!
Ichiyazuke
HUH?!
.....
WHY'D YOU BUY THAT?
MIKI WAS JUST SAYING SHE LIKED IT.

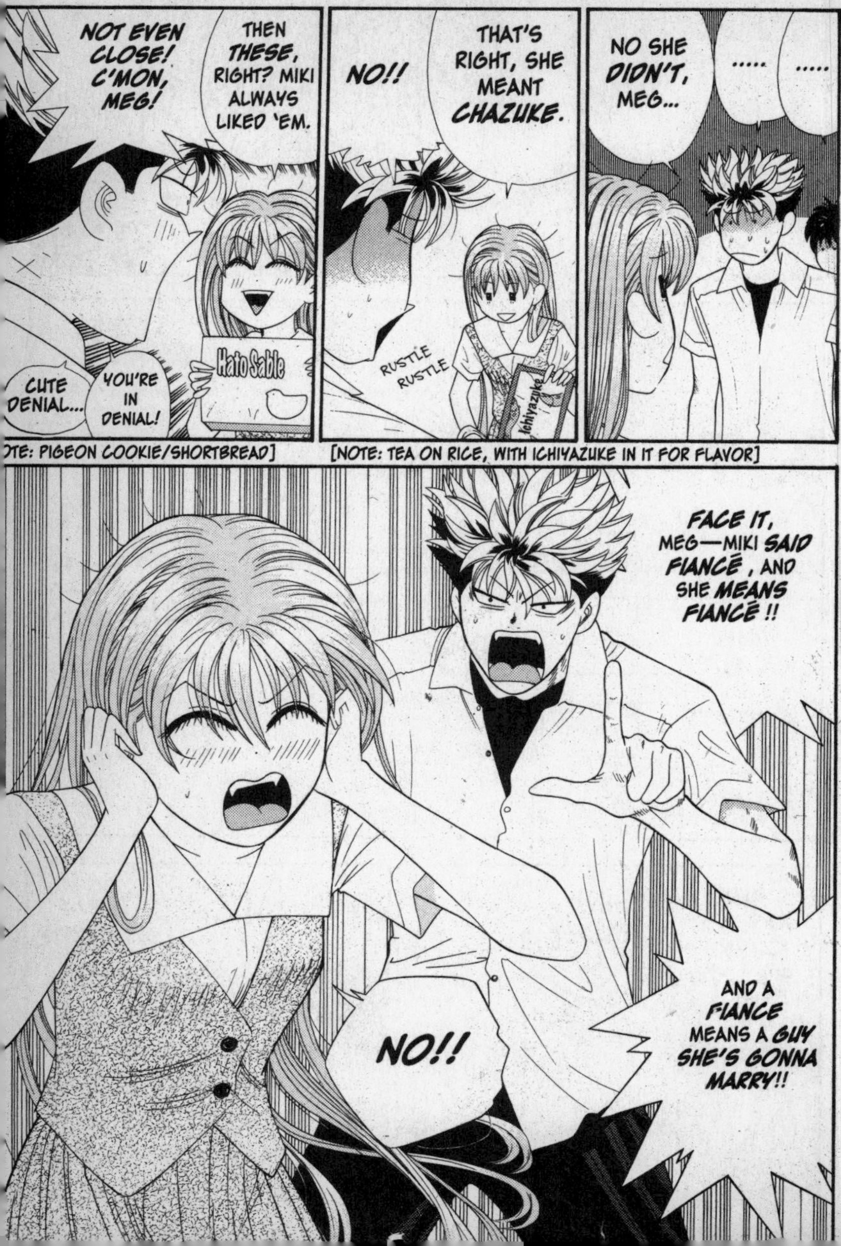
.....
.....
NO SHE DIDN'T, MEG...
THAT'S RIGHT, SHE MEANT CHAZUKE.
NO!!
RUSTLE RUSTLE
Ichiyazuke
[NOTE: TEA ON RICE, WITH ICHIYAZUKE IN IT FOR FLAVOR]
THEN THESE, RIGHT? MIKI ALWAYS LIKED 'EM.
NOT EVEN CLOSE! C'MON, MEG!
Hato Sable
YOU'RE IN DENIAL!
CUTE DENIAL...
OTE: PIGEON COOKIE/SHORTBREAD]
FACE IT, MEG—MIKI SAID FIANCÉ, AND SHE MEANS FIANCÉ!!
AND A FIANCE MEANS A GUY SHE'S GONNA MARRY!!
NO!!

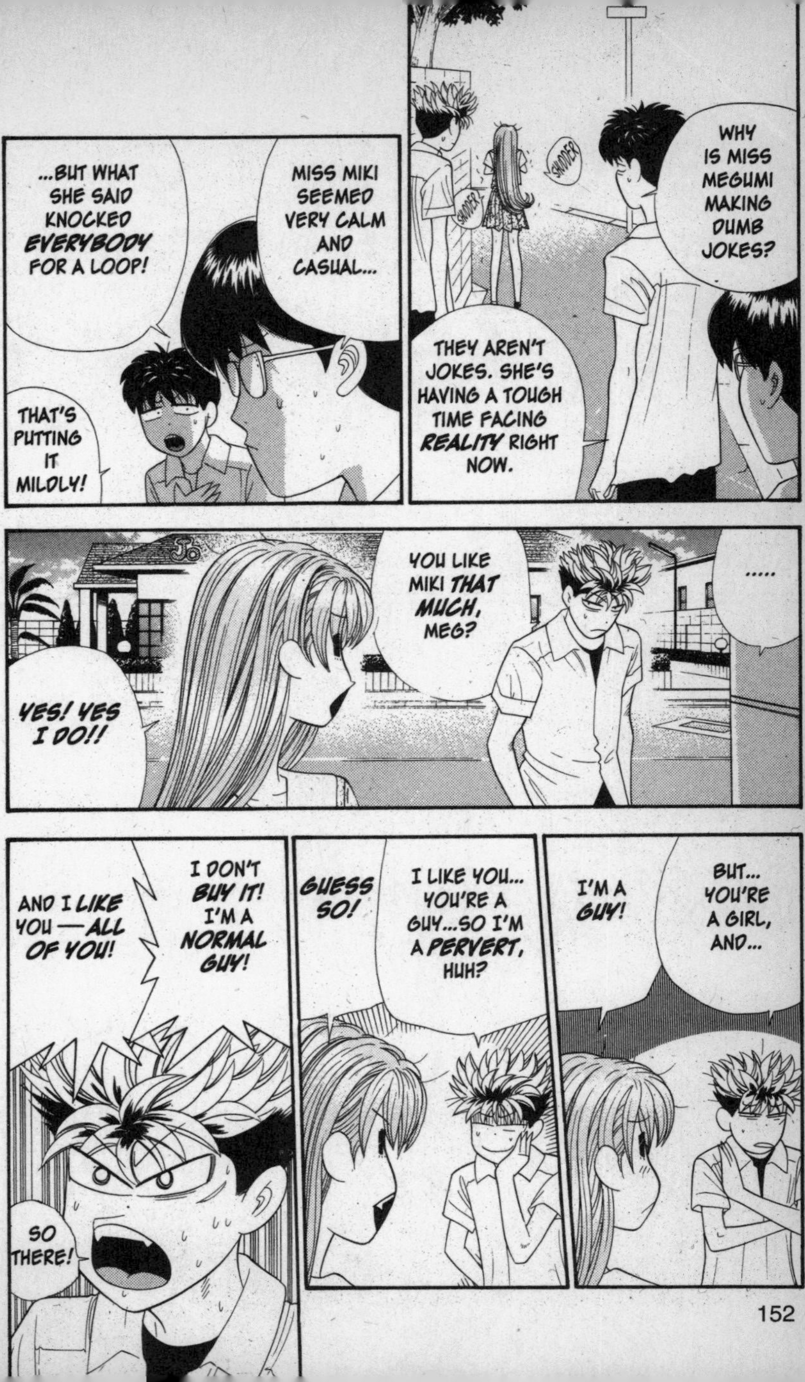
WHY IS MISS MEGUMI MAKING DUMB JOKES?
SHUDDER
SHUDDER
THEY AREN'T JOKES. SHE'S HAVING A TOUGH TIME FACING REALITY RIGHT NOW.
MISS MIKI SEEMED VERY CALM AND CASUAL...
...BUT WHAT SHE SAID KNOCKED EVERYBODY FOR A LOOP!
THAT'S PUTTING IT MILDLY!
.....
YOU LIKE MIKI THAT MUCH, MEG?
YES! YES I DO!!
BUT... YOU'RE A GIRL, AND...
I'M A GUY!
I LIKE YOU... YOU'RE A GUY...SO I'M A PERVERT, HUH?
GUESS SO!
I DON'T BUY IT! I'M A NORMAL GUY!
AND I LIKE YOU—ALL OF YOU!
SO THERE!

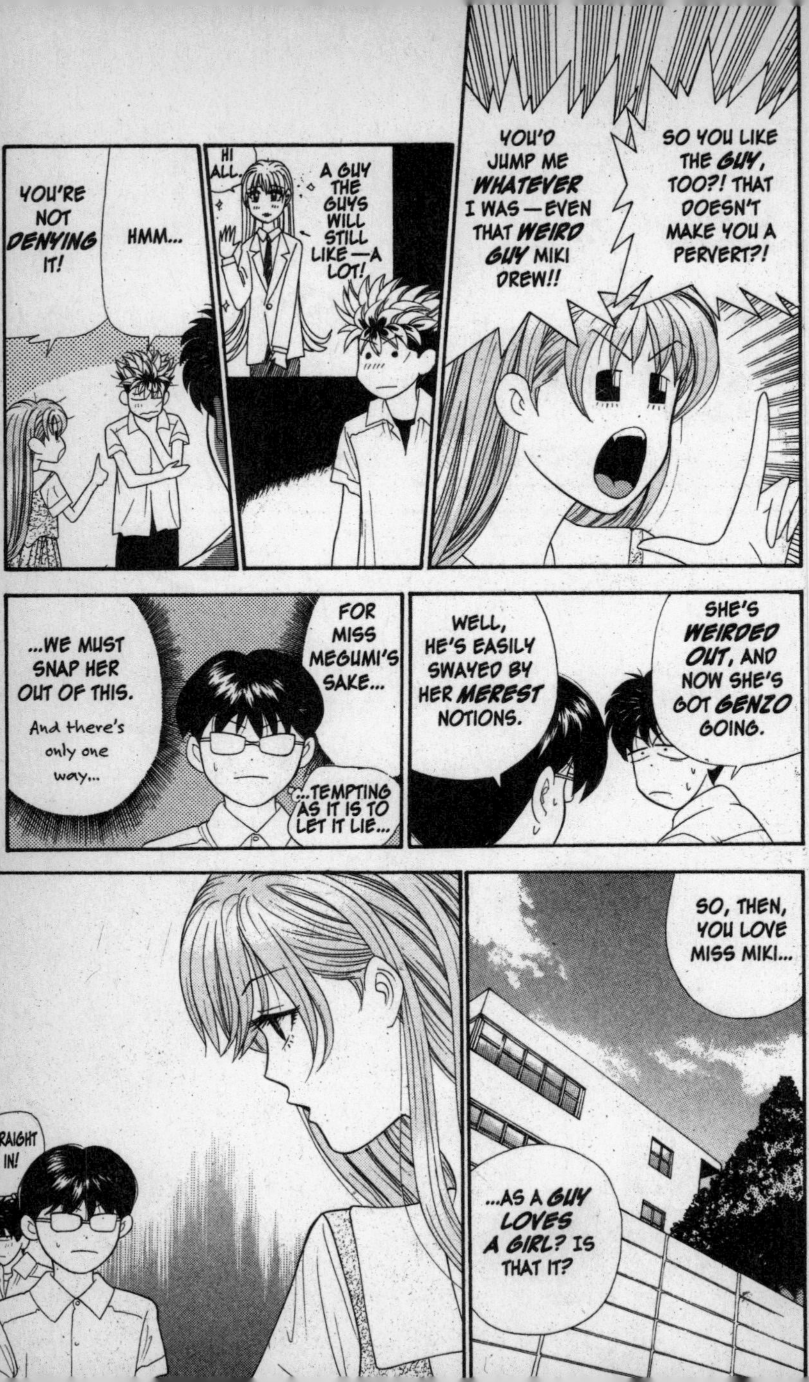
SO YOU LIKE THE GUY, TOO?! THAT DOESN'T MAKE YOU A PERVERT?!
YOU'D JUMP ME WHATEVER I WAS—EVEN THAT WEIRD GUY MIKI DREW!!
A GUY THE GUYS WILL STILL LIKE—A LOT!
HI ALL.
HMM...
YOU'RE NOT DENYING IT!
SHE'S WEIRDED OUT, AND NOW SHE'S GOT GENZO GOING.
WELL, HE'S EASILY SWAYED BY HER MEREST NOTIONS.
FOR MISS MEGUMI'S SAKE...
...TEMPTING AS IT IS TO LET IT LIE...
...WE MUST SNAP HER OUT OF THIS.
And there's only one way...
SO, THEN, YOU LOVE MISS MIKI...
...AS A GUY LOVES A GIRL? IS THAT IT?
STRAIGHT IN!

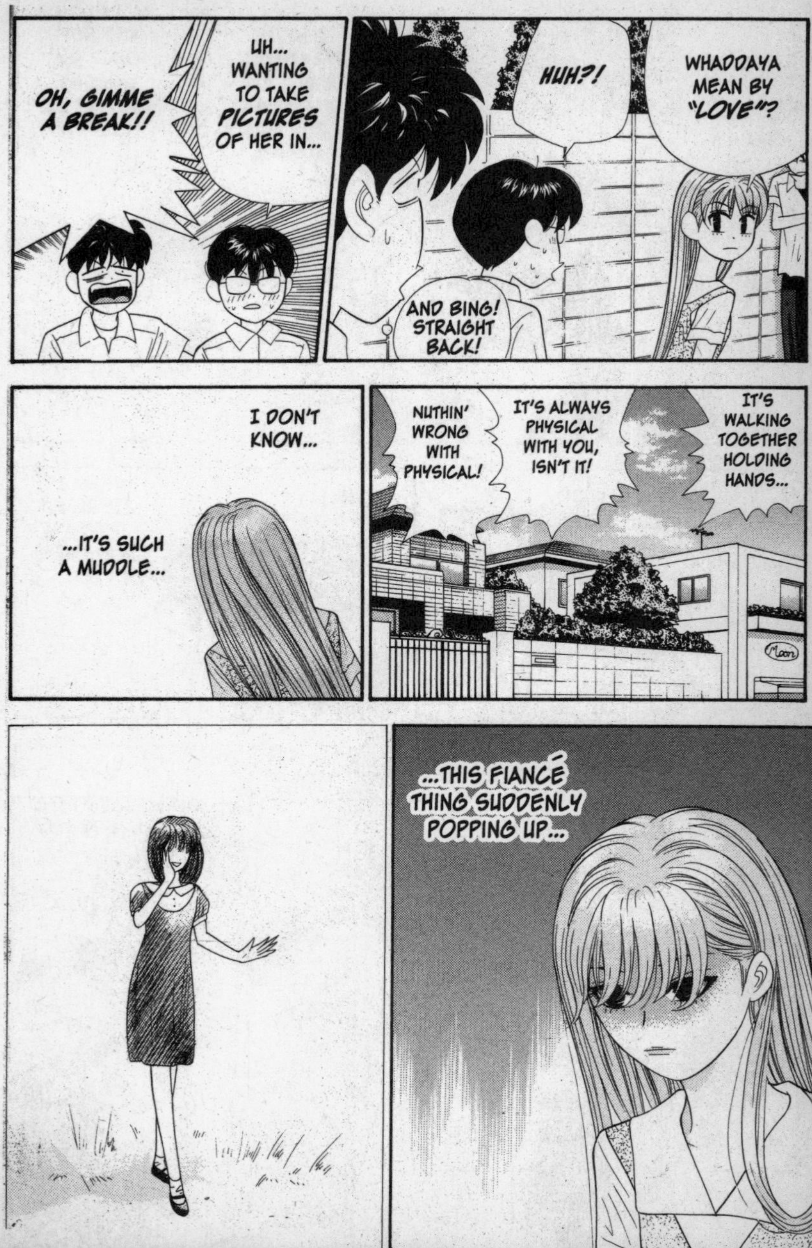
WHADDAYA MEAN BY "LOVE"?
HUH?!
AND BING! STRAIGHT BACK!
UH... WANTING TO TAKE PICTURES OF HER IN...
OH, GIMME A BREAK!!
IT'S WALKING TOGETHER HOLDING HANDS...
IT'S ALWAYS PHYSICAL WITH YOU, ISN'T IT!
NUTHIN' WRONG WITH PHYSICAL!
Moon
I DON'T KNOW...
...IT'S SUCH A MUDDLE...
...THIS FIANCÉ THING SUDDENLY POPPING UP...

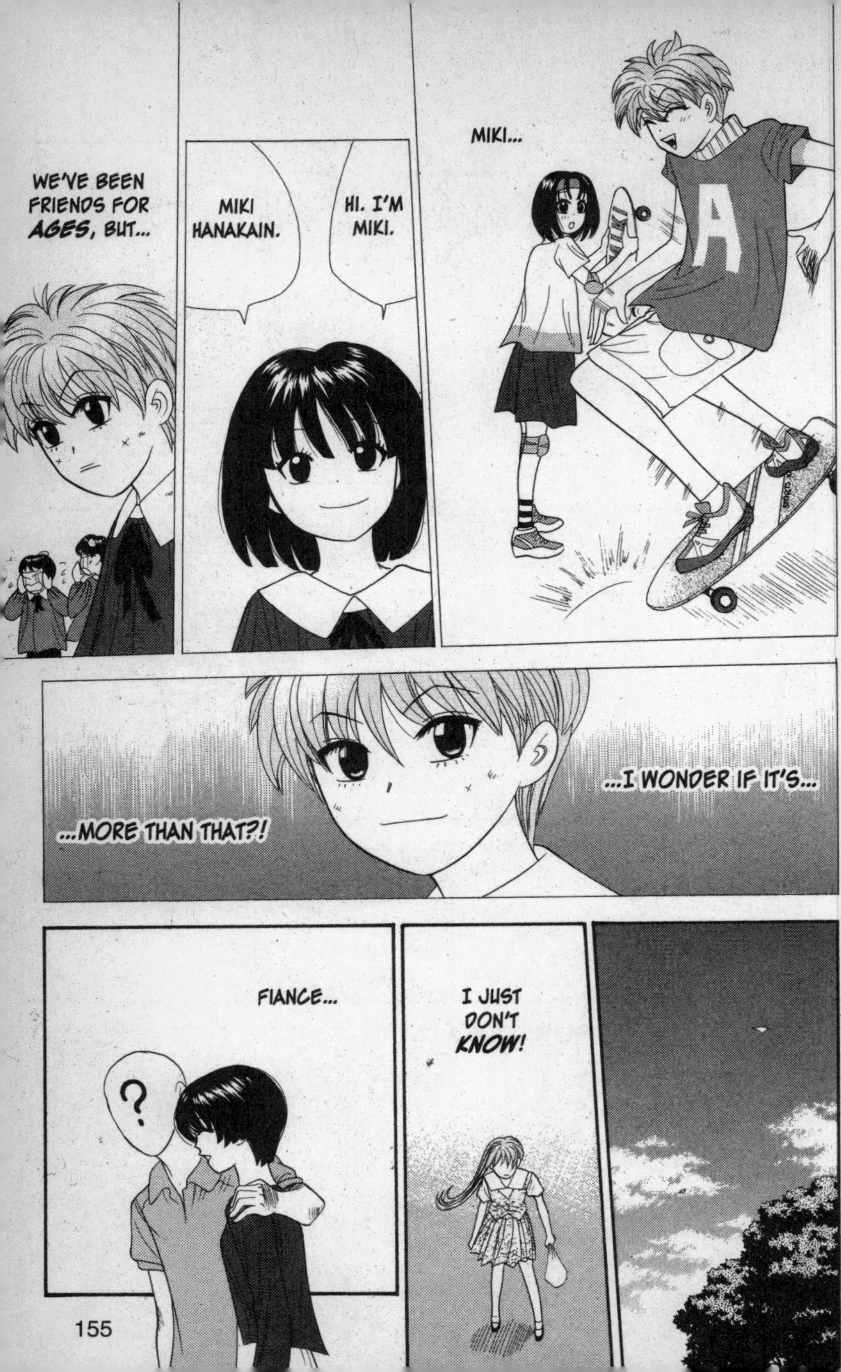
MIKI...
HI. I'M MIKI.
MIKI HANAKAIN.
WE'VE BEEN FRIENDS FOR AGES, BUT...
...I WONDER IF IT'S...
...MORE THAN THAT?!
I JUST DON'T KNOW!
FIANCE...
?

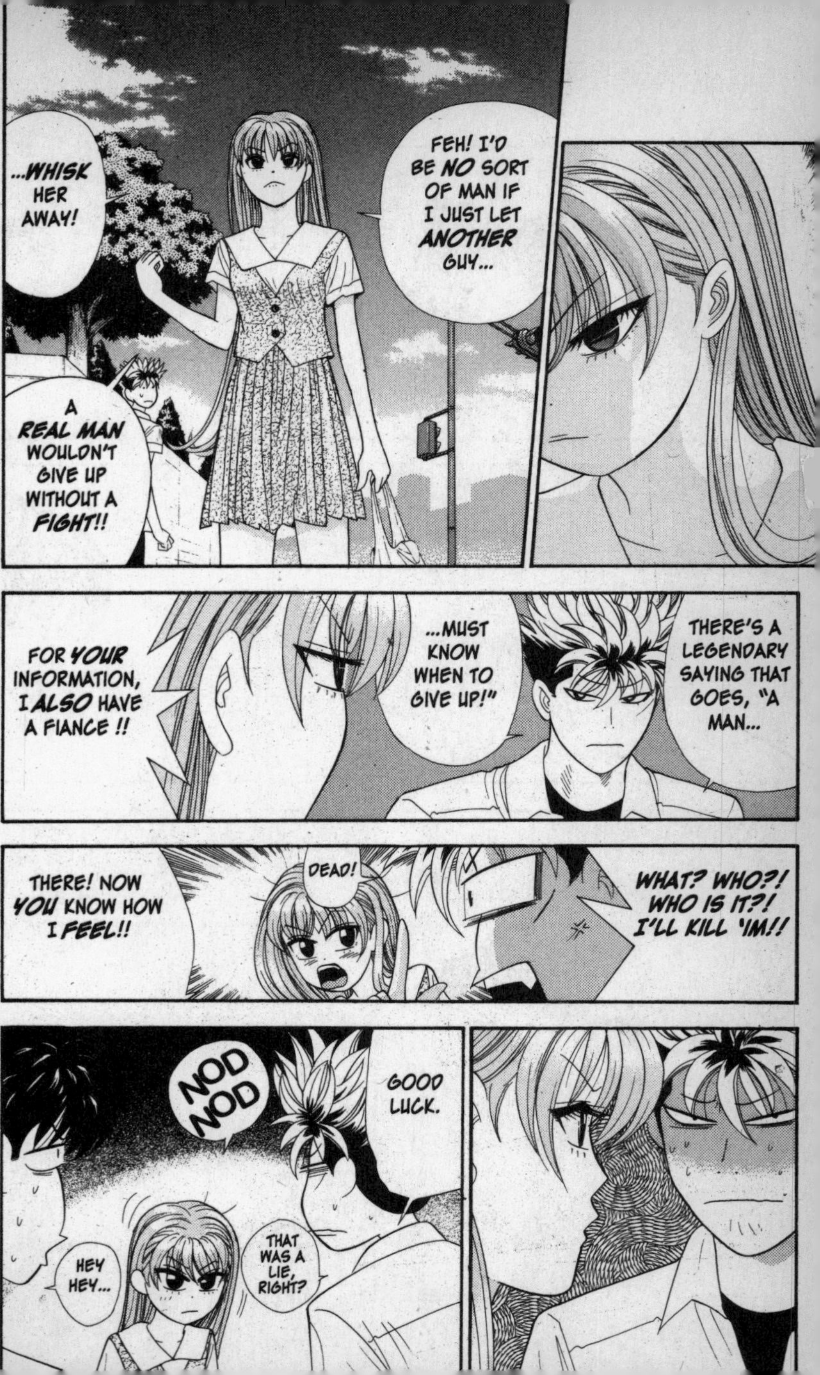
FEH! I'D BE NO SORT OF MAN IF I JUST LET ANOTHER GUY...
...WHISK HER AWAY!
A REAL MAN WOULDN'T GIVE UP WITHOUT A FIGHT!!
THERE'S A LEGENDARY SAYING THAT GOES, "A MAN...
...MUST KNOW WHEN TO GIVE UP!"
FOR YOUR INFORMATION, I ALSO HAVE A FIANCE !!
WHAT? WHO?! WHO IS IT?! I'LL KILL 'IM!!
DEAD!
THERE! NOW YOU KNOW HOW I FEEL!!
GOOD LUCK.
NOD NOD
THAT WAS A LIE, RIGHT?
HEY HEY...

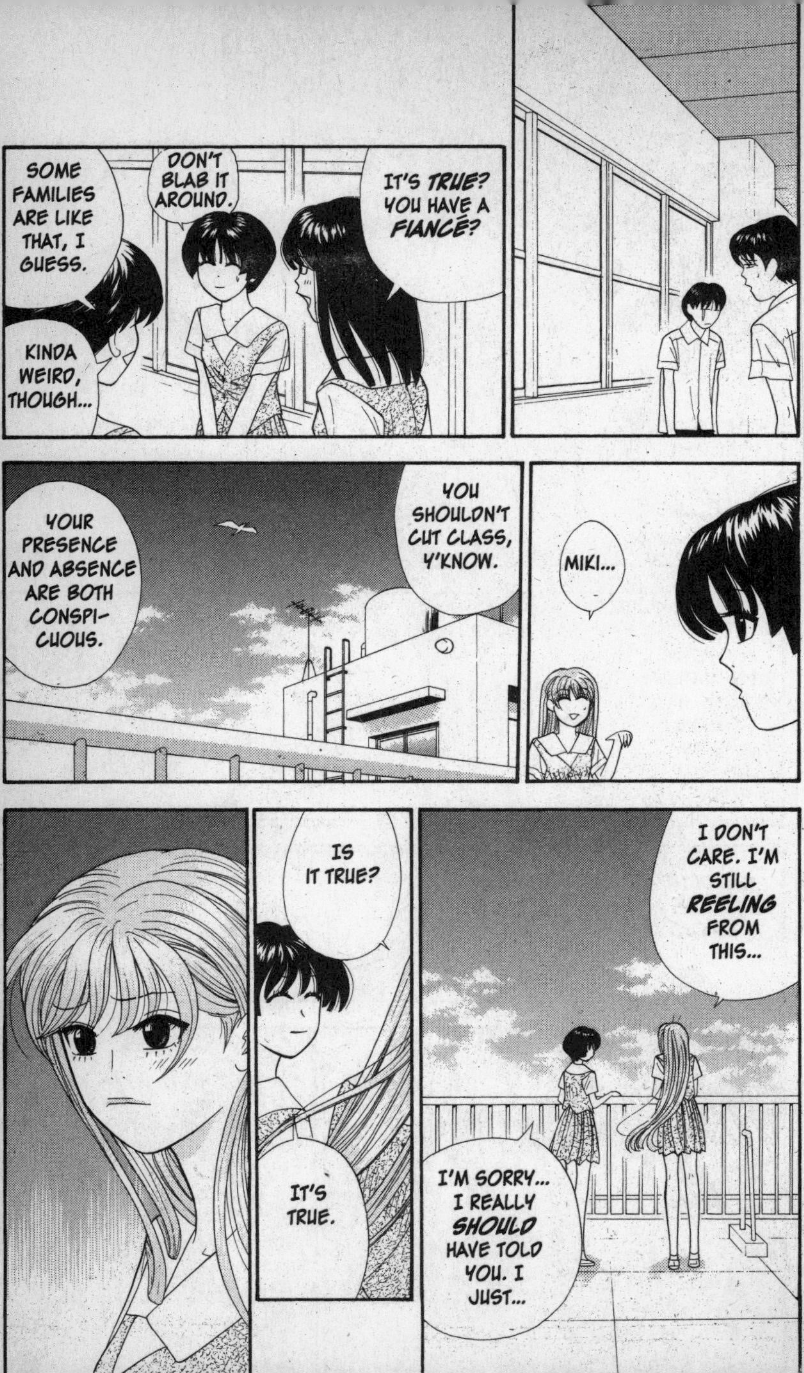
IT'S TRUE? YOU HAVE A FIANCÉ?
DON'T BLAB IT AROUND.
SOME FAMILIES ARE LIKE THAT, I GUESS.
KINDA WEIRD, THOUGH...
MIKI...
YOU SHOULDN'T CUT CLASS, Y'KNOW.
YOUR PRESENCE AND ABSENCE ARE BOTH CONSPICUOUS.
I DON'T CARE. I'M STILL REELING FROM THIS...
I'M SORRY... I REALLY SHOULD HAVE TOLD YOU. I JUST...
IS IT TRUE?
IT'S TRUE.

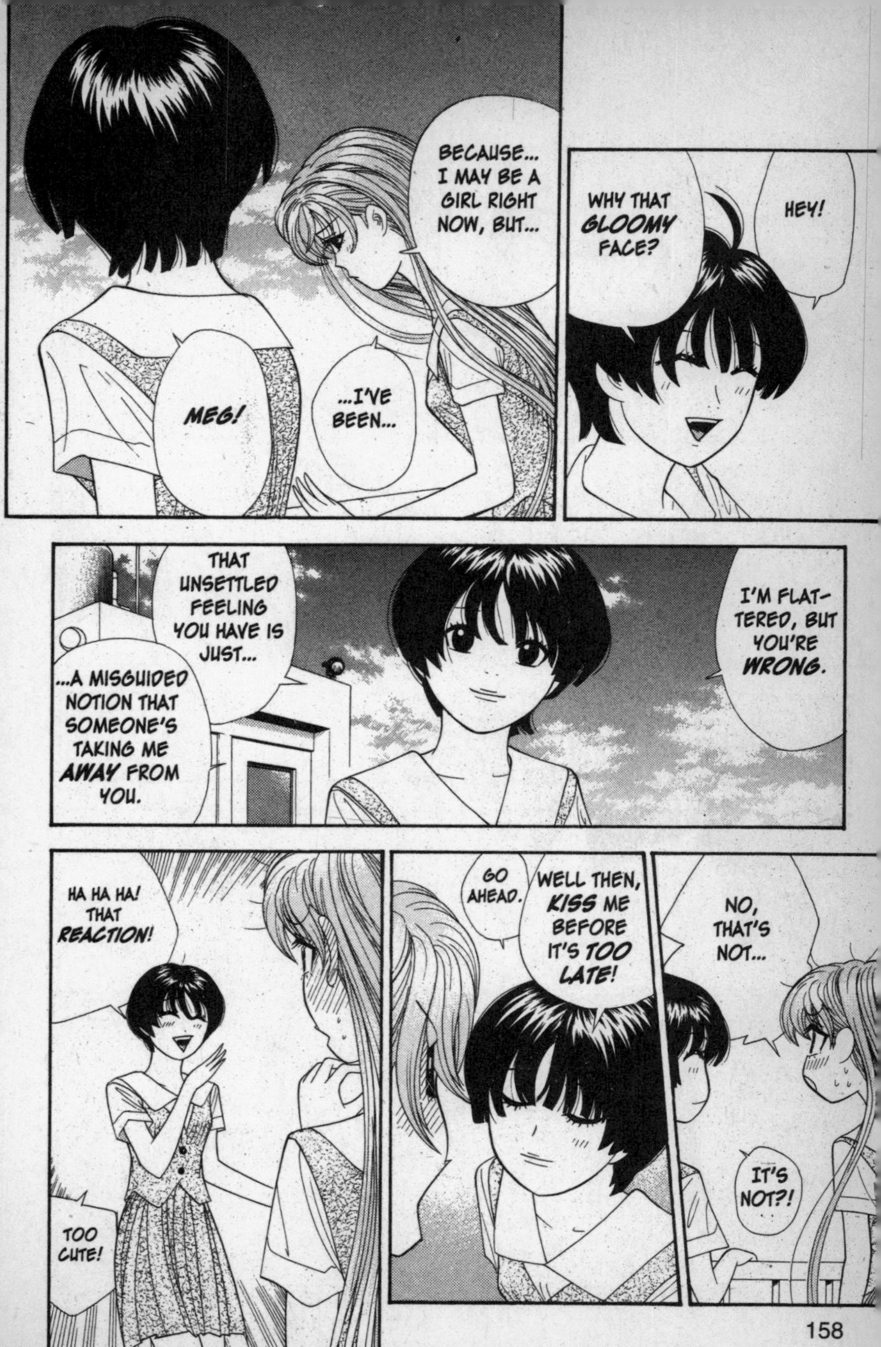
HEY!
WHY THAT GLOOMY FACE?
BECAUSE... I MAY BE A GIRL RIGHT NOW, BUT...
...I'VE BEEN...
MEG!
I'M FLATTERED, BUT YOU'RE WRONG.
THAT UNSETTLED FEELING YOU HAVE IS JUST...
...A MISGUIDED NOTION THAT SOMEONE'S TAKING ME AWAY FROM YOU.
NO, THAT'S NOT...
IT'S NOT?!
WELL THEN, KISS ME BEFORE IT'S TOO LATE!
GO AHEAD.
HA HA HA! THAT REACTION!
TOO CUTE!

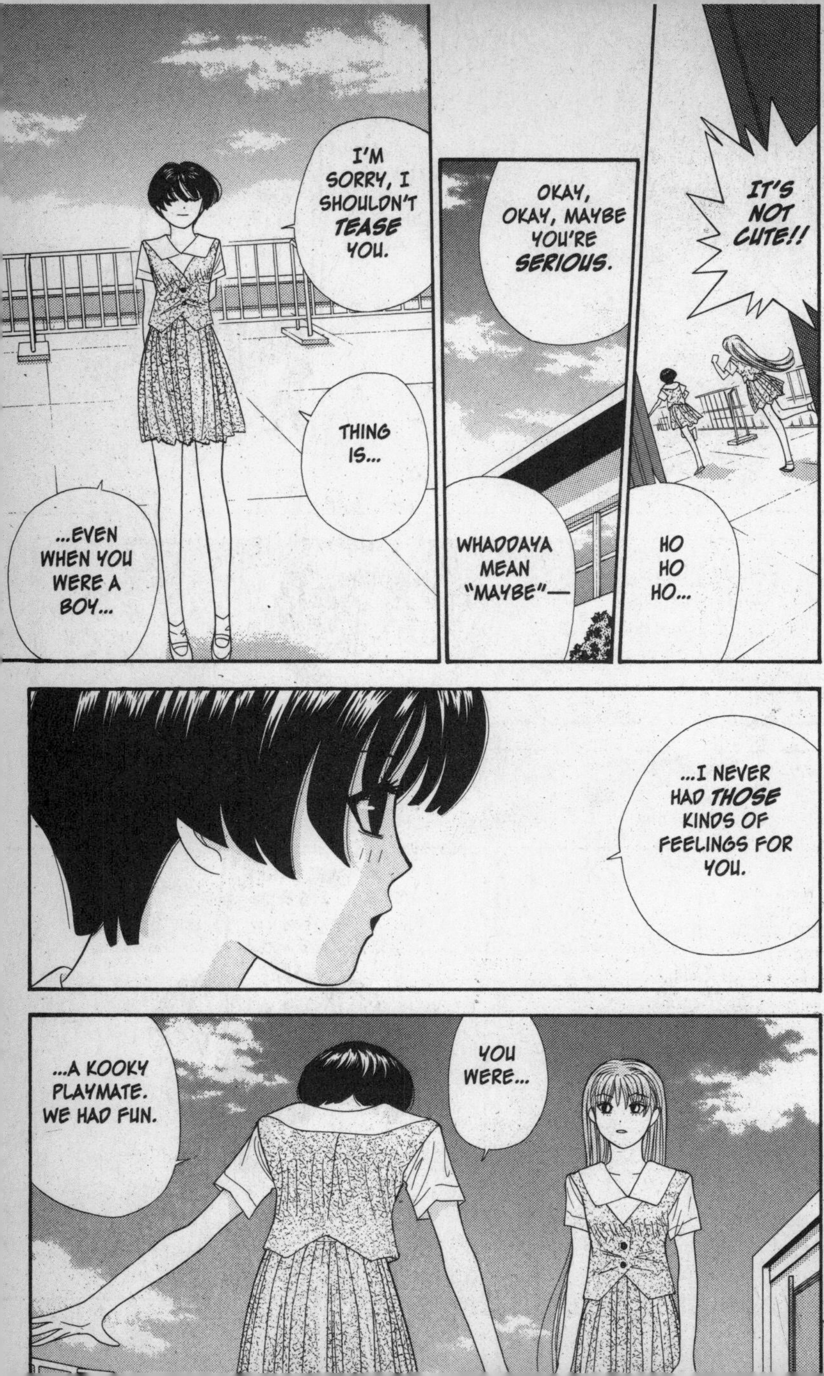
IT'S NOT CUTE!!
HO HO HO...
OKAY, OKAY, MAYBE YOU'RE SERIOUS.
WHADDAYA MEAN "MAYBE"—
I'M SORRY, I SHOULDN'T TEASE YOU.
THING IS...
...EVEN WHEN YOU WERE A BOY...
...I NEVER HAD THOSE KINDS OF FEELINGS FOR YOU.
YOU WERE...
...A KOOKY PLAYMATE. WE HAD FUN.

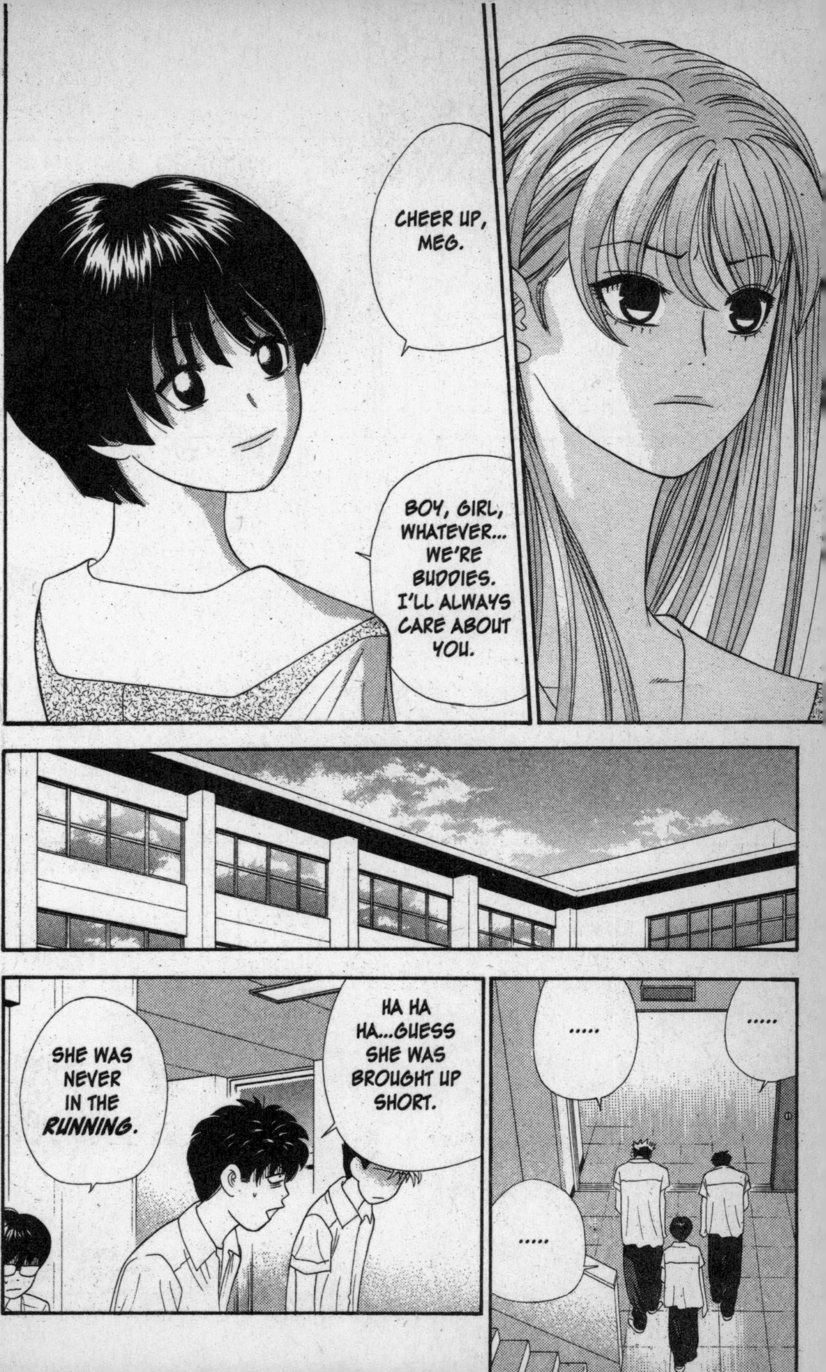
CHEER UP, MEG.
BOY, GIRL, WHATEVER... WE'RE BUDDIES. I'LL ALWAYS CARE ABOUT YOU.
.....
.....
.....
HA HA HA...GUESS SHE WAS BROUGHT UP SHORT.
SHE WAS NEVER IN THE *RUNNING*.

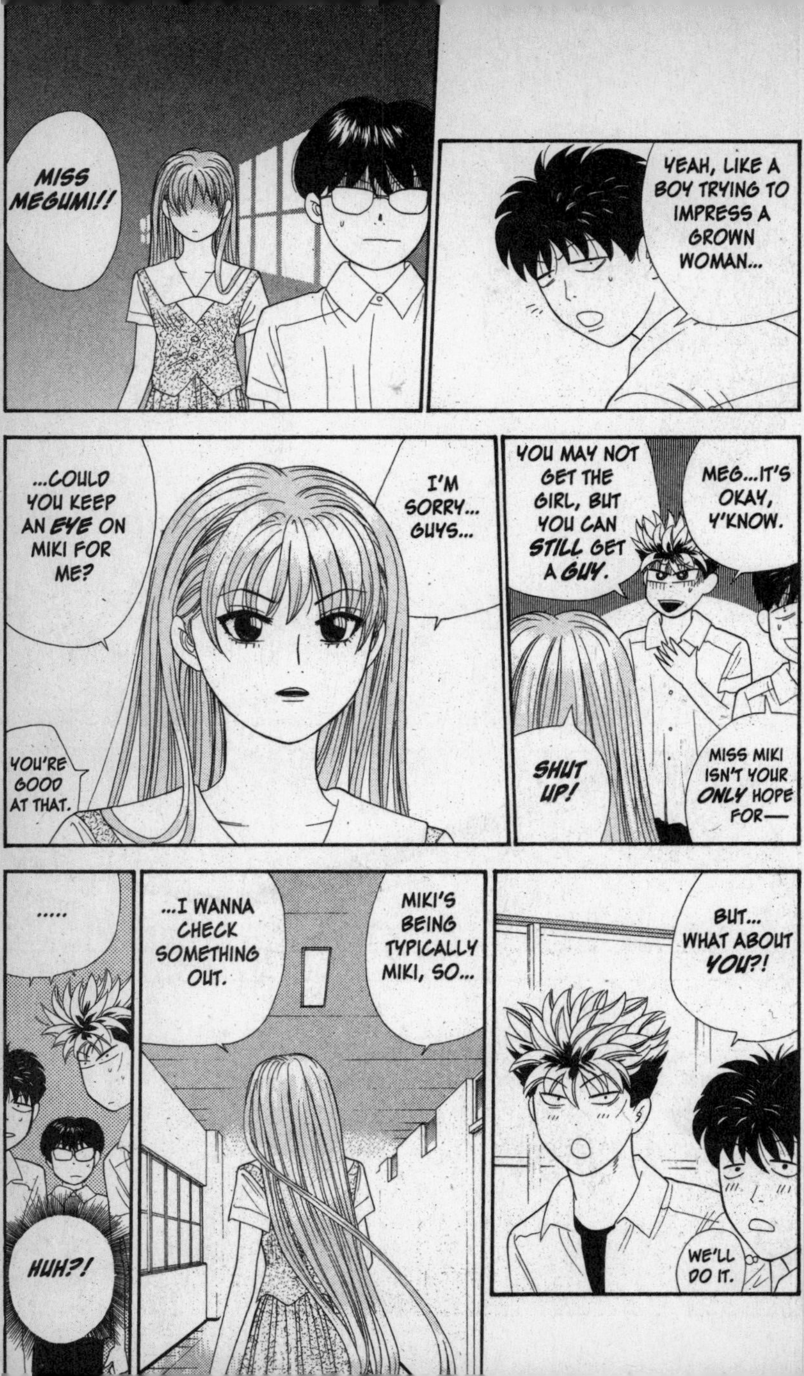
YEAH, LIKE A BOY TRYING TO IMPRESS A GROWN WOMAN...
MISS MEGUMI!!
MEG...IT'S OKAY, Y'KNOW.
YOU MAY NOT GET THE GIRL, BUT YOU CAN STILL GET A GUY.
MISS MIKI ISN'T YOUR ONLY HOPE FOR—
SHUT UP!
I'M SORRY... GUYS...
...COULD YOU KEEP AN EYE ON MIKI FOR ME?
YOU'RE GOOD AT THAT.
BUT... WHAT ABOUT YOU?!
WE'LL DO IT.
MIKI'S BEING TYPICALLY MIKI, SO...
...I WANNA CHECK SOMETHING OUT.
.....
HUH?!

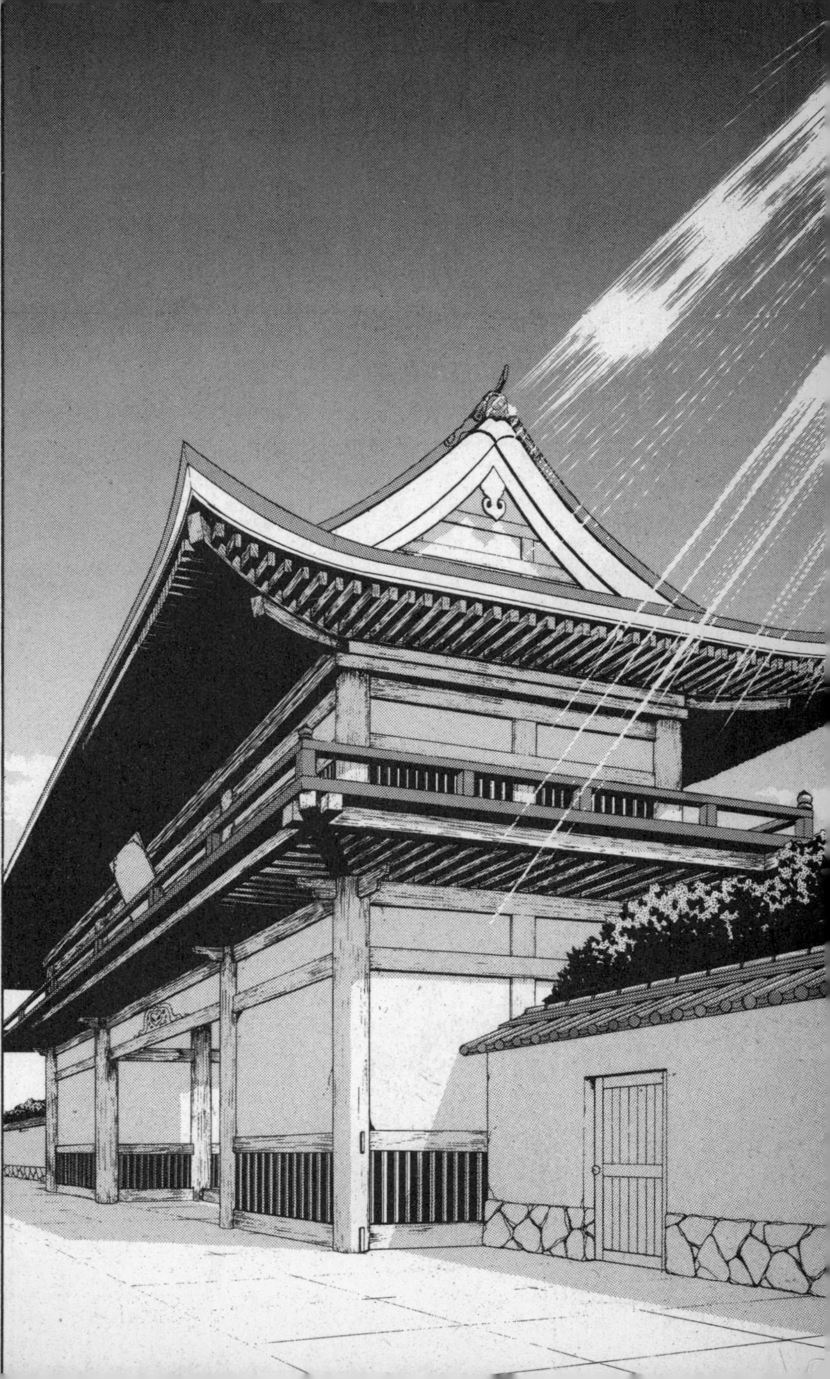

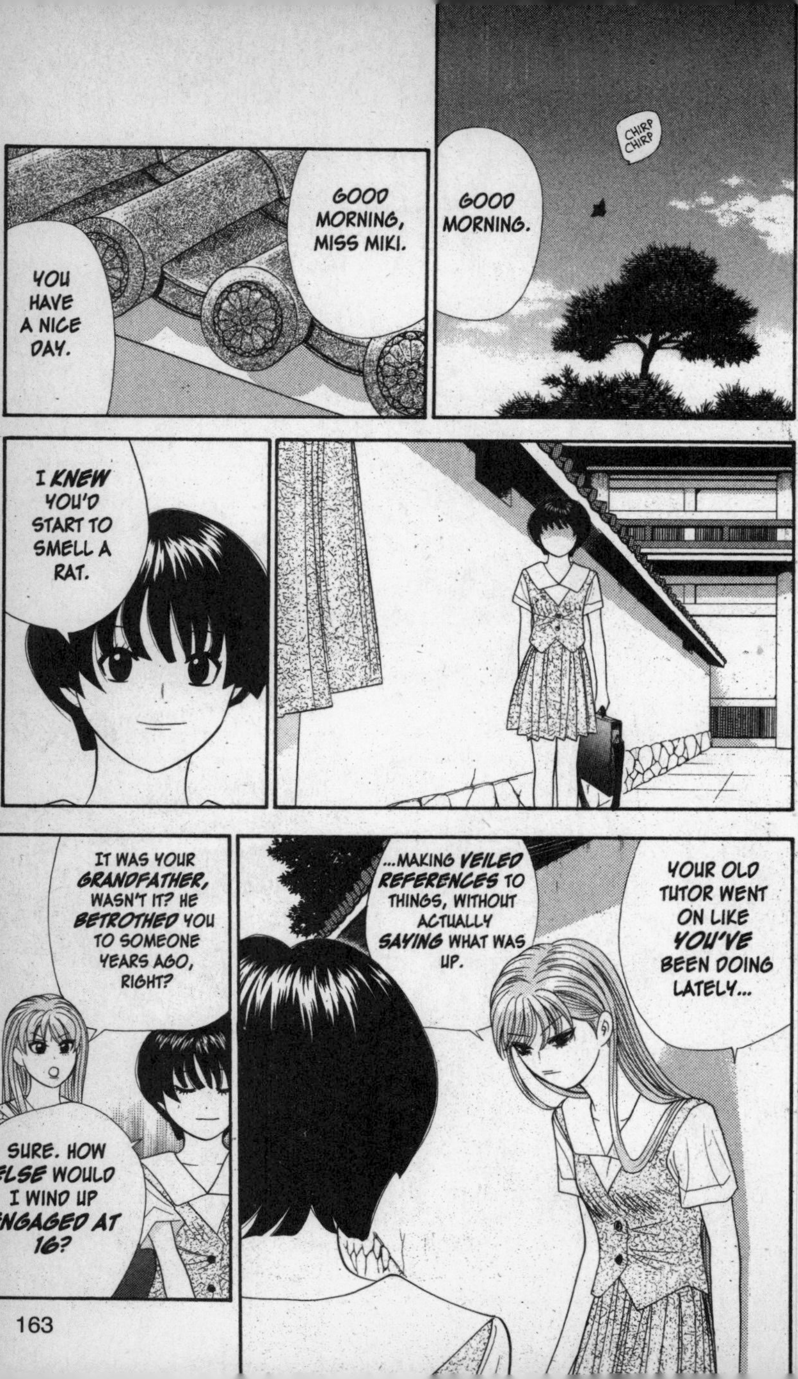
CHIRP CHIRP
GOOD MORNING.
GOOD MORNING, MISS MIKI.
YOU HAVE A NICE DAY.
I KNEW YOU'D START TO SMELL A RAT.
YOUR OLD TUTOR WENT ON LIKE YOU'VE BEEN DOING LATELY...
...MAKING VEILED REFERENCES TO THINGS, WITHOUT ACTUALLY SAYING WHAT WAS UP.
IT WAS YOUR GRANDFATHER, WASN'T IT? HE BETROTHED YOU TO SOMEONE YEARS AGO, RIGHT?
SURE. HOW ELSE WOULD I WIND UP ENGAGED AT 16?

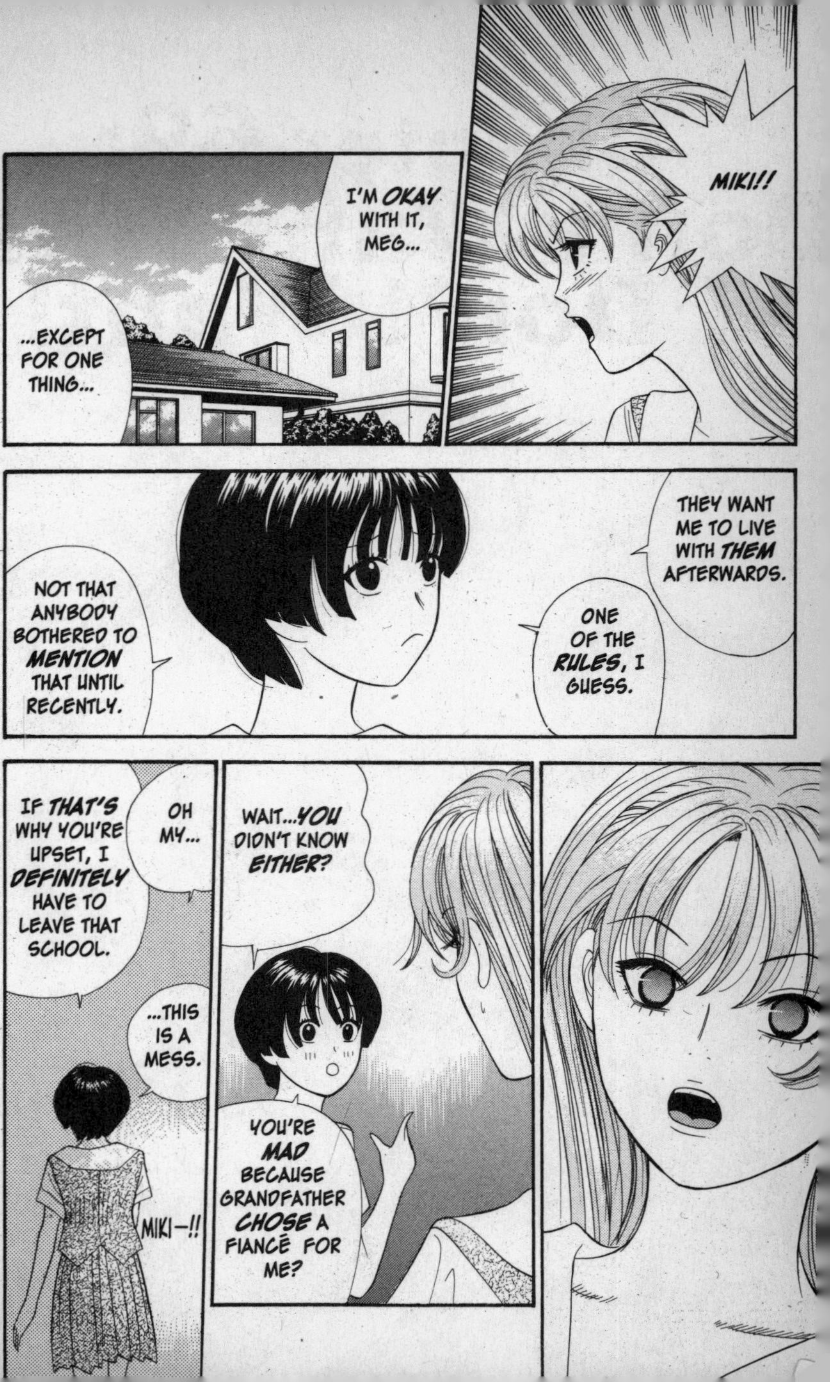
MIKI!!
I'M OKAY WITH IT, MEG...
...EXCEPT FOR ONE THING...
THEY WANT ME TO LIVE WITH THEM AFTERWARDS.
ONE OF THE RULES, I GUESS.
NOT THAT ANYBODY BOTHERED TO MENTION THAT UNTIL RECENTLY.
WAIT...YOU DIDN'T KNOW EITHER?
YOU'RE MAD BECAUSE GRANDFATHER CHOSE A FIANCÉ FOR ME?
OH MY...
IF THAT'S WHY YOU'RE UPSET, I DEFINITELY HAVE TO LEAVE THAT SCHOOL.
...THIS IS A MESS.
MIKI—!!

Chapter 69:
Don't Want What I Don't Want!

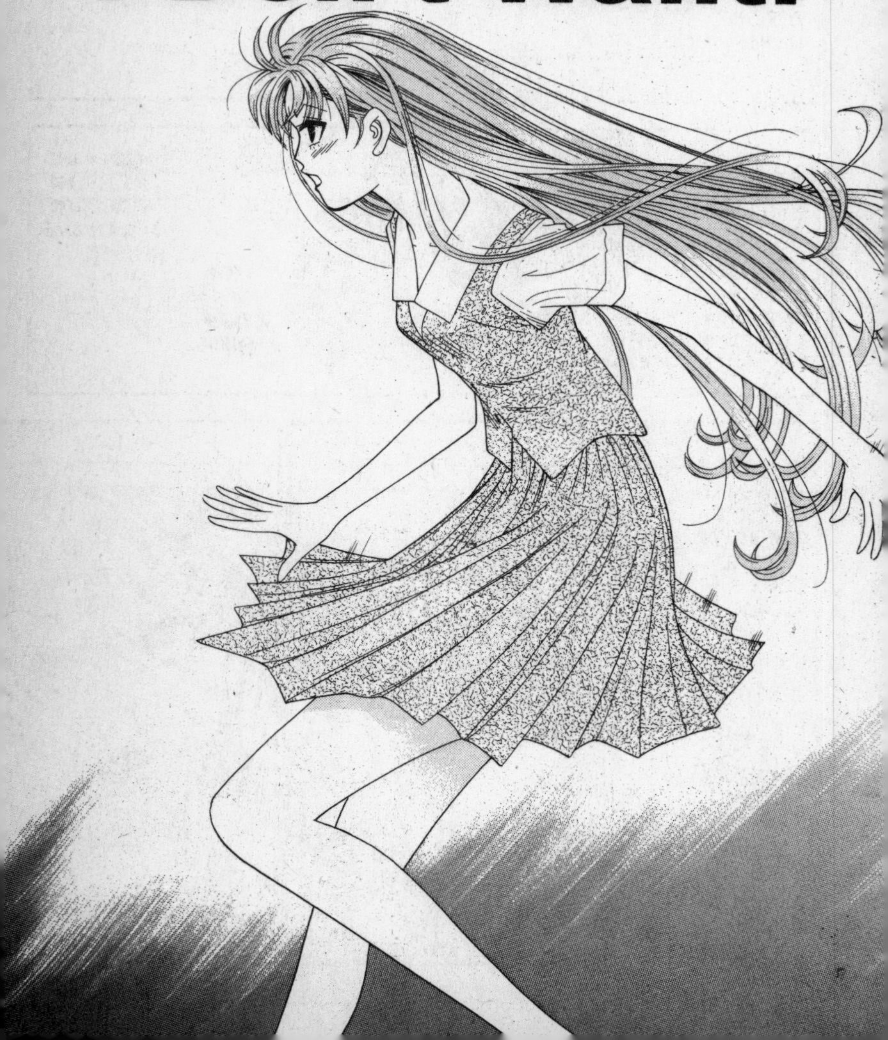

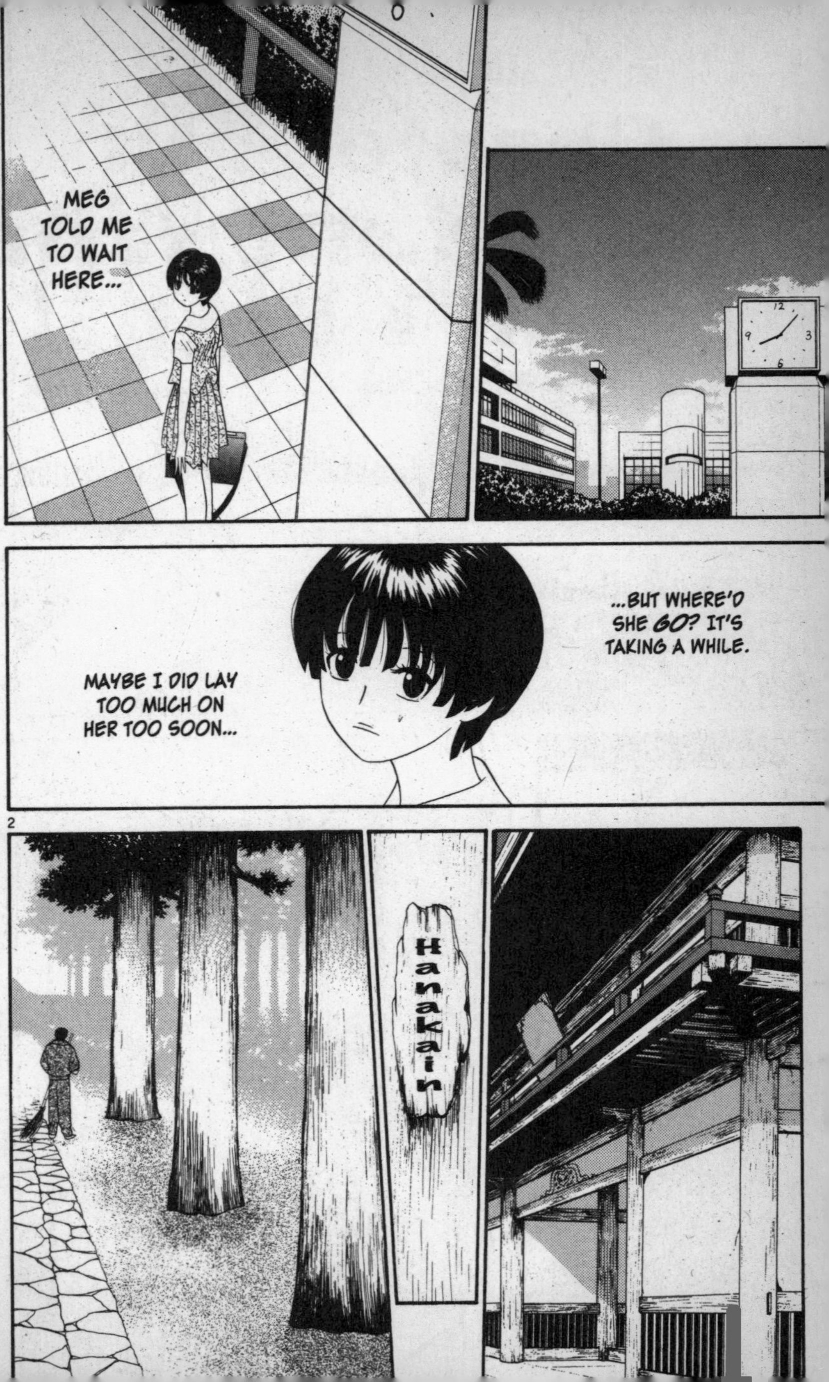
MEG TOLD ME TO WAIT HERE...
...BUT WHERE'D SHE GO? IT'S TAKING A WHILE.
MAYBE I DID LAY TOO MUCH ON HER TOO SOON...
2
Hanakain

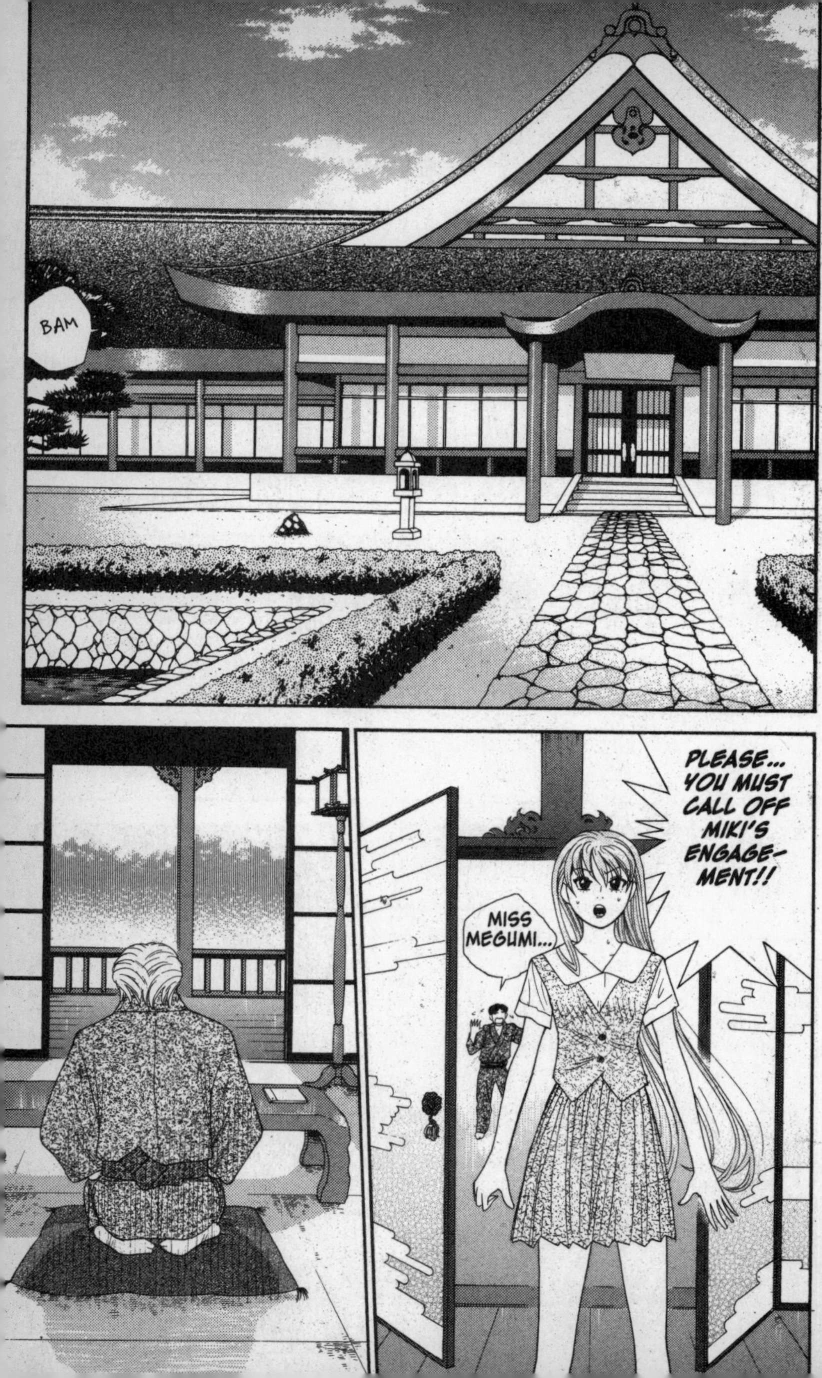
BAM
PLEASE... YOU MUST CALL OFF MIKI'S ENGAGE-MENT!!
MISS MEGUMI...

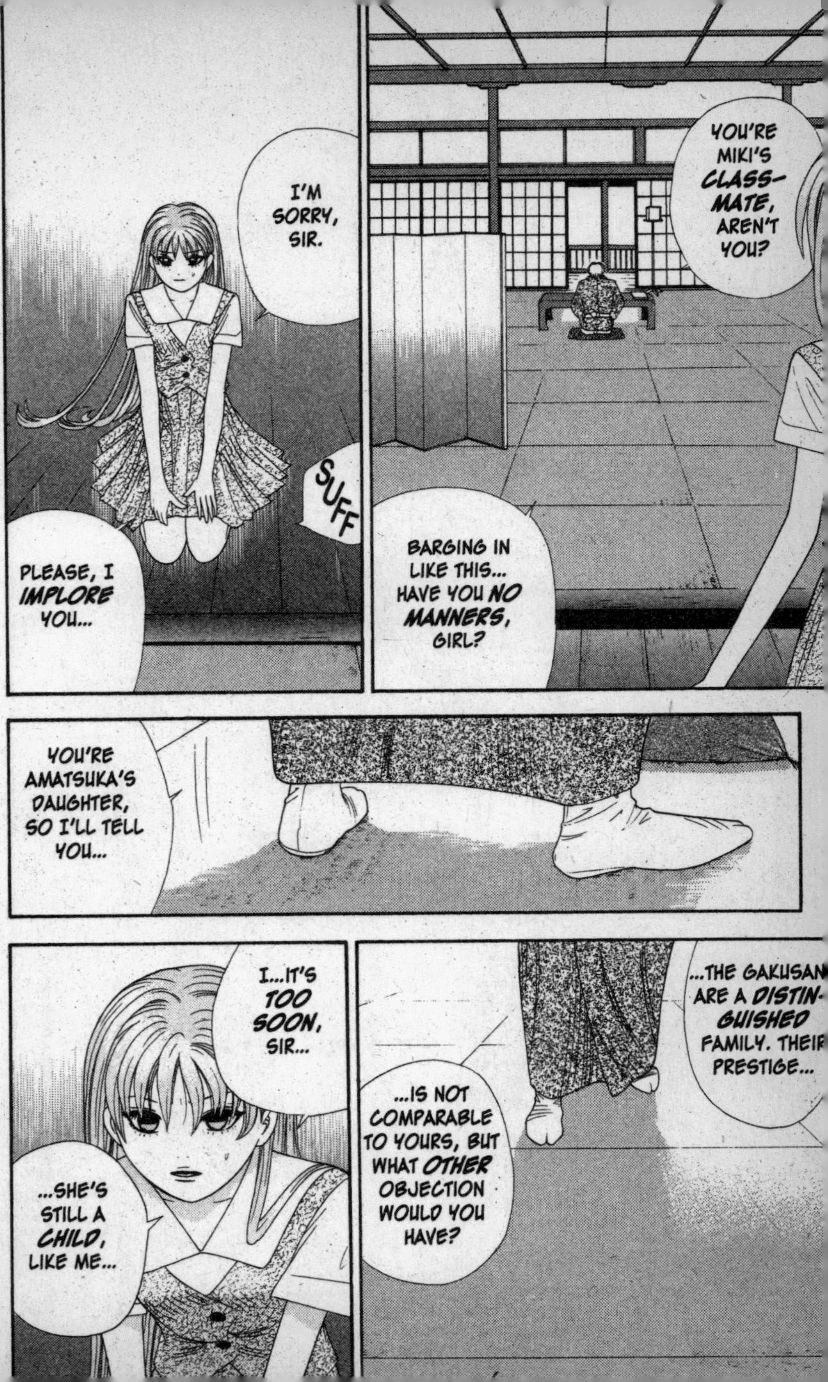
YOU'RE MIKI'S CLASS-MATE, AREN'T YOU?
BARGING IN LIKE THIS... HAVE YOU NO MANNERS, GIRL?
I'M SORRY, SIR.
SUFF
PLEASE, I IMPLORE YOU...
YOU'RE AMATSUKA'S DAUGHTER, SO I'LL TELL YOU...
...THE GAKUSAN ARE A DISTIN-GUISHED FAMILY. THEI PRESTIGE...
...IS NOT COMPARABLE TO YOURS, BUT WHAT OTHER OBJECTION WOULD YOU HAVE?
I...IT'S TOO SOON, SIR...
...SHE'S STILL A CHILD, LIKE ME...

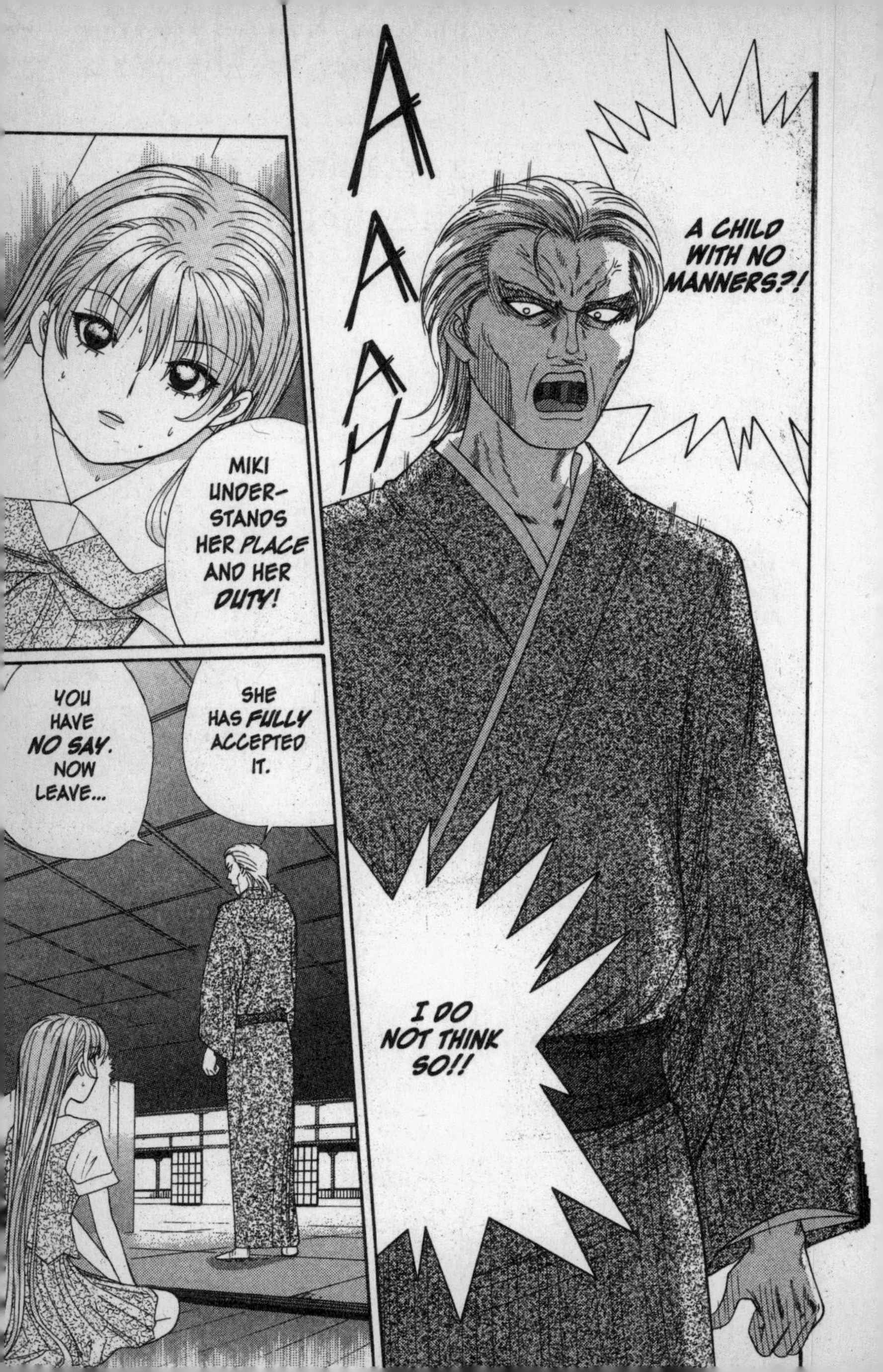
A CHILD WITH NO MANNERS?!
AAAAH
I DO NOT THINK SO!!
MIKI UNDERSTANDS HER PLACE AND HER DUTY!
SHE HAS FULLY ACCEPTED IT.
YOU HAVE NO SAY. NOW LEAVE...

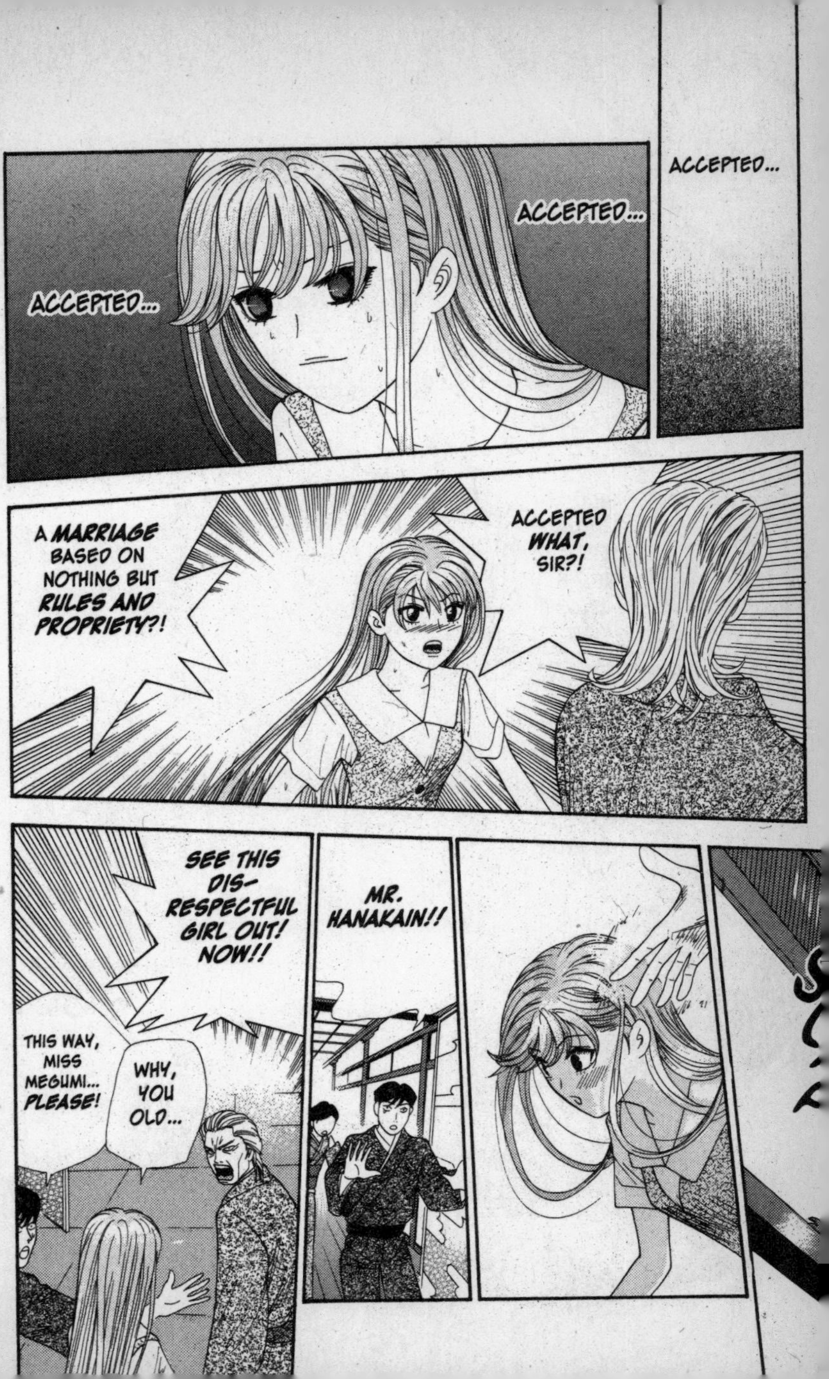
ACCEPTED...
ACCEPTED...
ACCEPTED...
ACCEPTED WHAT, SIR?!
A MARRIAGE BASED ON NOTHING BUT RULES AND PROPRIETY?!
MR. HANAKAIN!!
SEE THIS DIS-RESPECTFUL GIRL OUT! NOW!!
WHY, YOU OLD...
THIS WAY, MISS MEGUMI... PLEASE!

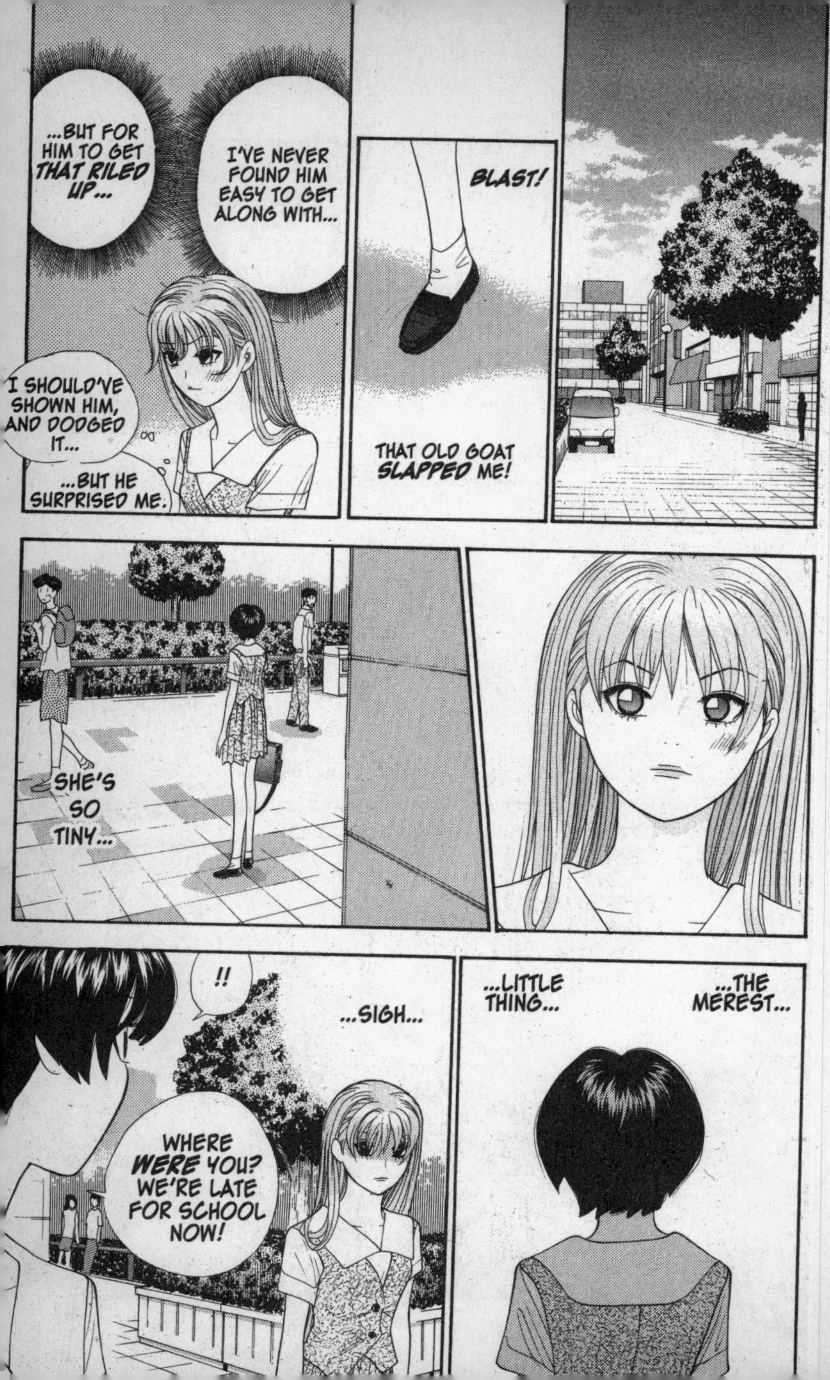
BLAST!
THAT OLD GOAT SLAPPED ME!
I'VE NEVER FOUND HIM EASY TO GET ALONG WITH...
...BUT FOR HIM TO GET THAT RILED UP...
I SHOULD'VE SHOWN HIM, AND DODGED IT...
...BUT HE SURPRISED ME.
SHE'S SO TINY...
...THE MEREST...
...LITTLE THING...
...SIGH...
!!
WHERE WERE YOU? WE'RE LATE FOR SCHOOL NOW!

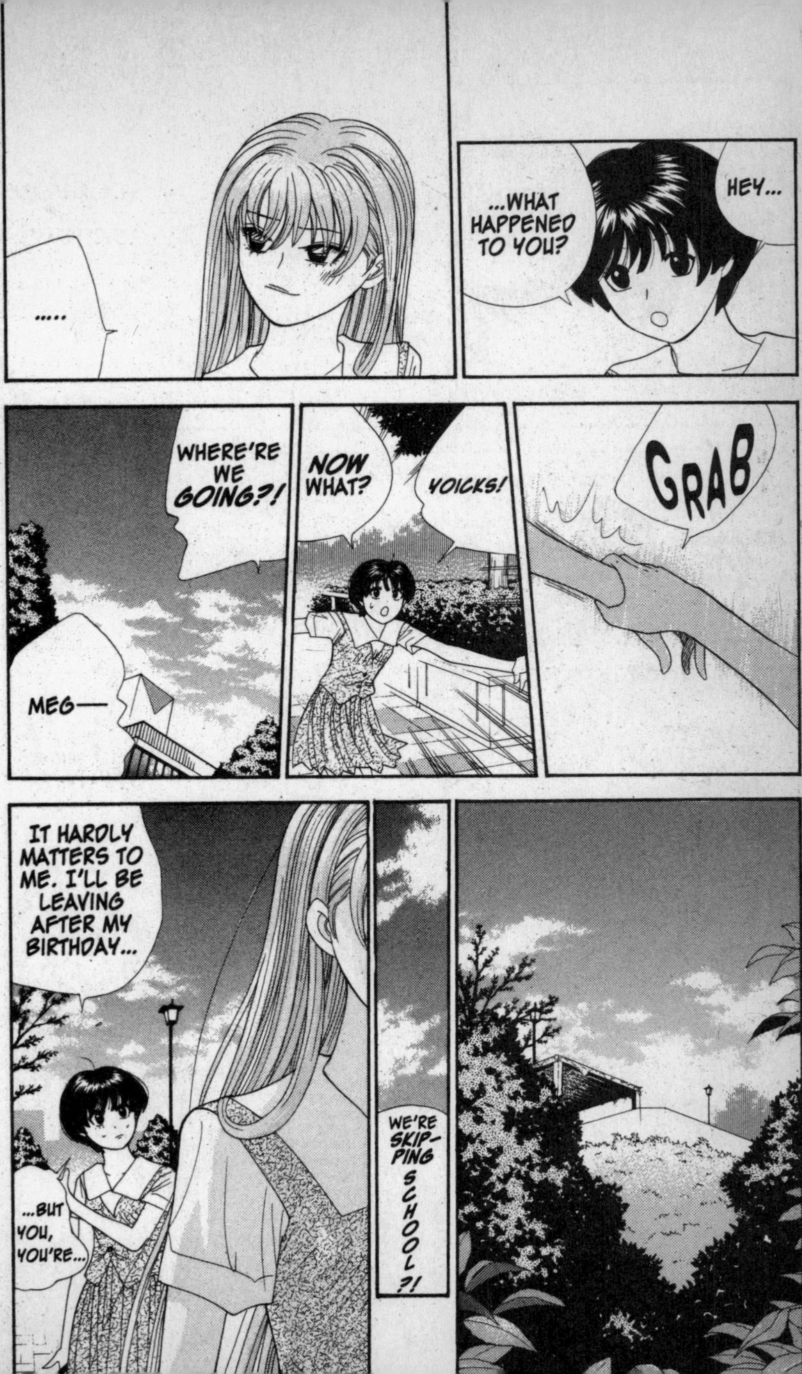
HEY...
...WHAT HAPPENED TO YOU?
.....
GRAB
YOICKS!
NOW WHAT?
WHERE'RE WE GOING?!
MEG—
WE'RE SKIP-PING SCHOOL?!
IT HARDLY MATTERS TO ME. I'LL BE LEAVING AFTER MY BIRTHDAY...
...BUT YOU, YOU'RE...

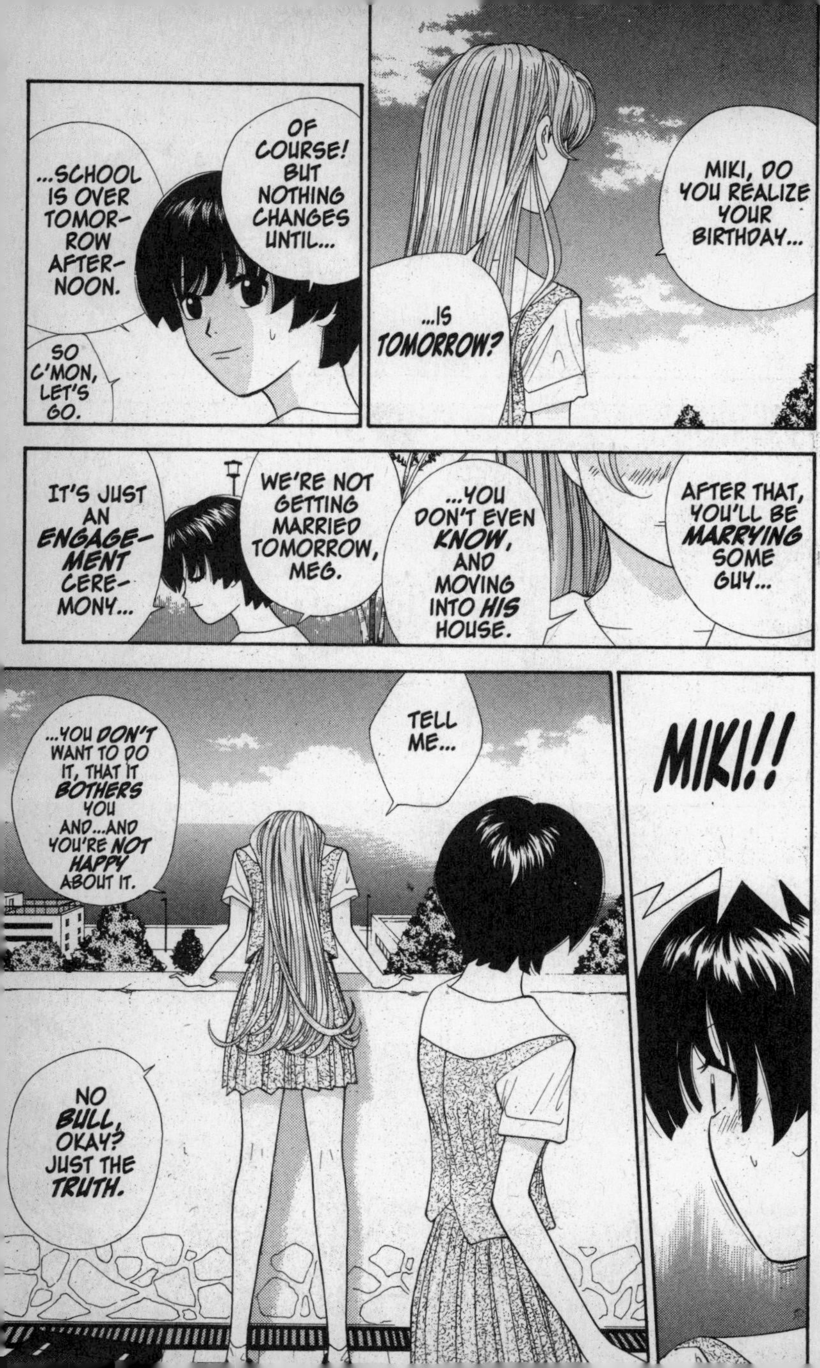
MIKI, DO YOU REALIZE YOUR BIRTHDAY...
...IS TOMORROW?
OF COURSE! BUT NOTHING CHANGES UNTIL...
...SCHOOL IS OVER TOMORROW AFTERNOON.
SO C'MON, LET'S GO.
AFTER THAT, YOU'LL BE MARRYING SOME GUY...
...YOU DON'T EVEN KNOW, AND MOVING INTO HIS HOUSE.
WE'RE NOT GETTING MARRIED TOMORROW, MEG.
IT'S JUST AN ENGAGEMENT CEREMONY...
MIKI!!
TELL ME...
...YOU DON'T WANT TO DO IT, THAT IT BOTHERS YOU AND...AND YOU'RE NOT HAPPY ABOUT IT.
NO BULL, OKAY? JUST THE TRUTH.

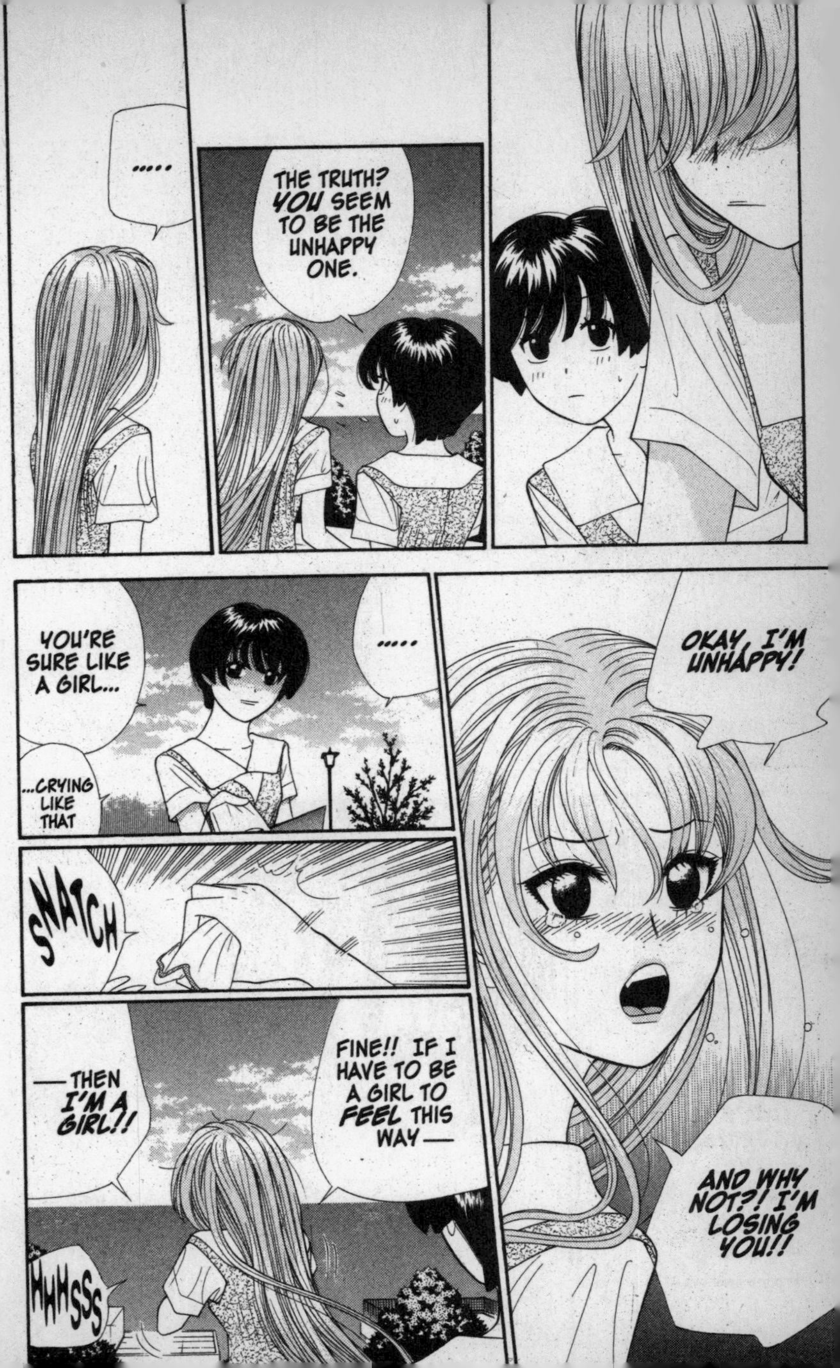
THE TRUTH? YOU SEEM TO BE THE UNHAPPY ONE.
.....
OKAY, I'M UNHAPPY!
AND WHY NOT?! I'M LOSING YOU!!
.....
YOU'RE SURE LIKE A GIRL...
...CRYING LIKE THAT
SNATCH
FINE!! IF I HAVE TO BE A GIRL TO FEEL THIS WAY—
—THEN I'M A GIRL!!
WHHHSSS

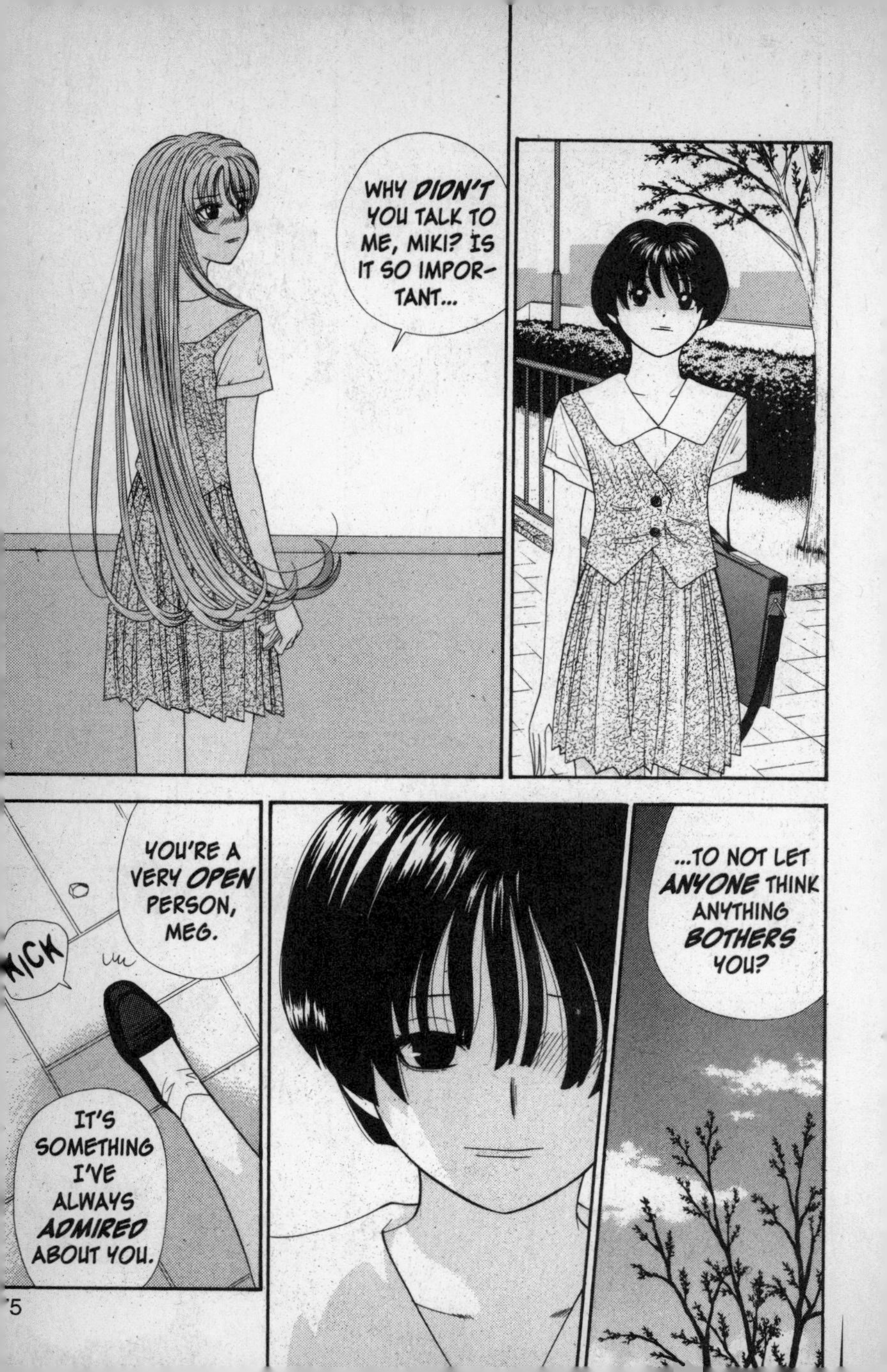
WHY *DIDN'T* YOU TALK TO ME, MIKI? IS IT SO IMPORTANT...
...TO NOT LET *ANYONE* THINK ANYTHING *BOTHERS* YOU?
YOU'RE A VERY *OPEN* PERSON, MEG.
KICK
IT'S SOMETHING I'VE ALWAYS *ADMIRED* ABOUT YOU.

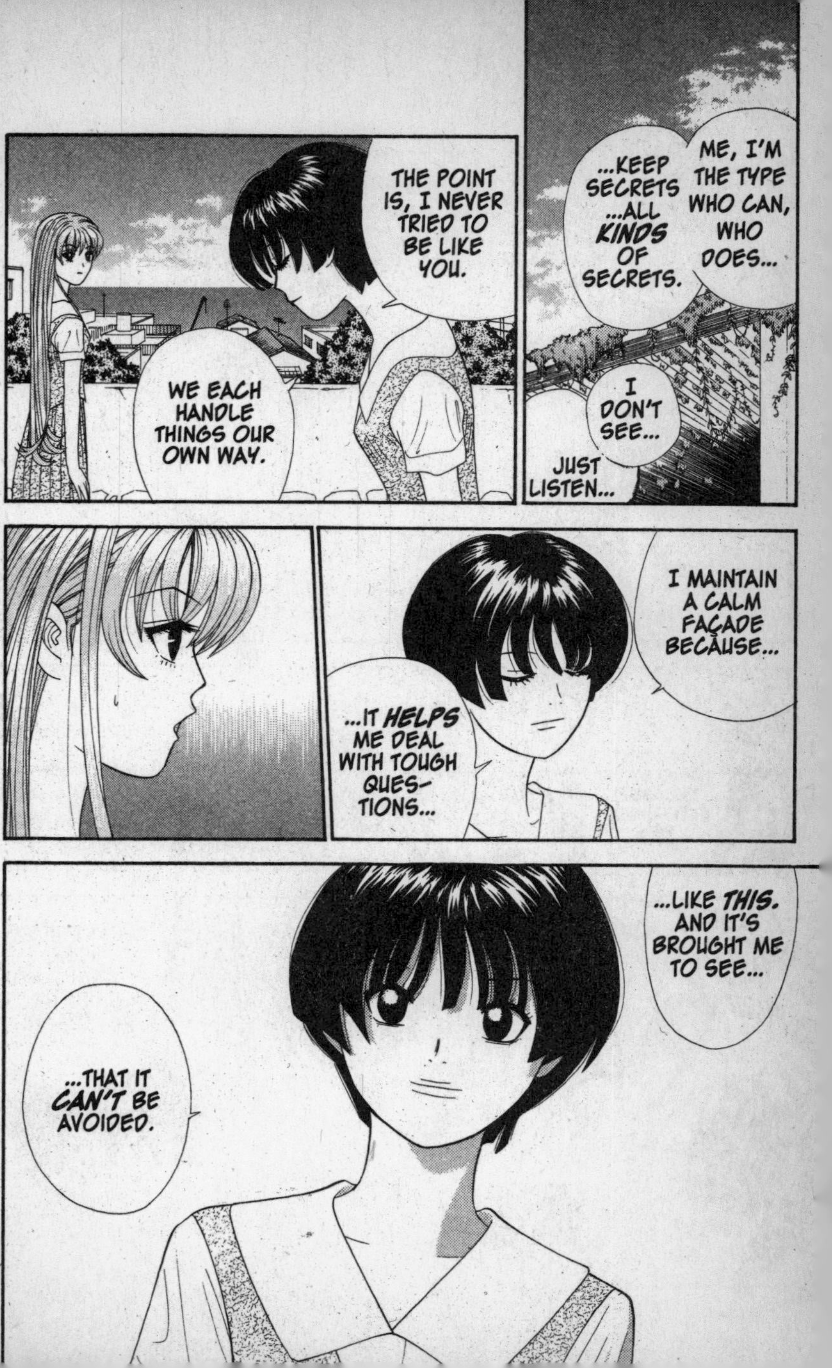
ME, I'M THE TYPE WHO CAN, WHO DOES...
...KEEP SECRETS ...ALL *KINDS* OF SECRETS.
I DON'T SEE...
JUST LISTEN...
THE POINT IS, I NEVER TRIED TO BE LIKE YOU.
WE EACH HANDLE THINGS OUR OWN WAY.
I MAINTAIN A CALM FAÇADE BECAUSE...
...IT *HELPS* ME DEAL WITH TOUGH QUES-TIONS...
...LIKE *THIS.* AND IT'S BROUGHT ME TO SEE...
...THAT IT *CAN'T* BE AVOIDED.

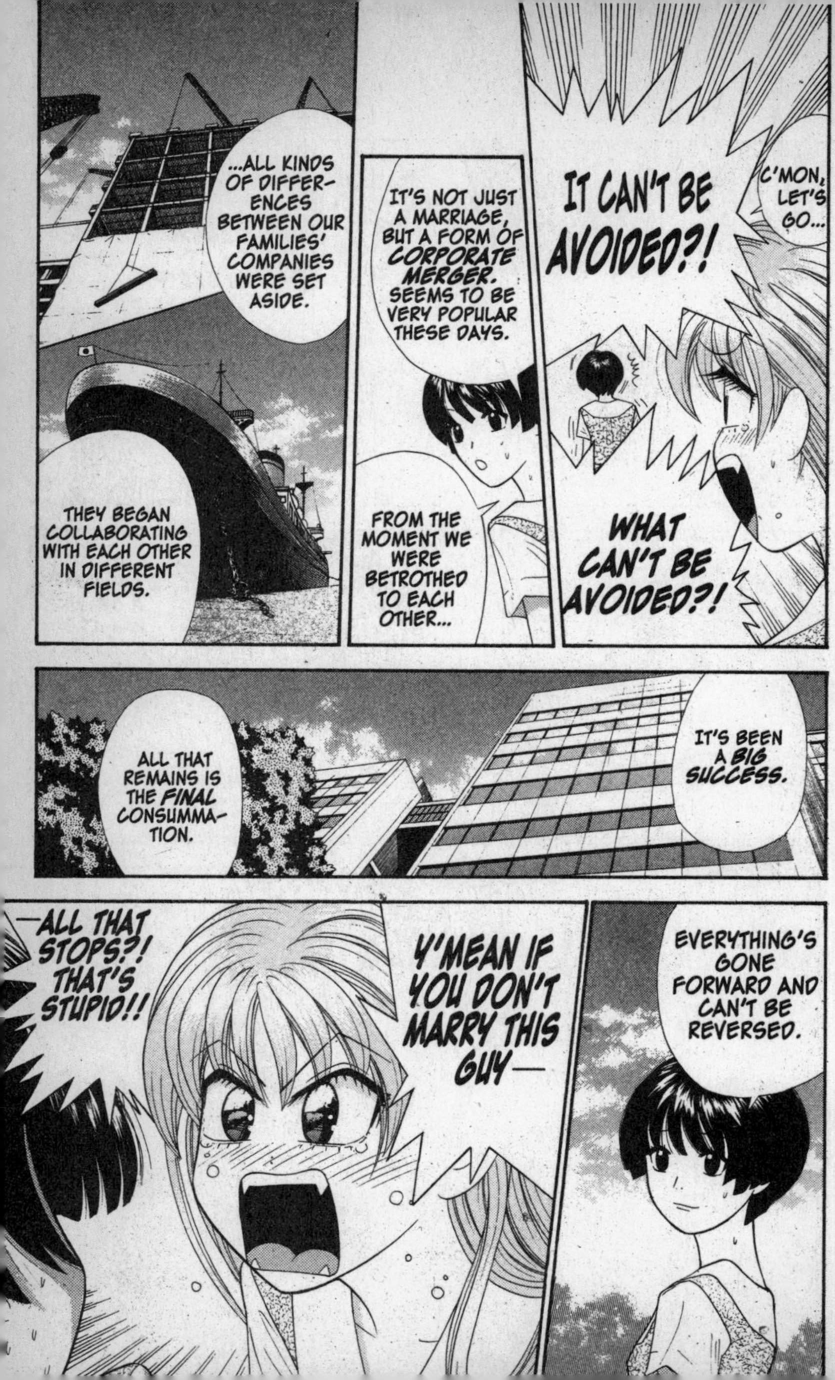
C'MON, LET'S GO...
IT CAN'T BE AVOIDED?!
WHAT CAN'T BE AVOIDED?!
IT'S NOT JUST A MARRIAGE, BUT A FORM OF CORPORATE MERGER. SEEMS TO BE VERY POPULAR THESE DAYS.
FROM THE MOMENT WE WERE BETROTHED TO EACH OTHER...
...ALL KINDS OF DIFFER-ENCES BETWEEN OUR FAMILIES' COMPANIES WERE SET ASIDE.
THEY BEGAN COLLABORATING WITH EACH OTHER IN DIFFERENT FIELDS.
IT'S BEEN A BIG SUCCESS.
ALL THAT REMAINS IS THE FINAL CONSUMMA-TION.
EVERYTHING'S GONE FORWARD AND CAN'T BE REVERSED.
Y'MEAN IF YOU DON'T MARRY THIS GUY—
—ALL THAT STOPS?! THAT'S STUPID!!

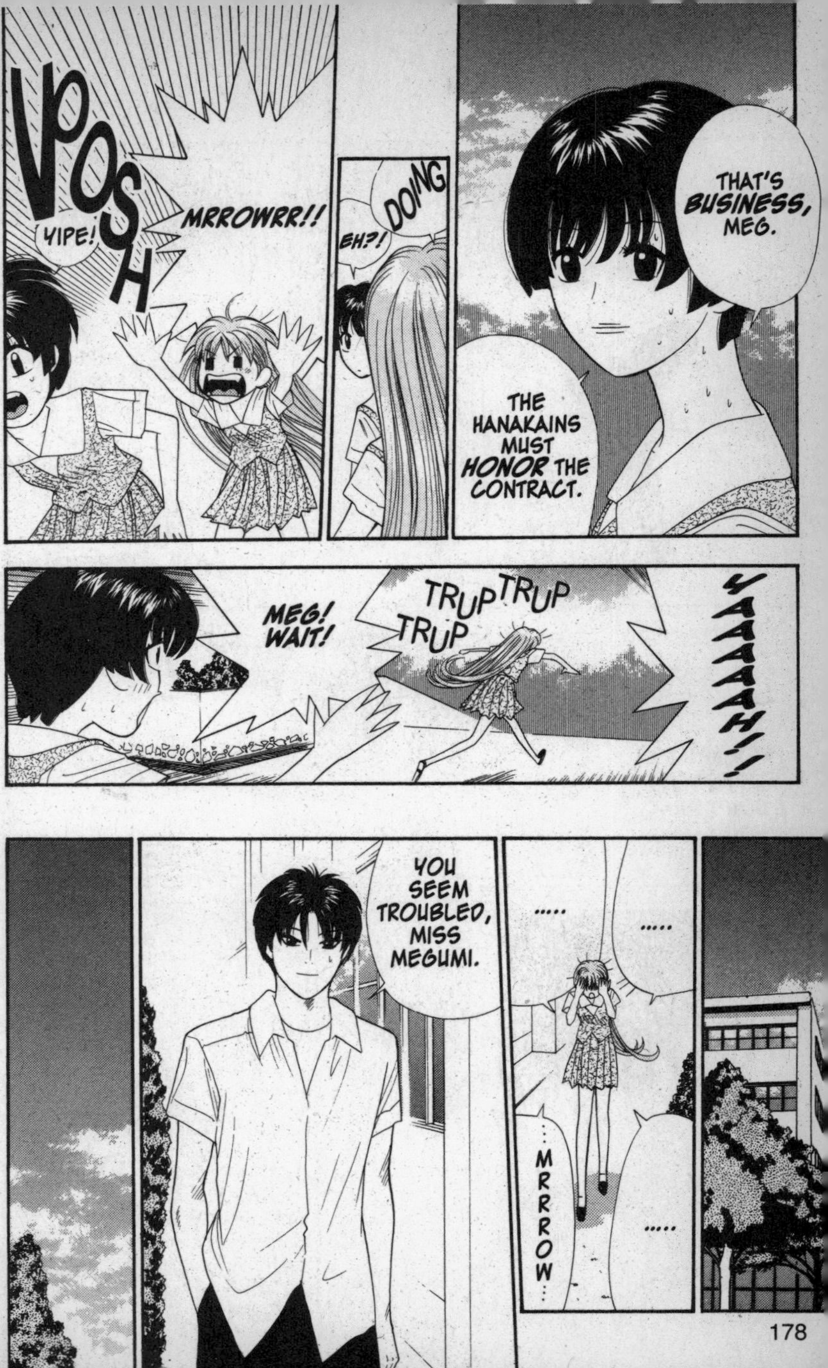
THAT'S BUSINESS, MEG.
THE HANAKAINS MUST HONOR THE CONTRACT.
DOING
EH?!
VOOSH
MRROWRR!!
YIPE!
YAAAAAAH!!
TRUP TRUP TRUP
MEG! WAIT!
.....
.....
.....
...MRRROW...
YOU SEEM TROUBLED, MISS MEGUMI.

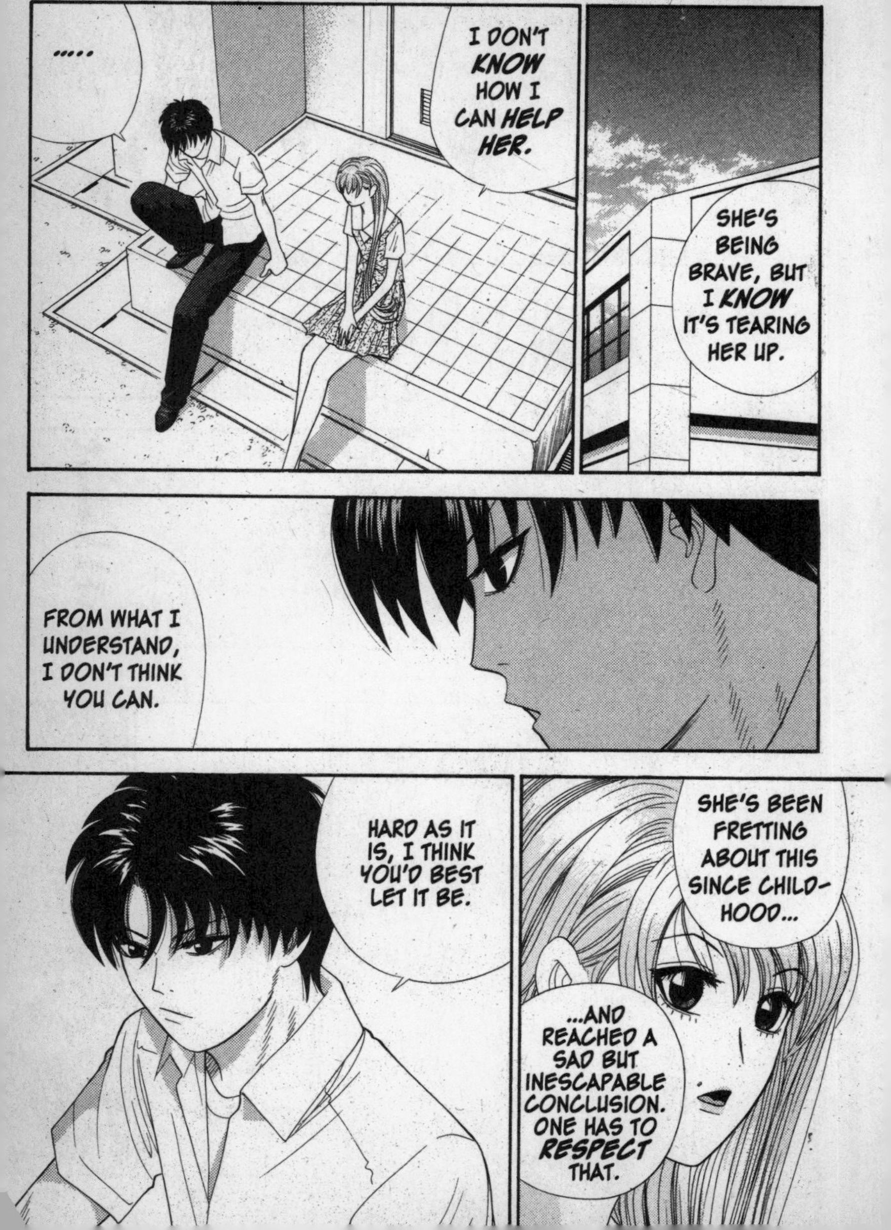
SHE'S BEING BRAVE, BUT I KNOW IT'S TEARING HER UP.
I DON'T KNOW HOW I CAN HELP HER.
.....
FROM WHAT I UNDERSTAND, I DON'T THINK YOU CAN.
SHE'S BEEN FRETTING ABOUT THIS SINCE CHILD-HOOD...
...AND REACHED A SAD BUT INESCAPABLE CONCLUSION. ONE HAS TO RESPECT THAT.
HARD AS IT IS, I THINK YOU'D BEST LET IT BE.

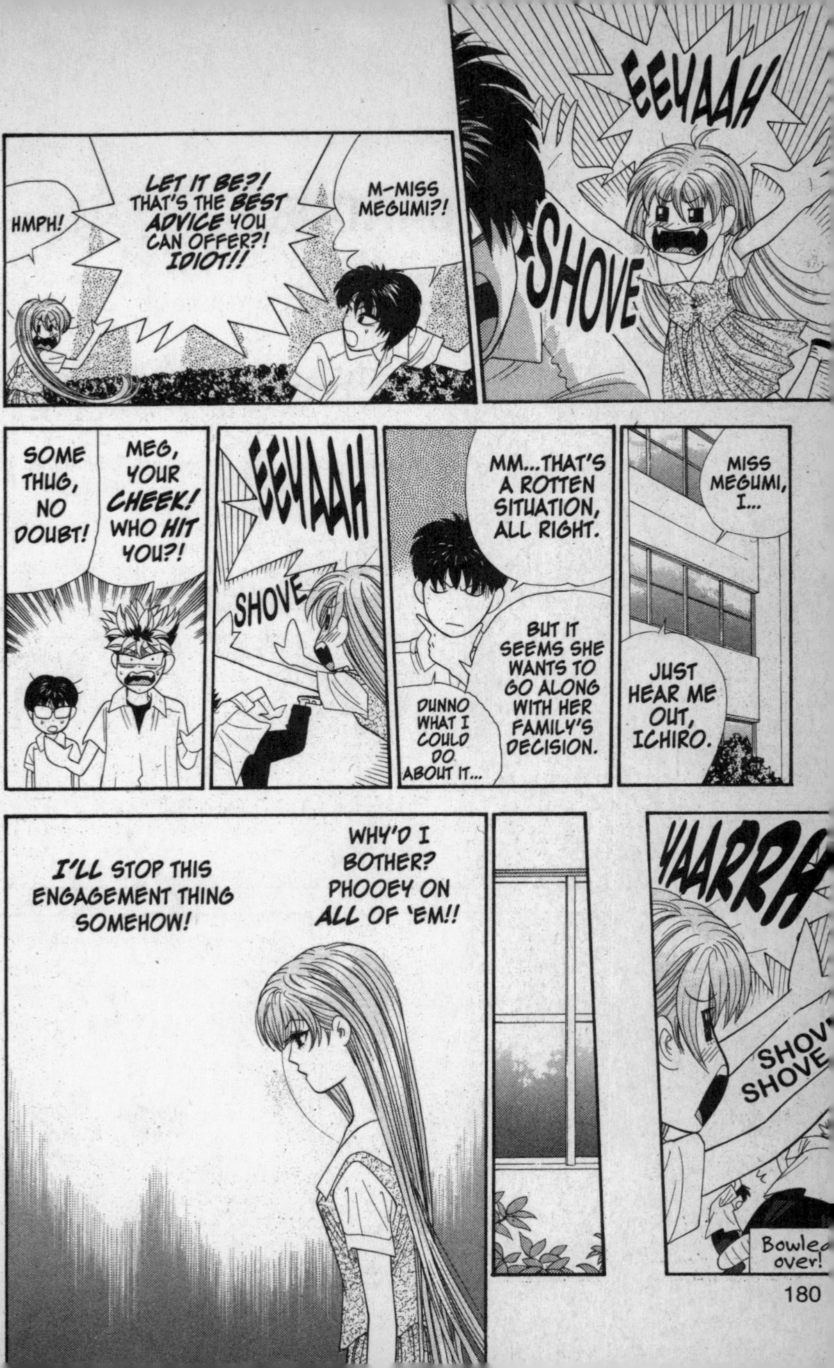
EEYAAH
SHOVE
M-MISS MEGUMI?!
LET IT BE?! THAT'S THE BEST ADVICE YOU CAN OFFER?! IDIOT!!
HMPH!
MISS MEGUMI, I...
JUST HEAR ME OUT, ICHIRO.
MM...THAT'S A ROTTEN SITUATION, ALL RIGHT.
BUT IT SEEMS SHE WANTS TO GO ALONG WITH HER FAMILY'S DECISION.
DUNNO WHAT I COULD DO ABOUT IT...
EEYAAH
SHOVE
MEG, YOUR CHEEK! WHO HIT YOU?!
SOME THUG, NO DOUBT!
YAARR
SHOV
SHOVE
Bowle
over!
WHY'D I BOTHER? PHOOEY ON ALL OF 'EM!!
I'LL STOP THIS ENGAGEMENT THING SOMEHOW!

EDITOR'S RECOMMENDATIONS

More manga!
More manga!

If you enjoyed this volume of

Cheeky Angel

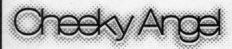

then here's some more manga you might be interested in.

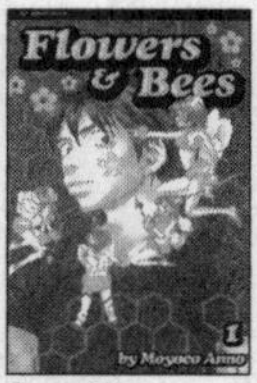
Flowers & Bees
1
by Moyoco Anno

Flowers & Bees
© 2000 Moyoco Anno/Kodansha Ltd.

Flowers & Bees
Masao Komatsu might deem himself a complete and utter loser, but high school life is never terrible enough that it can't get any worse. Gorgeous sisters Kiyoko and Harumi Sakurai are more than happy to bring out what's left of this shell of a young man—with each and every visit Masao pays to World of Beautiful Men, the men's beauty salon they own!

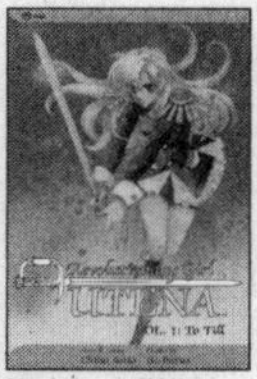

Revolutionary Girl Utena
© 1996 SAITO CHIHO/IKUHARA KUNIHIKO & BE-PAPAS/Shogakukan, Inc.

Revolutionary Girl Utena
Still searching for the mysterious prince who saved her life as a young lass, Utena must bear her biggest cross yet—the romantic gestures of Akio Ohtori. Can she trust the self-confident and obviously more experienced older man? After one night of heated love, Utena prays the overwhelming dominance of tender emotions will alter her destiny forever.

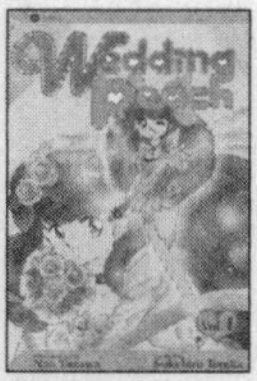
Wedding Peach

Wedding Peach
© 1994 Nao Yazawa/Sukehiro Tomita/Tenyu/Shogakukan, Inc.

Wedding Peach
Wedding Peach is about first-year middle school student Momoko Hanasaki and her friends Yuri and Hinagiku, who transform into demon-slaying supercharged angels when they aren't busy ogling the strapping captain of their soccer team.

COMPLETE OUR SURVEY AND LET
US KNOW WHAT YOU THINK!

☐ Please do NOT send me information about VIZ products, news and events, special offers, or other information.

☐ Please do NOT send me information from VIZ's trusted business partners.

Name: _____

Address: _____

City: _____ **State:** _____ **Zip:** _____

E-mail: _____

☐ Male ☐ Female **Date of Birth** (mm/dd/yyyy): ___ / ___ / ___ (Under 13? Parental consent required)

What race/ethnicity do you consider yourself? (please check one)

☐ Asian/Pacific Islander ☐ Black/African American ☐ Hispanic/Latino

☐ Native American/Alaskan Native ☐ White/Caucasian ☐ Other: _____

What VIZ product did you purchase? (check all that apply and indicate title purchased)

☐ DVD/VHS _____

☐ Graphic Novel _____

☐ Magazines _____

☐ Merchandise _____

Reason for purchase: (check all that apply)

☐ Special offer ☐ Favorite title ☐ Gift

☐ Recommendation ☐ Other _____

Where did you make your purchase? (please check one)

☐ Comic store ☐ Bookstore ☐ Mass/Grocery Store

☐ Newsstand ☐ Video/Video Game Store ☐ Other: _____

☐ Online (site: _____)

What other VIZ properties have you purchased/own? _____

_____

How many anime and/or manga titles have you purchased in the last year? How many were VIZ titles? (please check one from each column)

ANIME	MANGA	VIZ
☐ None	☐ None	☐ None
☐ 1-4	☐ 1-4	☐ 1-4
☐ 5-10	☐ 5-10	☐ 5-10
☐ 11+	☐ 11+	☐ 11+

I find the pricing of VIZ products to be: (please check one)

☐ Cheap ☐ Reasonable ☐ Expensive

What genre of manga and anime would you like to see from VIZ? (please check two)

☐ Adventure ☐ Comic Strip ☐ Science Fiction ☐ Fighting
☐ Horror ☐ Romance ☐ Fantasy ☐ Sports

What do you think of VIZ's new look?

☐ Love It ☐ It's OK ☐ Hate It ☐ Didn't Notice ☐ No Opinion

Which do you prefer? (please check one)

☐ Reading right-to-left

☐ Reading left-to-right

Which do you prefer? (please check one)

☐ Sound effects in English

☐ Sound effects in Japanese with English captions

☐ Sound effects in Japanese only with a glossary at the back

THANK YOU! Please send the completed form to:

VIZ Survey
42 Catharine St.
Poughkeepsie, NY 12601

All information provided will be used for internal purposes only. We promise not to sell or otherwise divulge your information.